£3.35

D1216882

THE SYMBOLIST
AESTHETIC IN FRANCE
1885–1895

A. G. LEHMANN

Second Edition

BASIL BLACKWELL
OXFORD
1968

First printed, 1950
Second Edition, 1968

631 10380 5

PRINTED IN GREAT BRITAIN
BY COMPTON PRINTING LTD., LONDON AND AYLESBURY
AND BOUND BY
THE KEMP HALL BINDERY, OXFORD.

PREFACE

IT is a common belief that modern European poetry dates from the age of Symbolism; and that in particular the French symbolists of the late nineteenth century brought into being a style of writing and an attitude to literature which were radically new, and which if they did not at once produce masterpieces, were already coherent, mature, and fairly complete. Nothing is further from the truth. When we examine this impression of coherence, we tend to find ourselves thinking of the poetry of Claudel and Valéry, of Yeats and Eliot, of George and Rilke, and of the appropriate criticism and aesthetic which accompany them; and these are all fruits of the second generation (in principle, if not in strict chronology). The *first* generation, which is in fact known more by repute than by its artistic achievements, lived in a climate of intense discussion, uncertainty, and relative incoherence. It is to find out exactly what this first generation did think and say, and to clear up a number of misconceptions on the beginnings of present-day aesthetic, that the present book has been written.

Some of the materials drawn on for its arguments are inaccessible and scattered; I have not hesitated to quote from them at considerable length where I find certain matters have been unsufficiently attended to. For fairly obvious reasons I have kept within the limits of the French tradition, as much a precursor in this age as the German was a century earlier. Even within these limits. I have had to make a choice out of the vast mass of available evidence; but I am confident that it is a representative one.

For reasons of space, too, little emphasis has been laid on the actual imaginative literature of the years under review. Not of course that it can be disregarded, for the link between theory and practice is as close here as anywhere else: a new field of enterprise in poetry puts the aesthetician or critic on his toes; and conversely the critic, laying his finger suggestively on a new trend, does much to encourage its cultivation by the writers of his age. Plainly some knowledge of the literary output of Symbolism will be found helpful, if the theme is not to appear too dry and abstract.

In the field of French literature, as of aesthetic philosophy, I have taken every advantage of earlier work of sorting and classification and of original theoretical writings. Whatever originality the following pages may be claimed to have, therefore, must lie solely in the attempt to effect a contact between the philosophy of art on the one hand and a well defined chapter in the history of literary ideas on the other, and, so far as possible, to see the one widened as the other is deepened. My own position is that of the catalyst rather than of the originator.

My thanks are due to the Committee for Advanced Studies and to the Curators of the Taylorian Institution, both in the University of Oxford, for financial aid towards publication of the present volume, the latter by a grant from the Gerrans Memorial Fund.

I should like to place on record my gratitude for help and advice in various stages of my work to Dr. E. Starkie, Professor P. Mansell-Jones, Professor C. M. Bowra, Dr. R. Niklaus, and above all to Professor G. Rudler, under whose guidance I originally designed this book. For its shortcomings, of course, the responsibility is mine alone.

A. G. LEHMANN.

Manchester
1948

PREFACE TO THE SECOND EDITION

TO bring up to date a study whose original conception was anchored in a set of pre-occupations now twenty years old is neither easy nor, perhaps, desirable. The starting-point of this book, it is plain, was a view of Aesthetics strongly dependent on Cassirer, Collingwood, and up to a point Croce; to abandon it would be to eliminate some of the questions asked of a particular set of writers and critics, and to forego the answers to these questions. This I see no great advantage in doing, partly because (it may be argued) that general standpoint itself grew out of certain literary attitudes formed in the latter years of the last century, along with much else. The work of Susan Langer in particular represents a development not taken into account in the pages that follow; but to redesign my argument would involve writing a different book.

On the other side, additions to scholarly investigation into French late nineteenth-century poetry have been numerous and important in the last two decades: monographs on individual writers (Professor Ireson's study of Gustave Kahn, Dr. Ll. Austin's work on *L'Univers poétique de Baudelaire*, Professor Guichard's *La Musique et les Lettres en France au temps du Wagnérisme*, or Dr. Raitt's *Villiers de l'Isle Adam*,

to name but a selection) have added much to detailed historical and
biographical knowledge and, in several cases, to critical insights also.
Some *minores* have also been rehabilitated (e.g., Marcel Schwab or
Elémir Bourges, to whom little or no space is allotted in my inquiry).
The still enigmatic Mallarmé has been extensively and frequently
examined, by J.-P. Richard, Léon Cellier, Jacques Schérer, among
others. Laforgue has been the object of one excellent little book by
Pierre Reboul. The purposes and argument of my own investigation
seem, on reflection, not to have been greatly affected by this flow of
scholarship; though on the other hand some of the books mentioned
(especially Professor Reboul's) help to reveal the very abstract nature
of any historical monograph on Aesthetics. One example, not perhaps
noted before: the *idéoréalisme* coined (or recoined) by Saint-Pol-Roux
has suggestive echoes of the same term as used by Proudhon half a
century earlier: but in general, a deliberate decision was taken not to
comment on the socio-political context of literary debate in Paris,
even though in certain cases (the critic Fénéon, Mallarmé even)
fruitful enquiry can be pursued into the background of Fourierist or
anarchist contributions to aesthetic speculation, or more generally
into ideological overtones.

Essentially, therefore, this book remains unchanged from the essay
in historical synthesis attempted two decades ago. One or two details
have been altered, and additions made, in footnotes, are designated
by square brackets.

A.G.L.

Reading
1967

CONTENTS

PART II

PART I

Chapter I

THE NATURE OF THE INQUIRY

> Orage, Lustral: et dans des bouleversements, tout à
> l'acquit de la génération récente, l'acte d'écrire se scruta
> jusqu'en l'origine...—MALLARMÉ

1. Aesthetic defined in its relation with the practice of art. 2. Aesthetic both
normative and descriptive. 3. Its historicity. 4. The position of symbolism in the
development of aesthetic consciousness.

I. AESTHETIC DEFINED[1]

THE main function of an aesthetic is to provide an answer to the
question: 'What is Art?' It is not to be supposed that to such
a general type of inquiry a simple and finally satisfactory answer
will ever be directly forthcoming; any aesthetic worthy of the name
has been and always will be finally content to render these questions
into a more approachable form; to limit the field of inquiry by first
deciding what we are referring to when we ask what 'art' is; and then
to examine in more detail its characteristic marks as well as those
features which it has in common with other human activities.

Pursued in this way, aesthetic comes mainly within the competence
of philosophy, as a branch of systematized and abstract inquiry;
and it is to the philosophers that we usually turn our minds when we
attempt to solve its problems. But at the outset, a difficulty arises;
the training of a philosopher in his particular technique (namely, clear
thinking), is no guarantee that he will be familiar with the material
he has to deal with when he enters the specialized field. The whole
fabric of his method, the habits acquired by previous work, may
indeed have been developed as the result of inquiry into quite other
fields than art (e.g. Taine); or may be irredeemably warped by the
presence somewhere in the background of a hobby-horse which must
be ridden on all and every occasion (e.g. Schopenhauer). That
unfamiliarity with the field of art need not necessarily prevent a
philosopher from making profoundly valuable observations on
aesthetics is evidenced by the case of Kant, among many others;

---

[1] It appears to be usual to describe as 'an aesthetic approach' any effort by literary critics
to discuss a poem or a book on other than historical or biographical terms. I need not insult
the reader's intelligence by asking him to put this usage out of his mind. 'Aesthetic' is throughout the following pages used as a synonym for 'philosophy of art'.

3

but the fruit of the *Critique of Judgement* is essentially a philosophic fruit, necessary to the systematic exposition of a way of thought, and not in the strictest sense a contribution to the study of art. By and large, it is undeniable that aestheticians fall into two classes: those with a highly developed critical apparatus but little or no direct knowledge of the material they are concerned with, and those (common in all ages) who have an extensive acquaintance with artistic activity in one form or another but little or no equipment for ordering and utilizing their experience. Into the first class falls the bulk of the professional philosophers; into the second the large majority of writers, critics, and so forth. Instances of those who combine both qualifications are infrequent.

It would seem from the way in which we have defined aesthetics that the second class of investigators could serve no useful purpose at all; but this is not true. If aesthetic means inquiring what art is, rather than what it might be, a historical factor enters for us on the scene. No one living since the eighteenth century will deny that art changes, even if only superficially (and not necessarily 'for the better'), from generation to generation,[1] and since the growth of anthropology at least, that it has from age to age changed very radically indeed, not only as regards media but also as regards intentions. This implies that not only must aesthetics be treated as an historical field of study but also that any aesthetic doctrine which is not purely a display of academic virtuosity must pay serious attention to the detail of such contemporary art as surrounds the aesthetician at the time of his writing. This requirement was much obscured in the past by the traditions of hellenic and latinist studies;[2] now that the ancients no longer exercise so despotic a rule over the world of art, it becomes self-evident. And it implies that the artist-critic, or even the critic pure and simple, spending his life in close contact with artists and presumably aware of their aims and intentions, is not a parasite living off dust-jacket 'blurbs' and the credulity of a bewildered public, but a man who, not entitled to the last word on the art of his times, is in certain circumstances entitled to the first. It becomes the task of the aesthetician, studying art in various media and the intentions of artists as professed elsewhere by themselves and their

[1] A good example of what happens when this is not realized may be found in Voltaire's *Letters on Œdipe*: not in any way a silly piece of writing, but the fruits of an a-historical frame of mind.

[2] 'Before theory could deal with what was native and familiar, it had to follow the toilsome clue afforded by the inheritance of the past, because it had been brought up to believe that there alone lay the treasure house of beauty.'—Bosanquet, *A History of Aesthetic*, 2nd ed. 1902, p. 252.

exegetes, to cast a more systematic glance on the tortuous, obscure, and often self-contradictory utterances of the literary *francs-tireurs*, and attempt to find in them some reasoned and consistent system of ideas; pointing out confusions where they arise, perhaps even venturing to re-interpret opinions which otherwise might seem nonsensical, and organizing the whole in relation to principles which seem to him valid.

Are we then to assume that the aesthetician, working quietly in his study, neither attempts nor can ever hope to influence the world of art personified in the artist and the public? that his sole duties are to himself, in answer to an entirely private craving for philosophic clarity, and that so far as the course of events are concerned he might equally well never have existed? This is evidently the view of a great many writers and poets; of whom Henri de Régnier is an example when he asserts that 'on peut avec les théories les plus médiocres, faire de belles oeuvres et aussi, avec les plus nobles théories, n'écrire que des oeuvres sans intérêt',[1] and dismisses at one stroke the possibility of aesthetics having any use for the artist. It is a view which has, of course, been extensively canvassed by the philosophers on the other side of the hedge; to quote from a standard work:

'Aesthetic knowledge is a branch of philosophy, and exists for the sake of knowledge, and not as a guide to practice. . . . The aesthetic theorist . . . desires to understand the artist, not in order to interfere with the latter, but in order to satisfy an intellectual interest of his own.'[2]

Such statements have the advantage of lucidity, but they are only half true. They are, indeed, a relic of an already venerable reaction to the 'moralizing' tradition of aesthetics; they are the property of people whose anxiety to disclaim the excesses of an earlier viewpoint has led them into excesses of an opposite but similar kind. Reflection on whatever one may be doing must interfere in this way or in that with the work it refers to. No one will pretend that conduct remains unaffected by even the most dispassionate reflection on ethics; equally, no artist can prevent reflection on his art by anyone whose work comes to his notice from affecting the way he treats it—even if only as the result of clarification or intensification of views which he already held before: since right clarification of one's views on art must lead to the elimination of confusion and mis-spent effort, and that is already a change.

To take an extreme example: suppose an artist to have assumed at

---

[1] Quoted in Le Cardonnel and Vellay, *La Littérature contemporaine*, 1905, p. 298.
[2] Bosanquet, op. cit., p. xi.

one stage that his true function was to paint exact likenesses of his sitters; and that at a later stage, after arguments with his friends or reflection on his own in the field of aesthetics, he revised his opinions and decided that his initial attitude hampered him in the execution of the sort of work he was really striving to produce. Then the intervention of aesthetics (either his own or someone else's) might not of itself lead to any improvement in his work; but at least it would powerfully assist in making such an improvement possible. Or again, the case of a poet such as Mallarmé is an extreme instance of the extent to which an aesthetic can mould the whole course of an artist's work: had he been less anxious to write poetry owing as little as possible to the material of ordinary experience, a lifetime of enormous activity would have produced more than the two or three slim volumes which preserve his memory; and it is impossible to imagine the sort of poetry which he would have written in maturity. Granted that in this case (as in all others) we must distinguish between a sphere of intention properly speaking aesthetic, and a sphere of preferences more properly individual, in some senses fortuitous; but the two are at many points linked together, and both have a hand in the eventual quality of his verse. We must, in fact, keep perfectly clear in our minds what we mean by aesthetic; and we can best introduce the required qualification at this stage by saying that aesthetic studies the conditions and assumptions on which any artist— and his audience—base their activities. Thus, if—as happened in Paris in the nineties—a whole group of writers and artists proclaimed that each man was a law unto himself, and that each man's aesthetic was a purely individual contrivance, we should, as aestheticians, know two things: first, that what was being referred to was not aesthetics at all but a system of individual preferences on an altogether much more specific level; secondly, that these assertions in the mass themselves constituted a most interesting piece of evidence for the aesthetic and literary historian.

So it would be altogether more judicious to suggest that in certain circumstances certain types of aesthetic speculation have little apparent influence on the shaping of art—are no more than mere gyroscopes steadying the keel—while in other times, particularly in times when a profound change in the general aesthetic consciousness is becoming noticeable, they are so intimately linked with the practical problems of art that to attempt to separate the two would do violence to both.

2. AESTHETIC BOTH NORMATIVE AND DESCRIPTIVE

This uneasy balance in the aesthetician's practical relations with artists and critics is an outcome of the nature of aesthetics as a philosophical science; that is to say, of the fact that it is neither exclusively descriptive nor purely normative. If indeed it were purely descriptive, it would have nothing to do save describe faithfully the ways in which people are observed to make art. It could do this either as psychology or as a sort of applied anthropology. The views of Freud as to what impulses drive a Leonardo da Vinci along his career represent fairly enough the former branch; the social historian, say Taine, may be taken to represent the latter. But it is demonstrable that the efforts of neither of these classes of researches, either alone or taken in combination, can answer even quite simple questions that we may legitimately put to aesthetics—nor say why they should be unanswerable—e.g. what we are basing our judgement on when we say '*this* picture is vastly better than *that*'. Nor can they give an account of the principles of their aesthetic philosophy, and relate art to these principles: yet by picking on certain material to describe and discuss, a descriptive science of art necessarily assumes such material to embody aesthetic principles in a way which other material, ignored, does not. It is plain that for a purely descriptive aesthetic (if it could exist) the evidence of artists and critics on what they are doing is of the highest interest; it is not plain that such evidence is adequately controlled.

If, on the other hand, aesthetic could be purely normative, and were to take no notice of what art is produced but, as it were, only show *a priori* how it should be, then it is evident that the aesthetician need not concern himself at all with the data available to the descriptive writer. He need not concern himself even with what he knows about art from personal experience; he can forget how he sings or paints, or how he listens to songs or looks at paintings—if he has ever done any of these things—and devote himself simply to determining the place of aesthetic in a philosophical system. But the excessiveness of his attitude is revenged on him: for not only will no one listen to his precepts and advice on how to write or paint: he himself will have no grounds for interest in his own subject matter, since he has rigidly divorced it from any field of application. The artist decides for himself what he is doing; the aesthetician can only offer to help and elucidate in so far as he himself is an embryo artist, and the artist will only listen to him in so far as *he* is an embryo aesthetician.

It might therefore be more plausible to define aesthetics as giving us an account of how artists and others think art *ought* to be produced. This formula includes both facts and ideals, and might therefore be thought to cover both sides of the matter—the descriptive and the normative. In fact, however, it is merely a disguised version of the descriptive programme; in which the ideals are reduced to the level of facts, and the aesthetician passes them on without comment, without an opinion on their truth. To acquire status as a philosophical science, aesthetic must not only say how people think (and have thought) that they ought to produce works of art; it must go on to say whether they were right, and if not, why not; and in this perspective, there are two possibilities open to it: either it can grant that all former attitudes to art are 'right', or it can criticize them by the application of explicit standards. If it takes the former course, it makes the assumption that the aesthetic ideal exists as an ideal in the minds of all persons connected with art; if it takes the latter, it assumes, or discovers, that the aesthetic ideal exists in their minds partly, and in an inchoate form, it being the object of critical discussion to bring the ideal more fully into the light. In either case, however, the philosophy of art is both descriptive and normative; and the aesthetician is forced on to his razor's edge: on the one hand he must consort with artists and critics, both living and dead; on the other hand he must keep step with philosophy—must analyse and criticize the artists and critics as thoroughly as he knows how, and in so doing make plain to himself the differences that separate their views from his: in a word, his historical study of aesthetic is at the same blow his aesthetic.

3. AESTHETIC IN THE CONTEXT OF HISTORY

The inevitably historical nature of such work is, however, a source of added difficulties; not by any means insuperable, though tricky enough if the aesthetician is not sufficiently attentive to history. The main difficulties are two in number, the second following from the first.

When we study the history of art, we notice two kinds of change. The first is the more troublesome. On the face of it, art from its earliest surviving examples down to its most recent productions is homogeneous, more or less. In galleries to-day we see paintings making use of line and colour, mass and form; and in Magdalenian caves we see things which are sufficiently like this to merit the name of paintings too. From this apparent homogeneity the casual observer might (I do not say he does) march gaily off with the belief that all art has always been art—of course!—the Magdalenian artist doing the same things that his modern 'primitivist' imitators are doing to-day, with the same intentions, the same attitude, and possibly even the same social status. Two sorts of gross error spring from this: the error either of treating Magdalenian man as a sophisticated London exhibitor, or—not so common, but more deadly—the Londoner as a primitive-minded Magdalenian. Comes the anthropologist and makes it plain that primitive 'art', so far from being an affair of the picture gallery, is an essential element in religious magic, and that this magic is best compared with propaganda, if an analogy with our own times is possible (we assume the critic to have outlived the days when magic was thought to be a substitute for the scientific control of nature). The artist, aesthetician, or art critic meditates afresh and brings out a theory of *littérature engagée*. But new difficulties then arise for him: plainly a great amount of modern popular art (cinema, detective novel, chocolate box pictures, and the like) is not remotely concerned with propaganda, or magic, or moral education, but is quite simply amusing, exciting, or 'escapist'; moreover, he discovers with more or less of a shock that the psycho-analyst has, all along, assumed it to be nothing else but that. He looks back for precedents, and finds among the more popular definitions one that states the purpose of art to be *miscere utile dulci*. If the *utile* is propaganda, the *dulce* is certainly amusement. Two theories then lay claim to his allegiance; and if he is honest he will not be content to leave his definition at this point of uncertainty. If the useful and the diverting are both aims of art, which is the more important? Which if either could be ignored without damage to art? Can he be sure that the two elements suggested are not mutually incompatible, that the one is not the direct antithesis in some way of the other? But usually he ignores these matters. He notes that by and large, successive ages have inclined towards one or other of the two wings of the definition: with primitive man there is little evidence of a search for 'amusement' or diversion—unless it is claimed that the ornamentation of this or that tool or weapon is not connected with his religion but is simply a nervous tic; that early Greek tragedy appears to have a definite educative and explicitly social function (see the trial of strength between Aeschylus and Euripides in Aristophanes' *Frogs*), later drama much less so; that in general, classical aesthetic oscillates between the two poles; that Christian mediaeval art tends to be as 'engagé' as Magdalenian, Renaissance art hardly at all—unless sheer display is thought of as making a secondary contribution to prestige; that present-day art is mainly amusing, except in Russia, where it is educative or propagandist; and so on.

Before these powerful claims to the title of art by two distinct—but not perhaps mutually exclusive—activities, the critic may very well begin to lose heart, but if he can persist in his inquiry, it may come to his notice that some art, and especially some very good art indeed, without regard to time or place, is neither specially 'amusing' and escapist, nor specially edifying, nor a mixture of both, but something more—or perhaps less; that what he specially likes about it is not the fact that it makes him forget his worries, nor the fact that it makes him more ready to face them bravely and confidently, but something else; and that this something else seems properly speaking the source of artistic value, to give it a non-committal name, and present in varying degree in all the things which rightly or wrongly he can ascribe to the realms of propaganda and amusement.

The further stages of his inquiry need not occupy us here; all that need be pointed out is the fact that art is to be distinguished from some of the uses to which it is put from time to time (practically always, in fact, when examined in the sociological context). No one would be so foolish as to claim that because rigorous thinking first developed in the matrix of the law courts, logic should be the exclusive property of lawyers in robes and wigs; or that because philosophy was, so far as we know, first developed by priests, its discussion should only be carried on from the pulpit; yet there are those who cheerfully believe that art is 'essentially' religious or magical (or propagandist) in its origins, and that its existence is tied to the life of religion or other similar activities; these people make no distinction between art as an activity and art in the service of some specific ulterior social need. In this case, the historical perspective leads the aesthetician into a round of serious pitfalls of reasoning, which he can only evade by being a good aesthetician—i.e., being able to propose the question clearly what art is and does, as opposed to what it has been used for at different times.

Another difficulty arises when we turn to consider something that intimately concerns the technician, the artist *qua* artist. A historical study of the field of art makes it plain that technical resources (a convenient if misleading expression) are to-day much greater than they ever have been in the past. A sculptor may cast a statue in bronze, if he likes, as well as any sculptor has ever cast them over a period of many centuries; but equally he may do it in some such substance as bakelite, not in existence before the twentieth century, but allowing him certain purely technical extensions to his technique (e.g. on grounds of its lightness). The architect may build in stone, like his Greek and Roman ancestors; or in brick, like the Tudors; but his resources are infinitely enlarged as compared with those of either earlier age by his having reinforced concrete, which they had not, and without which the designs of a Le Corbusier are unthinkable. The composer to-day has not only Elizabethan modal progressions, and nineteenth-century diatonic harmony (with all its chromatic distensions and developments): his language now includes much that Beethoven knew nothing of—polytonal and atonal systems. The French poet of 1890 may, if he chooses, write in Alexandrines as regular as those of Boileau: but his range of possibilities stretches far further than that of the seventeenth century—to *vers libre*, and rhythmic prose; his language is potentially the richer by all the devices of complex imagery exhaustively exploited; he may choose Iphigénie for his play's subject (Moréas did), but he may reach out too in any other direction open to him—and these directions are more various than those open to Racine. In short, the technique of art makes progress, at least as regards the possibilities before the artist.

To art itself the idea of progress is not applicable; no one can say that because an artist knows the work of a predecessor, or is able to lay his hands on a wider range of technical resources, he is *ipso facto* a better artist than that predecessor. The concept of aesthetic value is central and presumed fixed, like the concept of truth, though different ages have had different ways of expressing their views on it; in each case successive embodiments of the concept are constantly and necessarily changeful. Art does not become 'better' in the course of time, even though in principle[1] its technique becomes wider. This leads us to the second difficulty presented to the aesthetician by the historical nature of his work. On the one hand the aesthetic ideal is constant and fixed: when we judge a cave-man's painting, a tragedy by Aeschylus, a building by Wren, or a symphony by

[1] Though not of course always in practice: indeed the greatest ages in one art or another frequently follow after a rigorous pruning of resources bequeathed from preceding times—e.g. the literature of seventeenth-century France; or the age of diatonic music. The former case is a commonplace; less obvious is the latter, which developed from the elimination of all but two—Ionian and Aeolian—of the Elizabethan modes. From a wide range of choice a selected field is intensively cultivated. Against this tendency we must set the enormous diversity of techniques and styles opened up by historical research in the last century or two; the museum now shares with the studio the task of forming the artist's language. The issues raised by this fact are not new; they have been with us since the Renaissance, and to some extent in all art at all times.

Beethoven as beautiful—i.e. as aesthetically valuable—we go through the same process in each case; there is not one criterion for this and another for that work of art. But on the other hand we do not expect a uniformity of technique throughout the ages known to us. How then can we reconcile this fixed ideal with the idea of a developing—at any rate, constantly changing—philosophy of art from the earliest recorded opinions and behaviour down to the most recent?

The answer on which the inquiry that follows will be based is as follows. We may think we have developed a system of thought for ourselves out of the blue, or we may admit to having found it suggested in the work of previous thinkers; but whatever we believe, we occupy a position in an unfolding tradition of successive thinkers. Aesthetic, notwithstanding any claims to the contrary, is such a tradition; and if we examine attentively the development of the philosophy of art through the ages, we find that for every parcel of ideas that we reject from an earlier writer's views, there is still always something which is retained, and which, transformed in terminology and significance, survives in later aesthetics. We have in mind here something far more detailed than a mere broad synthesis, such as that which Bosanquet sees effected in modern aesthetic between the classical notion of form and the romantic notion of significance or expressiveness; if an example is needed, perhaps the relationship between the Greek view of form and that sketched out at the end of chapter v would serve. If modern thought retains in some sense the Greek idea of unity in multiplicity, it also rejects much else—the idea, for example, that art must of necessity be permeated through and through by the impulse to entertain or the impulse to teach. It demands perhaps some effort to reflect that until the eighteenth century, beauty was very generally held to reside in things rather than to be a function of human activity in connection with them; few educated persons would to-day go against this latter proposition: yet it is a bequest from writers as recent as Hume and Kant, or rather from the aesthetic consciousness as it was developing at that time. Again, though anticipated in part and sporadically in the nineteenth, it is the twentieth century that has introduced a systematic view of the essentially homogeneous *expressive* nature—what Croce somewhat misleadingly called the 'lyricism'—of all art: the fact that when we say 'this, as art, is wonderful (or wretched)', we are making one and only one sort of value-judgement, whether we make it of sonnets or symphonies, castles or chaconnes, and irrespective of whether the art is being turned to one or another ulterior use. The aesthetic ideal towards which we interpret all aesthetic theories that we examine to be partially aspiring, is one of which the present age—whichever it is—holds itself to be the specially privileged possessor. If we could see anything wrong or inadequate about our philosophy of art, we should correct or supplement it. But no one can seriously hope to have said the last word on aesthetic; and a subsequent generation will certainly find that in correcting what may appear at first to be simply one defect in the ideas that are handed to it, it is under the obligation of rejecting or modifying all the other views, and with them the historical perspectives, of its predecessors. This would seem to raise the question, whether historical perspectives are worth troubling to produce, whether it would not be much better to elaborate one's own aesthetic *ab ovo*? But once again, anyone raising this old skeleton would certainly be in the position of not understanding what an aesthetic is: for if on the one hand it is something that can be written out to look like a new and independent contribution to knowledge, on the other it can always be reduced to its primitive form—namely, judgements on the ideas of other people, picked up in one way or another, and either absorbed into or rejected from its system. A systematic philosophy of art, and a history of the philosophy of art are not two different things: they are one thing, looked at—or written out—in different ways according as circumstances dictate, and of course with different emphases. A philosophy of art can no more be non-historical than a history of the philosophy of art can be non-critical, i.e. non-philosophical.

4. 'SYMBOLISM' AND THE DEVELOPMENT OF THE IDEAL OF ART

It is not to be supposed, then, that a contribution to the history of aesthetic will be non-controversial. This need not mean that problems facing the symbolist artists (or problems we see to have faced them) are still facing us unsolved to-day. In the first place, Symbolism as a literary movement is more remote from us in certain ways than its terminology and slogans would suggest; and in the second place where we see problems (which have subsequently been resolved) they tended only to see a comfortable and easy *status quo*. This is natural enough: had they seen problems where we see them, they would have proceeded to solve them. It means that *our* solutions of these problems are controversial, at least in part.

At the same time, we are much closer to symbolism than to any other of the great artistic renascences of modern Europe, especially in the field of aesthetic; its younger generation—Maeterlinck, Claudel, Valéry—still command the veneration of a large reading public, and the thousand and one 'schools' and crazes of the last forty odd years (surrealism apart) are little more than apanages, setting forth to develop and explore lines first opened up by the symbolists' innovations. So far as aesthetics go, moreover, Symbolism stands on the threshold of our times. In a dozen major respects, which we shall examine in the proper place, it shows itself to be not perhaps contemporary in attitude, but very nearly so. Rid of its posturing, of an obsession with other people's reactions to it, of what we might be excused for calling its Aubrey Beardsley-ism, Symbolism displays an attentiveness to poetry, to poetic utterance, to the task of artistic creation shorn of irrelevances of purpose, which is our own to-day, and which contrasts with the disposition of most of its contemporaries. It is indeed a negative demarcation which most simply introduces the limits of Symbolism; successive stages in the inquiry will add precision and give fuller meaning to a preliminary definition of the facts.

Negatively, Symbolism is

(*a*) a refusal to be attracted by social, propagandist, and other strictly extra-artistic interests: which expressed in positive terms, puts us under the obligation of saying what is meant by *l'art pour l'art* (no easy problem) and noting a watery sort of literary mystique;

(*b*) a refusal to be bound by the conventions of writing which tended to atrophy when attention was withdrawn from them to (strictly) non-literary problems.

Both these negative definitions point towards the Symbolists' main positive link with our own day: a critical preoccupation with language as such, in the widest sense—the artist's peculiar field. And this positive link is on two planes equally—that of poetry and that of speculation on poetry. We might go so far as to say that the symbolist aesthetic is close to our own for what it *observes* about poetic activity. For a historical approach to aesthetic, it is evident that the value of any new theory, its main justification at any rate, is that it enables some new observed feature to take its place in the account dealt with by the philosophy of art. The theory is eventually discarded; but it leaves a precipitate, which is incorporated in the body of aesthetic knowledge. Any 'theory' of aesthetics is designed to correlate and systematize certain observations; the fact that it does so means also that it must exclude the possibility of attending to certain others. And there are no doubt other less tangible circumstances in every age which assist it in this latter function. Three geometrical points, looked at by a systematic mind, will be seen to form a triangle; and the aesthetician, occupied with the properties of his triangle, fails to remark the existence of a fourth point, situated outside his figure, and irrelevant to it as a triangle. But this fourth point, if irrelevant to this particular aesthetician, may be very relevant to art; and in another generation the triangle may be replaced by a quadrilateral as the shape of aesthetic theory.

The symbolists are in the position of a generation—perhaps one should say a generation and a half—which notes the existence of a fourth point but is not ready to see that the theorems of the geometry of triangles are on the one hand not sufficient for the geometry of quadrilaterals, and yet on the other hand not entirely irrelevant. This failure leads to two possible reactions: either geometry is denounced (in which case the points are said to be related together not by rational properties but by a mystic significance, a hidden meaning); or the attempt is made to reassert the triangle theorems— and the fourth point is conveniently forgotten again. In the metaphor, read 'positivist aesthetic' for 'geometry of triangles', and 'expressionist aesthetic' for 'geometry of quadrilaterals', and the equivocal position of the symbolists becomes clear. Their importance as systematic thinkers is quite negligible; their importance as artists calling out for new systematic thought is exceptionally great; and the ways in which they voiced these demands are of more than a little interest.

As always, it is impossible to give exact, and hard to give even approximate and helpful, chronological equivalents for intellectual moments: it is for this reason that the very term 'Symbolism' (and all others like it) is in constant dispute. Without going into a survey of literary history, a very few remarks on the historical flesh and blood of the moment may not be out of place. From the cénacles and groups that formed round outlandish titles and were a regular feature of nineteenth-century Paris, there seems to have developed in the early eighties a slightly closer fellow-feeling and community of bohemianism. This union of the young intelligentsia—almost a union *against* the mandarins of respectable criticism and orthodox art—found expression in a wave of independent and ephemeral reviews; the most famous pioneer being *La Nouvelle Rive Gauche* (later *Lutèce*). These leaflets provided a forum for discussion and new poetry, without leading to any crystallization of opinion and doctrine around a prominent figure. François Coppée, in 1882, was still looked on as an inspiration, together with writers such as Rollinat and Richepin; Verlaine makes a tardy entry on the scene; the epithet *décadent* is hurled, and sticks. By 1884, Jean Moréas assembles around him a small set of friends; they call themselves *les symboliques*; and it is against them that Verlaine later directs his epigrams, and René Ghil the disdainful wrath of his *Écrits pour l'art* (at least after 1889). Mallarmé is in Paris, building up a shadowy reputation among a limited circle, which however includes some names destined to be remembered (Manet, Villiers de l'Isle Adam, later Claudel, Gide, Viélé-Griffin, Valéry, Debussy . . .); in this year his repute is enormously advanced by Huysmans' novel *A Rebours*, but not without disadvantages. In 1885 Jean Moréas launches Symbolism with a capital letter in a series of manifestos; the next five years are a chaos of manifestos, slogans, definitions, and counter-definitions, marked by the superficial emergence of three 'schools'—Decadence, under one Anatole Baju; Symbolism, under Moréas; and *l'école instrumentiste*, under Ghil.   The turning-point comes in 1890.   The journalist Huret embarks on a famous *Enquête*, Moréas wearies of his companions and of the symbolist dinners, and by 1891 has broken away to form a more respectable school, the *école romane*, to which a small number of equally war-weary pamphleteers attach themselves. With the defection of its colourful chief, Symbolism begins to sink out of view; but at the height of its glory it loses its sectarian limitation, and is now applied to virtually all modernist writers who will accept it (or not reject it from dislike of Moréas): it means little or nothing as a fighting slogan. Of the four most interesting symbolist reviews, established in 1890 (*La Plume*, *l'Ermitage*, *Entretiens politiques et littéraires*, and the *Mercure de France*), none but the last survives far into the next century. By 1895, 'symbolist' attached to a writer's name signifies little more than friendship and reverence for Mallarmé, to whom the honour of literary chief has reverted as an unsolicited gift; and with Mallarmé's death in 1898, it passes slowly to its grave.

This cursory review gives, to be sure, little more than a skeleton of Symbolism; it ignores, for example, threads of political radicalism of one sort and another in individual poets, and even in some earlier numbers of *Le Décadent*, a movement grown to full and avowed socialism in the *Entretiens*, and curiously twisted in Ghil's Comtist 'Sociocracy'; it ignores an opposite anti-democratic trend which later becomes more pronounced: it ignores too the persistent and varied influences of Wagner and other considerable writers outside the movement. But it serves to recall the extremely hazy outlines of Symbolism as a movement of literature running by the side of Symbolism as a philosophy of art: from this hazy mass critics and historians of poetry have extracted pretty much whatever they choose, and gummed the label on. In the sense that it has bequeathed certain things to French poetry which are of lasting influence, it is fair to say that 'symbolism' lives in French poetry from Rimbaud's *Illuminations* down to the present day; in the sense in which Symbolism means the working-out of a reaction from the literary values of *Parnasse* on the one hand and naturalism on the other, it is about coeval with Mallarmé's life in Paris;[1] in the narrowest and most punctilious sense, it should be applied only to Moréas' literary campaign (1885–90)— a tiny movement in the republic of bohemian letters.

The literary confusion that reigned on the Left Bank throughout the last two decades of the century can be fully appreciated only by reading the reviews of the time, with their pretentious manifestos, petty squabbling, bizarre contents, and ephemeral duration.[2] No wonder then that opinions both then and since have been contradictory on what should count as Symbolism. Nevertheless, certain things seem to be more or less agreed upon. The distinction which we draw between the third and the remaining two of our definitions has the support of one who by reason of his active participation in both the early and the later days of Symbolism, had a special insight into these questions of convenience of classification:

'J'ai toujours professé qu'il faut distinguer deux temps dans l'évolution grammaticale du symbolisme: d'abord le "parler décadent" (proprement dit, celui de 1885-6-7-8) qui fut une explosion et qui du premier côup alla aux pires audaces; ensuite ce qu'on pourrait appeler le "parler symboliste", qui en est la continuation, mais une continuation notablement assagie, et qui comporte les mêmes particularités mais dépouillées des premières outrances.'[3]

If there are those who feel entitled to talk of a symbolist 'period' in literature, there have also been others who are more intent on individual differences than on generic similarities. In an age when, as we shall presently see, a consciousness of individualism was given

---

[1] Cf. 'A cette heure il y a deux classes d'écrivains — ceux qui ont du talent — les symbolistes; ceux qui n'en ont pas — les autres.' (Rémy de Gourmont, *L'Idéalisme* (1892) (reprinted in *Le Chemin de Velours*, 1902).

[2] The reaction of a not insignificant poet from these imbroglios is sufficiently amusing to be worth quoting:

' ... Comme tout est vanité, et que cette parole est encore une vanité, mais qu'il est opportun en ce siècle que *chaque individu* fonde une école littéraire, je demande à ceux qui voudraient se joindre à moi pour n'en point former, d'envoyer leur adhésion...' (Francis Jammes, 'Un Manifeste littéraire', *Mercure de France*, iii/1897, t. 21, p. 493).

[3] Ed. Dujardin.

quite undue stress by a number of theoretical and social considerations, it was natural for a writer, when asked for a definition of his position in the stream of literary history, to concentrate his attention on those points which marked him off from his fellows rather than on those which marked him and them off from his predecessors. Like the child in Locke's parable, denying that a child from central Africa was human because of its skin pigmentation, so Mauclair says, 'Le symbolisme comme école est insaisissable';[1] A. Retté, that there are 'autant de définitions du Symbolisme que de poètes interrogés, et que ce nom de Symbolisme n'est qu'une épithète commode et rien de plus';[2] and André Fontainas announces that 'aucun corps de doctrine n'a jamais réuni la pensée, les tendances, les aspirations des écrivains qui se sont appelés symbolistes'.[3] R. de Souza speaks to more point when he says: 'Le symbolisme n'accepta la servitude d'aucune doctrine. Chaque poète choisit l'armature morale ou philosophique qui lui convenait, la poésie, redisons-le toujours, n'étant pas dans cette armature. On ne cessa de l'affirmer: peine perdue! tout symboliste était un mystique plus ou moins rosecroix, occultiste et déliquescent.'[4] But his attempts to define poetry in the true symbolist garb are hardly more satisfactory than those he denounces. We need not be unduly put off: the definitions here referred to are the differentiae of species all belonging to the same genus—to a greater or lesser extent, at least—and it is the genus that interests us; though no doubt its larger features were the occasion of considerably less controversy and pamphleteering in 1890.

These larger features run parallel with, and in the closest relation to, certain unmistakeable new trends in French literature towards the close of the nineteenth century. The trends are in themselves not hard to describe, and historians of literature have produced effective descriptions of them as seen from the outside; we shall attempt to push a little more deeply into their analysis and to provide an account of them by outlining their effect on the assumptions and hypotheses of aesthetics. In so doing we shall be mainly concerned with Symbolism in the second context noted above; i.e. as a highly interesting ferment in literature and criticism between 1885 and 1895. Set out in this way, certain difficulties of historical presentation will inevitably arise; and it will not always be possible to adhere to a chronological sequence. That should not prevent us from taking note of the spiritual ancestry, so to speak, of Symbolism: of its claims

[1] *La Nouvelle Revue*, Oct.-dec. 1897.   [2] *Revue de l'Epoque*, 15/iii/1922.
[3] *La Plume*, 15/ii/1892.   [4] R. de Souza, *Où noux en sommes*, 1901, p. 81.

to be pursuing the aims of Baudelaire, or following up a venerable tradition of mysticism, or deriving a fundamental attitude from German speculative philosophy. But we shall be examining Baudelaire, or Schopenhauer, or Wagner, as the case may be, not as separate and distinct parts of an inquiry, but only with a view to finding out for what purposes their authority was borrowed—always, therefore, we shall look on remoter bodies of ideas through the lenses of Symbolism. Similarly with the virtually unending game of 'sources': that the period under review was in its interests one of the most heterogeneous that is known to the student of literature can hardly be denied; Tolstoy, Ibsen, Whitman, Wagner, all things German, and stray English writers as well, were welcomed as important to 'Symbolism', almost by virtue of their foreign provenance, and often in despite of protestations of hostility from the writer concerned;[1] and the professed debt to the past strains our credulity in more than a few individual cases. But fortunately we are excused the task of compiling an encyclopaedia of this kind. Analysis by sources has been summed up concisely: 'These methods of description are characteristic of that frivolous and superficial type of history which speaks of "influences" and "borrowings" and so forth, and when it says that A is influenced by B or that A borrows from B never asks itself what there was in A which laid it open to B's influence, or what there was in A which made it capable of borrowing from B.'[2] In examining what there was in the symbolist attitude which laid it open to such a diversity of allegiances, we shall be dealing strictly with an aesthetic problem; to go into too detailed enumeration of these influences would take us off the line of our inquiry.

A further point arises out of this problem of the relations between ideas held or adopted by different people. We have hinted already that the views on art held by such 'authorities' as Wagner or Schopenhauer differed vastly from those often ascribed to them by their acolytes; in this, ignorance may have played its part, as we shall attempt to show in the sequel; but ignorance alone would not adequately account for an unmistakable trace of creative endeavour in many of the interpretations which have come down to the present day. The truth appears to be, that the generations of the eighties and nineties were seeking to express a new (or partially new) view of art; in their aspirations they had not found their way to giving a clear

[1] Cf. Tolstoy's violent denunciation of Mallarmé and all things symbolist in the *Revue Blanche* (vol. xv, p. 259, 15/ii/1898).
[2] R. G. Collingwood: *The Idea of Nature*, 1945, p. 128.

account of themselves—they were, so to say, still at the subliminal
stage—but they knew roughly, and fragmentarily, what they
wanted, and were prepared in their haste to project what they were
looking for into what they were searching through: often with
grotesque results (for their search was in the highest degree un-
critical) and sometimes with positively harmful results, for they involved themselves in endless confusions and contradictions, and were
even led on to eventual disgusted renunciation of the whole business,
or at the least to bitterness and scepticism.[1] In a sense, it was simple
humility on their part that was to blame, plus the eclecticism of
youth; either not realizing or else forgetting that they were commenting a literature in the last degree novel as to its aims, they overlooked the plain fact that a new art makes new demands on aesthetic,
and that it follows from this that no former attempt to describe art
could in the nature of things prove fully adequate to their needs.
Moreover, theirs was a movement in the history of literature which
had not, at the time, any equivalent or parallel movement in Europe
with which comparisons might be made on a large scale. Yeats or
Stefan George came to Paris prepared to learn, not to teach, or even
compare. And even supposing for the moment that there had been
similarities between native and foreign trends, these could never
have been so close as to render unnecessary a more critical examination
of the notions of others than they were prepared to accord.

---

[1] As, for example, Téodor de Wyzéwa, who after filling most of the issues of the *Revue
Wagnérienne* with aesthetic essays, came out with the following: 'et puis, ne sait-on pas depuis
des siècles que les théories esthétiques sont de niaises et stériles clamitations d'eunuques?' (*Revue
Indépendante*, iii/1887, vol. II, p. 339).

CHAPTER II

THE STARTING-POINT OF AN AESTHETIC

1. Positivist theories. 2. The intellectualist formula. 3. Pre-symbolist roots of anti-positivism. 4. Symbolist anti-positivism. 5. Symbolist idealism. 6. Mystical influences in Symbolist theory. 7. Schopenhauer. 8. Schopenhauer and Mallarmé. 9. The inadequacy of Ideas in modern Aesthetic.

A. POSITIVISM

1. POSITIVIST THEORIES

THE symbolists, we have suggested, are mainly remarkable for contributions of aesthetic *fact* rather than system; and it would be as well to see briefly the shape of the prevailing system of aesthetics which they found too narrow to house their facts.

Positivism aimed broadly at extending to the anatomy of art certain principles which it assumed to be valid in the natural sciences, and which it saw no reason to abandon when it came to the human sciences. Its first attempt was on historical data, and to this end it adapted its conception of the scientific method. The positivists 'thought it consisted of two things: first, ascertaining facts; secondly, framing laws. The facts were immediately ascertained by sensuous perception. The laws were framed through generalizing from these facts by induction'.[1] If it could be shown that the laws of art thus discovered were in some way related to similar laws of society which it hoped ultimately to discover in a similar way, the first step would have been taken towards breaking down the intolerable mystery which surrounded the question, 'What is art?' All subsequent development of an aesthetic would then take the form of a minute investigation and detailed classification of artistic phenomena under headings provided by the theory of society. Art would, in short, be explained initially from a sociological viewpoint.

Sociology as dreamt of by Auguste Comte never materialized, and positivists tacitly gave up waiting for it around the sixties. So we may with some justice say that Taine's *Philosophie de l'art*,[2] which represents the sketch for the principles of an aesthetic, is not unlike a ship attempting to anchor in a sea that has never been sounded, or walls being set up for a house which it is never proposed to finish:

[1] R. G. Collingwood, *The Idea of History*, 1946, pp. 126–7. [2] [Although Taine cannot in any strict sense be regarded as a positivist philosopher, he was so treated in the eighties in France. The word, used loosely, had of course strong connotations in other fields—e.g., educational.]

is in fact an anachronism, in that the edifice of principles it embodies assumes a substructure which the temper of the age had given up hope of ever securing. Here, as elsewhere, confidence in the methodological security of positivist history prompted the aesthetician to venture on a search for 'laws' without previously looking to see whether this search was actually being conducted along the lines involved in the natural sciences.

The course of the argument used is well known, but worth sketching out briefly. Taine assumed that the 'data' of art are akin to those of botany or zoology; as in the one case the flora or fauna of a country are visibly affected by the type of climate in which they are situated, so in the case of art, the works produced in any age or roughly defined epoch are evidently influenced by the mental atmosphere in which they are formed. The orange tree would die in a Scandinavian winter; so would the delicate product of a culturally advanced society when transplanted into the harsh atmosphere of a more primitive community. The social forces which work on art like weather on the orange tree are extensively examined in the justly celebrated introduction to the *Histoire de la littérature anglaise*: they are there classified as Race, Milieu, and Moment. Presumably, therefore, the positivist history of art would have not only to cast a glance on the biographical circumstances in which a given 'work of art' appears, but also to borrow from economic and social history an account of all relevant data (such as the financial resources of an eighteenth-century German princely court in determining the size of its orchestra), and from sociology (the missing science) an account of all social characteristics which might have a bearing on artistic taste and preference. In the *Philosophie de l'art*, however, Taine is content to leave the 'atmosphere' undifferentiated, and to define the outward influences on art as falling under three heads: the social aggregate, the historical forces embodied in the artist's entourage, and those in the artist himself—three stages in ever-increasing precision.[1] The results of such an approach have been made familiar to us to-day by long tradition of academic biographical criticism—including, indeed, Taine's own study of La Fontaine. The ground gained in this kind of literary botany is plainly of importance—not least to the aesthetician; but to continue the metaphor, the botany evidently does not include an account of the central distinguishing feature of the plant; namely, the fact of its having life; in short, it is not an aesthetic.

---

[1] Taine, *Philosophie de l'art*, 2nd ed. 1872, p. 5.

Fully aware of this, Taine proceeds in the *Philosophie* to an investigation of art in general. It is an empirical investigation: that is to say, he draws on his wide knowledge of western European civilization to furnish himself with the subject matter of his generalizations. First in the determination of the arts is the claim that they are imitative—

'Ils ont tous un caractère commun: celui d'être, plus ou moins, des arts d'imitation.'[1]

As part proof of which he observes that in times when artists come to assume too readily that they know their subject matter, and neglect to study it closely, there is a decline in standards, and decadence sets in. Unfortunately, this argument is somewhat vitiated by Taine's omitting to tell us by what standards *he* can judge art to be decadent; and in the absence of a fuller treatment of the type of judgement exemplified in such an assertion, one cannot feel bound to accept this line of reasoning as support for the imitation theory.

Nevertheless, he claims to observe that imitation is the foundation-stone of art; but, he goes on, imitation alone is not enough. A rough sketch by Van Dyke is of greater worth than a finished portrait by Denner; moreover, there exists a representative art throughout which deliberate inexactitude is common; namely, statuary. Accordingly we have a first qualification: upon the art of imitation must be superimposed an act of picking out 'les rapports et les dépendances mutuels'. Even this is inadequate: 'l'Artiste, en modifiant les rapports des parties, les modifie dans le même sens, avec intention, de façon à rendre sensible un certain *caractère essentiel* de l'objet, et par suite de l'idée principale qu'il s'en fait. Notons ce mot, Messieurs. Le caractère est ce que les philosophes appellent l'*essence* des choses'.[2] As to the nature of this *caractère essentiel*,

'c'est une qualité dont tous les autres, ou du moins beaucoup d'autres, dérivent suivant des liaisons fixes'.[3]

2. THE INTELLECTUALIST FORMULA

Taine's final description goes as follows:

'L'œuvre d'art a pour but de manifester quelque caractère essentiel ou saillant, partant quelque idée importante, plus clairement et plus complètement que ne le font les objets réels. Elle y arrive en employant un ensemble de parties liées, dont elle modifie systématiquement les rapports. Dans les trois arts d'imitation, sculpture, peinture, et poésie, ces ensembles correspondent à des objets réels.'[4]

[1] ibid., p. 26.   [2] ibid., pp. 50–51. A curious identification, much criticised by posterity.
[3] ibid.   [4] ibid., pp. 63–64.

Music and architecture represent types of art whose parts are 'liées' but not 'imitatives': arts, in short, whose materials are simply 'des rapports mathématiques'; we might have thought that this in itself gave rise to powerful objections to the imitative axiom as a basic aesthetic principle; but Taine pleads that music at least has an analogy with the cries of living creatures; and a noted musicologist, in an effort no doubt to repair this breach in more substantial fashion, has argued, as against Helmholtz and Hanslick, that music contains a definite and acknowledged referential element, like speech, which entitles it to be called imitative, or at least representational, on the same terms as literature.[1] We shall have occasion to discuss this argument at a later stage.

It will be seen that already at this point Taine has committed himself by implication to a definite psychology (even if we had not the evidence of other works to confirm us in our findings). It may be summed up somewhat as follows:

1. The artist makes use of material presented to his senses and already interpreted intellectually before he comes to treat it in the way claimed to be peculiar to art (i.e. by bringing out the 'essential character' of the theme it combines to form). Therefore two elements alone need to be distinguished in aesthetic activity: a *passive* element of perception, and an *active* element of rational interpretation. The rest of the artist's work is pure routine: putting his material into communicable form.

2. The kind of attitude which the artist adopts in face of his material is intellectual, in the sense that he decides from a number of possible alternatives, what essential feature he *ought* to emphasize, or use as a guiding principle of design, and then proceeds to try and accomplish this self-imposed task of giving it requisite prominence. In short, he proposes to himself an end, and the business of art is the attainment of this end. It is in this sense that Taine can speak of posterity trying to *understand* a work of art,[2] and in this sense that his aesthetic is intellectualist.

The whole approach is open to the gravest objections. Suppose we were, say, to look at a wrinkled Dutch crone as some old master might have done; we study her carefully, and then say to ourselves something after this fashion: 'The essential character of this creature is a harsh and stubborn peasant earthyness. Her face reflects a hundred battles waged by her race against the havoc of the sea.' After which,

---

[1] Combarieu, *Les Rapports de la musique et de la poésie*, 1894, *passim*.
[2] op. cit., p. 13, 'comprendre'.

what further need is there to repeat the whole analysis by reproducing on canvas what is already perfectly clear in our minds? If art merely echoes a notion (for a 'caractère essentiel' is a notion)—a notion that can be expressed in half a dozen words—why should anyone spend days working at a canvas, at a novel, at a symphony? By these tokens all that art can ever contain is already there in the museum guide or the concert programme; and if that is so, how are we to judge whether our half-dozen words are prose, poetry, art, or nonsense? The most forceful presentation of the salient feature may be precisely the most offensively awkward and tasteless grouping of words—on every view, the least artistic. We know quite well that all these difficulties into which Taine has landed us do not really exist and need never arise; for nobody would seriously suggest that the painting of the old master is not infinitely higher in any scale of values than the half-dozen banal words in which we paraphrase its subject for the guide-book.

Taine has an answer to these objections, though not a very strong one. It depends for its authority on the existence, either actual or virtual, of a positivist sociology, and on examination is seen to consist in reducing art to the status of an inferior, because only approximative, science:

Man (he says) seeks to master the universe. 'Après tant d'inventions et de labeurs, il n'est pas sorti de son premier cercle, il est encore un animal, mieux approvisionné et mieux protégé que les autres, mais il n'a encore songé qu'à lui-même, et à ses pareils. A ce moment, une vie supérieure s'ouvre, celle de la contemplation, par laquelle il s'intéresse aux causes permanentes et génératrices desquelles son être et celui de ses pareils dépendent, aux caractères dominateurs et essentiels qui régissent chaque ensemble et impriment leurs marques dans les moindres détails. Pour y atteindre, il a deux voies: la première qui est la science, par laquelle, dégageant ces causes et ces lois fondamentales, il les exprime en formules exactes et en termes abstraits; la seconde, qui est l'art, par laquelle il manifeste ces causes et ces lois fondamentales, non plus en définitions arides, inaccessibles à la foule et intelligibles seulement pour quelques hommes spéciaux, mais d'une façon sensible, et en s'adressant non-seulement à la raison mais encore aux sens et au cœur de l'homme le plus ordinaire. L'art a cela de particulier, qu'il est à la fois *supérieur* et *populaire*, qu'il manifeste ce qu'il y a de plus élevé, et qu'il le manifeste à tous.'[1]

No one need be deceived by the italicized eulogy of art which comes at the end of this revealing passage—revealing not only for the way it shows up the simplicity of this truly rigorous thinker's course of argument, but also for the example it gives of the conclusion neces-

---

[1] op. cit., *ad finem*. Author's italics. It is worth noting that Taine here rejects the notion that art is either entertaining or of practical moral value: not explicitly, but by opening up a fresh vista of practical value, namely, that of positive knowledge.

sarily reached by any undiluted 'imitation' theory—even an imitation theory which allows art to represent emotions symbolically (as in music), or to bring affective factors into the play of the spectator's apprehension. To anyone capable of independent judgement, such a conclusion must come as a death-sentence on any view of art as a distinct form of human activity. The man whose intellectual faculties are insufficiently developed has, for lack of better means, to be approached through his sensibility, by which he is enabled to learn, for example, that 'Nature is harsh', 'life is a battle', etc. And since Taine undoubtedly believed—for much of his life at least—in the inevitable forward march of the intellect, it is plain that art is, on these conditions, destined ever to narrow its scope and finally disappear: a view which may appeal at times to Renan, but hardly one which an artist would ordinarily applaud. Although art is not in this definition differentiated in kind (but only in the degree of its rigour) from science, and thus not strictly speaking defined at all on this side, Taine never came closer to explicitly formulating an aesthetic. Hear him refuse to approach the problem by a different way:

'L'ancienne esthétique donnait d'abord une définition du beau, et disait, par exemple, que le beau est l'expression de l'idéal moral, ou bien qu'il est l'expression de l'invisible, ou bien encore qu'il est l'expression des passions humaines; puis partant de là, comme d'un article de code, elle absolvait, condamnait, admonestait, et guidait. Je suis bien heureux de ne pas avoir une si grosse tâche à remplir; je n'ai pas à vous guider, j'en serais trop embarrassé. D'ailleurs, je me dis tout bas qu'après tout, en fait de préceptes, on n'en a encore trouvé que deux; le premier qui conseille de naître avec du génie: c'est l'affaire de vos parents, ce n'est pas la mienne; le second, qui conseille de travailler beaucoup, afin de bien posséder son art: c'est votre affaire, ce n'est pas non plus la mienne. Mon seul devoir est de vous expliquer les faits et de vous montrer comment ces faits se sont produits. La méthode moderne que je tâche de suivre, et qui commence à s'introduire dans toutes les sciences morales, consiste à considérer les œuvres humaines et en particulier les œuvres d'art comme des faits et des produits, dont il faut marquer les caractères et chercher les causes: rien de plus'.[1]

Poeta nascitur et fit: by all means; but in studying the concretions of the mental activity of this strange creature, Taine admits the existence of only one kind of objects of study whatever: 'des faits ... dont il faut chercher les causes'; that is to say, the facts familiar to natural science; and only one way of approaching them—namely, as members of classes; so that when he says that there is only one way of studying art, this is evidently a way of studying art not as art, but simply as historical material; as historical material, moreover, in the service of a very special kind of history—in which the classification of 'data'

[1] op. cit., pp. 19–20.

under empirical generalizations for some ulterior sociology is the over-riding preoccupation.

Elsewhere, however, he concedes that the term 'genius' admits of some analysis; and announces that to be able to seek out the 'caractère essentiel' of a given subject for art, the artist must have 'une sensation originale'; by virtue of which 'il pénètre dans l'intérieur des objets, et semble plus perspicace que les autres hommes';[1] and one may always find in the true poet 'cet ascendant de l'impression involontaire'. Yet, he repeats, this alone is not enough; with all the will in the world, and the most sensitive and impressionable nature, the artist is lost if he goes against the dominant trend of the age:

'Pour faire de belles œuvres, la condition unique est celle qu'indiquait le grand Goethe: Emplissez votre esprit et votre cœur, si larges qu'ils soient, des idées et des sentiments de votre siècle, et l'œuvre viendra.'[2]

One cannot be sure that in his wish to make a case, he has not allowed himself to confuse different kinds of causes.

Such, briefly, is Taine's theory of art. It is hard to call it an aesthetic: rather it is an elaborate description of the method to be followed by a sociological history of art. Taine himself admits this[3] and adds with some emphasis that the two fields are identical:

'Supposez que par l'effort de toutes ces découvertes, on parvienne à définir la nature et marquer les conditions d'existence de chaque art: nous aurions alors une explication complète des beaux-arts, et de l'art en général; c'est-à-dire, une philo-sophie des beaux-arts; c'est là ce qu'on appelle une *esthétique*. Nous aspirons à cela messieurs, et non pas à une autre. La nôtre est moderne, et diffère de l'ancienne en ce qu'elle n'impose pas de préceptes, mais qu'elle constate des lois.'[4]

We have already noted above that the form of aesthetic speculation nearly always has a close relation with the other activities of the aesthe-tician. We cited the antithetical approaches made on the one hand by artists, and on the other by philosophers: here one would be tempted to find yet another standpoint: that of the professional critic, the historical critic. Sainte-Beuve may be said to have guided the development of literary criticism from the position of a mere apanage of the arts to an independent sphere of its own: Taine never knew the earlier position at all; for him, criticism of the arts was always an

[1] ibid., p. 61.   [2] ibid., p. 161.   [3] ibid., p. 184.
[4] ibid., p. 18. Cf. too this approving remark of a follower: 'La plupart des critiques n'ont essayé de montrer la nature des écrivains dont ils s'occupaient, que pour mieux apprécier leurs œuvres. M. Taine seul s'est à peu près dispensé de cette tâche secondaire' (Emile Hennequin, *La Critique Scientifique*, 1888, p. 64). This is the same as saying that Taine took no interest in estimating aesthetic worth—the reason being that he never defined it.

autonomous province of the mind, founded upon historical research into the art of the past, and treated as data for sociology; and he never appears to have recognized the fact that his criticism reaches the level of greatness only when it reflects a momentary abandonment of his principles—when, in fact, he ceases to look on his material as 'des faits et des produits dont on cherche les causes', and applies himself to evoking it vividly before his readers, and fusing interpretation and judgement in a way which his own theory excludes absolutely from any claim to being a valuable or indeed even possible activity.

Nor did it occur to him, or to anyone else until the turn of the century, that the historical approach could be anything other than this pseudo-application of the 'scientific method'; and accordingly we find that those who turned away in disgust from his whole conception never troubled to inquire whether history had any further interest for the aesthetician. Of the following generation, which incidentally gave symbolism to the world, it has been well said that it lacked greatly in sympathetic historical interpretation and criticism:[1] this in the world of letters only, of course; and while the judgement does little justice to the efforts, say, of a Jean Moréas to rediscover early French poetry, is too plainly true in such cases as Mallarmé's criticism (and especially his interpretation of *Hamlet*),[2] and does much to explain the motives underlying Laforgue's *Moralités légendaires*. The aesthetic doctrines of the symbolist movement are simply not designed to cope with the problems of historical relativism.

What we might call the loose ends, the inadequacies, of Taine's aesthetic may be set out under four counts. First comes the plain fact that he failed to distinguish the activity called artistic from the activity called scientific; that is to say, he ascribed to art the social functions already enjoyed by science. Secondly, and following on from this, he was unable to formulate a scale of values which was distinctive of aesthetics. His whole doctrine implied that art may be judged only by reference to its clarity—by its ability to convey information with the minimum of ambiguity. Rejecting all previous attempts to provide a scale, relative to the word 'beauty', he offered nothing in its place. Thirdly, he declined to offer an opinion on the

---

[1] Ad. van Bever, quoted in Le Cardonnel and Vellay, *La Littérature contemporaine*, 1905, pp. 210–11. Cf. Charles Morice's remark (in the name of the younger generation): 'Le sens historique est — fatalement et comme par définition, puisqu'on n'a d'histoire qu'à condition d'avoir beaucoup vécu — le signe de la vieillesse d'une race, une marque de décadence. Il s'éveille avec le sens critique, à l'âge critique des sociétés, pour brider en elles la spontanéité de la faculté créatrice' (*La Littérature de tout à l'heure*, 1889, p. 52.)

[2] See *Divagations* (Fasquelle), p. 371.

meaning of the word 'genius'—at first sight a trivial enough refusal, but a significant one: if he did not distinguish the difference between art and non-art, neither did he attempt to produce an account of what particularly *happens* in the creation of a work of art. Fourthly, he could offer a classification of the arts depending only on their superficial media, or the human organs involved in their reception: in this field the complement of French positivism is to be found in the work of Grant Allan, with its doctrines of the higher and lower faculties of perception, and the monstrous results that flow from this tempting hierarchy. And arising out of this, he found himself in serious difficulties when he attempted to incorporate music into a system of the arts.

It is not true that the position summarized above remains in all respects the same for the positivist tradition after Taine. The ever-increasing study of psychology and physiology redirected attention to one at least of the factors which differentiated art from other forms of knowledge—the emotional factor (Taine's aesthetic is at least free from the vulgar hedonism which slips in unquestioned among the assumptions of nearly all nineteenth-century efforts to found a positive science of art). Guyau, for example, studying poetry from the viewpoint of its rhyme and rhythm, along lines derived from Herbert Spenser, observed that all rhythmic gesture, indeed all gesture whatever, has a close relation to emotional states. Here already is an opening by which to admit music to the company of the other arts. And justifying the use of rhyme, Guyau recklessly uncovers other avenues of approach: from the fact that a vowel timbre derives from a 'harmony' between its fundamental note and its upper partials, he infers that rhyme produces a 'satisfaction' analogous to that of music. As developed by the physiologist, this satisfaction is dealt with in terms of nervous charge and discharge; and courageous attempts were made to give a full account of music, simple patterns and other easily handled objects, regarding their structure and laws, against this experimental background.

But it is especially significant that the underlying epistemological assumptions of Taine (not peculiarly his—they would have been thought of as belonging to common sense) were not only never modified, but never even called into question, at least during the nineteenth century. A new science or two entered the field, that is all; it continued to be taken for granted that the activities of the mind could be circumscribed, and with luck exhausted, within the limits of some kind of system constructed on analogy with one or other of the natural sciences, provided only that the net of the investigator was flung wide enough, and embraced all the data theretofore available. Each fresh positivist attempt was a new and wider throw of the net, as the increased perspectives of each generation gave its arm greater force; but each time it was still the same net that was used, each time something slipped through the meshes and was lost.

We must now return and examine the reaction that set in to those positivist doctrines that were familiar to the literary world of the eighties and nineties. These were, of course, the works of Taine and his followers; not indeed that the work of the physiologists and psychologists constituted a world unknown to the symbolists, for their findings were laid quite regularly upon the doorstep of symbolism through the popularizing work of Charles Henry, Jules de Gaultier, and others; it was a case of their being, quite simply, ignored.

3. PRE-SYMBOLIST ROOTS OF ANTI-POSITIVISM

The first and most striking feature of the symbolist aesthetic was its attempt to establish art as an autonomous branch of human activity.

It faced the task of distinguishing art from the history or science with which Taine and others had confused it; much as Baudelaire in an earlier generation had striven to distinguish art from moral propaganda or moral philosophy. And it is the symbolist attempt to deal with this problem which makes the generation of the 'petites revues' on balance modern in its aesthetic.

Such an attempt was plainly in the mind of Viélé-Griffin when he said:

'La rénovation du sens esthétique qui s'accomplit diversement entre 1885 et 1895 — la plus considérable depuis le romantisme — a fécondé toutes les branches de l'activité artistique et a nourri pour cinquante ans peut-être la cervelle contemporaine.'[1]

And the sequel has been treated by M. J. Benda to the point where contradiction on anything other than detail becomes useless.[2] There

---

[1] F. Viélé-Griffin, quoted in *La Littérature contemporaine*, 1905, p. 68.

[2] Julien Benda, *La France Byzantine*, 1944, *passim*. At the same time M. Benda's single-mindedness has resulted in his being unable to see any alternatives for the future besides surrealism and artistic philistinism. Already, in 1918, for instance, he makes his position clear: 'La présente société française demande aux œuvres d'art qu'elles lui fassent éprouver des émotions et des sensations; elle entend ne plus connaître par elles aucune espèce de plaisir intellectuel' (*Belphégor*, 1918, p. 1). And in his most revealing work to date, we read: 'Je sais par cœur de nombreux vers, voire des plus exempts de réelle pensée, comme ceux de tel poète

can be no doubt that since the recognition of Henri de Régnier or
Valéry, the poet in France has been left free to sing without the
imposition of degrading or at least distasteful public functions.
But that this was not so at an earlier date is brought vigorously to
our notice in Baudelaire's polemics against philosophical art. Though
more than twenty years old, these polemics had lost none of their
topicality for Symbolism; here as in much else their author was an
avowed master:

'Il en est de la condition de moralité imposée aux œuvres d'art comme de cette
autre condition non moins ridicule que quelques-uns veulent leur faire subir, à savoir
d'exprimer des pensées ou des idées tirées d'un monde étranger à l'art, des idées
scientifiques, des idées politiques, etc... Tel est le point de départ des esprits faux,
ou du moins des esprits qui, n'étant pas absolument poétiques, veulent raisonner
poésie. L'idée, disent-ils, est la chose la plus importante (ils devraient dire, L'idée et
la forme sont deux êtres en un); naturellement, fatalement, ils se disent bientôt:
puisque l'idée est la chose importante par excellence, la forme, moins importante,
peut être négligée sans danger. Le résultat est l'anéantissement de la poésie.'[1]

The attack on the old aesthetic takes on, for Baudelaire, largely the
character of an attack on the old distinction between content and
form; and to a pre-symbolist generation, this was the essential and
burning problem of art. By idea, plainly, Baudelaire means nothing
more than the subject of a piece, be it a poem or a picture; something essentially intellectual, therefore. 'Medea stabbing her children',
in Delacroix' picture, makes an unedifying spectacle from the viewpoint of moral instruction; therefore, 'all other things being equal',[2]
a less revolting subject makes a better picture. For Baudelaire, the
weakness of the position, especially *without* the qualification, was
obvious: a subject, a theme, are not simply colourless objects of
intellectual apprehension, to be judged by the standards of some
non-aesthetic science (e.g. ethics); on the contrary, there enters into
every such apprehension a factor of emotion, a factor entirely independent of any extraneous criteria, standing on its own merits, valued

mallarméen, et me les récite souvent avec amour. Mais j'éprouve peu de considération pour
cette activité et pour le goût que j'en ai. Je les trouve volontiers enfantins... En somme, je
crois que le sort de l'humanité est intéressé à l'avènement de cet âge dont parle Renan, où sortie
de l'enfance, elle ne respectera plus l'homme qui fait œuvre d'art, mais seulement qui lui dit la
vérité' (*Exercice d'un enterré vif*, 1944, pp. 11–14). Evidently we cannot accept unreservedly
much of M. Benda's account of the symbolist and post-symbolist aesthetic (he takes no trouble
to distinguish any developments as between Mallarmé and Eluard); but on the point here in
question, i.e. the search for artistic autonomy, there is no great distortion in his interpretations,
grouped under his heading: 'Volonté d'une littérature actuelle de constituer une activité
spécifique'.

[1] *Art Romantique* (ed. Crépet), p. 320.

[2] 'Toutes choses égales d'ailleurs, l'œuvre qui exprime un caractère bienfaisant est supérieure
à celle qui exprime un caractère malfaisant' (*Philosophie de l'art*, II, p. 289, 1921 ed.). Taine's
phrase is vigorously attacked by Laforgue in his correspondence.

for itself. 'Il y a des moments de l'existence où le temps et l'étendue sont plus profonds, et le sentiment de l'existence immensément augmenté',[1] we read: there can be little doubt that the type of experience indicated by this remark is the source of Baudelaire's approach to mysticism and to art; these two things are for him merely different faces of the same experience, art being the vehicle for realizing a state of mind which has no interest for science or for ethics in the ordinary sense. No doubt Baudelaire would have rejected forcibly any suggestion that his theory of art could be reconciled with a rational philosophy of art, or his experiences with a rational psychology; but to-day there seems to be little justification for his having recourse to a Swedenborgian mysticism as the term of his aesthetic observations.

It being granted that an affective factor is indispensable to any true account of aesthetic experience, runs Baudelaire's argument, it follows that the truly artistic element of style, or form, as he calls it, which generates this factor, cannot be treated apart from the matter which it clothes; or rather, in art, the subject cannot be regarded in isolation from the way in which the artist approaches it, nor the work of art be divided into two watertight sections, subject and form, with the former prior to, and more important than, the latter. For the instant the artist seizes on his subject, he has already formed an attitude towards it. To isolate 'subject matter', when talking of art, is to introduce an intellectual abstraction which has no place at all in the world of art. We are here anticipating somewhat the theorizing of two generations later on language; but this approach to the subject-form controversy is fundamental to the modern aesthetic; and to Baudelaire must go a large measure of credit for anticipating the refutation of Taine.[2]

Whatever we may complain of in the matter of Baudelaire's incomplete and disjointed exposition (scattered through a dozen or more critical articles and fragments), here, at least, is a first vital distinction between the positivist view and what was later to be the

---

[1] *Fusées*, p. 81.

[2] Though we find in the correspondence of one of his more distinguished contemporaries a rather extreme and apoplectic version of the same thing: 'Pour moi, tant qu'on n'aura pas, d'une phrase donnée, séparé la forme du fond, je soutiendrai que ce sont là deux mots vides de sens. Il n'y a pas de belles pensées sans belles formes, et réciproquement. La Beauté transsude de la forme dans le monde de l'art, comme dans notre monde, à nous, il en sort la tentation, l'amour; de même qu'on ne peut extraire d'un corps physique les qualités qui le constituent, c'est-à-dire, couleur, étendue, solidité, sans le réduire à une abstraction creuse, de même on n'ôtera pas la forme de l'idée, car *l'idée n'existe qu'en vertu de sa forme*' (Flaubert). The last phrase is questionable and confusing; but the general notion of art being other than the mere statement in symbolic form of an abstract notion is unimpeachable.

symbolist view: art is to be distinguished from science by the fact that it embodies in it an absolutely indispensable element of form, which is more than a mere convenience of presentation. For Taine, at least in the *Philosophie de l'art*, form is ascribed by implication to the level on which a printer decides what the width of the margin shall be in his book—utilitarian standards relating to the attentiveness of the reader: for Baudelaire it occupies a quite crucial position. At a later stage we shall have to return to the concept of form with Baudelaire and examine it in relation to the category of the symbol; for the moment it is enough to note his major disagreement from the positivist view on the status of the material of art. It is one which we find in attendance wherever 'art for art's sake' is invoked in the nineteenth century; often, unfortunately, in confused form.

For the step forward which Baudelaire and Flaubert both attempted to make was attended by difficulties of the most extreme kind. As distinguished by them from content, form could hardly stand as an end in itself; Flaubert's practice and constant choice of themes for his greatest works belie some of his incautious pronouncements on craft. And the attempt to distinguish art from anything else by drawing attention to its *form* did not help very much when they were really trying not only to draw distinctions but to lay down an autonomous province within which the artist was to be the exclusive legislator. A moralist or a scientist could both, without prejudice to their prospective aims, set forth their views in artistic forms; they would be artists then, but not by virtue of taking part in any specifically artistic activity—unless it were possible to ignore completely the fact that they were giving utterance to notions and arguments which were in fact the prime reason for their writing at all. Under such circumstances, it would be possible to defend the artistic approach to their work only by saying that art could be compared in some way with science or ethics and found in every respect to be more important. This latter is the solution that suggests itself to Valéry, and indeed to Edgar Allan Poe in *Eureka*; but it involves the supposition that any activity whatever is artistic activity and virtually nothing besides; which is as much as to solve the problem of distinguishing art from all other forms of activity by denying absolutely the existence of the latter. And although such a radical view has from time to time been adopted by both philosophers and poets, it does not usually commend itself for any great length of time, or to a very wide circle of artists—or thinkers.

4. SYMBOLIST ANTI-POSITIVISM

At any rate, the age of Symbolism was not prepared to set out on such a venture. Instead it restricted itself to revealing the faults inherent in Taine's position: that is to say, without ever going so far as to say that all science is art, it vigorously attacked the suggestion that all art is science. And whereas in their positive doctrines regarding aesthetics the symbolists reveal extraordinary confusion and contradiction of one another, in this purely negative stage their unanimity is remarkable. From every Eleusinian grove comes a standard condemnation of Taine. On the wing of pure mysticism, Ernest Hello fulminates against the current embodiments of positivist aesthetic:

'Le réalisme pur, ni au théâtre ni ailleurs, n'a pris un nom, ni adopté une forme. Là où il passe, il détruit l'art, mais ne se propose pas pour le remplacer. Il fait le vide. Le réalisme a donc, dans l'histoire de l'art, la place du scepticisme absolu dans l'histoire de la philosophie. Il est l'expression du désespoir...'[1]

Another noted mystic, critic, and well-known figure in symbolist controversy, Péladan, founds a whole aesthetic upon an emotionalist theory which binds art closely to the mystic intuition of divinity; and the resulting confusion is recognized as being incompatible with any kind of intellectualist or analytic approach whatever:

'La culture qui prépare un plaisir d'art se détache radicalement de l'enseignement universitaire ... l'émotivité ne résulte pas de l'érudition... Les bons commentaires sont ceux qui naissent de la contemplation et qu'on n'écrira jamais.'[2]

Moving towards the less extravagant spheres of criticism, we come upon Bernard Lazare attacking Taine's whole approach on the grounds that it has in fact nothing to do with art as a creative activity;[3] upon the gifted young symbolist theorist G.-A. Aurier undertaking to refute all so-called historical attempts to explain (or explain away) art, and accusing Taine, Hennequin, and Sainte-Beuve (the latter, to be sure, for no valid reason at all) of looking on works of art as corpses to dissect rather than as creatures to bring to life:

'Et en effet, M. Taine sans l'avouer explicitement, s'insoucie fort de la valeur esthétique absolue et intrinsèque des œuvres. Celles-ci ne l'intéressent que comme phénomènes de l'esprit humain ou comme documents historiques... Ceci une fois posé, la méthode qu'en déduit M. Taine est logique. Il ne perdra point son temps comme ces critiques dogmatiques d'autrefois, à vous expliquer pourquoi une

---

[1] Ernest Hello, *L'homme, la vie, la science, l'art*, p. 372.
[2] Péladan, *L'Art idéaliste et mystique* (précédé d'une réfutation de Taine), p. 56.
[3] Bernard Lazare, in *Entretiens politiques et littéraires*, No. 25, vol. iv, p. 170, avril/1892.

œuvre d'art est belle, il ne vous parlera même que fort peu de cette œuvre. Il se bornera, à propos de l'œuvre en question, à des considérations logiques de psychologie, de sociologie, et d'histoire, convaincu qu'il a fait ainsi de la critique d'art.'[1]

Zola's press in the symbolist reviews was always bad; but the reasons for hostility were not always so frankly and tellingly set forth as in the following anonymous review of his sincerest attempt to come to grips with the mentality of the artist (*L'Œuvre*):

'Le roman sera toujours hybride et bâtard... Chacun de ses protagonistes a dû le torturer pour lui donner du sérieux. M. Emile Zola l'a porté vers l'enquête sociale; ne serait-ce pas plus simple de dire sans fabulation aucune (car toutes sont leurre) les impressions d'un artiste sur les faits ambiants? N'empiète-t-on pas sur le territoire futur de la science sociale maintenant à faire, et qui serait probablement établie si M. Zola y eût appliqué ses grandes qualités? La science sociale est ainsi embryonnaire dans les romans de Balzac. Elle expliquerait et légitimerait le rôle de l'artiste et du théoricien si méconnus de ce monde capitaliste. Certes le roman n'est que transition. Evoquer et non raconter; fouiller les personnelles et sincères analyses, rythmer les poèmes qui diront les symboles, tel est à la minute présente le but de l'art. Le reste est du passe-temps, ou de la demi-science.'[2]

Charles Morice is impelled to much the same sort of attack on realism and naturalism in general:

'Ce point de vue historique, très notoire aussi dans les prétentions des *Rougon-Macquart*, est à la fois secondaire, faux, et dangereux. Secondaire et presque inutile, car qu'importe, en somme, la réalité historique des mœurs et la physionomie sociale d'une civilisation aux civilisations futures? L'héritage des pensées et des images traverse les révolutions et importe seul: l'habit que portaient les hommes, morts depuis longtemps et dont la parole nous gouverne encore, ne peut solliciter qu'une curiosité oisive. Mais ce point de vue est faux car il n'est pas humain: il oblige celui qui s'y place à se supposer au lieu des hommes qui viendront dans deux cents ans. Pourtant rien n'est urgent et capital que de vivre sincèrement sa vraie vie, sa vie contemporaine, et de faire le plus bellement fleurir en soi ses pensées d'homme de ce temps.'[3]

This is not a very powerful argument; and we have the impression that at no point in his career was Morice quite in a position to argue his case against Taine convincingly; in the quotation above, it is not plain where we should draw the line between the face of past society (irrelevant to-day) and the images of it formed in the minds of its artists (still valuable); what is required is a more precise definition of the 'images' in question. Morice has, on the other hand, two powerful alternative arguments with which to confront the historical novelist of the times and his dependent aestheticians. In the first place, there is a well-worn, but none the less valid, argument that no

---

[1] 'Préface pour un livre de critique d'art,' *Mercure de France*, t. vi, p. 311, xii/1892.
[2] *Vogue*, No. 2, pp. 68–9, 18/iv/1886.   [3] *La Littérature de tout à l'heure*, p. 194.

art can ever be strictly descriptive—'A rigoureusement parler, il n'y a pas de description *exacte* possible';[1] and he supports this view with the assertion that in the case of at least one outstanding realist so called (Balzac) the greatness of his work is entirely dependent on the power of the imagination which informs his materials—that power which he quotes Carlyle as calling 'L'organe par lequel nous percevons le divin'.[2] The second argument strikes harder at the whole problem of determinism in art, at the narrow view which asserts a rigid causality between environment and art and ignores any other field of investigation. Elsewhere Morice may well have had one eye on Hegel's impressive classification of the historical and logical stages through which art had passed, when he asserts a course of aesthetic development in principle independent of the growth of societies:

'Cette fécondation de l'Art en conséquence des évolutions externes n'est peut-être pas indispensable au développement de l'idée esthétique, qui du moins n'en subit pas aveuglément et fatalement le contre-coup, mais accomplit, de période en période, une ascension qui s'affirme étrangère aux progrès hasardeux de la formule sociale.'[3]

While a more illustrious colleague in the field of journalism, Rémy de Gourmont, asserts, in the passage which we quote below, as a sufficient refutation of the positivist aesthetic, that the data of aesthetics do not fall into the sort of classes necessary for so-called scientific treatment:

'L'Individu est anormal: on ne le classe que par les limitations à ses manifestations extérieures; intérieurement il est anormal, il est un être dissemblable des êtres qui lui ressemblent le plus. L'Art (que je considère ici comme une des *Facultés* de l'âme individuelle) est donc de même que l'individu lui-même, anormal, illogique, et incompréhensible.'[4]

Though the language used is misleading enough, the sense is pretty clear; and it expresses what to-day would pass for a common-sense view. Not too much notice should be taken of the arresting term 'anormal', nor should it be necessary to try and correct the notion of individuality being either illogical or incomprehensible. But at least these phrases serve to show that Rémy de Gourmont was fully alive to the formal impossibility of a positivist science, which divides its phenomena into classes marked by exact properties, making any sense whatever of a mass of material in which the only point of similarity between its members was their essential individuality. We could multiply almost to infinity the examples of objections

---

[1] ibid., p. 165.　　[2] ibid., p. 168.　　[3] ibid., p. 74.
[4] *L'idéalisme*, reprinted in *Le chemin de Velours*, 1902, p. 217.

raised between 1880 and 1900 to the system of ideas put forward by Taine and purporting to be, in the entirety, an aesthetic. Many show little real understanding of the essentials at stake; some, among them *obiter dicta* of Laforgue, contradict Taine formally at the same time as they construct a rival view on almost equivalent lines;[1] most of them base their arguments on the assertion that positivism leaves no place for an artistic freedom of which they were intuitively conscious, but which they could not theoretically justify; all, however, have a strong feeling that positivism has not adequately propounded—let alone solved—the problems of aesthetic which were vital to their activities.

And it is to the alternative foundations of an aesthetic which they attempted to provide for their art that we must now turn our attention.

B. SYMBOLISM

'A cette heure, la théorie idéaliste n'est plus guère contestée que par quelques canards enclins à se plaire dans les vieux marécages.'[2]

'Cet idéalisme est la clé métaphysique de la plupart des esprits de la génération qui compose l'école symboliste.'[3]

5. SYMBOLIST IDEALISM

Without there being ever so rigid an antithesis as a brief schematism would suggest, it is true to say that to the curious but uninitiated literary world of after 1870 two 'systems' offered themselves, the first positivist, realist, naturalist, the second speculative, idealist, anti-naturalist. The first was in its origins largely French, its lineage including Auguste Comte, Littré, Taine, Renan, a host of physio-psychologists, the first students of evolutionary biology, and a wing of historians; the second was represented mainly by early nineteenth-century German philosophy enjoying an Indian summer in a tropical climate—Kant, Fichte, Schelling, Hegel, Schopenhauer. It is interesting to reflect that but for the collector's enthusiasm which largely promoted the translation of the Germans, and was sustained not only by eclecticism after 1830 but by positivism in the sixties and onward,[4] this efflorescence might never have taken place. From every point

---

[1] *Vide infra,* chapter IV, 7. Laforgue puts a metaphysical determinism of the Unconscious in place of Taine's more straightforward determinism founded on sociology.

[2] Rémy de Gourmont, *L'Idéalisme* (in *Le Chemin de Velours,* 1902, p. 198).

[3] Henri de Régnier, quoted by Ed. Dujardin, *Mallarmé,* p. 33.

[4] That same attitude which did so much at an earlier date to encourage the study of oriental thought in France.

of view, however, this vogue must appear as an anachronism; a dual approach of dogmatism and (in its more guarded moments) of historical retrospection exemplified by Charles Bénard's whole work,[1] or by Ribot's *Schopenhauer*. The relation between the two traditions becomes at times almost quaint: Taine's *L'Idéalisme anglais*, a work aimed principally at Carlyle, alternates between respect for his subject's personality and disgust for his theories; and even Taine does not venture on a root-and-branch refutation of his adversary's stand-point: while Ribot's study of the German philosopher is thoroughly impartial—one might almost say non-committal. It seemed as though the speculative method bore a charm which saved it in essential parts from attack by positivism: retaining from an earlier period a prestige so great that even those wedded to the piece-meal accumulation of fact hesitated to interfere with it in its search for some general organizing principles of human thought.

The first important entry of German transcendental philosophy into France dates from the popularizing work of Victor Cousin, notably the published lecture-courses of 1816-19 and the *Fragmens Philosophiques* of 1826;[2] and the study of the great German classical philosophers from Kant to Hegel grew in volume, under the indulgent eclecticism of official philosophy after 1830.[3] Having once made its appearance, German idealism was not easily dislodged. Powerfully entrenched in the academic hierarchy, the tradition was supported by frequent translation from the originals, which made the leading works of speculative idealism accessible not only to the student but to the general public as well. The result of this acquisition of a foreign tradition was to give the works translated a rather unusual force of authority, since in the earlier stages at least no attempt was made, except in specialist circles, to bring to view the great volume of controversy, and the bulk of rival and disintegrating development by disciples and critics in Germany and elsewhere, which clung round the central themes and problems treated in the works translated. To the writer of 1880, Kant or Schopenhauer (almost indifferently) were simply 'idealists': enormous figures, whose work, seen through a mist, appeared only in the vaguest outline. Less famous philosophers (i.e. those whose works, though perhaps important, remained

---

[1] See, for example, his 'Problème de la division des arts dans son développement historique et dans l'esthétique allemande,' *Rev. Phil.*, t. xvi, septembre/1883.

[2] Mme de Staël's *De l'Allemagne* can hardly be counted as an anticipation. German philological research of course had already produced important repercussions in France, notably through Fauriel.

[3] See, for example, the controversy around Jouffroy's debt to Kant in his posthumously published *Cours d'esthétique* (1841).

untranslated) were figures entirely blotted out from sight, though doubtless inferred to stand at one point or other of the compass by relation to the Great Names; the rest of the German landscape was a void. It does not require a great deal of perspicacity to observe the results of such desultory 'knowledge'; Barrès' novel *Les Déracinés* gives them in caricature; and we may do worse than turn to hear the moral pointed by another novelist at a slightly later date:

'Au ve· siècle grec nous trouvons un développement harmonique de la pensée grecque. C'est admirable de régularité, c'est une combinaison parfaite. C'était le moment où l'éducation consistait, suivant l'expression de Platon, "à mettre du rythme dans les âmes". On pouvait parler du rythme grec, de la pensée grecque. Mais y a-t-il une pensée française? Non. Nous sommes sous l'influence de tous les philo-sophes allemands, que nous les ayons lus ou non. Bien peu ont lu Hegel, et cependant presqu'aucun n'échappe à son influence... On prend des coins de pensées comme on prendrait un livre dans une bibliothèque; on prend des fragments de l'idéologie totale. Il y a un total, mais ce total n'est pas une somme, parce qu'il n'y a pas de classement harmonieux et logique.'[1]

Nothing indeed can be more amazing than the obscurity in which, for the general public at least, Ravaisson, say, and Renouvier and Lachelier lived and taught, when compared with the lively interest professed for German Idealism. Modern French thought in this field hardly came into its own before the turn of the century.

With such a lack of solid familiarity and in the absence of any perspective view, it was inevitable that the writings of the German philosophers, like massive lumps of authority to be thrown about, should be simple playthings invoked in arguments in no way resembling those which they had been developed out of and designed to deal with, and a shining example of their abuse is provided by that branch of knowledge with which we are here concerned: aesthetic. Characteristic in their essential feebleness of hold upon French ground were the cases of Schopenhauer and Wagner, first-comers in a long sequence of 'crazes'. The reasons for Schopenhauer's popu-larity in the first years of the third republic have been frequently analysed, and with a fair measure of unanimity—in terms of a wave of national disillusion and frustration coinciding with a thorough-going pessimist creed. But there is more in the problem than that; and we shall not be digressing if we study in some detail a few examples of those general philosophic views which went with the literary generations of 1880 and 1890 by the name of 'idealism'.

[1] Marcel Prévost, quoted in Le Cardonnel and Vellay, *La Littérature contemporaine*, 1905, p. 296.

A succinct version has been provided by Rémy de Gourmont, at a time when he himself would not have refused the label:

'Une vérité nouvelle est entrée récemment dans la littérature et dans l'art; c'est une vérité toute métaphysique et toute d'*a priori* (en apparence), toute jeune, puisqu'elle n'a qu'un siècle, et vraiment neuve, puisqu'elle n'avait pas encore servi dans l'ordre esthétique. Cette vérité, évangélique er merveilleuse, libératrice et renovatrice, c'est le principe de l'idéalité du monde. Par rapport à l'homme, sujet pensant, le monde, tout ce qui est extérieur au moi, n'existe que selon l'idée qu'il s'en fait.

'Nous ne connaissons que des phénomènes, nous ne raisonnons que sur des apparences; toute vérité en soi nous échappe; l'essence est inattaquable. C'est ce que Schopenhauer a vulgarisé sous cette formule si simple et si claire: le monde est ma représentation. Je ne vois pas ce qui est; ce qui est, c'est ce que je vois. Autant d'hommes pensants, autant de mondes divers.'[1]

Here already, in a writer who was certainly one of the more intelligent exegetes of symbolism, is a reproduction of a view of Schopenhauer's which for adequacy leaves much to be desired. One might suppose from it that Schopenhauer's idealism was perilously near a vulgar solipsism; that outside a world of precarious images nothing may be held to exist at all. Rémy de Gourmont, in common with other popularizers of his time who aimed at a similar grounding for a symbolist aesthetic, says nothing of the pan-thelistic monism which, rather than his theory of knowledge, is the essential feature of Schopenhauer's philosophy, and provided the main problems for his German disciples and critics to face. We are, in fact, in the presence of our first example of what might be called selective misinterpretation; where the real aims of Rémy de Gourmont (briefly hinted at in the reference to 'l'ordre esthétique') remain as it were 'off the picture'.

A slogan similar to Schopenhauer's 'Die Welt ist meine Vorstellung' was Ed. Dujardin's 'seule vit notre âme', prefaced to his unusual novel *Les Hantises* (1886) and quoted *ad nauseam* by its author and by Téodor de Wyzéwa in the *Revue Indépendante*. And yet, despite the lucidity of Ribot's study on Schopenhauer (1874) (expressly recommended by Wyzéwa to all prospective 'idealists'), it cannot have been easy to form any other view of the philosophy of Schopenhauer in times when a presumably informed and certainly exalted reporter, writing in the *Revue des deux Mondes*, could give the following *glose* of the famous doctrine:

'Le monde est ma représentation. Supposez le spectateur autrement constitué—doué par exemple d'une autre organisation cérébrale, — le spectacle change; supposez-

---

[1] Rémy de Gourmont, *Le Livre des Masques*, I, 1896, pp. 11-12.

le entièrement supprimé, la scène elle-même s'abîme dans la nuit. Si vous imaginez qu'il en subsiste quelque chose, c'est qu'il vous est difficile d'effacer de votre esprit jusqu'à l'idée d'une intelligence possible.'[1]

Here, if anywhere, is the solipsist myth; a solipsism which if it admits of no answer, certainly produces very little conviction on anyone considering it on its own merits. But this solipsism was not considered on its own merits by the writers with whom we have to do; it lingers on for several decades, owing its retention to the notion that it was essential as a presupposition to any aesthetic whatever that *allowed a place to the individual choice and style of the artist.* At a much later date, at the end of the symbolist vogue, in fact, we find in André Gide's *Journal* such traces of it as the following:

'Mon esprit ergotait tant, pour savoir s'il faut d'abord être pour ensuite paraître, ou paraître d'abord pour être ce que l'on paraît.'[2]

and again:

'Je ne parviens jamais à me persuader tout à fait de l'existence réelle de certaines choses. Il me semble toujours qu'elles n'existent plus quand je n'y pense plus ... le monde m'est un miroir, et je suis étonné quand il me réflète mal...'[3]

which position leads him more and more to conclude that a life of pure 'introspection' is alone logically admissible, at any rate to the writer: and he quotes with enthusiasm from Lavater:

'Je le dis à tous mes adversaires; je le pense à tous les jours de ma vie: méditer sur soi-même est la vie de la vie; et nous y méditons si peu! Combien rarement faisons-nous notre vie pour la vie (intraduisible; il y a: wie selten machen wir unser Leben zum Leben !).'[4]

That these are no mere chance coincidences down the years is evidenced on all hands; for the case in point, that of Gide, it suffices to repeat his own testimony:

'Il semblait qu'en ces temps nous fussions soumis plus ou moins consciemment à quelque indistinct mot d'ordre, plutot qu'aucun de nous n'écoutât sa propre pensée ... Soutenu par Schopenhauer ... je tenais pour "contingence" (c'est le mot dont on se servait) tout ce qui n'était pas "absolu", toute la prismatique diversité de la vie.'[5]

It is not difficult to envisage this state of mind: the hero of Gide's novel *Paludes*, and Valéry's almost contemporary figure, Edmond Teste, are idealizations of this spirit of *disponibilité* which goes so closely with the literary 'idealism', and which seems, in 1880,

---

[1] Challemel-Lacour, *Revue des Deux Mondes*, 15/iii/1870. The theory of the will is not entirely ignored in his article, but it is accorded little prominence.
[2] Gide, *Journal*, 7/viii/1891. *Œuvres* (NRF) í, p. 482.   [3] ibid., 10/vi/1891.
[4] ibid., 1894.   [5] Gide, *Si le grain ne meurt*, 1928, p. 264.

to presuppose it by contrast with realistic and naturalistic literature's appeal to positive knowledge.

For such versions, plainly, and for such disregard of the intentions of the 'authorities', anything was good enough; and we shall not be surprised to find the symbolists pushing every German name they knew into a single class and then claiming allegiance to the principles they profess to find incarnate in all. The results are sometimes amusing; Edouard Dubus, in a study of the *vers libre* of Marie Krysinska, sets out the proposition that this kind of verse abandons the principle of a unified style, dependent on a steadily repeated ground-rhythm. To clinch his formal argument, he goes on:

'Si, comme le veut Kant, la variété dans l'unité est la condition essentielle de la beauté...'

then it must follow that either Kant is wrong or free verse is not beautiful.[1] And the free verse is beautiful. . . . One wonders what particular vendetta could have caused him to single out for castigation the sage of Königsberg; but it may well be that no such hostility is intended; at any rate, scraps such as this, ridiculous as they are, appear to have passed with tolerable success for learning among M. Dubus' friends. More often, however, the display of learning is not so much amusing as pathetic; and as an outstanding example we may observe the strange case of Villiers de l'Isle Adam. All evidence points to the fact that enthusiastic contemporaries and juniors held this colourful figure to be an authority on the idealist speculations of the German school. Mallarmé is not alone when, in his funeral oration, he refers to his 'considerable' reading, in Kant, Hegel, and divers other metaphysicians;[2] but when Villiers' cousin tells us of his early initiations, we begin to see what this is all turned to:

'La philosophie allemande [generically, it would seem] passionnait alors le maître du logis; elle s'empara bientôt de l'esprit profond de Villiers de l'Isle Adam. Son ami l'initia aux brillantes théories spiritualistes de Hegel, dont il était le fervent disciple ... la vraie poésie du penseur allemand, la largeur et la magnificence de se vues l'enthousiasmaient au plus haut degré: il commence à exposer les théories de la philosophie spéculative dans l'étrange nouvelle de Claire Lenoir.'[3]

The fruits of this plunge into unknown realms of thought are

---

[1] *Mercure de France*, xii/1890.   [2] *Divagations*, pp. 70, 71.

[3] R. du Pontavice de Heussey, *Villiers de l'Isle Adam*, 1893, p. 65. Claire Lenoir features in 'Tribulat Bonhomet'. Her husband dies in the presence of the swan-shooting rationalist caricature of a doctor; and a year later she herself expires, under the stress of terrible haunting. Bonhomet inspects the pupils of her eyes through an opthalmascope, and see there the image of her husband in the guise of a vampire. This finally convinces him that what passes by the name of reality is simply the sum total of figments of the imagination. The conversion of Bonhomet is preceded by a good dozen chapters of discussion of 'Speculative philosophy'.

hardly the sort of thing that would have pleased their begetter; Villiers, to judge by what he wrote (and there is nothing to suggest that he ever wrote insincerely), formed an opinion of 'Hegelianism' so hazy that it allowed him to vary his exposition between the limits of (1) the plainest solipsism, influenced by a Fichtean vocabulary, and (2) a kind of common-sense view of the obvious relativity of any perception at a given moment. The first view is set out at some length in *Axel*:

'Sache une fois pour toujours qu'il n'est d'autre univers pour toi que la conception qui s'en réfléchit au fond de tes pensées, car tu ne peux le voir pleinement, ni le connaître, en distinguer même un seul point tel que ce mystérieux point doit être réel en sa réalité... Si tu veux posséder la vérité, crée-la! comme tout le reste! tu n'emporteras, tu ne seras que ta création... Son apparaître (celui du monde) quel qu'il puisse être, n'est en principe que fictif, mobile, illusoire, insaisissable...[1]

The second attitude, somewhat less intransigent, appears in the following, which—perhaps on grounds of redundancy—was omitted from one of his phantasy novels, *L'Eve future*.

'Maintenant je dis que le Réel a ses degrés d'être. Une chose est d'autant plus ou moins réelle pour nous qu'elle nous intéresse plus ou moins, puisqu'une chose qui ne nous intéresserait en rien serait pour nous comme si elle n'était pas — c'est-à-dire, beaucoup moins, quoique physique, qu'une chose irréelle qui nous intéresserait.

'Donc le Réel, pour nous, est seulement ce qui nous touche, soit les sens, soit l'esprit, et selon le degré d'intensité dont cette image *réelle*, que nous puissions apprécier et nommer tel, nous impressionne, nous classons dans notre esprit le degré d'être plus ou moins riche en contenu qu'il nous semble atteindre, et que, par conséquent, il est légitime de dire qu'il *réalise*. Le seul contrôle que nous ayons de la réalité c'est l'*idée*.'[2]

It is to be presumed that such passages were intended—and received—as expositions of an 'idealist' view; but an idealist view of what? Certainly not of nature, of a world of phenomena; this is no longer solipsism, but a system of valuation for experiences; and if Villiers intended his 'idealism' to relate not to a theory of knowledge but to a psychology of conviction, there was nothing very Hegelian in that. But whatever he intended bore no great resemblance to Hegelian philosophy; in the words of a contemporary critic, 'il y a dans tout cela plus de poésie que de clarté et de précision, et ce sont visions de prophète plus que théories de philosophe...'[3] Not only poetry, one might add, but myth.

What is true of Villiers is true of all those writers and critics who contributed in one way or another to a symbolist aesthetic. Each one of them had his Claire Lenoir to justify as an artistic creation against

---

[1] *Axel*, p. 201.   [2] Page inédite *L'Eve future*, in *Mercure de France*, viii/1890, p. 259.
[3] Charbonnel, *Les mystiques dans la littérature présente*, 1897, pp. 69–70.

the canons of naturalism, though few were so calmly fabulous. Intent on the introduction of a new way of writing, they had recourse to the philosophers essentially as a means of combating opinions on art which ran counter to their own and were accepted as obvious by the literary public of the times; a few of the more clear-sighted among them ventured to oppose aesthetic doctrines promulgated in philosophic circles, and for that turned to find authorities on whom they might lean—Laforgue, for example, or the much less well-known Aurier—in their polemics against Taine; but for the vast majority the process of thinking was carried on at what has been called 'a zero level of efficiency'; and at that level 'idealism' meant simply the inalienable right to look on the world in whatever way one pleased; or to invent worlds, on an equal with the 'common-sense world', and entitled to the same respect both from the point of view of art, and, what is more serious, of anything else. The fatal attraction exercised by 'idealism' in this rather unusual form on highly imaginative groups of writers has another classic victim in its collection— namely, the 'Jena school' of German romanticism (notably Novalis) with its rendering of Fichte's *Wissenschaftslehre* along lines very similar to those we are considering here. The reasons we can venture for the latter are largely valid for the former.

The result of such loose thinking was that those who had started out with great hopes of what the imported philosophy would do for art soon fell back on less ambitious kinds of interpretation; and by the turn of the century we find that Rémy de Gourmont, when he claims that 'l'idéalisme est la doctrine régnante en philosophie',[1] is staking out a claim for a doctrine no more ambitious than that

'dès qu'il y a vie, il y a idéalisme, c'est-à-dire il y a, selon les espèces ou même les individus, des manières différentes de réagir contre une sensation externe ou interne',[2]

thus renouncing all attacks upon the central problems of epistemology; indeed, so far from 'idealism' being any longer a possibility of interpreting the whole of knowledge, a self-sufficient totality, it is reduced to a subsidiary position where it can account merely for irregularities in response to stimuli, and by extension for such individuality as we find in artistic vision. That is, of course, all that Rémy de Gourmont was interested in the last resort in doing. The fall in status is given typical expressions in the following passage from a true-blue 'symbolist':

'Tout objet a deux aspects: l'aspect matériel et l'aspect idéal. Il y a donc bien authentiquement deux mondes: l'un phénomenal, frappant l'âme par les sens et

---

[1] *Promenades philosophiques*, I, p. 79. *Les Racines de l'idéalisme* (1904).　　[2] ibid., p. 61.

s'y introduisant en notations directes, l'autre intuitif, produit de l'âme, et empruntant pour se traduire les formes du premier ... il s'ensuit que le réalisme et l'idéalisme sont deux tournures de l'esprit, deux manières d'envisager la vie...'[1]

So far as can be judged, what is here meant is that perceptions as accounted for by a realist epistemology, are subject to distortion when the processes of an affective factor are allowed to play upon them. And it is no more than this which Rémy de Gourmont has in mind when, examining at length the implications of the doctrines whose apparent supremacy he had announced in the early *Livre des masques*, he concludes that not only 'l'idéalisme se fonde en définitive sur la matérialité même de la pensée, considérée comme un produit physiologique',[2] but moreover that 'les raisons de l'idéalisme se plongent dans la matière et à l'inverse matérialisme veut dire idéalisme.[3]' Following his train of thought Rémy de Gourmont calls judgement, the form in which thought appears, 'une accommodation, une moyenne', springing presumably from the need to offset randomness in the physiological structure of the brain.[4] He speaks of 'la rélativité de l'extérieur', implying not that it is a different world for each spectator, but that each spectator wears differently tinted spectacles. Finally he tramples on the view that mind is in any way independent of material forms—with a violence that suggests the irritation of a man slightly ashamed of his own past assertions:

'Les sens doivent correspondre à des réalités extérieures. Ils ont été créés non par l'être percevant, mais par le milieu perceptible. C'est la lumière qui a créé l'œil, comme, à nos maisons, elle a créé les fenêtres. Dans les milieux sans lumière les poissons deviennent aveugles.'[5]

Further,

'Le dédoublement de l'homme en deux parties, l'un considérant l'autre et prétendant le contenir, n'est qu'un amusement philosophique qui devient impossible dès que l'on garde tout son sang-froid. Il y a en effet une physiologie de la pensée; on sait que c'est un produit, puisqu'on peut la tarir en lésant l'organe producteur. La pensée est non seulement un produit mais un produit matériel, mesurable, pondérable.'[6]

So much for the 'idealism' of one of the more intelligent and thoughtful critics and writers of the symbolist literary background.

The result of this return to 'sang-froid' may be seen in Rémy de Gourmont's later interests as an art-critic—philological interests above all; its logical conclusion for the philosophy of art would seem to be the belief that since what is measurable may be controlled, the reactions of the mind to art might also be forecast; and if forecast,

---

[1] Dumur, 'Aurier et l'évolution idéaliste', *Mercure de France*, t. viii, p. 293, viii/1893.
[2] *Promenades philosophiques*, I, p. 104.   [3] ibid., p. 105.   [4] ibid., p. 98.
[5] ibid., p. 98.   [6] ibid., pp. 102–3.

produced by design, by coldly reasoned design—in the way we have come to associate with Edgar Allan Poe's *Genesis of a Poem*.

That nothing in the symbolist literary attitude—assuming for the moment that we may talk of such an attitude—was in fact essentially and rootedly linked to uncompromising 'idealism' otherwise than as we have suggested, is implied by the case of Gustave Kahn. Here, if ever there was one, was the typical symbolist poet-critic of the eighties and nineties—far more typical than Jean Moréas and infinitely more concerned with the aesthetic presuppositions of his art. Yet here too was a man who held that all processes of thought are rigidly determined by factors to which he gave the approximative name of laws of association; laws which brooked no interference by the individual choice of the thinking subject; for whom, therefore, writing poetry was nothing more than plucking out on the emotional strings of his readers those chords which the association laws sanctioned; and whose whole work was directed to securing conditions in verse writing in which, as he thought, these (virtually) impersonal laws should be the least impeded by outward convention—namely, *vers libre*. Of him a sympathetic observer writes:

'Ce n'est pas par les tendances mystiques que Kahn est amené au symbolisme, ni par une conception religieuse des choses, ni par les conclusions de quelque métaphysique spiritualiste ... s'il est idéaliste, d'une certaine manière, ce n'est pas pour transformer l'esprit en un absolu. Mais plutôt il est matérialiste et sensualiste.'[1]

Similarly, in the *Revue Wagnérienne*, a stronghold of the new aesthetic where one would least expect to find such a view cropping up, Téodor de Wyzéwa sets forth a theory of experience in which association is assigned a part that makes nonsense of any idealist theory of knowledge.[2] Though he is careful to call every datum of experience an 'illusion', in his effort to present a properly idealist account of knowledge, his position drives him to demand of art a rather thinly veiled version of the literary realist's claim;[3] even to the point of ignoring his mentor Wagner's tastes in the matter. No coincidence, again, that within the decade Wyzéwa had repudiated all ties with a field of thought which he, more than almost any of his fellow-writers, had publicized in the venturesome years of the *Revue Wagnérienne* and the *Revue Indépendante*:

'Je vois très nettement combien de dommage a déjà causé à l'esprit français l'influence allemande, depuis vingt ans qu'elle sévit librement, constamment, dé-

---

[1] André Beaunier, *La Poésie nouvelle*, 1902, p. 109.
[2] Wyzéwa, *Nos Maîtres*, 1895, pp. 32-33, reproduced from *l'Art Wagnérien*, in the *Revue Wagnérienne*, vi/1886.
[3] ibid. Namely, 'l'analyse complète et minutieuse des faits les plus ordinaires'.

mesurément sur lui. Elle a failli lui faire perdre les plus précieuses de ses vertus, son besoin d'ordre et de clarté... Je dis que ce génie est à l'opposé du génie français, qu'il saurait malaisément se concilier avec lui, et que, pour l'avoir admiré plus que de raison, nos artistes et nos écrivains se sont déjà trop détournés de la voie qui leur était naturelle.'[1]

Here speaks the authentic voice of one who to overcome his shyness has drunk somewhat too freely of an unusually strong liquor; and then blames the brewer for the excesses which he subsequently commits.

Examples might be multiplied; and it is hard to escape the conclusion that the symbolist critic treated the high-sounding propositions that he gleaned always as *slogans*; and slogans, which always have a considerable affective value, are prone on examination to reveal a greater or lesser degree of imprecision. The typical symbolist knew roughly what he wanted of an aesthetic; and faced with the choice between a flourishing positivism seemingly committed to Zola and an alluring strange new field, chose the latter as better complying with the polemical requirements of the times.

We shall in due course attempt to analyse these requirements, and see in what way they led so persistently to pastiche 'idealism'. For the moment it is convenient to sum them up under one principle: the writer, in that complex of literary developments which we call Symbolism, was seeking his liberty as a creator, and would pay any price for it; was seeking an unrestricted range of expression, free from the formal and emotional patterns imposed by a realistic art; and turning from a philosophy whose avowed aim was a reasoned account of the exact determining forces in every sphere of knowledge and experience, found for a time his haven in garbled versions of idealist epistemologies:

'Enchaîné dans la caverne, le prisonnier se lamente et s'effraye parce que d'épouvantables fantômes se heurtent sur le mur devant ses yeux,' we read; but 'dès qu'il se connaît la seule cause, il est libre, et le prisonnier de la caverne devient le mage divin, le Mage créateur.'[2]

The artist, the creative magus, can ignore the grim patterns of heredity and environment, the social problems of the day, since he is not obliged to report them. It is easy to see how such a liberation quickly turns into an attitude of refusal, of escapism, the selective preciosity of the ivory tower.

[1] Wyzéwa, *Mercure de France*, iv/1895, t. xiv, p. 31.
[2] Téodor de Wyzéwa, 'Le pessimisme de R. Wagner,' *Revue Wagnérienne*, iii/1886. The author, in common with all advanced literary circles, took Wagner as the typical exponent, *mutatis mutandis*, of Schopenhauer's doctrines: a view which, to my knowledge, was never corrected in the symbolist era.

We might mention here another type of relapse from crude solipsism. It is represented by the mental development of Jules Laforgue. Of him it has been said that 'tout ce que réalisa le symbolisme, il le contient et l'exprime avec une plénitude telle (celle du génie) qu'il est vraiment le symbole du symbolisme'.[1] This is a big claim, and one which on the face of things is not borne out by the realities of the case; apart from a year in Paris, before his death in 1887, Laforgue moves only on the fringe of symbolist activity; his posthumous glory in the *Entretiens politiques et littéraires* and in the *Revue Blanche* is hardly to be ascribed to the value of the incoherent notes and jottings published in these reviews by the diligence of his executors; and the hollowness of these executors' enthusiasm has been strikingly demonstrated by Mauclair.[2] On the positive count, however, his immediate hostility to the positivist approach, and his treatment of the question of artistic freedoms and constraints, bring him well into the orbit of our inquiry. In this sense Fagus was not only perfectly correct, but even understating his case: Laforgue was indeed a pioneer of symbolism, even though his lonely position made his influence in the late eighties and nineties potential rather than actual. It will come as no surprise to us to find that he too started his adult career around 1880 as an inveterate devotee of Schopenhauer, with verse written in the vein of ironic pessimism and reference to the illusory nature of all experience.[3] Yet in his case, it does not appear that he took an interest in solipsism as a line of argument for the liberation of poetry from realist 'contingency'; in effect, all that survives to us of his attacks on Taine points rather to a different objection to naturalism; and accordingly when Laforgue abandons Schopenhauer, it is not to go over to the enemy's camp, as is virtually the case with Rémy de Gourmont, but to move on to new ground. The philosophy of the Unconscious to which he attached himself in Germany did not play an important part in the symbolist aesthetic; nor did Edouard von Hartmann's *Aesthetik*, for instance, which appeared only in the year of Laforgue's death, raise so much as a shiver of interest in Parisian literary spheres (outside the philosophic reviews): Laforgue's enthusiasm for Schopenhauer's famous disciple was not emulated or developed. What was emulated, or at least warmly welcomed, was again his reasoning on artistic originality, based largely on an analogy with Darwinian evolutionism, and linked to a theory of literary unrestraint. The notion that an artist may do as he

---

[1] Fagus, *Revue Blanche*, 1903, quoted Ruchon, *Laforgue*.
[2] Mauclair, *L'Art en silence*.   [3] *Le Sanglot de la Terre*.

pleases is not incompatible with naturalism, though a Taine would have added that in any given *milieu* only one course will lead to great art; but in Laforgue's development of the notion, in the form that only by dint of being unique, unequalled, can an artist ever attain to genius, the clash with positivism becomes evident. For Taine, an artist is a kind of automatic telephone exchange, successful when a certain pair of lines have been connected; for Laforgue, he is a lunatic exchange operator, whose highest function is to promote unexpected encounters among the subscribers. Whatever the importance of this distinction, however (and its very real importance to a number of aesthetic questions may be imagined), it did not obtrude itself on the current discussion of philosophical viewpoints: the imagination is freed, which is the important thing.

Certain other aspects of the idealist vogue cannot be subsumed under this general heading; the views ascribed by common consent to Mallarmé and his closest followers (the young André Gide of the *Traité du Narcisse*, or the early Mauclair of *Eleusis*, for example) resemble those already noted in that they are logically projections back from an aesthetic desideratum to a philosophical justification rather than the other way round; but the desideratum in this case is a different one, and relates not so much to a theory of poetic imagination as to a theory of language. It has a direct bearing upon the nature and definitions of symbols, for instance; but in this it is concerned not with the literal conformity of a 'symbol' with a real object, but rather with what makes the symbol artistically effective: we may recognize the distinction between on the one hand arguments designed to show how the material of poet, painter, and musician leads to distinctive experiences which we call aesthetic, and on the other arguments designed to show why the artist need not be simply a mirror of all he sees. The one field is a positive contribution to the philosophy of art: the other a sweeping-away of loose cumber.

At the same time it would be wrong to draw a hard and fast line between the two fields; the distinction, while apparent to us, was rendered a good deal less so in the last century; Mauclair, for instance, gratuitously called his analysis of the nature of symbols 'un théorème d'idéalisme hégélien'[1] and evidently considered it closely related to the conception of a subject creating his own world of experience; the notes we find in Gide's early *Journal* relating to these two parallel problems of art are too completely interwoven to permit us to think that he distinguished their separate functions; while Mallarmé's

[1] Mauclair, *Eleusis*, 1894, *Du Symbole*, p. 87.

Divagations, where 'idealism' and language theory dwell side by side, are claimed by their author to treat of 'un sujet de pensée unique'.[1] Moreover, it must be remembered that Mallarmé, well in advance of the principal wave of symbolist activity, had arrived at a solipsism which the following generation did not surpass: already when engaged on his youthful *Hérodiade*, he wrote to a friend:

'Malheureusement, en creusant le vers à ce point, j'ai rencontré deux abîmes, qui me désespèrent. L'un est le Néant, auquel je suis arrivé sans connaître le Boudhisme, et je suis encore trop désolé pour pouvoir croire même à ma poésie et me remettre au travail, que cette pensée écrasante m'a fait abandonner.'[2]

A highly plausible attempt to interpret the bulk of his later poetry as expounding this same attitude was made in the heyday of symbolism.[3] Mauclair, in an article written shortly after Mallarmé's death, was trying to make substantially the same point when he said that:

'Son œuvre est la pierre de touche de la théorie hégélienne,'[4]

and (with allowances for that fine off-hand disregard for exactitude which, we have noted above, marked all symbolist claims of kinship with the giants of German tradition) René Ghil wrote of Mallarmé's most notorious venture:

'Nous avons lieu de croire que cette œuvre, si elle êut pu etre construite et écrite, êut reproduit en son essence philosophique un idéalisme à notion du Moi incarnant l'Idée créatrice du Monde — où l'on êut retrouvé Platon, Fichte, Hegel, Schelling.'[5]

Mallarmé, no less than his close friend Villiers de l'Isle Adam, is on his own showing bound to be an 'idealist'; since being a *poet* implies for him the creation of the world, as much as being *alive* does for Claire Lenoir.[6]

6. MYSTICAL INFLUENCES IN SYMBOLIST THEORY

From a different quarter symbolism received equal support in its anti-realist drive; from mysticism. Hard as it is to define with precision the way in which young writers of the eighties embraced German idealism, our task becomes harder still when we try to

---

[1] *Divagations*, Foreword.
[2] Letter to Henri Cazalis, March, 1866. Quoted in *Propos sur la Poésie*, ed. Henri Mondor, 1946, p. 59.
[3] By Téodor de Wyzéwa, 'Le symbolisme de M. Mallarmé,' *Revue Indépendante*, ii/1887.
[4] L'Esthétique de Stéphane Mallarmé, *Grande Revue*, xi/1898.
[5] R. Ghil, *Les Dates et les Œuvres*, 1923, p. 234.
[6] For a detailed examination of this point, see *Les Lettres*, numéro spécial consacré à Stéphane Mallarmé, June, 1948, and in particular M. Charles Mauron's essay on 'Igitur' and 'Un Coup de Dés'.

assess the importance to them of so vague and indistinct an attitude as that implied by the term 'mysticism'. Nothing is easier than to profess to be a follower of Swedenborg or a student of oriental asceticism; nothing is more difficult to challenge; when all is said, however, the only sphere in which it is possible to define a mystic's ideas with any precision at all is when he comes to attack those intellectual standpoints from which his own position is invariably a revulsion. Of all men the mystic is the most eclectic: he will forage behind the enemy's lines regardless of the danger of being cut off; when such forays prove disastrous (as with the phenomena of electricity early in the nineteenth century), he will fall back on his strong point: his conviction and his inner voices; no rational army can ever hope to attack him there, and but for the fear of decay, he would never feel bound to issue forth again. Perhaps the defining feature which unites all mystics lies in that direction. The traditions of mysticism are at least as venerable as any others; and the mystic's freedom from obligations towards rational thinking and historical precision introduce into them a timelessness which to the adept is a source of strength. Since, essentially, mysticism is not only irrational but anti-rational, its periods of most vigorous growth coincide in modern times with the disappointment of excessive hopes and claims by the current representatives of the rational persuasion. So with Mme. Guyon, or Pierre Poiret, for whom a Cartesian account of the human mind did insufficient justice to the claims of the emotional life; so too in the nineteenth century, when the march of naturalism in its crude and uncompromising attacks on the problems of the human mind did violence to the experiences of a whole range of thinkers, among them dreamers and poets. Especially poets; for the weakest point in the whole naturalist front comes at the point where it attempts to give an account of the individual mind in the presence of art.

In the face of such relative failure, the appeal of mysticism in one or another of its forms was bound to be strong: any problem which threatened to prove insoluble, any factor which promised to escape analysis, was a finger pointing towards a system of *comprehensio incomprehensibilis*; where rational criteria give place to those of emotional sympathy, where opposed doctrines are not necessarily contradictory, and where the widest freedom of personal choice supplants the tight reins of a methodology.

The strength of literary mysticism in its various forms in the eighties has been variously estimated, according to the types of credo included in this generic title. Victor Chardonnel, writing in 1895, included in its sphere not only Melchior de Voguë,[1] but also Paul Verlaine—evidently for him the anti-realist ticket was sufficient claim to inclusion. By those standards it would be hard to exempt any of the symbolists from it; but luckily it is possible to outline some of the more important groupings, such as Péladan's Rosicrucianism. Orliac,[2] among many others, finds in the whole course of French literature a subterranean thread of mysticism, making its appearance in Chateaubriand, Lamartine, in Balzac even;[3] and (in the period under review) in the illuminism of de Guaïta, Papus, M. Barrès, Paul Adam, Dubus, Morice, Schuré, Vulliaud, Péladan, and others. Téodor de Wyzéwa, writing in the *Revue Indépendante* in 1887, gives a long list of recently published works of mystical tendency which certainly suggests a flourishing market for this literature;[4] and in a rather witty article which follows this list Wyzéwa applies the beliefs of contemporary spiritualism to the task of rehabilitating an old Russian fairy tale, told him by his nurse; he succeeds in showing how telepathy, magnetism, and a whole gamut of occult forces can between them render credible each of the fantastic events that figure in it. But for the verve of Wyzéwa's restitution, we might be tempted to complain that it is wasted labour: the important point is that mysticism affects aesthetic theory not by enabling its adepts to 'believe anything', but by giving them, or attempting to give them, an explanation why they find art valuable at all. This explanation always takes the form of a variation upon one given theme: that in the aesthetic experience man is brought into more or less direct communication with his God. The classical account of this process belongs by right of precedence to Plotinus, virtually the first philosopher to advance a definitely 'symbolic', as opposed to imitative outline of the metaphysic of art; and it is an account which, infinitely flexible, has lived through many centuries already. In a sense it is the essence of Schelling's theosophy, with which symbolism was quite as familiar as with the works of Kant and Hegel; it recurs over

---

[1] Author of a famous best-seller, *Le Roman russe*, written in a deeply pious vein, hostile to French realist tendencies in the novel.

[2] *La Cathédrale symboliste*, 1933.

[3] When 'Séraphita' is claimed to be 'une de ces balustrades sculptées par quelque artiste plein de foi et sur lesquelles les pélerins s'appuient pour méditer la fin de l'homme, en contemplant le chœur d'une belle église' (quoted from Ch. Morice, *La Littérature de tout à l'heure*, 1889, p. 194).

[4] *Revue Indépendante*, ii/1887, vol. 2, p. 201 (reproduced in *Nos Maîtres*).

and over again in Carlyle, an author very much read by the generations with which we are dealing:

'The Universe is but one vast symbol of God; nay, if thou wilt have it, what is man himself but a Symbol of God? . . .'

'Another matter is it, however, when your symbol has intrinsic meaning and is of itself *fit* that men should unite round it. Let but the Godlike manifest itself to sense; let but Eternity look, more or less visibly, through the Time-Figure (Zeitbild)! . . . Of this latter sort are all true works of art: in them (if thou wilt but know a Work of Art from a Daub of Artifice) wilt thou discern Eternity looking through Time; the Godlike rendered visible.'[1]

and it will be remembered that Baudelaire, himself one of the most direct formative influences on the symbolists, rested his theory of poetic symbols on an uncompromisingly mystical foundation.[2]

A striking example of the grip of mysticism on sections of the world of literature is provided by the case of Ernest Hello. This fiery but unsuccessful prophet and writer died, embittered and disappointed, in the provinces in 1884. In 1894, when all traces of him might be supposed to have been lost, he came into his own with a lengthy eulogy by Léon Bloy, in the symbolist stronghold, the *Mercure de France*. Following the same lines of argument as Carlyle, he asserts that: 'L'art est le souvenir de la présence de Dieu'.[3] And the opinion is not confined to prophets: if in other writers the specifically religious inflection is restrained, or allowed to remain unexpressed, there is nevertheless a persistent harking back to mystical and transcendental realities which evade all rational explanation, and whose closeness is felt to an unusual degree in the enjoyment of art. There cannot have been many readers to disagree with Viélé-Griffin's aphorism:

'*Mysticisme artistique:* ces mots me semblent constituer un pléonasme; toute idée d'art impliquant celle du mystère.'[4]

'Mystère': a commodious term, rich in suggestive vibrations, applicable to almost any situation in which the emotions are aroused to an unusual degree (as before an outstandingly great work of art); and where the humdrum account of nervous excitation offered by the physio-psychologist, or by the psycho-therapist, seems more than usually insufficient. Countless times this word is forced into service:

---

[1] *Sartor Resartus*, Bk. III, ch. 3. Brought to notice no doubt by Taine, in his *Idéalisme anglais*, he is quoted extensively and often in the *Entretiens politiques et littéraires* (1890–); his *Sartor Resartus* is translated *in toto* in the *Mercure de France* (1897–); Mauclair writes, for example, in the *Mercure de France* of xi/1897, p. 391, 'et j'ai aussi Carlyle, Poe, Laforgue, et c'est à peu près tout mon viatique, tous mes antidotes'.

[2] See Pommier, *La Mystique de Baudelaire, passim.*

[3] Hello, 'L'Homme, la vie, la science, l'art', p. 367.

[4] F. Viélé-Griffin, 'Les Forts,' *Entretiens*, viii/1890, vol. 1, p. 163.

by all poets, critics, novelists, playwrights, pamphleteers, grouped around the various banners of decadence, symbolism, and the rest; the mystery of dreams, of the unconscious, of great art, of anything. If it performed no other useful function, the mystic tradition at least provided a sense of cohesion to the symbolists from their common use of this slogan. 'Nous ne nous grandissons qu'en grandissant les mystères qui nous accablent.'[1] Morice and Mauclair in their principal expositions of the new literature, both devote a chapter to 'le Mystère'. Mallarmé so far conforms to the customs of his audiences as to use it freely (and most misleadingly in the context of his views) when discussing aesthetic creation. It penetrates into every nook and cranny of poetry and criticism; not in any standard form, of course, but to suit the task in hand. 'Il y a mille mysticismes divers', we read:[2] very likely there are as many mysticisms as there are mystics to make a profession of faith; but for all of them the starting-point, the central experience, is a mystery arising from introspection. And for a great many writers at this time, there is little doubt that the label of mystic was automatically linked with an obstinate denial of ordinary 'bourgeois' values in literature, of the type ridiculed earlier by Baudelaire in his *Art Romantique*.

Virtually, then, the mystic's approach to literature differs in little but its terminology from that of the 'idealist'; each sees in poetry, and by extension in every other form of art, the communication not of 'information' but of some strong emotional experience. Moreover, so great is the reaction from the idea of imitative or didactic art, that there is a tendency, frequently observed in late nineteenth-century literature, to claim that the affective aspect of art can exist quite independently of the imitative—on occasion, that it must do so. The yogi pursues his dreams regardless of the existence or otherwise of a human world around him; nothing in his perfected state of inner harmony need ever cause him to yield to the essentially social claims of rational discourse. From there, it is but a single step to the kind of self-sufficiency which we find, much later, in *dada*. There is, as we shall observe, a pronounced correlation in modern times between the growth of anti-intellectualism and the heritage of symbolism. For lack of a rational psychology, for lack of a systematic account of feeling, the nineteenth-century poet, whenever he stood out against a dry and repellent positivist aesthetic, capitulated in this side of his theory of art to the successors of Swedenborg. For a time, a very few years, around the turn of the century, literary opinion hovers over

---

[1] Maeterlinck, *Les disciples à Saïs*, 2nd ed., s.d., p. viii.   [2] ibid., p. xx.

an intermediate position; we see a maturer Viélé-Griffin, for instance, or a Verhaeren,[1] seeking an escape between the horns of the dilemma; but this escape was in the main never realized; and the dominant forces in aesthetic standpoints became more and more sharply divided between positive study of the *phenomena* of art, and irrationalist accounts of the *experience* of art. The first course is naturally repugnant to the artist; the second wearies common sense. If quasi-scientific approaches in the late nineteenth century are responsible for the former diversion from rational inquiry, the symbolists have their share of responsibility for the latter.

7. SCHOPENHAUER

We have already mentioned that *Die Welt als Wille und Vorstellung* and its sundry appendices (the *Parerga und Paralipomena*) enjoyed an enormous if not very firmly grounded popularity amid enlightened circles from about 1870 onwards. Schopenhauer's *magnum opus* dates from 1818, and its author died only in 1860; however, as by general consent it is acknowledged that the theories laid down in it suffered no noticeable change in his later works, which were no more than a clarification of some of its obscurities and a development of some of their less obvious implications (and that not in the sphere of aesthetic) we may without danger confine ourselves here to a brief sketch of its third book to map out the sort of position which it commended to its admirers.

Schopenhauer, in his search for a fundamental Principle, sees the operation of a metaphysical entity which he calls the Will, blind, impersonal, and totally indifferent to all man's efforts towards happiness, goodness, or truth. The Will is objectified mediately in all experience on which man has erected what he is pleased to call knowledge; its impulsion may be discerned throughout the range of practical activity; and Schopenhauer observes that all human efforts are continually frustrated by its disregard of our aims. The Will itself has no aims; it drives forward incessantly, leaving in its train misery, disaster, and the defeat of human aspiration.

There are two ways by which humanity can escape from the Will's all-enfolding net; one temporary and fallible, one permanent and entirely reliable. The latter does not concern us here; it is the path of contemplation, of Buddhist renunciation of the ways of the flesh, leading firmly to the extinction of the human race, and with it

[1] See, for instance, 'Le Verbe' in *La Multiple splendeur*, 1902.

all human misery. The former, less drastic, is the cultivation of art; and it is important to examine the reasons which allow art to be a means of escaping from the snares of a worldly and practical existence.[1]

The first stage in the determination of art concerns a renovated theory of Platonic Ideas. It is a theory which has been described as magnificent but fantastic;[2] magnificent for its challenging originality, fantastic for its self-contradictory elements: whatever its merits and demerits it is extremely hard to define with that degree of precision which excludes the possibility of ambiguity. Schopenhauer returned again and again to the elucidation of his terminology; and it will be seen in the sequel that this care proved insufficient for at least one section of his readers. All the more reason then that we should attempt to put his position in the clearest possible light before going on to discuss the use made of it by symbolist aesthetics.

First, an Idea is not a concept; nor is it a mental image. 'The concept is abstract, discursive, within its bounds entirely undetermined, only determined by its boundaries, capable of being attained and grasped by anyone possessed of mere reason, communicable by words without any further mediacy, and able to be completely exhausted in its definitions. The *Idea*, on the other hand, may perhaps be defined as the adequate representation of the concept; it is entirely within the sphere of intuition, and although it represents an infinite number of single things, is for all that completely determined. It is never the object of knowledge to the individual as such, but only to the mind which has raised itself above all Willing and above all individuality to the position of a subject of pure contemplation; therefore it may only be reached by Genius; hence by the mind which has developed its powers of pure contemplation, largely through the operation of Genius, and is thus in the condition of genius.'[3] Genius is here that activity or ability of the mind to act in such a way as to contemplate the objects of its cognition in a completely detached and impersonal way: genius is the ability to 'leave all interests, all act of will, all intention, completely out of account.'[4] The difficulties attendant on this notion are manifest: 'The Idea is, by reason of the temporal and spatial form of our intuitive perceptions, a unity dissolved into multiplicity; on the other hand, the concept is a unity reconstructed out of multiplicity by the power of abstraction exercised by our

---

[1] *W.a.W.u.V.*, 3rd ed. 1859, II, ch. 29, p. 413. By comparison with asceticism, it is only transitory.
[2] S. Alexander, *Beauty and other forms of Value*, 1933, p. 147.
[3] *W.a.W.u.V.*, I, § 49, p. 276.   [4] ibid., p. 218.

reason; the latter may be described as *unitas post rem*, the former as *unitas ante rem*.'[1] Art deals with Ideas as its subject matter, not with concepts. 'The object of art, whose presentation is the artist's aim, and knowledge of which must therefore precede his work as its kernel, as its very source, is nothing more nor less than an *Idea*, in Plato's sense. Not a single thing, the object of common perception, nor the concept, which is the object of rational activity and of science.'[2] Thus art is the state of the most complete mental objectivity;[3] and aesthetic delight is nothing other than the complete absence of those pleasures and pains which all derive from the working of the Will: a negative definition, but this did not unduly worry its author. It may be seen what a singular accord there is between anti-conceptionalism here and in Baudelaire's aesthetic.

The fuller implications of this recondite view of the subject matter of art will be noted later in the sections devoted to the various topics under which they fall. But it is important to grasp from the start that the doctrine of Ideas has some unusual results throughout the fabric of Schopenhauer's aesthetic. As Plato had noted many centuries before, there is no limit to the possible number of Ideas, any more than there is a limit to the number of distinct forms of thought open to the mind. And just as Socrates confesses his inability to set a limit, so Schopenhauer makes no attempt to circumscribe the field in which the artist moves among Platonic Ideas. Anything apprehended intuitively, by a mind set free from the Will, is suitable material for art. Kant's condition of 'disinterestedness' has been erected into the crucial test, and magnified into a full-scale metaphysical doctrine. The position is not without its disadvantages: fully adhered to, it leaves no room whatever for comparative judgements of value. Call a work of art bad because it excites your appetites, and you lay yourself open to the charge of being yourself not enough of a genius! To a fully-fledged genius, anything whatever is matter for aesthetic delight. To begin with, Schopenhauer refused (quite consistently) to distinguish between the beauty of art and the beauty of nature,[4] except in so far as a work of art lightened the task of self-detachment. A further point which Schopenhauer did not pursue, and which the symbolists left strictly alone, is that art differs from nature precisely in so far as a work of art is a deliberate attempt to communicate the artist's disinterested contemplation.[5] Secondly, a system of classification of the arts which gave prominence to this

[1] ibid., p. 277.   [2] ibid., § 49.   [3] ibid., p. 218.
[4] ibid., pp. 229–30. [5] ibid., p. 229.

dominant attitude of the artist was necessarily founded on a table of
the senses dictated by current psychology, in which the eye achieved
the greatest measure of objectivity, whereas hearing already was
bound up with the affective and even passionate reactions, and the
sense of touch and smell (Kant's 'subjective senses') were virtually
excluded from aesthetic mediation, by reason of their close connections with the manifestations of the Will.[1] Schopenhauer parts
company with his times only in the pre-eminence conferred for
extraneous reasons on music, an art of hearing.

Turning for a moment to valuation in art, Schopenhauer admitted
two ingredients to man-made art: the one being genius, the other
sheer technical skill. The one is innate, the other acquired. Thus he
perpetuates in a new form the distinction between 'great art', that of
genius, and 'good' or technically brilliant art. There are in fact *two*
aesthetic criteria; with all the difficulties that this dualism involves.
Schopenhauer ignores the point: essentially, it is a reflection of the
romantic myth of the 'mute inglorious Milton'; and when aesthetic
overcomes these irrelevances, or at any rate these myths, it comes
under the necessity of producing a theory in which genius and
technique are more closely linked than Schopenhauer's teaching
allows.

More serious perhaps than any of these objections is the fact that
Schopenhauer considers art, in treating of Ideas, to deal not with
individuals but with whole classes of things. The Platonic Idea is 'the
permanent form of this whole class of things'. The artist 'knows
Ideas thoroughly well, but not Individuals. Hence a poet can have a
profound knowledge of Man, but only a very superficial one of
Men.'[2] If this is so, then it appears as though the difference between
Ideas and Concepts is being dangerously narrowed. Schopenhauer is
steering his aesthetic to catch the wind of the doctrine that art has a
cognitive content; that by knowing *Hamlet*, we learn better how men
behave under certain circumstances, and that this knowledge is an
element in aesthetic value. But he does so at the risk of allowing a
dangerous element into his philosophy of art: one which we have
noticed to pervade Taine's *Philosophie de l'art*, and which consists in
separating artistic form from artistic content. This once done, a
painting and a catalogue 'blurb' are equally good for calling the
spectator's attention to the 'Idea' represented; and then how is the
distinction of aesthetic value to be made between the two on grounds
of 'technique' except as a matter of sheer complexity? The dualism

[1] ibid., p. 230.   [2] op. cit., I, p. 229.

noted in the preceding paragraph brings Schopenhauer down, and subsequent attempts to patch the theory together lead to nonsense.[1]

And yet, woven into so dubious and ambiguous an account of art, there is a profoundly important psychological observation, one which has in more recent times been picked upon to bear the whole burden of aesthetic speculation. It is the fact that when we are intent upon a work of art, we feel ourselves entirely taken up in it; the logical relation of subject and object—we the subject, the art the object—vanishes entirely from our consciousness. Schopenhauer makes great play with this observation:

'We can withdraw from all suffering equally well by means of present or of remote objects, provided we can raise ourselves on to the plane of a purely objective contemplation of them, and thus produce in ourselves the illusion that only these objects, and not ourselves, exist; in such circumstances, relieved of our suffering selves, we, as the pure subject of cognition, become completely one with our object, and it (the object) becomes at such a moment as remote from us, as our suffering is remote from it.'[2]

The merit of Schopenhauer's philosophy of art, over and against that of Taine, may be set down under the following heads:

1. It gave an account of art as distinguishable from any other form of mental activity;

2. It defined, at least in some measure, those qualities which distinguish the artist from his fellows;

3. Ignoring questions of historical determination, it gave rein to the idea of creativeness in art; and

4. It suggested that art, so far from being confined to relatively large-scale, catalogued, and acknowledged works of art, is rather something which can arise at any moment of human experience.

Thus, to a greater or lesser degree, each of the four main defects which we have noted in Taine's philosophy of art are avoided by Schopenhauer; and aesthetics is established in its own right. At a high cost, granted: but it is not within our purpose to weigh up the numerous, and flagrant, objections which can be lodged against the foundations of Schopenhauer's doctrine. Our sole purpose in giving a sketch of his system is to illuminate certain otherwise unaccountable features which we come upon when we attempt to disengage one or two threads of doctrine especially associated with the name of

---

[1] E.g. Schopenhauer's fantastic theory that in speech, essentially conceptual in its parts, the concepts as it were 'cancel one another out' to leave only the Idea. He accounts in this way for the use of figurative language, as in Homer: the best poetry must therefore be that most charged with adjectives, metaphors, and so forth.

[2] *W.a.W.u.V.*, I, Bk. III, § 38, p. 234. Compare too Baudelaire, *L'Art Romantique*, p. 119, for a similar observation.

Mallarmé among other symbolists. Some aspects of *Die Welt als Wille und Vorstellung* and its theory of art are plainly incompatible with more recent views of art: Schopenhauer's idea that art, as a temporary relief from the misery of practical existence, is only a second-best to a thorough-going asceticism, would hardly prove attractive to those, who, like most poets or painters, think of it as entirely sufficient within its own sphere, an activity justifying itself; or again, his obsession with distinterestedness has long outlived its novelty or precision. Yet, as we shall see, elements of Schopenhauer's doctrine are continually, and almost unexpectedly, cropping up in symbolist exegesis; and lead one to suspect that here and there, for all the lack of organized and critical reflection, a fruitful or perhaps merely striking train of thought has been suggested by some remark issuing from this unique imaginative writer.

8. SCHOPENHAUER AND MALLARMÉ

It has been customary in the past to associate Mallarmé in things poetical with Baudelaire, largely on the strength of his earlier writings; yet there is little but tradition to recommend this view. And when we come to study the presuppositions of these two great poets it is impossible to overlook radical differences, not to say oppositions. Baudelaire gives an account of poetry which leans heavily on the notion of a blindingly beautiful supernatural realm to be glimpsed by the inspired artist; he never attempts to place the poet's activity there; furthermore his theory of language is not in any way remarkable, save for the doctrine of 'correspondances'; and outside of this last, he held no original views on a possible synthesis of the arts. Mallarmé, on the other hand, gives an account of poetry in which the poet is permanently sited in a non-phenomenal world, not in any sense the same as that glimpsed by Baudelaire's poet-priest; formulates a startlingly new theory of language; and virtually ignoring the notion of 'correspondances' goes on to the idea of future art-forms in which poetry, drama, music, dance, will all play their part. Baudelaire's admiration for Wagner is unbounded; Mallarmé's is only guarded. There is nothing in Baudelaire's view of the integrity of art which Mallarmé could not have learnt equally well from Théodore de Banville. And so on. From the very start there is nothing to be gained by treating Mallarmé as the 'successor' of Baudelaire, at least in what concerns his philosophy of art.

On the other hand, when we come to observe Mallarmé's view of the basic stuff from which poetry and indeed all art is made, we cannot but be struck by remarkable similarities with those notions which we have just been examining—that is to say, Schopenhauer's theory of Platonic Ideas; and although it is beyond our means to find out exactly to what extent the former did undergo the influence of the latter,[1] the resemblances are sufficiently numerous to justify our placing Mallarmé in a rather special position *vis-à-vis* his contemporaries. For it has been noticed by all who interest themselves in symbolist literature that he cannot conveniently be associated with any grouping of the younger poets at all; such intellectual traffic as there was between him and them was entirely one-way; they venerated him, though few copied him, but he himself appears to have gone his way unscathed: accepting their homage, indeed, but never bending to accommodate himself, or his ideas, to their opinions. It is customary to speak of him, and of his closer disciples, as essentially 'intellectual' in their approach to poetry; the label is certainly a false one, but it dates from long before Mauclair's important article which appeared on his death, and seems to have expressed even in the earliest days of the symbolist vogue a clearly felt sense of difference between him and his contemporaries, none of whom would ever have dreamt of aspiring to the title of literary logician.

A leading symbolist critic, Téodor de Wyzéwa, has interpreted a large number of his poems as having for their subject matter the fundamental unreality of the phenomenal world—its *contingency*, in fact. If this is correct, they would be a sort of popular transcription of the first book of *Die Welt als Wille und Vorstellung*, though there is nothing to suggest that Mallarmé ever set out to illustrate Schopenhauer's doctrine in verse:[2] indeed we have seen already that this sense of 'le néant' was with him from a very early stage of his life. Equally well, there is nothing to stand in the way of our treating his distinction between the two uses of language (as also his doctrine of Ideas) as a free translation of Schopenhauer's Third Book. We can assert no direct relationship, nor indeed a completely identical presentation of the notion; we are therefore not concerned with producing evidence that Mallarmé had ever read or even heard of the German philosopher (though from the time he came to Paris, in 1874, it would have been hard for him to avoid doing so): all we are concerned with here is the suggestion that there are similarities beneath the superficially so

[1] Mallarmé's biographers, as well as his own writings, are curiously silent on the matter.
[2] But see T. S. Eliot's treatment of him as a *metaphysical* poet (*NRF*, xi/1936: 'Note sur Mallarmé et Poe') quoted in ch. iv, p. 190 n. below.

different expositions; and it is these similarities which we shall now proceed to lay bare.

A famous passage in the *Divagations* distinguishes two uses of speech: the first commercial, 'reportage', the second literary. The characteristic of the literary use of language is that it involves more than the mere exchange of 'human thought', such as is involved in narration, teaching, or even description. All these actions have practical ends, and are in fact of no value except in their role of means to these ends; whereas in literature, or art in general, we feel the presence of some residual value. And Mallarmé identifies this residual something as the apprehension of 'la notion pure':

'A quoi bon la merveille de transposer un fait de nature en sa presque disparition vibratoire selon le jeu de la parole, cependant; si ce n'est pour qu'en émane, sans la gêne d'un proche ou concret appel, la notion pure.

'Je dis: une fleur! et, hors de l'oubli où ma voix relègue aucun contour, en tant que quelque chose d'autre que les calices sus, musicalement se lève, *idée même et suave*, l'absente de tous bouquets.'[1]

Here Mallarmé is talking of poetic images, nothing more; he attacks the realistic view, on which the painter's duty is to arrive as closely as possible at the imitative perfection of Zeuxis' grapes, and the writer's duty to utter the sort of language which enables the reader to 'visualize' as closely as possible an image conforming closely to his experience of the world around him; and instead propounds the poet's task as being to live in, and write of, a world of 'pure notions'. From the description he gives of the Idea, there cannot be much doubt that he is referring to something like a Platonic Idea; the recipe for reaching the 'Idea' of a flower would seem to be to abstract from one's mind one by one every feature which serves to distinguish one flower from another; such as a specific colour, a specific smell, shape, size, and so forth. The question remains, however, whether once these abstractions have been made, anything is left over at all; this question is of some importance for the whole Mallarméen aesthetic.

It is usual to acknowledge that a flower, or indeed any of the objects we think of as unities, are constructs formed by an essentially logical activity of the mind from the large number of sense-impressions that are involved as 'raw material'; in this sense, of course, a flower, as an object of ordinary everyday perception, is for Schopenhauer ruled out as a creature of the intellect. And yet, if we try to ignore the details of any particular flower, and make our poetic word 'une

---

[1] *Divagations*, pp. 250–1. My italics.

fleur' refer to Flowers, as a whole species known from repeated observation of numerous different members of the species, our word is doing duty as a sign for a concept, for something essentially the result of a logical activity; which again is inadmissible for Schopenhauer. In the case of Mallarmé, moreover, there is evidence that this latter interpretation is wholly alien to his intentions. Words capable of being used to refer to species of objects are not the only members of the group of means whereby he evokes 'Ideas'; a dancer's gestures, individual to a degree, also serve:

'Le ballet ne donne que peu: c'est le genre imaginatif. Quand s'isole pour le regard un signe de l'éparse beauté générale, fleur, onde, nuée et bijou, etc., chez nous, le moyen exclusif de le savoir consiste à en juxtaposer l'aspect à notre nudité spirituelle afin qu'elle le sente analogue et se l'adapte dans quelque confusion exquise d'elle avec cette forme envolée—rien qu'au travers du rite, là, énoncé de l'Idee, est-ce que ne paraît pas la danseuse à demi l'élément en cause, à demi humanité apte à s'y confondre, dans la flottaison de rêverie?'[1]

Again, speaking on one occasion of the problem of scenic presentation, he advances the view (later modified, but without prejudice to the position of the Idea) that the art of the future is destined to be the Dance, which he says, is 'seule capable, par son écriture sommaire, de traduire le fugace et le soudain jusqu'à l'Idée';[2] and elsewhere, too, he speaks of the ballet, or rather of the movements of the dancer, as the 'incorporation visuelle de l'idée'.[3] Now it could hardly be claimed that, however formalized the movements of a dancer may become, they are ever the vehicles for referential statements about classes of things. 'Flower' might refer to a botanical species; a pirouette would not ordinarily refer to a species of thing at all; and it need not indeed 'refer' to anything whatever.

We are forced to the conclusion that Mallarmé's Idea is Schopenhauer's in one respect: it is an object of pure contemplation or intuition. Mallarmé states in the *Divagations* that the poet is 'chargé de voir divinement'; he is an intuitor, and intuition is the autonomous sphere of art. But this is the difference, that Mallarmé adjusts his perspectives to link artistic worth closely with artistic competence as Schopenhauer never did: vision and skill of vision are for him one thing, where for Schopenhauer (in mid-tide of the romantic movement) they are two.

Indeed, with this reservation granted, we may wonder why Mallarmé clings to the theory of the poet as 'idealist': the play of

[1] ibid., pp. 157–8.   [2] ibid., p. 142.   [3] ibid., p. 177.

words once overcome, what he has to say about poetry far transcends the nineteenth century's arsenal of terms and definitions; and this adds to our difficulties as his readers. On the other hand, he and the generation following him *do* theorize as though on the basis of Schopenhauer's aesthetic; especially when they are attempting to explain what they mean by a 'Symbol'. And this fact, if no other, must prevent us from dismissing once for all at this stage the aesthetic category of the 'Idea': for without remembering its presence in the tangle of controversy we cannot follow certain awkwardnesses in Mallarmé's philosophy of art.

There are two further not unimportant aspects of symbolist art that the theory of Ideas was well able to reflect. First, the practitioner of a world of 'Ideas', whatever these may be, is indulging in an activity which demands a high degree of mental discipline, and is therefore not immediately accessible to the majority of people. The poet is, in fact, a specialist in a difficult technique, and his art thus becomes a rite, almost an esoteric practice. We shall see in the next chapter the lengths to which this conclusion was taken, reinforced by a variety of strictly non-aesthetic considerations. Schopenhauer and Mallarmé here, after avoiding the specialization introduced by Taine into the artist's sphere, fall into a precisely similar trap on quite other grounds. Art has ceased to be a technique of scientific notation, and instead become something akin to a religious experience, in the most sectarian possible limitations.[1] No doubt theory here does no more than mirror the circumstances of the times, but it presents the artist with a course of action which leads unavoidably to literary suicide.

Secondly, we have to consider the uses to which the theory of Ideas was actually put by Mallarmé in his *Divagations*. Up to this point we have deliberately omitted to deal with this problem, preferring to isolate the metaphysical element and judge it on its own merits. In the event, however, Mallarmé does not leave the matter at this point; he connects it to a number of observations regarding the way people do behave, in the presence of artistic activity; and this connection, or rather confusion, has not up to the present helped towards a clearer understanding.

If we turn again to the *Divagations*, in search of a clue to what the poet is doing when he uses words or images to express 'ideas', we find that Mallarmé has given a very full account of what a writer

---

[1] Cf. Mallarmé's slighting references to 'l'art officiel qu'on peut appeler vulgaire' (*Divagations*, p. 162).

sets out to do. We have seen that Ideas are not confined to the realm of intelligible, or rather intellectual, speech, but may be found in any form of art, and especially ballet ('... les jambes, comme un instrument direct d'idées...'[1]); and we are led to the conclusion that for the poet, poetry or art is something very much wider than the communication of opinions—it is symbolic gesture in the widest sense: the expression of attitude. We give two examples of the way in which spoken or written language displays this underlying quality of gesture or attitude:

'Abolie la prétention, esthétiquement une erreur, quoiqu'elle régit [*sic*] les chefs-d'œuvre, d'inclure au papier subtil autre chose que par exemple l'horreur de la forêt, ou le tonnerre muet épars au feuillage: non le bois intrinsèque et dense des arbres. Quelques jets de l'intime l'orgueil véridiquement trompetés éveillent l'architecture du palais, le seul habitable; hors de toute pierre, sur quoi les pages se refermeraient mal.'[2]

A more adequate, if less simply expressed, example is the following:

'Les monuments, la mer, la face humaine, dans leur plénitude, natifs, conservent une vertu autrement attrayante que ne les voilera une description, évocation dites, *allusion* je sais, *suggestion*: cette terminologie quelque peu de hasard atteste la tendance, une très décisive peut-être, qu'ait subie l'art littéraire, elle le borne et l'exemple. Son sortilège, à lui, si ce n'est libérer, hors d'une poignée de poussière ou réalité sans l'éclore, au livre, même comme texte, la dispersion volatile soit l'esprit, qui n'a que faire de rien outre la musicalité de tout.'[3]

A movement of the limbs, a metaphor, an image, a musical phrase—all therefore occupy the same position relative to the evocation of the Idea. And the thing they have in common is an affective value, the horror evoked by the forest, not the actual trees; the majesty of the palace, not the reproduction of its architecture. The Idea, in short, with whose chief exponent the majority of critics associated an uncompromising intellectuality,[4] is here no more than the justification of an affective factor in art.

As for musicality, this is not the place for a digression into the usage

---

[1] *Divagations*, p. 184.   [2] ibid., p. 245.
[3] ibid., pp. 245–6, quoted from *La Musique et les Lettres*.
[4] Cf. 'Ce fut un logicien parfaitement organisé... St. Mallarmé développait une méthode logique et philosophique...' (Mauclair, 'L'esthétique de Mallarmé,' *Grande Revue*, t. iv, p. 189, xi/1898). Or again, 'L'œuvre que dirige la pensée, l'œuvre avant tout logique qui s'adresse à l'intelligence, celle qui développe avec des gradations, des proportions calculées...' (Mockel, 'Mallarmé, un héros,' *Mercure de France*, xi/1898, t. xxviii, p. 368). 'Mais M. Mallarmé se manifeste ici même [in his early poems] un logicien et un artiste' (Wyzéwa, 'Mallarmé,' Notes, *Vogue*, 5/vii/1886, p. 366). The instances might be multiplied: but in every case the term 'idée' is plainly the original source of confusion—and it appears to have confused Mallarmé too: 'Anatole France m'appelle logicien, croyant peut-être que je suis ainsi comme on est voleur, honnête homme, etc. Que ne s'aperçoit-il que l'avocat aussi qui défend une cause est logicien, mais il ne comprend pas ce qu'est la logique éternelle' (Mallarmé quoted by E. Bonniot, *Les Mardis de Mallarmé* (*Mardi*, 17/i/1893), reproduced in *Les Marges*, 1936, quoted Mondor, *Vie*, p. 655).

in symbolist aesthetics of this key term;[1] but here again, we shall see in a later chapter that the musical element in art, that condition to which the poetry of the eighties and nineties so ardently aspired, may be reduced in the last resort to the affective factor in all language; and therefore to the affective element in words to which Mallarmé might choose to give the name of Idea. That is not to say that Mallarmé was canvassing a hackneyed romantic view of art as a vehicle for the expression of personal emotions, in the limited sense in which this was taken at the beginning of the nineteenth century. There is a whole world of difference between expression in this latter sense, a kind of transliteration of conventionally recognized emotions, and the kind of 'emotion' which exudes from every line of, say, *L'Après-midi d'un faune*; and it is more than probable that Mallarmé deliberately avoided the ordinary word for the affective element in poetry simply because for him it was inextricably tied up with the earlier kind of poetry.

The gentle persuasion of Mallarmé's voice and views, in the remoteness of his drawing-room in the Rue de Rome, was a powerful instrument in the aesthetic education of young poets. Less powerful, no doubt, but infinitely more strident, was Moréas' proclamation to all France of the birth of Symbolism in *Figaro* on September 18th, 1886. Moréas, we are told, 'avait séjourné en Allemagne. Ce fut lui, si je ne me trompe, qui l'un des premiers parla à ses camarades de Schopenhauer.'[2] Whether it was from Schopenhauer's works direct, or from Mallarmé that he learnt of the importance of 'Ideas' to art, is impossible to determine, so hazy is he in his reference to the matter; here are his own words:

'Ennemi de l'enseignement, de la déclamation, de la fausse sensibilité, de la description objective, la poésie symboliste cherche à vêtir *l'Idée* d'une forme sensible qui, néanmoins, ne serait pas son but à elle-même, mais qui tout en servant à exprimer l'Idée demeurerait sujette. L'Idée à son tour ne doit pas se laisser voir privée des somptueuses simarres des anologies extérieures, car le caractère essentiel de l'art symbolique [*sic*] consiste à ne jamais aller jusqu'à la conception de l'Idée en soi. Ainsi dans cet art, les tableaux de la nature, les actions des humains, tous les phé-

---

[1] The fact that both Schopenhauer in 1818, and the symbolists in 1885, ascribed such extreme importance to music may be taken as a coincidence, at least in principle: for we have no means of assessing to what an extent the arguments for the supremacy of music, in Schopenhauer, were fully understood in literary circles. But if it is a coincidence, it is all the more significant for that; and we shall have to ask, not so much what music is, as what the symbolists took it to be. There is little evidence that for the French literary scene of Schopenhauer's own times this art had anything like the importance we find in the eighties. See Baldensperger, *Sensibilité musicale et romantisme*, 1905, *passim*.

[2] Morhardt, 'Les Symboliques,' *Nouvelle Revue*, t. LXXIV, p. 768, 15/ii/1892.

nomènes concrets ne sauraient se manifester eux-mêmes: ce sont là des apparences sensibles destinées à représenter leurs affinités ésoteriques avec des Idées primordiales.'[1]

It will be seen that Moréas, with a flair for leadership and publicity which is far from being his least claim to fame, and the tactician's sense of obligation to all his divers supporters, improves on Schopenhauer: Platonic Ideas have become 'des Idées primordiales'—more than a glimpse, there, of Wagnerian legend—while Ideas and their representations are now linked by 'esoteric affinities'—a concession to the mystics. The 'symbol' (which Schopenhauer incidentally spurns violently as conceptual and anti-artistic) is here foreshadowed as a necessary touch to German idealism: according as the symbolist speaks of Mallarmé or Baudelaire, the symbol of an Idea will be either a word or any object in the external world.[2] At all events, the Idea is strongly ensconced, and brings to symbolist doctrine the authority of the most famous German thinker in late nineteenth-century France.

9. THE INADEQUACY OF IDEAS IN AESTHETIC

The way in which it was linked up will become more apparent in our next chapter, when the study of poetic Imagination leads us to examine the place occupied by definite 'themes' and 'subjects' as material for Mallarméen poetry; but we may so far anticipate our findings as to suggest that in Mallarmé's case at least, and probably also in the case of many of his contemporaries for a large part of the time, the 'subject', as (say) Lamartine or Hugo made use of it, was in itself void of aesthetic value. An image, something present to the eye or ear, a particular combination of words even, makes an appeal to the poet; but any form of mental activity in which an intellectual element is involved (for 'subject matter' is inevitably an appeal to the intellect) is excluded from the sphere of aesthetic contemplation. So soon as it ceases to be the mere product of words combined on other aesthetic grounds, and becomes an element standing above, standing, as it were, over and against the images, the phrases, the Ideas, and the Symbols, this subject becomes an organizational abstraction; it is no longer the poet's property, but something accessible (as the circulation of the poetry of the romantic era well

---

[1] Reprinted, *Les premières armes du Symbolisme*, 1889.
[2] An attentive and unusual student, who had read Challemel-Lacour's article on Schopenhauer in 1870, absorbed enough of it to write at a slightly later date: '... Encore tout enfant j'admirais le forçat intraitable ... je voyais *avec son idée* le ciel bleu et le travail fleuri de la campagne' (*Saison en enfer*, 'Mauvais sang'. Rimbaud's italics.)

shows) to the meanest creature who finds an appeal in the spectacle of Abnegation in a poem by Vigny, or religious fervour in the *Harmonies* of Lamartine. And although we are not concerned in this type of inquiry to explain symbolist views in terms of their protagonists' social foibles, it is hard to escape the suspicion that all this aesthetic wrangling, designed in every case to free the poet from the shackles of what is conventionally called his 'theme'—whether it be a plot in a novel or a play, or the classical sonata form in music, or the heroic subject in painting, or the definite setting and situation in a poem—did perhaps have its motive in a wish for art to be completely different from anything else men do, and for symbolist poetry in particular to branch away from anything previous schools and movements had aimed at and 'bourgeois' orthodoxy approved. There is no doubt that the *deliberateness* of the tendency is harmful; that even in the world where willy-nilly the poet of 1880 had to live, it was not possible to avoid experiencing strong feelings about quite straightforward 'intellectual' subjects which he could have embodied in poetry; and that the deliberate banning of all traffic in this field was at the root of certain weaknesses of all European poetry of the time seen as a whole—for the fact that no poet grew up in its atmosphere whom we can in the ordinary sense call 'great', that the symbolist masterpiece, which alone would have justified it in the eyes of the world and its own followers, never saw the light;[1] and that all literature of any note that has stemmed from symbolism has not so much intensified its tenets to the exclusion of all else as operated a fusion between its innovations and the products of quite other traditions in art.[2]

This is a serious accusation to bring against the doctrine of Ideas; yet it is not one which can be easily refuted. We have seen that in Mallarmé's theory the Idea, for all its significance to art, still resembles a Platonic Idea inasmuch as it extends only to single 'units' of experience. One could hardly say that *L'Après-midi d'un faune* is the expression of an Idea, one and indivisible; in the context of language, an Idea might extend over a group of words, a line, a stanza even; from the aspect of poetic material, it might be covered by an image, a description; but it could never correspond to an organizing

---

[1] Cf. the great hopes placed in Moréas' *Pèlerin Passionné* by all the faithful; see too Dujardin's *Mallarmé*, and Ghil's *Les Dates et les Œuvres, passim,* for the eagerness with which Mallarmé's apocryphal 'œuvre' was awaited.

[2] The symptom here discussed is simply a more advanced stage of the tendency noted by Arnold in mid-nineteenth-century England: or by Sainte-Beuve in his article 'Des Soirées Littéraires' (*Portraits Littéraires,* 2nd ed. 1863, t. I, p. 430 *seq.,* and especially pp. 433–4).

principle such as one finds a *plot* to be; to some overall conception of a poem which determines the place of each Idea, lays down its relations to neighbouring Ideas (contrast, reinforcement, modification, and so forth), or presides over the vitally important task of preventing confusion and frustration of effort.

For Mallarmé's immediate disciples the same limitation holds. André Gide's early *Traité du Narcisse* (1892), a beautifully precious piece of imaginative writing, gives us no hint as to how Ideas are to rise above their association with the merely unitary elements of art. For him, the 'Chaste Eden, jardin des Idées' is virtually the same as Plato's world of Ideas:

'Le Paradis est toujours à refaire, mais il n'est point en quelque lointaine Thule. Le Paradis est sous l'apparence. *Chaque chose* détient, virtuelle, l'intime harmonie de son être.'[1]

Five years later, he writes, as if aware that something rather important has been left out in the cold by Mallarmé's theory:

'Une œuvre bien composée est nécessairement symbolique. Autour de quoi viendrait se grouper les parties? Qui guiderait leur ordonnance? Sinon l'idée de l'œuvre, qui fait cette ordonnance symbolique';[2]

and again:

'L'œuvre d'art est une idée qu'on exagère.'[3]

Yet it should be plain that the objection he is meeting in these remarks is not the same objection that we have lodged. The difference between the two problems is precisely equivalent to the difference in the aesthetic problems raised on the one hand by his *Voyage d'Urien*, and on the other by *L'Immoraliste*—both early works, but the one definitely symbolist, the other definitely not. In the former, one might well say that the formal composition of a long narrative depends entirely on the unity of its atmosphere, on a certain underlying intention to create and give sustained expression to a state of mind (as Gide himself declares[4]) through the symbolic use of a landscape—playing on what he is pleased to call the ideal properties of images and scenes. In the second, the plot, perfectly plain and orthodox, is there for all to see. And Gide is no longer a symbolist.

---

[1] *Traité du Narcisse, Entretiens politiques et littéraires*, vol. 4, pp. 20–28, iv/1892.

[2] Gide, *Réflexions, Œuvres* (NRF, vol. 1), p. 424. First published in 1897 (in the *Mercure de France*).

[3] ibid.

[4] 'Emotion et manifeste forment équation; l'un est l'équivalent de l'autre. Qui dit *émotion* dira donc *Paysage*; et qui dit *paysage* devra donc connaître *émotion*' (*Mercure de France*, xii/1894, p. 354). Although referring specifically to the *Voyage*, the same formula would also hold good for *Paludes*, despite its rather different material.

For Camille Mauclair, too, at one time a faithful disciple of Mallarmé, the Idea has the same limitations as for the Master. In an article which he devoted to the relations between the 'Idée pure' and the 'Symbol', any 'object' is said to comprise (a) its phenomenal qualities, and (b) its idea—'qui s'incarne en son nom, et qui est l'unique cause de son existence, puisque nous concevons idéalement'.[1]

'Les objets sont les caractères hiéroglyphiques, où s'inscrit complexement l'idée pure, et en cet assemblage de formes, comme en toute géometrie, la connaissance profonde et le soigneux formulaire de l'écriture ou des figures aident à la compréhension et dédient à la lecture plus de clarté.'[2]

There can be no doubt that the relation between ideas and 'objects' or the material of poetry, images, scenes, landscapes, and the like, is a one-to-one relationship. And the problem of an intellectual content in art remains unsolved.

The same difficulty attends with equal force on the theory of the symbol. In this case, admittedly, the symbolists themselves found a means of escape from their dilemma by playing on the ambiguity of the term;[3] by surreptitiously allowing an element of allegory to become implicated in it, and by failing to define with sufficient precision what they meant by myths or legends, they brought an intellectial content back by the side-door into the house from whose main entrance they had expelled it with such noise. It is at least questionable whether, as Téodor de Wyzéwa alleges, the whole of the *Après-midi d'un faune* constitutes a single 'symbol', without making nonsense of that term; but if we examine his argument, we can see that this elusive word does not yet provide a solution for the problem we are facing:

'Je crains que nos jeunes poètes et peut-être aussi M. Mallarmé lui-même, ne reprochent à cette églogue de n'être point assez symbolique. Je crois au contraire que *l'Après-midi d'un Faune* est le modèle excellent du véritable symbolisme artistique. Ce faune est un personnage concret en des conditions particulières et déterminées. Les émotions restituées sont celles du Faune à un moment donné, non des émotions abstraites et générales. Et cela n'empêche point les émotions de ce Faune d'être aussi les nôtres; elles sont l'universel regret das âmes après la joie, et nos inquiétudes, et notre course vers le rêve qui doit nous rendre la joie évanouie. Mais notre âme, pour éprouver ces émotions, doit lui donner une forme précise et concrète: et l'émotion est plus vivante d'autant qu'elle est plus précise et concrète en nous: c'est pour cela que nous ressentons profondément notre émotion lorsque le poète nous restitue avec plus de netteté l'image spéciale de cette âme émue que, grâce à lui, nous devenons. La meilleure façon de symboliser dans l'art un sentiment

---

[1] 'Notes sur l'idée pure,' *Mercure de France*, t. viii, ix/1892, p. 42.   [2] ibid.
[3] See below, ch. VI.

ou un raisonnement universel, c'est encore d'en faire les sentiments et les raisonnements très définis d'une spéciale âme vivante. Car chacun de ceux qui ont en leurs âmes, ce sentiment ou ce raisonnement, le retrouvent, en revivant cette âme créée par l'artiste; et ils le retrouvent précis et réel, puisque l'artiste s'est attaché à le recréer dans les plus précises et réelles conditions de la vie.'[1]

No doubt the symbolic aspect of the whole poem rests on a completely integrated group of 'émotions restituées'; but it is a group belonging to 'un moment donné'; and there is much in the background of the poem which is not to be contained in an instant of time. Indeed, the surface obscurity of the whole thing is due precisely to the fact that Mallarmé has pushed his 'Plot' (necessarily, without any doubt, in the interest of its subtleties) so very far into the background; witness the efforts of a whole succession of notable exegetes to help the reader by reconstructing what has *happened* to the musing faun. This plot is hardly the symbolic content of the poem; but for all that it is perfectly real, and necessary to a work of that length; and reluctance to study such a feature in composition is closely linked with the relative failure of symbolist ventures in spheres outside the lyric poem.

Yet it is unfair to blame symbolist doctrine for lacking a theoretical perspective able to accommodate the material of intellect within the sphere of art. Two reasons should restrain us from such an indictment. The first is, that as we have already claimed, aesthetic theory is not independent of the practice of art, and for a variety of reasons, more properly the province of a history of literature, the symbolists were nearly without exception moving away from 'intellectual' art. This is indeed the outstanding tendency in their work, and it is only to be expected that their aesthetic doctrines should reflect it. The second and perhaps more important reason is, that it is undoubtedly true that poetry can be written, pictures painted, music composed, from which the working of intellect seems almost absent; in which evident conceptual relations between parts do not occur; in which the writer or artist is attending not to a diversity of images, experiences, states of mind, or occurrences, linked together by conceptual ties, but to one only: such as the experience of seeing one single and particular sunset—a single and indivisible experience or response—or perhaps something even more simple than that. The symbolist is by his own logic entitled to claim that this is true art which he is engaged on developing, and moreover that it is an activity sharing nothing with other forms of human activity. If he turns to writing a long poem about nature (like Lucretius) he can be accused of over-

---

[1] Téodor de Wyzéwa, 'Les Livres,' *Revue Indépendante*, iii/1887, t. ii, p. 339.

lapping with the scientist; Shakespeare may be encroaching on the ground of history; Dante on philosophy—what he does not go on to recognize in each of these cases is that where intellect supervenes, it is doing so under the auspices not of its own criteria (namely, truth and error) but rather of those of art, aesthetic criteria. This, of course, is precisely the argument to which Schopenhauer's stubborn separation of concepts (*Begriffe*) and Ideas (*Ideen*) cannot lend itself; the situation which cannot be dealt with in the light of Mallarmé's rigid division of language into reportage and poetry. Ironically, it is the commonest of all situations that an aesthetic has to deal with; yet here is a literary movement whose leading protagonists (we shall presently see the same conclusion from different premises) adopt and develop a doctrine that denies the possibility of its arising. Aspirations of practice are faithfully reflected in the enunciations of theory.

This state of affairs represents a distortion exactly opposite to those noticed earlier in speaking of Taine. There, intellectual elements dominate to a point where they prevent the aesthetician from establishing any essential characteristics of art distinct from science (in the nineteenth century's sense). Here, certain essential characteristics of art are established at the expense of intellect in such a way as to inhibit a full and unstunted tradition of art from forming itself. The bulk of the profound human problems which are from time to time expressed in great works of art are put out of court, without right of appeal. The inevitable development from this position is Bergson—for whom the artist can *never* stray into the field of thought without destroying the uninterrupted flow of his intuitive consciousness; and the ultimate equivalent of this in the practice of art is Surrealism.

On a preliminary survey of symbolist thought in the philosophy of art we see, then, two broad positions; one is called idealism, the other, anti-intellectualism. The first, it has been suggested, amounts to no more than a claim to be rid of a naturalist tradition: against theories built on the statement that careful observation of fact controls and assists artistic creation, it advances theories based on the equally valid statement that servility to historical fact can cramp artistic endeavour. The second position is concerned with a rather more fundamental problem; the attempt to find an autonomous field for art, distinct from science or history, and without interference from their intellectual criteria of truth; and with this field, a primary *function* distinct from such secondary duties as education, persuasion, or distraction. These two general positions are seemingly distinct;

but as soon as we explore them they appear to be in fact very closely related. Anti-intellectualism, if it is not to relapse into irrationalism and Surrealism, must give a clear account of what sort of process the poet or composer goes through in composition; this account will in turn reshape the whole issue of 'real' versus 'imaginary' material in art, and so put the 'idealist' vogue in proper perspective. Some element is evidently missing from the naturalist account of knowledge, both artistic and historical, if art is to be autonomous in the way suggested by poetic experience.

Reverting to our geometrical analogy, a fourth point, somewhere outside the triangular system, calls out for a new figure; there are certain facts about art, not by any means observed for the first time, but only now demanding with insistence a new theory capable of embracing them; and this means upsetting traditional positivist assumptions. The work of upsetting assumptions was undertaken piece-meal by the writers of 1880–1900; and the subsequent work of reconstruction was taken as far as the statement of a new central fact regarding poetic knowledge; but the development of a new theory of art implied by newly acknowledged facts was the work of others after them.

CHAPTER III

POETIC KNOWLEDGE

Inventer ce n'est que se comprendre.—VALÉRY

I. THE REVULSION FROM AESTHETIC INTELLECTUALISM

THE philosophy of art developed by Taine and rejected by the symbolists was both strong and weak. It was strong in so far as it stepped outside the purely *a priori* speculation of a Cousin, a Jouffroy, or a Levêque, in which aesthetic was little more than a stopgap inserted to complete the pattern of a methodical philosophy—in which, in other words, the philosopher rode a purely normative high horse and suffered the usual fate for such work. For Taine aesthetic was something which started with the facts—the *phenomena* of the world of art, certain features which the historian detected in the course of his labours on works of art. Aesthetic did not stop there, however, for all that Taine may have said to the contrary: implicitly attached to its descriptions was another, a normative aspect, in the light of which our respect for Taine recedes. It is out of the question to write off as simply bad luck or lack of artistic appreciation the circumstances that led him to build a crooked tower of theory from which to survey the facts: it is not in keeping with the ways of so thorough a master-builder to start straight and develop a list as he went upwards. If the edifice went askew, it must be that the foundations were not laid on the level. These foundations are, of course, none other than the principles of knowledge implicit in all naturalist discussion of the operations of the artist's mind. And it is to these that we shall now turn our attention.

We have seen that for Taine the function of the artist seems to be to impart knowledge—inaccurate knowledge no doubt, by the standards of science, and sometimes knowledge of a trivial nature, but nevertheless knowledge not essentially different from, if more palatable than, that of the scientific monograph or the history book.

74

Even if the knowledge was (as in La Fontaine's fables, for instance) in one sense obviously 'untrue', the criteria by which it was judged remained those of science or history: the fable was subjected to 'interpretation'. The artistic narration must bring to the audience's notice a *characteristic*, clearly and explicitly: clarity and explicitness are stylistic criteria of historical and scientific discourse. This characteristic element is lodged in a composition which makes use of shapes, sounds, colours, rhythms, and so forth: the material of sense perception.

The artist (like any other man) opened his eyes, and colours were present before them; he turned his ear, and sounds of various pitch struck it. Sometimes he was subject to hallucination; this was troublesome, because there was on internal evidence no way of distinguishing real perception from hallucination; the former were *hallucinations vraies*. Not Taine, but several generations of artists and writers who had no quarrel with his views, moreover, joined to this rough and ready handling of the material of art, the view (called 'realism' in literary criticism, but in this point not materially different from 'naturalism' in the same technical vocabulary) that art should properly be a mirror of real or at least historically possible events, and strictly avoid the fantastical; the works of the Goncourts make, and were intended to make, an ideal hunting-ground for the follower of Taine who should equate literary criticism with social history.

Against this identification of art with history (not to say with science), the symbolists react strongly. In the first place, they claim (and posterity agrees), the material for art is not necessarily 'truthful': it is no defect in painting as against sculpture that it pretends to put three dimensions before you on a two-dimensional canvas; or that no talking crows or foxes have ever existed; *Salammbô* is no worse for the fact that Flaubert's historical scholarship is bad; in a word, that truthfulness is a relative term, and 'imitation' ambiguous. In the second place, it is of no interest to the spectator whether the work before him is a member of a species, or whether the species links interestingly with sociology or anthropology: art refuses the call of science, and the merits of the Rougon-Macquart cycle are independent of opinion whether drunkenness is inheritable. A work of art is valued for its individuality, not for its particular embodiment of a general truth. In a subsequent section, we come upon an apparent contradiction of this assertion; but the contradiction does not invalidate the claim that the symbolists made a sharp division between art and the positive sciences. Equally, when we come to discuss the literary symbol, we shall meet with the view that the aesthetic importance of symbols (for some persons, at least) lies in the fact that they embody some general proposition, about some 'caractère saillant' of the universe regarded as a mystical whole; but we shall also see that the grounds for this view are far from being such as would have met with Taine's approval; and that in effect this explanation of the value of symbols results from a more radical inability to define adequately the nature of aesthetic value. Taine's criteria are rejected, but the new ones are not fully formed; and in the interval, though the intention is plain, the means are insufficient. Two stages in the definition of a work of art emerge accordingly from preliminary negative demarcation: it is not a contribution to scientific knowledge, since it features an individual experience and nothing more; it is not even a contribution to historical knowledge, since its value has no relation to veracity.

Given these two stages, there are powerful inducements to go a stage further and say that art is not concerned with knowledge at all; that is to say, with knowledge of the objective world. The special interest of German idealism for artists in the eighties was, we have suggested, precisely that: in the solipsism into which writers like Villiers de l'Isle Adam attempted to transform the idealisms of Fichte or Hegel, history and science tumble down from their pre-eminence and take a humble position as the study of organized illusion; and art is once again on an equal footing with its haughty sisters.[1] There are, however, other grounds on which the question could be decided; and a mystical streak in the literary movement was always eager to find an activity which could be clearly pointed to as its special method of cognizing the world.[2] A third alternative offers itself, however, which is neither trivial nor obscurantist: one towards whose development the symbolist movement made signal, if only semi-conscious, contributions. This is the view—not by any means unfamiliar to philosophy—that in the aesthetic act no cognitive element[3] is present but that this act is nevertheless in principle an indispensable foundation to all knowledge which can be classified as true or false.

The symbolists' reaction to the argument for a cognitive content

[1] Cf. 'On demande comment la Science et l'Art feront le grand accord sur quoi compte l'avenir? Pascal, Balzac, Edgar Poe, M. Villiers de l'Isle Adam le savent. L'art touchera du pied la Science pour prendre en elle l'assurance d'un fondement solide et d'un élan la franchira sur les Ailes de l'Intuition' (Morice, *La Littérature de tout à l'heure*, 1889, p. 203).

[2] See below, § 4.

[3] We shall use the term 'cognitive element' in referring only to the work of art as a *reference* that is to say, coming under consideration not for its aesthetic adequacy but for its truth or erroneousness: an intellectual criterion.

follows from the attempt to find links between poetry and certain elements in experience which, in the times at which they were writing, were ignored by positivism and the object of very little attention on the part of the public. These elements were dreams and other manifestations of mental activity which did not lend themselves to so-called 'common-sense' analysis as a harmonious combination of perception and reasoning and which seemed to make nonsense of the criterion of 'imitation'. The links and associations could take a number of forms; e.g. the view that poetry can make use of material drawn from memories of experience when the conscious and deliberate activities of the mind are apparently at rest; or that the whole fire and force of poetry depends on certain energies which are beyond the reach of such control; or that the poet's task is to encourage unwilled and uncontrolled experience to supply him with the forms and patterns of his conscious art; or that poetry is simply the renunciation of what is usually understood by deliberate composition, and indulgence in an activity whose nearest analogy for non-poetical people is to be found in the act of dreaming, or day-dreaming.

Literary discourse, to be sure, had long recognized the interest of such strange visitors to poetry, and continued to welcome new-comers: while the French romantic tradition makes constant reference to the '*rêverie*' of the eighteenth century, and through Rousseau finds in it the source of a wide range of poetic material, the symbolists at half a century's remove are eager to define their art in terms of '*rêve*'; and some of them light on the notion of the subconscious as an agent in literary creation. But all these terms are in the highest degree ambiguous; no coherent theory of poetic knowledge can possibly use them without a very close precision of what they are intended to define; and our examination of symbolist usage will put one thing beyond the possibility of doubt: that neither individually, nor all together, can such terms form the basis of a systematic theory able to replace Taine's formidable construction. They are protests, isolated if suggestive details for a future synthesis: they have not within themselves the making of a synthesis. For the special case of '*rêverie*' this will be made plain enough in the sequel. For the category of '*rêve*' the situation is different; a word with a host of connotations, the symbolists will be found making use of it in two distinct ways: to describe the texture of poetry, and (with a great extension of meaning) to define the nature of poetic knowledge.

This last is indeed the core of the problem. It is easy enough to see how, say, *Salammbô* accords with Taine's demand for 'imitation;'

not so easy to reconcile the latter criterion with the (historical) innocence of Mallarmé's *Faune*. The 'thought' in such a poem is plainly not of such a kind as can be readily taken up into the science of man; yet at the same time poetry is evidently more than the sort of passive experience which for Taine constitutes perception simple. Again, art is in some sense 'true': but its truth does not lie in its making verifiable statements about objective facts. All points to the suspicion that Taine classified experience too rigidly into the two elements *perception* and *reasoning*—the former passive, the latter active; that art is an activity, but not one of reasoning—a kind of perception, but not passive. Taine's return to the *Traité des Sensations*, in short, makes it impossible for him to reckon with the discoveries of the *Critique of Judgement*. The sections which follow show how the symbolists apprehended the difficulties of the situation, and attempted to satisfy their conscience by all means short of actually overturning the assumptions of positivist epistemology. What they were aiming at was the establishment of a category perhaps similar to that of Imagination, as we find it in Kant and also in the English tradition; but coloured at every stage by literary preferences, which impinge so powerfully on all their aesthetic controversy as greatly to hinder the formation of any firm and universal criteria. In this general position, they represent an important and no doubt unique phase in the history of aesthetic in France: a phase which passes away with the appearance in the twentieth century of Bergson and Bergsonism, and which is as remote to-day from the *ulterior* requirements of Existentialism or Thomism, as it is anathema to Marxian discussion of the arts.

Not that it is absent from the French scene. In direct line of descent from the symbolist movement, for example, stand Gide and Valéry: not so much the Valéry of *Teste* and *La jeune Parque* as of the *Introduction à la mèthode de Léonard de Vinci*, the *Calepin d'un poète*, or, best of all, the ripely matured *Poésie et Pensée abstraite* of 1939; influenced no doubt greatly by Mallarmé, and standing in much the same relation to the perfection of a certain strain of poetry as Gide stands to a certain strain of novel-writing. For Valéry, the aesthetic problem *par excellence* is that of poetic knowledge; and looked at from the viewpoint of the specialist user of language, the solution is bound to be presented largely in terms of the relation of poetic knowledge to creation. Quite simply, the relation is one of identity; creation *is* poetic knowledge, therefore self-knowledge: the definition of the poet's attitude, with a lesser or greater degree of precision, according as he is a good or a great poet. 'Inventer c'est se comprendre.' The attitude studied is necessarily a concrete one: that is to say, in any individual situation in time and space the poet is working to define what is latent in his mind by saying it;[1] by taking a vague sensation and rendering it more precise through working on its poetic form. For Valéry the task is paradoxically made easier by the introduction of difficulties, but that is the incidental contribution of one man's tastes. The essential is the discovery of the poem, taking place as an act of language, and identical with the discovery of feeling. Under all circumstances the artist is not claiming the sort of 'truth' for his art that Zola claims for his 'roman expérimental', and he is agitated by none of Renan's difficulties of relating art to science; he claims no *discursive* truth for his work, only an intuitive or imaginative truth— what one might call genuineness, the validity of consistency built upon truthful facing of experience. The more complex and refined the attitudes he desires to express, the more difficult becomes the work, as compared with the expression of simple responses to simple occasions; but the subtleties of rhythm and balance, for example, provide not distinctions in kind but only of degree between various similar acts of creative imagination.

Thus the realist's criterion of *imitation* is irrelevant; whether a piece of imaginative knowledge is 'truthful' or not does not arise, because it is knowledge of the concrete and the individual, and discursive truth is concerned with relations *between* individual elements of knowledge. Artistic vision can be subjected to immanent, but not to transcendental, criticism; when judged as art, we decide on its adequacy; when we discuss it by reference to other criteria, we are no longer strictly talking about it as art. 'Real' and 'illusory' are meaningless terms for it; 'truthful' and 'erroneous' are irrelevant.

The status of this poetic knowledge has been briefly set out by an English philosopher in a way that generally reflects the intentions of modern literature;[2] and it is important to notice only one further point. If imagination, or consciousness of individual situations, is the mastering of brute sensation by directing attention towards stimuli, then a scale of artistic value of exactly the kind implicit in all our literary judgements stands right at the core of the position. Awareness of, say, Fear results not from the involuntary act of

---

[1] By 'saying' Valéry also, in the *Introduction*, explicitly means painting, which is a parallel activity of bodily gesture serving to sharpen consciousness. The notion of language can be similarly extended to include singing, dancing, and so forth: an important extension when we are considering Mallarmé's views.

[2] R. G. Collingwood, *The Principles of Art*, 1937, esp. Part II.

shrinking back or screaming, but from a direction of attention towards whatever it is we shrink from, and the formulation of an attitude in language: by so doing we escape to some extent from the world of uncontrollable impulses; the more we can make plain our attitude, the more we enjoy this freedom. The act of artistic creation lies in that link between the world of determination and the world of freedom whose first postulation was Kant's great achievement; and it is for this reason that formulating an attitude, or *expressing* it, is not a purely mental act, but a mental act grounded on a physical act of language.[1]

From this in turn it seems to follow—and whichever way we turn critically-minded writers and poets of the present century seem to appreciate clearly—that consciousness is an activity that can be pursued well or ill; that at some times we are more conscious than at others; that the language which shapes consciousness can be, as it were, more linguistic or less linguistic, a more or a less adequate formulation of attitude; and that the activity called poetry is nothing other than the development of certain aspects of language to the maximum point of expressiveness or imaginative lucidity. If at the highest level poetic creation shows language in its clearest forms, we should expect to find the language of poetry more highly *organized* than that of more ordinary everyday discourse; and in one or other of many possible ways this is always so. Similarly, the lowest levels of imaginative consciousness are so far from the organization we expect from language that at certain limiting points we may doubt whether we are in the presence of this sort of activity at all: certain states of auto-hypnosis seem so light and indefinable that they seem almost free of attitude, so passive that active processes of conscious attention seem to be suspended. And similarly certain utterances are sometimes so 'inarticulate' as hardly to appear to be language in any formalized sense.

These two latter limiting cases seem to be independent; yet in a surrealist world, for example, they rub shoulders in a striking way; and an undercurrent of European thought for over a century and a half persisted in relating art to special cases of consciousness such as these. Almost invariably this happens as a reaction from some form of dogmatic intellectualism; but whether intellectualist like Taine, or anti-intellectualist like Bergson, there is always a tacit assumption that poetic knowledge can be sited only in one of two spheres:

[1] The point is clearly argued against Croce by Alexander in *Art and the Material*, 1925. The linguistic implications of the argument become relevant in the next chapter.

intellection or sensation. The symbolist movement as a whole tries to avoid both of these alternatives; and although it is not able to give its position explicit shape, there is no doubt that implicitly it was *working towards* a conception of imaginative creation such as we can isolate in Valéry. And, since that name has been mentioned, it is worth repeating that the poet who came nearest in the nineteenth century to formulating this conception was Stéphane Mallarmé.

The symbolist position, then, was an attempted evasion of two parallel dangers. Before expounding it, we will first take the second, anti-intellectualist, alternative and consider a literary category (*rêverie*) at its very fountain-head. When we have done this we shall have before us all the main streams of aesthetic speculation at the opening of the symbolist era in literature, and it will be a simple process to see the writers of 1885 in proper perspective.

2. 'RÊVERIE'

The grandfather of anti-intellectualist French aesthetic is Rousseau; and Rousseau occupies in many people's eyes a place apart as one of the founders of the modern Bergsonian approach to art: both these on the strength of the posthumous *Rêveries du promeneur solitaire*. Essentially, Bergson's intuition, for example, and Rousseau's *rêverie* are an attempt to define (I will not say 'invent') a state of mind from which intellectual activity is absent, a state undistorted (as they say)[1] by language forms and other such products of deliberate activity, in short a consciousness enjoying all the hypothetical advantages of a passivity, without the attendant disadvantage—namely, that into a state of complete mental passivity no consciousness could enter. Thus in his fifth *Promenade* Rousseau writes:

'Quand le soir approchait, je descendais des cimes de l'île et j'allais volontiers m'asseoir au bord du lac, sur la grève, dans quelque asile caché; là, le bruit des vagues et l'agitation de l'eau, fixant mes sens et chassant de mon âme toute autre agitation, la plongeaient dans une rêverie délicieuse, où la nuit me suprenait souvent sans que je m'en fusse aperçu. Le flux et reflux de cette eau, son bruit continu, mais renflé par intervalles, frappant sans relâche mon oreille et mes yeux, suppléaient aux mouvements internes que la rêverie éteignait en moi, et suffisaient pour me faire sentir avec plaisir mon existence sans prendre la peine de penser. De temps à autre naissait quelque faible et courte réflexion sur l'instabilité des choses de ce monde, dont la surface des eaux m'offrait l'image; mais bientôt ces impressions légères s'effaçaient dans l'uniformité du mouvement continu qui me berçait, et qui, sans aucun concours actif de mon âme, ne laissait pas de m'attacher au point qu'appelé par l'heure et par le signal convenu je ne pouvais m'arracher de là sans efforts.'[2]

[1] See Bergson, *La Pensée et le Mouvant*, p. 35.
[2] Rousseau, *Rêveries, Œuvres*, V, 1883, t. i, p. 427.

The impressions of the outside world lose their meaning except in so far as they kept alive in him the feeling of existence; when they offer food for thought ('sur l'instabilité des choses de ce monde') they are in effect interrupting the *rêverie*. But—and here we come closer to Bergson—this reflective approach to the impressions of nature is not the only one possible:

'... L'occasion sans doute était belle pour un rêveur, qui sachant se nourrir d'agréables chimères au milieu des objets les plus déplaisans, pouvait s'en rassasier à son aise en y faisant concourir tout ce qui frappait réellement ses sens. En sortant d'une longue et douce rêverie, me voyant entouré de verdure, de fleurs, d'oiseaux, et laissant errer mes yeux au loin sur les romanesques rivages qui bordaient une vaste étendue d'eau claire et cristalline, j'assimilais à mes fictions tous ces aimables objets; et me trouvant enfin ramené par degrés à moi-même et à ce qui m'entourait, je ne pouvais marquer le point de séparation des fictions aux réalites, tant tout concourait également à me rendre chère la vie recueillie et solitaire que je menais dans ce beau séjour!'[1]

Nature in this second passage is no longer food for thought, but rather a supplement to day-dreaming; and as such, says Rousseau, not indispensable:

'De quoi jouit-on dans une pareille situation? de rien d'extérieur à soi, de rien sinon de soi-même et de sa propre existence; tant que cet état dure, on se suffit à soi-même, comme Dieu. Le sentiment de l'existence, dépouillé de toute autre affection, est par lui-même un sentiment précieux de contentement et de paix, qui suffirait seul pour rendre cette existence chère et douce à qui saurait écarter de soi toutes les impressions sensuelles et terrestres qui viennent sans cesse nous en distraire, et en troubler ici-bas la douceur.'[2]

At the very outset of this argument an invincible objection arises to the conception of *rêverie* being a wholly self-sufficient state of consciousness. How *can* there be a pure intuition of existence? But let that pass. What is the relation between this (probably only hypothetical) state of *rêverie* and the doctrine of imagination offered in modern aesthetic? In the first place, void though it may be of impressions—or, as we should say, of imagined ideas—it is yet a conscious state. It is describable by language; but in another sense, if we may anticipate a little, it cannot, if it is a conscious state, be completely divorced from all sorts of language whatever. It is at least an attitude; a state of feeling which has a pleasurable emotion embedded in it; it therefore rests on a form of constructive activity no doubt infinitely cruder than imaginative language in art as we recognize it, but not entirely dissimilar. Inasmuch as the dreamer empties his mind first of reflective thought, then progressively of attention to

---

[1] ibid., p. 429.　　　　[2] ibid., p. 428.

impressions, he is moving towards the limiting point of consciousness—a lower limit; though he does not reach it. So that *rêverie*, seen as an activity of the mind, can hardly be called a highly developed aesthetic act; and Rousseau's account, if we look on it as a piece of artistic writing, is something quite other than the *rêverie* itself; it is a totally distinct act of imagination, into which the *rêverie* enters as part of the material—that part which might be singled out and described as the 'subject matter' by a literary critic. Romantic literature pays a great deal of attention to *rêverie*, but always in this way, as something to write about; the writer himself is in anything but a state of *rêverie* as he writes.

At the same time, there is much that is of importance to aesthetic in *Rêverie*; for however humble a degree of consciousness it represents, it is for all that imagination. In it, for instance, Rousseau detects no distinguishing boundary between 'real' and 'fictitious'—that is to say, the impressions of nature he attends to and the memories of former attentions which he revolves almost at random in his mind. And this is natural: for that distinction does not belong to imaginative thought but to reflection. All that we can quarrel with is the language in which he expresses the fact: for an image is not a 'chimère' or a 'fiction' until its thinker has reflected on its relation to other images in the synthesis of his experience; and such reflection is no part of the state of *rêverie*. Here indeed is the side in which Rousseau's account of *rêverie* or Bergson's account of intuition appeals most strongly to aesthetic; no artist would agree that art is necessarily based on a simple 'sentiment de l'existence dépouillé de toute autre affection'; even if such a state existed it would in itself and as such furnish no basis for art; but the one and the other thinker's insistence that *rêverie* or intuition has nothing in it of practical purposive thought strikes close to the central aspiration of aesthetics—to show how art seats its value concept in something other than rational truth or one or another sort of practical utility or moral criterion.

In a confused way, then, the *Rêveries du promeneur solitaire* is an important signpost to the future, and one which was understandably neglected by both a rationalist and a positivist age. The central confusion, however, based on the assumption that existence can be an object of consciousness apart from all other 'affections', points towards a curious sequel—surrealism. And this in the following way. Consciousness, isolated not only by Rousseau in the eighteenth century, but by Bergson in the twentieth, from all activity whatsoever, becomes an anachronism; something for which no useful function can be found; an outcast; an epi-phenomenon. If it is true that no conscious willed activity is relevant to *rêverie* (or intuition in Bergson's sense—for Bergson defines intuition as something to be reached by stripping off, one by one, all those intellectual acts which he holds to be the sum total of mental activity), then it is at least reasonable to suppose that art, as the representation of our innermost *passive* reaction to the world around us, will suffer from our attending to it; and this is precisely the gist of André Breton's famous definition of surrealism.[1]

A final point in Rousseau's *Rêverie* will claim our attention in another context: namely, the fact that the images which (protestations notwithstanding) crowd his mind as he day-dreams (how else would it come about that he does not distinguish between the 'real' images of his surroundings and the fictitious ones with which these mingle?) are not controlled and organized by consciousness: they come at the bidding of his phantasy-building mechanisms with which he has no call to interfere. As such they are, presumably, materials which would be of the highest interest to the psycho-analyst (we need only think of Rousseau), and by reason of their apparent randomness, they again appeal strongly to the surrealist, anxious as he is to avoid anything which has the least taint of deliberate organization (deliberate organization implies convention, convention implies banality).

In this respect, surrealism owes nothing whatever to Symbolism. Alike as the two movements appear in various attitudes—worship of idiosyncracy, flouting of tradition, fierce anti-intellectualism—there is yet a quite fundamental difference between them which shows up on the touch-stone of the idea of *rêverie*, and makes it impossible to succeed in the claim (which we shall later see Dujardin making) that surrealism is the logical fruit of symbolist aspiration. In point of fact, the generation of 1885 had very little use for the *term rêverie* as a fighting slogan; that may be because it carried with it too strong a flavour of romanticism, of the worn-out battles of fifty years back, of the *literary* heritage of Rousseau. This same revulsion from the associations of the word is perhaps one reason why the term '*rêve*' is so firmly entrenched at its expense in the symbolist aesthetic; but

---

[1] 'Surréalisme, n.m. Automatisme psychique pur par lequel on se propose d'exprimer, soit verbalement, soit par écrit, soit de toute autre manière, le fonctionnement réel de la pensée. Dictée de la pensée, en l'absense de tout contrôle exercé par la raison, en dehors de toute préoccupation esthétique et morale' (*Manifeste du Surréalisme*, 1924). There is something extraordinarily old-fashioned in this last phrase: Breton is still in revolt against a long-standing view that part of the value of art *as art* lies in its being educative, purposive. Some of the success of surrealism was surely due to the fact that this old bogey still exists in corners of the educational system.

iᵗ is not the main reason. The next section will make clear that all the principal writers associated with Symbolism claimed from the new field of experience not disorder but order; were not prepared to be catalysts, but demanded to be the central figure in the drama of poetic creation; and that so far from the change of allegiance pointing to a decline into chaos and nightmare, the symbolists were fully alive to the importance of structure and deliberate composition in art.

3. 'LE RÊVE'

With this term issues become at once important and confused; for 'rêve' is a word so intolerably ambiguous that the generation which introduced it into artistic jargon is frequently unable to make any satisfactory and constructive use of it. The word floats like a slogan; the depths of its user's implications remain unsounded. If we consider the interest that the experience of dreaming (the dreaming of sleep) can have for poetry, two possible lines of approach present themselves. On the one hand, dreams afford us a wealth of surprising imagery and new and strange combinations; something incomparably more varied than anything that we find in waking everyday life.

(*a*) As in much else, Baudelaire seems to lead the way. For him, 'le rêve', equivalent to the significant experience in the crucible of the poet's art, is not the simple opposite of 'reality'; it is the world in which the criteria of truth and falsehood are abolished; in which the poet is not bound by the rules of realistic composition;[1] in infusing it into art the poet produces an experience in which the work of art and the artist are fused into one (into one activity);[2] in which the artist or spectator undergo experiences of heightened lucidity and sometimes terrifying exhilaration—which he ascribes to the beneficent effects of communion with a mystical universe, a 'puissance supérieure', or at least to 'une véritable grâce';[3] in which are to be found all the most mysteriously powerful turns of language and imagery, the profoundest plunges of 'awareness'.[4]

[1] 'L'imitation exacte gâte le souvenir' (*Cur. Esth.*, 138). Yet elsewhere he praises Delacroix for attempting to 'traduire très nettement le rêve' (*Art Rom.*, p. 10). Evidently dreams have a special aesthetically favourable property. But the word is not innocent of the connotation of a *goal to be aspired to*.

[2] 'Qu'est-ce que l'art pur suivant la conception moderne? C'est créer une magie suggestive contenant à la fois l'objet et le sujet, le monde extérieur et l'artiste lui-même' (*Art Rom. L'art philosophique*, p. 113).

[3] See *Paradis artificiels*, ed. Calmann, p. 159.

[4] 'Le rêve absurde, imprévu, sans rapport ni connexion avec le caractère, la vie, et les passions du dormeur! ce rêve, que j'appellerai hiéroglyphique, représente le côté surnaturel de la vie' (*Fusées*, 136).

It is wrong to suppose, as some critics evidently do, that the enjoyment of the realm of Dream (or enormously wide freedom in imagination) as a reservoir of poetic creation comes only at the end of a succession of purificatory disciplines.[1] No urchin that whistles on his way to school, no Gauguin setting up his easel in Brittany, has to fight destructive battles against his intellect: it is only the inveterate philistine, the man arguing his way from *a priori* principles back to the enjoyment of art that has to go through so horrid a penance. Baudelaire condemns hashish and the 'paradis artificiels'—because such addiction 'empêche le travail successif et la contemplation': but these latter are nothing but the act of writing poetry seen under its various aspects. For dreaming (*rêve*) in Baudelaire's sense is not going to sleep and waiting to see what visions will favour us: it is staying awake and working hard: *composing* poetry. In his case a typical and favourite activity is the search for metaphor—not simply in words but in images. This is a matter—for him—of long practice; and something which—for all artists—becomes more easy and more accomplished with practice.[2] In his case the practice reaches the point where he can hardly leave off, where composition, playing with 'dreams', becomes an obsession. The occurrence is a common one.

But this deliberateness is of great importance. The poet says: 'These black tresses demand a metaphor, an analogy. There must be one I want. Which is it?' and he bombards his critical judgement with suggestions, not necessarily at random, but rather as one lights on possible words to fill a crossword clue. The surrealist satisfies his dream worship by picking the first words that come into his mind;[3]

---

[1] 'Echapper au temps pur par la perte de la conscience et le silence des facultés superficielles, ce n'est encore pour Baudelaire que la première étape sur laquelle vient se greffer d'abord la méditation en ensuite l'effort esthétique' (Béguin *L'âme romantique et le rêve*, II, 404). The terms of this description are of course in the Bergsonian jargon. Cf. too the following passage from the same work: 'Non seulement il est interdit à l'homme de "déranger les conditions primordiales de son existence" et de recourir à la magie d'autant plus infernale qu'elle est infaillible; mais l'usage de la drogue annihile la volonté, empêche le travail successif, et la contemplation. Celui qui s'y livre, même s'il y pouvait découvrir un moyen de connaître, serait incapable d'exprimer ce qu'il a vu; car le poète doit autant au travail qu'à l'extase' (ibid.). To such an argument it may be answered that if the 'extase' and 'travail' are two *separable* steps in composition, an interval might be supposed to be allowable between them for the effects of the drug to wear off and leave the mind clear for Contemplation and Work. This indeed is the Rimbaldian procedure. In point of fact, the poet's ecstasy is not in the living of an experience but in the poetic expression of it: in the act of creation which uses experience—as it uses words, colours, and the rest—as the material of art, as the vehicle of an attitude. An ecstatic experience might be a powerful inducement to a poet to write: it is not itself the poem.

[2] 'Il faut vouloir rêver et savoir rêver. Evocation de l'inspiration' ('Mon cœur mis au nu,' quoted by Béguin, op. cit., II, 399).

[3] The customary phrase might be 'comes to the tip of his pen'; but that figure glosses over a first-class delusion. It is no more possible to write words 'automatically' than it is to make a motor-car in one's sleep. The fact that the writer's attentiveness is not strained is not the same as the suggestion that it is entirely absent.

not so Baudelaire. His 'dream', when it is finally composed, is the result of conscious effort:

> Architecte de mes féeries,
> Je faisais à ma volonté,
> Sous un tunnel de pierreries
> Passer un océan dompté.[1]

And it is the relief of final success—or relative success—which produces in him the feeling of 'grâce'.

There is accordingly no place in Baudelaire's aesthetic of dreams for passivity:[2] though in another place we shall see that his insistence on the *activity* of artistic endeavour is not so fully explored as it might be. Small wonder; for what he has already mapped out in a theory of poetic knowledge, is already remarkable for his time. The organizing of 'dream' images is precisely that creativeness which is an important aspect of poetic imagination, and which makes the artist the creator that he is, in place of the catalyst that the surrealist would have him be.

(*b*) A fundamentally like view emerges from the writings of a contemporary of Baudelaire to whom posterity has paid more attention than his own generation did: Gérard de Nerval. For Nerval, the art of the modern poet—soon to be baptized the symbolist —consists in 'L'épanchement du rêve dans la réalité':[3] or in plain speech, the abandonment of imitative or realistic canons of art. '*Le rêve*' here means simply the figments of the imagination undifferentiated into true and false; but this is far from meaning that the poet may sit back and allow any odd images to string themselves together that may chance to find their way into his distracted and

---

[1] Quoted by Béguin in this context (op. cit., I, 399).

[2] Though this might seem obvious, more than one writer has failed to see the force and bearing of this fact. E.g. Fiser (in *Le Symbole littéraire*, 1945) writes on the one hand: 'Le monde est rempli de rêveurs incapables et impuissants. Le rêve pris en lui-même est un relâchement de l'attention à la vie. C'est un état de régression psychologique où les forces de l'esprit sont détendues et où l'esprit abandonné à lui-même se complait dans son propre néant. Ce n'est pas ainsi que Baudelaire conçoit le rêve' (op. cit., p. 113). Yet three pages further he can write: 'Prenons une autre sensation: celle d'un parfum. Le poète rêve, il assiste *au libre jeu de ses souvenirs*. Tout à coup il constate la présence d'un parfum. Ce parfum est analogue à celui dont se servait la femme aimée. Voici donc que le parfum — sensation présente — devient le véhicule d'un souvenir ancien — de la femme aimée — et cela grâce à la reconnaissance d'une analogie entre ce parfum présent et le parfum de la femme disparue' (ibid., 116). The confusion exactly mirrors the confusion (to use an old terminology) between the Fancy and the Imagination. From such confusions stems the whole legend of pre-surrealism. For the poet no more 'is present' (merely) at the free exercise of his memories than he is under the obligation to accept what they throw up.

[3] *Aurélia*. A debt to German Romantic practice from Novalis to Hoffmann and to earlier tastes for the macabre must not blind us to Nerval's arresting qualities, which secured him (as did Baudelaire's) an uninterrupted popularity in the bohemian undercurrent of letters— through Gautier, Rollinat, and others—down to the age of symbolism.

careless mind. On the contrary, Nerval, in admittedly controversial terms, expresses much the same opinions on structure as Baudelaire:

'Pourquoi ne point enfin forcer les portes mystiques, armé de toute ma volonté, et dominer mes sensations au lieu de les subir? N'est-il pas possible de dompter cette chimère attrayante et redoutable, d'imposer une règle à ces esprits des nuits qui se jouent de notre raison?'[1]

To be strictly accurate, the 'sensations' he here speaks of—it is irrelevant for the moment whether in waking or sleeping—that force their way into his mind *are* already very faintly dominated by the mere fact of awareness, faint or distinct. Their fullest domination is the act of the fullest attention to them: the fullest degree of transformation from passively responded to sensations to actively grasped 'ideas of the imagination'. This position, exactly equivalent to that of Baudelaire, has been clearly enough stated and correctly evaluated by a discriminating critic:

'C'est de lui (Nerval) qui vient la grande leçon de l'organisation du rêve dont procéderont les symbolistes pour créer la féerie intérieure, tandis que par une inexplicable régression, sous prétexte de remonter aux sources mêmes du génie quelques nouveaux venus en littérature étaleront tout le bric-à-brac de l'inconscient et mêleront aux rares fulgurations des trouvailles de décevantes trivialités. Or, Gérard de Nerval, dont ils se réclament volontiers, a nettement proclamé que l'art a toujours besoin d'une architecture précise, d'une forme absolue au delà de laquelle tout est trouble et confusion.'[2]

How this architecture (cf. Baudelaire's *Architecte de mes féeries*) is produced, what actually happens when a sensation is raised by attention to the level of imagination, is the province of language, the concrete imaginative expression. At this stage it is sufficient to remark that creating this architectural order, this formal element, is nothing if not a deliberate and conscious act; and that this is what marks off the deliberate awareness of the poet from the helpless submission momentarily imposed by the nightmare. Corollary to this is the obvious fact that when a Baudelaire or a Nerval talk of organizing and giving order to dream images, they are not aspiring to intervene into the moments of sleep, to pick and choose just what dreams they shall undergo—we have seen that this would destroy the very notion of a dream; they are claiming the artist's privilege and duty to organize such chaotic streams of visions and experiences, as he organizes all else that goes into his work, according to standards self-imposed in waking, conscious life—aesthetic standards.

(*c*) In the writings of a third principal symbolist figure, perhaps

---

[1] ibid.   [2] Orliac, *La cathédrale symboliste*, 1933.

the most important in this connection, Mallarmé, the same use is made of the concept of dream.[1] We have already touched on the supposed motives and justification offered by contemporary thought for this; as an ardent disciple put it:

'Il admit la réalité du monde, mais il l'admit comme une réalité de fiction. La nature, avec ses chatoyantes féeries, le spectacle rapide et coloré des nuages, et les sociétés humaines effarées, ils sont rêves de l'Ame; réels: mais tous rêves ne sont-ils point réels?'[2]

Here is that solipsism of which mention has been made: this time in the most intimate context of aesthetic speculation. The description of Mallarmé's attitude is a fair one, so far as it goes, and centres on the argument that for the artist the realm of material elements is not limited by the data of the 'real world'—art is not in essence imitation; and that since in simple inspection—or introspection—there lies no way whatever of distinguishing between 'real' and 'illusory' (i.e. dream-) images, there is no reason to suppose that any given image is not illusory, or that in consequence any ideas whatever of the outside world are not 'fictions'. The essential point to remember in a critique of this view is that for images the distinctions of true or false, or rather real or illusory, are irrelevant, non-existent; that such criteria are applicable in intellectual thought which establishes relations between ideas, not in imaginative thought which simply thinks them. As Collingwood put it, 'the concept of illusion is resolved into the concept of error'.[3] This line of argument is not commonly to be found in symbolist aesthetics at all; Baudelaire can scrape by without it, but Mallarmé, with his much greater persistence in aesthetic speculation, is seriously embarrassed by the points which it covers. A thorough-going solipsism is, on paper, an impregnable position; but in life, in the stream of practical activities which even the

---

[1] Mallarmé's view is elegantly set out in the opening paragraph of *Un Spectacle interrompu*: 'Que la civilisation est loin de procurer les jouissances attribuables à cet état! on doit par exemple s'étonner qu'une association entre les rêveurs, y séjournant, n'existe pas, dans toute grande ville, pour subvenir à un journal qui remarque les événements sous le jour propre du rêve. Artifice que la réalité, bonne à fixer l'intellect moyen entre les mirages d'un fait, mais elle repose par cela même sur quelque universelle entente: voyons donc, s'il n'est pas dans l'idéal, un aspect nécessaire, evident, simple, qui serve de type. Je veux, en vue de moi seul, écrire comme elle frappe le regard de poète, telle Anecdote, avant que la divulguent des *reporters* par la foule dressés à assigner à chaque chose son caractère commun (*Divagations*, p. 20). The most striking thing here is Mallarmé's insistence in the closing sentence on the individuality of art, tempered it may be with the rarifications of dandyism in revolt against the crowd: but what theoretical view ever rises fully above its historical context? We need pay no further attention to the hint of the Idea, 'l'aspect nécessaire...'; the idea of *dream* as implied here does not depend on it.
[2] Wyzéwa, 'Mallarmé' (*Vogue*, No. 11, p. 375, 5/vii/1886). The interpretation is in fact based on a quotation from *Un Spectacle interrompu* (see above).
[3] *The Principles of Art*, 1937, p. 190.

'poète de tour d'ivoire' cannot escape, it is implicitly denounced at every instant; and we find a gap opening between the dream-life of poetry and every and any other feature of day-to-day life.

Art is shut off; Mallarmé speaks of

'L'antagonisme du rêve chez l'homme avec les fatalités à son existence départies par le malheur.'[1]

Poetic dreaming (a word misleading enough in Mallarmé, and which Valéry shortly expels from the vocabulary of aesthetic speculation) is certainly 'real'—it certainly takes place; no one can deny that an image I imagine is an image; but failing a clear view of the position of this reality *vis-à-vis* the reality of 'real life' the temptation is great to think that the two realities are incompatibles. And once embarked on this course, there is no stopping before the conclusion that the images dealt with by art are in some sense, some *mystical* sense cognitive, and afford a profound insight into the nature of the universe and its powers.

'La Poésie est l'expression, par le langage humaine ramené à son rythme essentiel du sens mystérieux des aspects de l'existence: elle doue ainsi d'authenticité notre séjour et constitue la seule tâche spirituelle.'[2]

Leaving this matter aside for a moment and considering only how it affects the poet's conception of his images, as indistinguishable from dream-images, we find Mallarmé, in answer to a questionnaire from a clinical psychologist, speaking of 'le poète qui véritablement rêve éveillé',[3] meaning thereby that no more cognitive value need be attached by the common-sense view-point to his images than to those of sleep; we find him, too, reproaching a close admirer (unjustifiably, but perhaps coquettishly) for suggesting that he discriminates unfairly between 'real' and 'illusory' images in his poetry:

'Vous constatez mon manque d'hésitation à me jeter au gouffre du rêve apparu quand je pouvais rester aux jardins anciens, parmi les fleurs ordinaires et certaines

---

[1] Mondor, *Mallarmé*, 1941, p. 407. In a sense the implied opposition between dream and reality corresponds in the symbolists' mind to the opposition between symbolism and naturalism. As we can see, the correspondence is crude and untenable; but it cannot be overlooked when we study the awkward definitions of a Wyzéwa or a Mauclair. Compare too the following criticism on Nerval, by Charles Morice: 'Cette perception de deux existences simultanée, se correspondant en une seule âme, il n'a que le tort de l'avoir soit arrêtée trop court dans la voie vers le symbole, soit de la séparer trop net de l'ensemble de la vie normale' (*La Littérature de tout à l'heure*, p. 187).

[2] *Vogue*, 18/iv/1886, No. 2, pp. 70–71. The negative side of such a creed is summed up by Maurice Barrès: 'La réalité, qu'il s'agisse des choses d'aujourd'hui, de l'histoire, ou de la mythologie n'offre aucun intérêt artistique. Elle est même un mot dépourvu de sens...' (there follows an argument from the uniqueness of each individual's experience, *à la* Rémy de Gourmont) (Barrès, 'Jean Moréas, Symboliste,' in *La Plume*, No. 41, 1/i/1891, p. 8).

[3] Mondor, *Vie de Mallarmé*, p. 735.

Voilà qui m'atteint très doucement ... je ne cherche point à m'illuminer de feux de Bengale.'[1]

From this last dissociation it would appear that Mallarmé's view of '*rêve*' cannot be entirely comprised within the compass of a definition; that there is something ordinarily associated with dreams other than the fact that they need not be conformable with reality; this being the fact that they are *striking*. Now from the fact that an image, a contrast, an orchestral combination of sound, an event, is *striking* it does not follow that it will *ipso facto* confer excellence on the art in which it is embodied; bright colour in a painting may sometimes be not so much overwhelmingly wonderful as garishly shocking; an unexpected contrast ineptly introduced may be no better than incongruous; but there is no doubt that live art has a constantly expanding margin of new and striking effects—cf. Baudelaire's 'correspondance' metaphors, a typical product of romanticism, and of which more hereafter. When commonplace situations of everyday life have had their interest exhausted by too frequent treatment, the realm of faery may offer new resources. Maeterlinck succeeds Sardou. When Mauclair in his novel *Le Soleil des Morts* figures Mallarmé as Calixte Armel, Mallarmé in a letter of appreciation writes:

'J'ai suivi cette figure jusqu'où j'y pouvais prétendre; ... puis l'accompagnai au delà de moi *vers ses proportions de rêve.*'[2]

Calixte Armel, then, is a heightened Mallarmé; and in this sense the word 'heightened' means not simply that he exceeds limits set by imitation, but also that in doing so he is more vivid, impressive. These two sides of the word illustrate Mallarmé's two connotations for the idea of dream. They may be inseparable, but they are distinct. Similarly, when acknowledging a copy of Kahn's *Premiers Poèmes*, he writes:

'Comme cela se groupe et se construit à la manière des architectures mobiles musicales, toutes les probabilités que contient une riche substance de rêve tout à coup s'érigeant, illuminant et souriant.'[3]

[1] Letter to Rachet, 18/v/1887 (in Mondor, *Vie de Mallarmé*). Yet Rachet is not the only one among his admirers to find in Mallarmé what all the symbolists expected to find—indeed looked for—in the truly poetic outlook: cf. 'Il [Mallarmé] savait que l'Art est un travail, différant de la Vie banale, et par ce motif il l'aimait. Cette destination artistique est facilement perçue dans les premiers vers du poète: c'est une sincérité, un effort à éprouver les émotions qu'il traduit; c'est encore la préférence à toutes images naturelles, d'images plus affinées; une curiosité des parfums exquis, des meubles, des tapisseries, des étoffes, très rares. Les sujets même, pareils à ceux de Baudelaire, disent un choix d'artiste. M Mallarmé voyait ce monde de nos réalités, et au dessus, le monde plus joyeux de l'Art' (Wyzéwa, 'Mallarmé,' *Vogue*, No. 11, p. 367, 5/vii/1886).
[2] Letter to Mauclair, 1898, quoted in Mondor, *Vie*, p. 795.
[3] Letter to Kahn, ix/1897, ibid., p. 779.

The 'riche substance de rêve' is much richer than that of the 'fleurs ordinaires et certaines', more resourceful not only in images and combinations but in their effects also. But let it again be noted that these products of the 'riche substance', these 'probabilités',[1] are dependent on constructiveness—on architectural qualities. The same dependence is noted in a more famous passage from the *Divagations*:

> 'Décadente, Mystique, les Ecoles se déclarant ou étiquetées en hâte par notre presse d'information, adoptent, comme rencontre, le point d'un Idéalisme qui (pareillement aux fugues, aux sonates) refuse les matériaux naturels et, comme brutale, une pensée exacte les ordonnant; pour ne garder de rien que la suggestion. Instituer une relation entre les images, exacte, et que s'en détache un tiers aspect fusible et clair présent à la divination...'[2]

This 'tiers aspect' is, in Mallarmé's terminology and doctrine, the Pure Idea culled from Schopenhauer; in point of fact, though, there is no need to appeal to anything so elusive: if we rid ourselves of such prepossessions, it is clear that the 'tiers aspect' is a new image, a new formal construct. It makes no difference whether, as he wrote these words, Mallarmé had in mind only the special case of metaphor, the subtle play with blending images which are so particularly associated with his style; what applied here applies, *pari passu*, to the larger constructs of greater complexity such as whole poems. Last, a distinction is drawn between the 'brutal' order of purely scientific thinking and the orderly systems of 'exact relations' (here speaks Mallarmé the 'logician'!) set up in a work of art. Mallarmé argues as if the two were mutually exclusive; a more consistent aesthetic would be content to show that between the logic of imagination and the logic of reason there is not opposition but distinction.

At all events, the point to be established has been satisfactorily made: Mallarmé plainly recognized in the material of poetry a kind of structure that is quite lacking in dreams, taking that word as referring to the flux of confused imagery that later experiment in verse and painting set its hopes on.

(*d*) Even Rimbaud, whom we would least expect to find in agreement on points of technique with the hard doctrines of Mallarmé, gives a brief and most fascinating side-long glance in the *Illuminations* to the task of organizing the materials presented in dreams; and here,

---

[1] In Mallarmé's mouth this has a highly personal flavour; for if anything serves to characterize his poetic technique it is the studied ambiguity and flux of imagery that clings like a haze to his verse. In the words of Rémy de Gourmont, 'L'Œuvre de Mallarmé est le plus merveilleux prétexte à rêveries qui ait encore été offert aux hommes fatigués de tant d'affirmations lourdes et inutiles' (*La Culture des Idées*, p. 132); but this is pointing to empirical differences in the style of language rather than a fundamentally new element in poetic creation.

[2] *Divagations*, p. 245.

of course, is meant dreams natural and otherwise, the nightmare and the 'Paradis Artificiel'. True, he appears to look on this organization as independent either of the process by which images come before the mind's eye or of the process by which they are later *translated* by speech into communicable form; that is, given language equivalents. The passage that illustrates his awareness of the problem is in *Veillées*:

'... Tu en es encore à la tentation d'Antoine. L'ébat du zèle écourté, les tics d'orgueil puéril, l'affaissement et l'effroi. Mais tu te mettras à ce travail: toutes les possibilités harmoniques et architecturales s'émouvront autour de ton siège. Des êtres parfaits, imprévus s'offriront à tes expériences. Dans tes environs affluera rêveusement la curiosité d'anciennes foules et de luxes oisifs. Ta mémoire et tes sens ne seront que la nourriture de ton impulsion créatrice. Quant au monde, que sera-t-il devenu? En tout cas, rien des apparences actuelles.'

This glimpse of a putative next stage in Rimbaud's career as a poet should not be taken as evidence that the world, by his spectacular renunciation of poetry, has lost masterpieces. There is every possibility that a task half-glimpsed, like Mallarmé's projected *Oeuvre*, might have proved too great an undertaking: it is one thing to develop incredible intensity on a small canvas, quite another to transfer the newly-acquired powers on to a large-scale work. We must remember that Rimbaud's most widely-spanning poem to date was *Le Bateau Ivre*, which as a test of coherence, of constructive unity, is already behind many of the *Illuminations*—almost adolescent, indeed, if one can talk in such terms about so altogether unusual a figure.

But the interest and significance of the passage lies not so much in the course it charts for the future as in the evidence it provides of what Rimbaud himself thought of his work to date—namely, the *Illuminations*. It seems to show that these were to him no more than trial pieces—studies in technique (the technique of imagination and of words together, of course): occupying roughly the position of, shall we say, a painter's sketch-books. The present century has passed through a phase of literary opinion in which it has been the fashion to think of the *Illuminations* as the *nec plus ultra* of poetry—a phase, be it added, in which the two concepts of style and constructiveness have been brutally held apart—and in which, as a result, Rimbaud has been looked at as a sort of godfather of surrealism. The very core of surrealism being the worship of extravagant aimlessness, it can only be supposed that misapprehension of the artistic significance of the *Illuminations* has been greater than one is entitled to expect: that either terms of criticism have been grossly abused in discussing them, or else that critics have so far failed to find understanding audiences for Rimbaud (and surrealism, naturally) that hypocrisy and cant have slipped in to glorify them as something they were never intended to be.

From an altogether different point of view, which indeed takes us back to the central theme of this chapter, the surrealist claims on Rimbaud stand partly condemned out of the mouth of their idol. Their recipe for the attainment of 'superrealism' is the suppression of conscious application, as is well known; and we should suppose, therefore, that this would be a tenet with Rimbaud also. In support of the argument that it is so, all the well-known (and well-worn) phrases and quotations are recalled—

'... Il s'agit d'arriver à l'inconnu par le dérèglement de *tous les sens*.'[1]

'... Le poète se fait *voyant* par un long, immense et raisonné dérèglement *de tous les sens*.'[2]

'... *Je* est un autre... Cela m'est évident: j'assiste à l'éclosion de ma pensée: je la regarde, je l'écoute'[3]—

with the result that even Béguin, with his powers of sympathetic understanding and attention to fact, is led to remark:

'Le poète peut "arriver à l'inconnu", mais à condition de se créer une ascèse particulière qui le délivre de ses facultés superficielles [the cloven hoof, here, in this ominous terminology!] et ne laisse plus s'élever en lui que cette voix qui n'est plus à lui seul. Il se propose de prolonger, de rendre permanente l'expérience de ces états où le moi, cessant de se percevoir lui-même, n'est plus que le lieu d'une présence.'[4]

Evidently, in any exegesis of Rimbaud, we are skating on thin ice: there is so little extant information on what he actually thought about his poetic activities, that two or three texts, torn out of a couple of letters and *Une Saison en enfer*, come to be held sufficient evidence for almost any 'theory' whatever. For that reason, any arguments that we may put forward here are also to be regarded as provisional; with the rider that it is unlikely that anyone in the future will ever find scope for any very much more exact knowledge of what went on in the young Rimbaud's fabulous mind. But this is not a study on Rimbaud alone; we are concerned to trace certain threads in the minds of a considerable number of people, and it is difficult to resist the temptation of essaying our problems on his quicksilver in company with the metal of others we discuss. With this caution, we can still

[1] Lettre à Izambard, 13/v/1871, in Carré, *Lettres de la vie littéraire*, 1931, p. 55.
[2] Lettre à Demeney, 15/v/1871, in Carré, op. cit., p. 62.
[3] ibid., p. 60. All perhaps no more than an outburst against conventional mind-habits.
[4] Béguin, *L'âme romantique et le rêve*, II, pp. 413–14.

claim that the surrealist exegesis is unduly perverse, which looks on all unusual poetry of the nineteenth century as leading forward to, and often brilliantly prophesying, the realization of its own ideal, the exclusive claimant to the higher dignity of art. Another point may be noted. He was twenty when he turned his back on Paris. It is hardly to be supposed that in perhaps a tenth of the working life of Mallarmé, he should produce a coherent, unambiguous, or single-minded account of poetry, and if we look carefully at the wild Rimbaldian outbursts (with running through them the possible faint trace of a dissatisfied and self-conscious youth seeking after effect) we find that almost any single passage we care to choose is susceptible of half a dozen interpretations, so loosely are they phrased; a view over the sum total of Rimbaldiana gives us no confidence that a grand doctrine of art can ever be fairly reconstructed from it; how can there be reconstruction for what never existed? But to start at the beginning, several pointers are unmistakable: in the great programme which he formulates in his two letters of May 1871, he wrote:

'La première étude de l'homme qui veut être poète est sa propre connaissance, entière. Il cherche son âme, il l'inspecte, il la tente, l'apprend.'[1]

This is unequivocal; to any plain man it means not a regrettable lapse into effete romanticism, but that Rimbaud prescribes a self-attentiveness, a conscious devotion to experience, which cannot but be anathema to the surrealist. Not the sentimentality, the loose outpourings usually associated with romanticism in decay—for that he has no patience—but a scrupulous and urgent curiosity about what Mallarmé or Valéry called one's 'état d'âme', and what we find more convenient to call one's imaginative knowledge. But while Mallarmé is content to spend almost an infinity of time in clarifying to himself the most insignificant experience, Rimbaud (what else would one expect?) goes to the other extreme—after other material. A youth, desperately at odds with all features of everyday provincial life, and with the ethos of a tyrannical household in which he is not allowed to grow up, cannot bring himself to take an interest in the normal, or more normal material of art—to be fired with enthusiasm by simple events, even as a ground for elaboration. His own normal attitudes, infected by unhappy memories, are not the field for him to develop peacefully. That is why he declares that the poet studies his experience and then,

'Dès qu'il la sait, il la doit cultiver... Il s'agit de faire l'âme monstrueuse, à l'instar des comprachicos, quoi! Imaginez un homme s'implantant et se cultivant

[1] Carré, op. cit., p. 61; lettre à Démeney, 15/v/1871.

des verrues sur le visage... Le poète se fait voyant par un long, immense et raisonné
dérèglement de *tous* les sens... Ineffable torture où il a besoin de toute sa foi, de
toute la force surhumaine, où il devient entre tous le grand malade, le grand criminel,
le grand maudit — et le suprême savant! — car il arrive à l'inconnu.'[1]

If Charleville cannot fire his imagination, then the hallucination of
drugs, the nightmare after exhaustion, drunken vision, can. We may
set aside for a moment his claim that such experience makes of the
poet 'le grand savant'—we shall have plenty to say about this in a
minute. At any rate it gives him a larger palette to paint with. In
place of Mallarmé's subtle play with tones, Rimbaud stretches out
his hand and snatches more violent colouring, splashes it on with
bolder strokes. Each path has its validity; each an appeal to a different
temperament.

Evidently there is a difference between Baudelaire and Rimbaud
on the matter of the 'Paradis Artificiels'; but it is not so fundamental
as the surrealist exegete would make out. Where the one takes
whatever images, seen or remembered, lie within his reach, the other
goes out to find new ones for himself; or at any rate allows new and
strange juxtapositions to rise and occupy his attention. The natural
phenomenon which to Mallarmé is a complex sensum, and becomes
an image when he looks at it attentively (whether directly, or afresh
in the memory) and tries to see it more by speaking about it, has its
equivalent for Rimbaud in some bizarre combination, manufactured,
he thinks at random, and thrown before the mind's eye in a 'dream',
which he recalls on waking and brings to mind as a remembered
image, and then proceeds to embody in his *Illuminations*. In either
case, attention to the given—the sunset or the phantasmagoria—is
imaginative: the exploration of what it looks like and what it feels
like to be looking at it are not separable. And it is almost a commonplace that the painter paints as part of the act of seeing more sharply:
the poet makes poems as part of his act of conscious experience,
of attention to something given from outside, of knowing what he is
seeing and hearing and feeling.

Rimbaud has no idea—no explicit idea, that is—that the poet's
vision (to translate his terminology) is bound up with his work of
moulding and expressing it; for him the poet is poet only by virtue
of his extraordinary hallucinations: by the fact that *different experiences*[2]
force themselves on his attention. Continually he dwells on the rich-

---

[1] Lettre à Demeney, 15/v/1871, op. cit., pp. 61–2.

[2] What Béguin calls 'Les obscures images de la rêverie ... et les associations apparemment
fortuites des objets dans la vie végétative de la pensée, que l'on prétend substituer à la perception banale des sens et de la raison' (*L'âme romantique et le rêve*, II, p. 406).

ness of his material—this artificial extension of the outside world:

'Les hallucinations sont innombrables... Je m'en tairai: poètes et visionnaires seraient jaloux. Je suis mille fois le plus riche, soyons avare comme la mer.'[1]

And again:

'Je suis maître en fantasmagories.'

The process is extended into waking life:

'Je m'habituai à l'hallucination simple: je voyais très franchement une mosquée à la place d'une usine...'[2]

The richest dreamer is the greatest poet: there in seven words is Rimbaud's hasty conclusion in the philosophy of art. To this, even, we must add two cautions: in the first place, who will dare to assert, given the limits of what we know of him, that Rimbaud rejects nothing from his dreams, in the *Illuminations*; that he accepts just any and every figment of the fancy[3] without questioning its relevance to his purposes? Of his discrimination in this field we know nothing whatsoever; but it seems at least highly improbable that the poet of *Le Bateau Ivre* should have abdicated all power of mental revision as he wrote. 'Free chance', or however we term the force which he hoped to find still in dream worlds far from everyday, regimented life, offered the visions: but surely he, the 'voyant', accepted them or not as he thought fit? The second caution is, that not even he would suggest that the artistic value of his dreams is entirely apart from the way in which they are presented in speech. It is one thing to say that poetry owes its magic to its imagery: it is quite another to say that this magic can shine through any formal presentation whatever; indeed, if the former can never be more than partly true, the latter is plainly false. We cannot and do not ever think of these fragments, these well-styled *Illuminations*, apart from the hard brilliant phrases they live through and in. And even if it is true that Rimbaud was engaged for several years in forming the view that the poet is a seer, a 'voyant', and that this implied the passivity of the mystic, not the activity of the artist, he realizes without much difficulty when he reviews his *past* literary activity that a part at least of the magic of poetry is 'in the words':

'... Puis j'expliquai mes sophismes magiques avec l'Hallucination des mots.'[4]

[1] *Saison en enfer*, 'Nuit de l'enfer'.   [2] ibid., Délires, II, 'Alchimie du verbe'.
[3] 'Fancy' in Coleridge's sense.   [4] *Saison en enfer*, Délires, II, 'Alchimie du verbe'.

Why 'Hallucination'? Partly, perhaps, the expression is simply a loose one, used in the rather special atmosphere of the *Saison*, to denote no more than the impelling force of poetic utterance in general, and so in keeping with the tone of his quasi-mystical attitude; but almost certainly also because he knew very well the sense of necessary cohesion that comes with poetry, the feeling that what has been created surrounds and informs a moment of existence. Anyone with the obviously astounding mastery that Rimbaud had over language could, in the circumstances of the *Saison en enfer*, hardly fail to make some reference to this side of his achievement. But, as we have said, he nowhere shows any sign of thinking the whole of artistic creation to be comprised within the single activity of imagination, under that or any other name, with the concomitant idea of language as the form in which imagination is carried on.

From Rimbaud we learn that the dream in relation to art has its importance from both the active and the passive side. From the passive, inasmuch as the dreamer does not control the visions that come before his attention—and because he is asleep, cannot even arrest the experience in the way we can shut our eyes when we grow weary of a sunset: a sunset in a dream is quite as much an independent object as a sunset in front of my house. From that point of view, dreams as phenomena, have as little artistic worth in them as sunsets viewed by dull and unintelligent people. And in proportion as the poet 'imagines' them less and less, below the point where he turns his attention to them into language and is instead merely aware of having dreamt them, his memory of them in waking life approximates more and more closely to a Rousseau-esque state of *rêverie*. In sleep, they are hardly more than a flux of sensation—though not quite, since to 'have' a dream means usually to have paid sufficient attention to it to 'have' it in your memory, and the pure flux of sensation devoid of conscious attention cannot leave traces in the memory. On the other hand, taken up into artistic activity and incorporated in imaginative work, they take their place beside other sources of experience as material for art. What to the nineteenth-century poet was so startling a feature of dreams—their strangeness, their lack of conformity in many ways to the experiences we expect to meet with—turns out to be nothing more than an empirical distinction: a very suggestive one, no doubt, but not such as to overturn all our views on what art is, and make us conclude that poetry using material suggested by dreams is essentially different from all other poetry. If that were so, the poems of St. John of the Cross, of Wordsworth, of Rilke, would each have to have their special aesthetic too—to cover the case of poetry deriving from different varieties of experience; and once launched on this venture there would be no end to the number of possible 'aesthetics'. But aesthetic is concerned with what is present in all art; once we start establishing distinctions *of kind* between this poetry and that, we are away from aesthetic into the world of literary criticism and literary history, and there is no stopping before we reach the point of recording the individuality, the uniqueness, of every single work of art.

Rimbaud undoubtedly thought—and many others have done so too—that in a world of ever-increasing uniformity and restriction, dreams offered the only safe refuge for a poet anxious to expand his individuality and enjoy that measure of freedom which is necessary for the cultivation of metaphorical warts on the face. The attitude is understandable, but fallacious: firstly, because the strangeness of a dream is no guarantee that a poem written out of it will be good poetry; secondly, because not long afterwards it became plain that dreams are not quite as 'free' as he had hoped. Rimbaud's merits as a poet rest on something very different from his capacity to have strange dreams in greater number than anyone else, just as Van Gogh's greatness is something more than an insistence on yellow. The strange dreams and the yellows are not excluded from the greatness: they are used by it.

(e) When we come to the minor dignitaries of the symbolist movement, to the generation of 1885–90, the term '*rêve*', used in relation to the material and the nature of poetic vision, loses almost all clear meaning and becomes little better than the slogan it continually tends to degenerate into. Where a Mallarmé had given it an approximate function in an organized theory of art, the late-comers handled it wildly; and it picked up a large number of connotations, each corresponding to the particular interest or bent of its user, and not always easily separable from its neighbours.

(i) Laforgue, one of the earlier symbolist adepts of 'German idealism', uses '*rêve*' simply as a handy term for reminding his readers that the world they—and he—lived in is a world of 'Fiction'— 'une simple légende':

'Je suis un pessimiste mystique ... la vie est trop triste, trop sale. L'histoire est un vieux cauchemar bariolé qui ne se doute pas que les meilleures plaisanteries sont les plus courtes. La planète terre était parfaitement inutile. Enfin, peut-être Tout n'est-il que *rêve*, seulement celui qui nous rêve ferait bien de hâter le cuvage de son opium.'[1]

---

[1] *Mélanges posthumes* (1882), p. 280. Cf. *Le Sanglot de la Terre, passim.*

He also confused the possibility that we are somebody else's dream
(like Alice and the Red King) with the possibility that what we see
(or what we think) has no more objective validity than one of our
dreams: that both are equally the products of illusion:

'... ne sachons que nous enivter des paradis sans fond de nos sens et fleurir
sincèrement nos rêves sur l'heure qui est à nous.'[1]

Here we are verging on the problem of our knowledge of the
external world, in which (at least for the greater part of his adult life)
he professes a simply solipsist view.

(ii) For Charles Morice '*rêve*' signifies rather different aesthetic
problems and artistic preoccupations.

'... Y a-t-il d'autre Vérités,' he asks, 'que le Rêve lui-même, en Art, le rêve
propre de chaque artiste?'[2]

This could simply mean that the artist is interested only in imaginative truth, and not in relational: a denunciation of Taine's demand for
realistic art. A dream is neither illusory nor real, unless we interpret
it in the context of our life in the same way as we interpret more
normal forms of experience in waking life: it is simply what it is,
and so is art. The artist does not make his picture or his poem as a
signpost or as a piece of information; he is making not a proposition
but an utterance. But I do not believe that this was the significance
of '*rêve*' for Morice; he goes a great deal further, and tries to relate
it to the pervasive doctrine of eternal Ideas, along the pattern of
Schopenhauer's aesthetic or Moréas' manifesto.[3] In doing so he falls
into the error of making 'dream' (that is to say, images) not prior
to, and innocent of, truth and error, but simply the opposite of reality
—in short, fiction; the concept of illusion is fathered on imagination,
and the 'dream' is the illusory image, the poet's stock-in-trade. So it
comes about that Wagner is criticized for not choosing sufficiently
'dream-like' subjects for his music-dramas:

'Wagner fait la Synthèse des observations et des expériences dans la Fiction.
Mais cette Fiction, quelle est-elle? Historique, encore qu'elle recule l'Histoire,
jusqu'aux limites de la Légende. Elle évoque une heure, un lieu connus. Il eût été
bien digne de Wagner de conclure (après tous les efforts des poètes précédents vers
le rêve au moyen de ce subterfuge: l'éloignement dans l'espace et dans le temps)
par la suppression du temps et de l'espace, par l'épanouissement du Rêve en sa

[1] ibid., p. 208.   [2] *La Littérature de tout à l'heure*, 1889, p. 265 n.
[3] 'Hors du monde, et non pas seulement des dates et des sites connus: voilà la loi constitutive
de toute fiction. Hors du monde, mais point hors de l'humanité ni de la nature. Une âme,
une fleur, un corps, sont dans l'éternité. Même l'instant contemporain du Poète peut — je dis
peut, et non pas "doit" — rester l'*heure de départ* du Poème: car il y a une joie à voir le beau
Rêve sortir du temps et le dépasser' (ibid., pp. 373–4).

propre patrie qui est sans heure et sans lieu, non pas l'oublie, mais l'inconnu, non pas le trop distant du sol précis qui porte nos pas, mais ce beau Pays qu'on ne verra sur nul continent.'[1]

One supposes that for Morice the ideal of the dramatic poet is the sort of thing evolved by Maeterlinck, in which shadowy characters whom one classes as 'legendary' but ascribes to no known cycle enact themes which one classes as symbolical but knows to symbolize nothing. If this is so, an aesthetic concept (the 'Idea') has made an irruption, an unfortunate irruption, into fields where it does not belong; it has descended from its judge's tribunal and taken sides in the matter of fashion, in the choice of poetic material. In any event, the problem of embodying eternal Ideas, with the least possible intervention from the field of familiar experience, leads Morice into the error of thinking that art must gather its material from the fanciful, the impossible, the illusory: and this view cannot but warp his critical judgement.[2]

(iii) René Ghil's use of 'le rêve' is so confusing and confused as to be most often meaningless; but we can glimpse through the mass of tangled verbiage the prototype on whom he bases his aesthetic, at least at the outset, as when he treats us to:

'Le réel et suggestif symbole d'où, palpitante par le *rêve*, en son intégrité nue se lèvera l'Idée prime et dernière, ou Vérité.'[3]

(iv) From much the same fountain-head Mauclair pieces together his typically 'symbolist' views on the nature of dream in relation to art. Nevertheless, it is not always easy to guess his intention. For example, on three successive pages of *Eleusis*, which is little more than a somewhat laborious elaboration of some of the main threads of the *Divagations*, we find first of all this:

'Ce que nous appelons le rêve n'est pas non plus une lueur en dehors de nous. C'est l'état primordial de notre esprit.'[4]

Which in the context suggests something along the lines of Mallarmé's doctrine of the image as the basis of all poetry. This view seems to be strengthened when we read on the following page:

'Le rêve, c'est de nous connaître nous-mêmes, et libres.'[5]

[1] ibid., p. 198.
[2] And incidentally also confuse his ideas on the nature of poetic symbolism. It is curious that at another part of the self-same book, Morice seems to contradict himself categorically; in a fanciful account of the rites of art when the aesthetic millennium arrives, he adds a little rider on the activities of the artist-priests: 'Rien dans ces prémisses n'exclut les ressources de l'observation, soit psychologique de Stendhal, soit physiologique de M. Zola' (op. cit., p. 69). One supposes that even to a critic who views the historical sense as a mark of decadence, the psychological material of Stendhal and the description of Zola are hardly 'hors du temps', or 'hors des dates et des sites connus'.   [3] *Traité du verbe.*
[4] *Eleusis*, 1894, p. 62. Most of the more serious parts of this work are pastiches of Mallarmé.
[5] ibid., p. 63.

And finally confirmed a few lines later:

'Ce que nous nommons le rêve n'est que l'état idéal de notre esprit, et nous sommes continuellement sur le point d'y atteindre—mais nous n'y atteindrons que par l'abolition complète des choses inharmonieuses et des circonstances malavisées, et il nous faudrait mourir... Le rêve c'est le désir du Soi. C'est l'innocence de la raison pure.'[1]

But even when we make allowances for the strange terminology, and overcome our antipathy for the pomposity of phrasing, all is not yet clear. We might be tempted to see a dissonance between the statement that 'le rêve est l'état primordial de notre esprit' and the statement that it is unattainable. What is disquieting is indeed this latter remark—that 'le rêve' is an ideal and unattainable state. It stems evidently, in a curious way, from the doctrine of Ideas; and suggests that Mauclair, looking at a landscape painting, cannot quite banish the old Adam in him which wants to eat the cabbages in the foreground. But that is preposterous: no artist was ever troubled either by the problem of 'disinterestedness' or by the irruption of rational preoccupations—least of all the symbolist poet! And yet the 'ideal' state is claimed to be unattainable, and the limiting case for the poetic activity is not unimaginably fine art, but death. Can it be that Mauclair is haunted by Schopenhauer's buddhist tendencies which go beyond art in their search for ultimate 'release'? It is impossible to see clearly what he is trying to express—unless perhaps it is an ineffable awe before the mystery of art. Such an example of symbolist writers lapsing into the unintelligible is not uncommon: it is a powerful obstacle to any attempt to evaluate symbolism in positive terms. For the inability to find ideas current in the thought of one's time for expressing important but inarticulate truths is only a negative characteristic, never a positive: it is infinitely easier to see what the symbolists were not than what they were. For, of course they knew the former and had not yet learnt the latter.

(v) For Rémy de Gourmont the problem of dreams is a simple one. He has already solved the problem of imagination to his own satisfaction, and set all philosophy to rights in a few trenchant articles on idealism, materialism, and other like topics. Dreams, to his way of thinking, are relevant to the poet's art because they are unexpected, novel, and colourful, and because they afford the dreamer a means of escape into an easy world, where he can abandon all effort to reconstruct the poet's original creation, and simply muse. Thought, set out in language, demands that one follow in the footsteps of its

---

[1] ibid., p. 64.

original thinker; but poetry, being according to the trend of the times 'suggestive' rather than 'descriptive', merely sets you off on your own track, the poet has fired his guns without aiming them, and you may choose your own objectives. *Rêve* for him is simply *Rêverie*; the latter includes the former. We have seen (see page 92 above, note 1) how he characterizes Mallarmé's writings as a pretext for *rêveries*; the larger part of a well-known article is devoted to expanding the theme that Mallarmé's poems are simply an invitation to the reader to make his own poem, starting from a few suggestive but entirely ambiguous snatches. What goes for Mallarmé may be presumed to go for Nerval's sonnets too, and Rimbaud, indeed for all poetry in which a content of 'thought' is not too plainly and aggressively present. His attitude has called forth a well-earned and justly-famed rebuke from Thibaudet,[1] who feels intuitively that so far from the poet's 'meaning' being irrelevant to our enjoyment of his work, it is the only thing worth while about a poem. But neither Gourmont nor Thibaudet gets beyond a simple opinion on this matter: as Thibaudet leaves the dispute, it is all still a matter of preference: some preferring to day-dream, others to search the text. Gourmont does not appreciate that the very nature of art demands that the artist's experience should be re-lived by the reader, that if his expression of it is penetrating and good art, the reader's recreation or rediscovery of it can be correspondingly so, and that if it fails to be, it impairs the artistic experience but need not destroy it entirely; that *rêverie* being not even usually recognized as a linguistic expression, a reader who weaves a day-dream around some improperly understood poem is no more enjoying the *poem* than if he stops to think how comfortable his chair is; and that any 'filling-in gaps' in what he understands is as little use to the poem as a bad restoration is to a picture. And yet there is something still to be said on Gourmont's side: for our recreation of a poetic experience can never be 'better' than an approximation to the poet's, must always fall short of the original vision, is always therefore less sharp, is always therefore *more*

[1] *La Poésie de Stéphane Mallarmé*, 1913, pp. 38–9. After quoting Gourmont's views, which in their full context are in fact excessively provocative, he boldly asserts: 'Au contraire de M. de Gourmont j'admets à chaque ligne de Mallarmé un sens réel, objectif, qu'a voulu l'auteur ou qu'il a accepté de son inspiration, comme cela se passe dans n'importe laquelle des pages de prose et de vers qui furent jamais écrites.' What he overlooks is that there are limits around the use of language, to surpass which necessarily increases the ever-present possibilities of misinterpretation, of unsuccessful recreation of the poet's attitude: and that Mallarmé on many occasions presses against these limits. Again, many commentators still strangely ignore the idea of multiple ambiguity as the most subtle weapon available to a very subtle poet: that as Mallarmé's mind worked, two or three 'real and objective' meanings were perhaps present at the same time in a poem like 'Victorieusement fui le suicide beau'.

like a *rêverie* than the original; and there is nothing shocking in the impossibility of a uniform response to a poem, provided we admit within the class of interpreted 'meanings' a scale ascending always towards the poet's original intention.

4. ART AND MYSTICAL COGNITION

In ordinary usage 'dreamer' means indifferently the man who day-dreams and the man who dreams asleep—it is a general term used in contradistinction to the practical, worldly man whose rise to power and influence increasingly distressed the nineteenth-century poet, and whose philistinism is the butt of Villiers de l'Isle Adam's most violent mockery. It was to this world of 'contemplative' men that Edgar Allan Poe addressed his strange cosmogony *Eureka*, translated by Baudelaire in 1859.

'Aux rêveurs et à ceux qui ont mis leur foi dans les rêves comme dans les seules réalités, j'offre ce livre de Vérités, non pas spécialement pour son caractère véridique mais à cause de la Beauté qui abonde dans sa Vérité, et qui confirme son caractère véridique. A ceux-là je présente cette composition simplement comme un objet d'Art — disons comme un Roman, ou si ma prétention n'est pas jugée trop haute comme un poème... C'est simplement comme poème que je désire que cet ouvrage soit jugé.'[1]

Eureka is a long and tedious essay in universal cosmology, not very original or assured in its speculations on nature (which appear to have been common fare since Kant's *Natural History of the Heavens*, 1775) and perhaps rather shoddy in its sentimental pantheism. Under the first head, the Universe is visualized as an alternately expanding and contracting natural system; under the second, these pulsations are described as the breathing of God—the systole and diastole of the divine heart. Into the endless complications and digressions[2] of this thesis it is not our business to enter; we shall not even be tempted by the rather startling tail to his thesis:

'Et maintenant, ce cœur divin, quel est-il? C'est notre propre cœur.'[3]

Our business is with the problem raised by the provocative introduction. Although Poe appears to have taken a good deal of trouble with his mathematics, it is on the second line of defence that he especially counts—namely, on intuitive certainty that the universal

---

[1] *Eureka*, trad. Baudelaire, Préface (Conand ed.).
[2] Some, such as the assertion of intuition of past existences in terms strikingly like those of *Correspondances*, may have helped Baudelaire to take the decision to publish his translation (e.g. pp. 145, 147).
[3] *Eureka*, Baudelaire, *Œuvres*, 145.

periodicity has a mystical import. The recurring explosion and subsequent destruction of Universes was perhaps the most sublime conception in the field of natural science that he could envisage; what more fit to be the connecting-link between the mystical and the scientific than this vast and terrifying instance of the 'law of periodicity'? At any rate the reader is invited to accept the 'poem' not because of its argument, but because it relies on our inner conviction, because it is grand, impelling, *poetic*.

The special virtue which poetry possesses may be presumed to have its source, according to this view, in the power of mystic insight: art does no more than reproduce the profounder vision of the seer. What the seer sees is variously described, though the formulae seldom move outside the repertoire of mystical tradition: it may be the 'essence of things' or the 'spirit of things'—two phrases that dovetail neatly enough into a theory of Platonic Ideas, and seem not to need further definition;[1] or alternatively it may be the 'visible form of God'[2] so recalling a tendency latent in Baudelaire but strongly encouraged in the work of Hegel and Schelling (assuming the symbolists to have studied these writers) to treat art as in some way sacred, a quasi-religious rite, or at least on a par with religion as one of the absolute forms of mind;[3] or it may be, as in Mallarmé in his more eloquent and less exact moments, 'le commentaire des signes purs,

[1] 'Le mur de séparation entre fable et vérité, entre passé et présent, est tombé; et c'est la foi, l'imagination, la poésie, qui nous dévoilent l'*essence* du monde' (Novalis, quoted by Thorel, 'Les Romantiques allemands et le symbolisme français,' *Entretiens politiques et littéraires*, ix/1891, No. 18, p. 163). Or again in the same review, as if specializing in this side of symbolist interests (though in fact nothing could be farther from the truth: it was largely a medium for socialist propaganda by middle-class intellectuals)—'La Poésie est le perpétuel effort vers l'expression de l'esprit des choses, effort qui, dépassant le corps brut, pénètre sa vie et sa raison d'être, et voit, derrière l'effet éphémère et fugace, la nécessité immanente de sa cause' (Emerson, quoted as an epigraph in *Entretiens*, 1/ix/1890, t. 1, p. 169). See too Béguin's *Nerval and Poésie et mystique* (1936) for a sympathetic modern expansion of the theme that poetry in some way reaches down into the essences of life.

[2] 'Cette théorie (du symbole) fait de l'art une manifestation mystique. Une des conséquences de l'hégélianisme est de relier l'esthétique à la religion. L'étude des formes au point de vue de la beauté est en effet, suivant Fichte, l'étude des formes visibles de Dieu. La ligne et la couleur sont des éléments abstraits, imposés à la matière et distincts d'elle, car ils sont immatériels. Ce sont les traces du divin dans le monde. Le poète et l'artiste sont donc en quelque sorte, des prêtres. Ils apprennent aux hommes à voir Dieu sous les symboles. C'est aussi l'opinion de Emerson. Pour s'en tenir à la poésie, cette théorie est conforme à ses origines mêmes, qui furent religieuses. La génèse du Langage poétique appartient aux prêtres qui prononçaient les prières et les oracles en langage rhythmé et chanté, ou accompagné par des instruments... La poésie est donc un chant exprimant musicalement et par symboles une idée religieuse' (Mauclair, 'L'art en silence,' *Esthétique de Stéphane Mallarmé*, p. 87). The confusion of historical with logical precedence is too patent to need more than pointing to.

[3] The atmosphere of Bayreuth springs at once to mind in this context. Villiers de l'Isle Adam among several who made the regular pilgrimage (under the auspices of the *Revue Wagnérienne*) is the link between Wagner's religious art and the symbolists' religion of art.

à quoi obéit toute Littérature, jet immédiat de l'Esprit'[1]—sometimes
perhaps a little closer to necromancy than to any of the acknowledged mystical strains of Christianity. Nearly every symbolist
critic, at one time or another, bowed down at the altar of irrationalism
in one form or another; we need not spend time on the prophets—
Péladan, Hello, Guaïta, Schuré, and how many others—who at some
distance in time seem uncommonly 'bogus' (in common with the
philistines of their own times); but when we come to a practising
writer and critic like Charles Morice, and find in his aesthetic writings
a persistent (if not always consistent) return to mystical arguments
for the supremacy of art over all other forms of human enterprise,
usually compounded out of an analgum of Schopenhauer and Baudelaire;[2] when we find Mauclair (the straw that blows with the more
powerful breeze of Mallarmé's influence) advancing the view that
what is mystic and apparently 'irrational' in art arises from a mystic
and irrational faculty in man, and that there are 'total universal
laws' ascertainable by mystic insight, which artists attempt to
formulate;[3] when we find every *petite revue* carving out its path on

---

[1] Quoted by Mondor, *Vie de Mallarmé*, 1941, p. 520. See too *Divagations*, 'Magie,' p. 324,
and article in the *National Observer*, 28/i/1893, on the same topic. Mallarmé's linking the
doctrine of 'Ideas' with magic is, of course, entirely gratuitous and probably whimsical rather
than serious.

[2] 'Le Livre, l'objet d'art, la phrase musicale, la pure pensée elle-même — je dis avant même
son expression formelle — sont des éternisations du Moi. C'est que nous en faisons autant de
moyens et dès qu'il échappe aux contingences, le Moi recourt — comme une vive branche
ployée reprend l'attitude verticale dès qu'on l'abandonne à sa liberté naturelle — au foyer de
l'Absolu — *au lieu métaphysique des idées* — *à Dieu*, (*La Littérature de tout à l'heure*, 1889, p. 30)
This twist of Schopenhauer's tail brings Morice into line with Péladan, when the latter, fresh
from his Kirkegaard, claims art as the 'commentaire des transcendantales pensées, relations
de l'homme avec l'Absolu, transitions du temps avec l'éternité (*L'Art idéaliste*, etc., p. 41). We
seem to hear the echo of Baudelaire when we read, in a discussion of the definition of Beauty
'Mais qu'est-ce que cette jouissance des "sens spiritualisés" sinon le rayonnement de la Vérité et
des symboles qui la dépouillent des sécheresses de l'Abstraction et s'achèvent dans les joies du
Rêve?' (ibid., pp. 33–4). Cf. the following: 'N'est oeuvre d'art que celle qui précisémen
commence où elle semblait finir, celle dont le symbolisme est comme une porte vibrante don'
les gonds harmonieux font tressaillir l'âme dans toute son humanité béante au Mystère...
(ibid., p. 34) '. . . Ainsi entendu l'art n'est pas que le révélateur de l'infini: il est au Poète un
moyen même d'y pénétrer... De nature donc, d'essence, l'Art est religieux' (ibid., p. 35); and like
Mauclair, Morice supports this historically with examples from the Jews, Egypt, India, China
Greece, mediaeval Europe, etc. We have already seen how art-religion subordinates science to
its purposes (ch. 4, p. 76, n. 1); presumably *Eureka* would count as an illustration of this relationship. Even sixteen years later, answering an Enquête, Morice clings to the same (by then
outmoded formula): 'Essentiellement, le poète est un ordonnateur de fêtes, le maître des céré
monies de la religion de la vie'; the context is different ('ce n'est pas l'art qui est une religion')
'pourtant l'artiste officie' (*La Littérature contemporaine*, 1905, p. 63).

[3] *Eleusis* starts off with the affirmation that all consciousness whatever is self-consciousness
'Les lois de l'esprit proclament que la sensation existe en cela seul qu'elle est perçue, et la perception étant une propriété intellectuelle, l'homme en pensant les phénomènes, ne peut que
prendre conscience de son intellect, c'est-à-dire constituer de ses perceptions sensitives une
notion assimilable à son esprit par une série d'états analogues à l'assimilation gastrique d'aliment
... cet état d'esprit ... est simple. Je veux dire que tout s'y subordonne, que sur lui nulle
influence sociale ne prévaut' (pp. 4–5)—this act of 'assimilation' sets up a 'rhythm'; and also

the assumption that its readers treat art as a religious exercise, if not as a mystic one;[1] then we do not necessarily conclude that the symbolists have won through, as they all profess, to a new and intuitive grasp of the outside world and its universal truths, or even, as some of them seem to profess, to new fields of positive knowledge of the self; but we do admit that there must be something, some pre-possession of importance—a worry to express something about art, lurking obstinately aside from the paths of orthodox (nineteenth century) aesthetic categories and notions.

The whole matter turns on the definition of the word 'know-ledge'. As we have interpreted the *intention* of nineteenth-century anti-positivist aesthetic, centred on Mallarmé, 'knowledge' in the sense of what is permanently won by rational thinking, discursive know-ledge, is outside the proper domain of art, except in so far as it is assimilated into imaginative material. But at the same time, the artist revolts instinctively against a parallel idea dear to another and even more influential wing of positivist tradition—the idea that art is 'play', a gratuitous and constructively useless activity which canalizes surplus energy and safeguards a psychological equilibrium: he feels, and no doubt rightly, that the artist on completion of his work has *gained* something, has attained a deeper hold on the conditions of his existence, and that his life is permanently the richer for it. He is in a dilemma. The accepted contemporary epistemology offered him two alternatives: either to *play* at reproducing objects of perception, an exercise offering no scope for a principle of aesthetic valuation; or to develop rational knowledge about objects of perception, in which case aesthetic value is assimilated to rational value, and a stultifying

'la notion nouvelle élargit par son adjonction le champ de la conscience, et tout ensemble l'excite à d'autres adjonctions; car elle fortifie l'instinct primordial, dont il sera reparlé, qui est: *la connaissance des lois totales, de la cause ou du mystère*' (ibid., pp. 6–7). There are some curiously frank instructions for would-be mystics: 'Nous sommes les créateurs de notre mystère; nous l'engendrons comme un suc: nous sommes les abeilles de notre sensibilité; nous nous en nourrissons et nous la recréons pour nous en alimenter encore...' (ibid., p. 48). 'C'est en nous exerçant à fonder une hypothèse sur tout objet au lieu de nous tenir à la décision de nos sens que nous acquerrons progressivement l'habitude aisée des tacts et des propositions mystérieuses' (ibid., p. 49). 'Le mystère qui gît dans un objet vient de nous. Il émane de notre aperception' (ibid., p. 52). Indeed, what need of ghosts and banshees in the world?—'pourquoi inventer un monde des choses terribles? Nous les avons toutes en nous.' Nevertheless, lest anyone should be tempted to think that Mauclair's mysticism, if it come so completely from the fancy, can equally well be expelled by a caprice, I would remind the reader that we have to do with a young man already given over to solipsism (though he now calls it 'Idéoréalisme'—'la formule d'art de l'idéalisme'—a term coined at this time by, it would seem, Saint-Pol-Roux).

[1] A last-minute twist is given to the fashion by the earthly-minded Baju, anxious to please, but not to be fooled: 'Ce qui assure le triomphe de cette littérature, c'est son rôle éminemment éducateur, rôle qui fut celui de la Religion. Le Prêtre mort, la direction morale (des) esprits appartient à l'Ecrivain' (*Le Décadent*, 3e. année, No. 20, 1/x/1888).

naturalist turn is given to the aphorism that 'Beauty is Truth, Truth Beauty'. The problem is further complicated by the fact that the concept of Truth in art, as we see, has two implications: it may be the Truth which Taine sees in art, i.e. freedom from error, rational consistency; or it may be the truth which Mallarmé sees, i.e. freedom from artistic blemish, imaginative adequacy. But in the symbolist's day, this distinction, although persistently apprehended in a vague way, is never set out explicitly (except by Mallarmé, and Mallarmé's expositions, though luminous, are never popular). For a positive gain in experience of some sort to emerge from poetry (either writing your own or reading someone else's), the 'play' theories, with their somewhat derisory view of the triviality of art, must be rejected as not going far enough; for this positive gain to be interpreted in terms of a peculiarly aesthetic category and none other requires that we should stop short of the intellectual criterion of Taine. Somewhere between the two a way out must be sought.

When we consider the history of aesthetic in France up to around 1880, and the educational tradition under which the young intelligentsia formed their first views of art, it is not surprising that the way found by the symbolists was not a true escape. The only satisfactory way out of a dilemma is to smash both horns, not to slip between; by leaving the intellectualist tradition alive and able to influence them in a hundred indirect ways, many of the generation of 1885 failed to assure a solid foundation for other aspects of aesthetic theory. They recognized well enough that art had the character of knowledge but were misled as to the nature of this knowledge. Instead of realizing that we find in art imaginative, not discursive knowledge, they mostly took it for granted that anything entitled to the name must deal with material abstracted from and distinct from the knowing subject. This material was however not known discursively; the kind of cognition involved recalls rather Schopenhauer's intuitive knowledge of Ideas as opposed to his discursive knowledge of concepts; and because in 1885 as in 1949 it is not acknowledged that any such knowledge can exist in a context of rational thought, they were content to call it an irrational knowledge, and say that their grip of the universe was a mystical one.[1]

---

[1] In point of fact, this attitude is in no way new. When Rousseau cried, 'Non, de vaines argumentations ne détruiront jamais la convenance que j'aperçois entre ma nature immortelle et la constitution de ce monde, et l'ordre physique que j'y vois régner: j'y trouve dans l'ordre moral correspondant, et dont le système est le résultat de mes recherches, les appuis dont j'ai besoin pour supporter les misères de la vie' (*Rêveries*, III; *Œuvres*, 1883, t. i, p. 413), he was perhaps doing no more than echo a sentiment that is ageless; and of his successors Béguin said 'Les romantiques admettent tous que la vie obscure est en incessante communication avec un

The fruits of this attitude are with us still. One of the first acts of the post-symbolist aestheticians was to divide all experience into two mutually exclusive fields; on the one side of the fence was placed 'perception' for practical ends and the 'utilitarian' sciences; on the other 'contemplation' with its attendant practices—art and religious mysticism. Thus, speaking of the supposedly radical nature of symbolist philosophy, a justly renowned critic, Albert Béguin, announces:

'A l'origine ne fut pas l'action, la conquête des pouvoirs utilitaires, mais la contemplation, cette autre prise de possession de l'univers';[1]

as though these were two entirely unrelated genealogies of human endeavour. The philosophic isolation of much late French aesthetic, aside from empirical studies connected with the sociology of art, is evidence of the impasse produced by this unfortunate diversion of symbolist aims and by the hardening of over-rigid distinctions.

The problem turns now on the sense in which we must understand 'mysticism'. In its strictest sense, it must be reserved for the religious ascete who aspires to, or achieves, communion with divinity without the mediation of symbols of religion: for whom, indeed, the religious experience becomes incapable of adequate description. But in a wider and more tolerant usage we may revert to the suggestion that any belief or practice is mystical which is not simply irrational (for that would make most stupidities mystical) but also connected with some system of predominant emotions grouped around it. On the one hand, under this definition, there would fall all religious symbolism which was asserted as *true*; all imagination on which intellectual interpretation failed to assert its authority; and in this regard Lévy-Bruhl speaks of the mysticism of primitive peoples: on the other hand we could instance the aesthetic of Schopenhauer, with the emotional motivation of an irrational theory of Ideas. For the refutation of the symbolists' mystic theorizing we cannot be content with a survey of its results in the early twentieth century;[2] nor with pointing out that the mystical cognition theory cannot possibly

---

utre réalité, plus vaste, antérieure, et supérieure à la vie individuelle (*L'Ame romantique et le Rêve*, p. xxix). What is more serious is that present-day critics should blandly, and without apology, advance similar opinions on their own account. See in this connection G. Michaud, *Message Poétique du Symbolisme*, 1947, t. iii, pp. 641-2.

[1] *L'Ame romantique et le Rêve*, t. i, p. 105.

[2] Cf. J. Rivière's confident statement, 'la poésie tend de plus en plus à se différencier du jugement et même de la perception; elle s'ouvre de plus en plus sur cet abîme que nous portons en nous, différent à la fois du cœur, des sens et de l'esprit, et elle se dévoue avec une docilité croissante à en recueillir les incertains murmures' (quoted triumphantly by Dujardin, *La vivante continuité du symbolisme*, p. 71).

square with any account brought forward of the place of language
in art (though Schopenhauer's aesthetic is felt by the symbolists to
succeed here). We must in fact see if there is implicit in the theory
any radical objection to it on grounds which admit no refusal, which
escape the verbalizing quagmires of obscurantist argument, and yet
impose themselves on the mind of anyone who has anything to do
with art, whether as artist, critic, or audience. It so happens that
such an objection is easily found; we have seen it applied in the
narrower field of Schopenhauer's theory; now, as if to confirm again
the conclusion that the latter is itself wildly irrational, we see it operate
against avowedly mystical doctrines in a precisely similar way. In
each case it is relevant to say that there can be no estimation of
aesthetic value when all art is held to be a glimpse of a supernatural
Reality: for on this assumption, the artist either makes a masterpiece,
an evidence of the divine wisdom, or something which cannot
properly be called a poem or a picture at all. There is no such thing
as a poem of which we can say, 'This is a poem, but that is a bad line
in it'; no such thing as a proposition, 'Beethoven's 7th symphony
is better than Strauss' Blue Danube Waltz'. To borrow Mauclair's
words, 'Toute comparaison est anti-esthétique';[1] and this must go
not only for comparison between two recognized pieces of art but
for comparisons between the poem or performance as someone
else has written or performed it and the poem or performance as
you yourself would prefer it to have been executed. The latter is no
different from the former instance, for a modified poem or performance is a different entity. So that if we allow that all comparison is
anti-aesthetic, we must go on to allow that all criticism is too, and
that all the 'critic' (perhaps his title should be changed to policeman,
or temple-guardian) can and should attempt is to hurl thunderbolts
at impudent counterfeits masquerading as music or paintings or plays.
Mauclair's own subsequent career as a practising art-critic—to look
no further—gives the lie to his own earlier theories.

But it may be said, granted the artist's share in creative activity is
not to be judged as either good or bad, an element of differentiation
can still be slipped in on the *other* side: the mystical reality may be
divided up into more valuable and less, and the problem of worth
as between two works of art solved by making it a simple pendant of

---

[1] *Eleusis*, p. 200. Combarieu complained against Schopenhauer's theory of music, that it
fails to distinguish good from bad. To the amateur that Schopenhauer or many Symbolist
were, however, such distinctions are always tentative, and accompanied by a feeling that no
serious reliable criteria exist in judgements of taste. The nineteenth century as a whole is
on this point almost uniformly anti-Kantian.

a difference in the supernatural realm of Ideas, essences, manifestations of God, etc. The artist, set down before his little slice of Reality,
had no say in what he was doing: he was not a free agent but took
what was handed to him, and with it all its merits and demerits as
art. This indeed is a picture not very unlike that drawn by Jules
Laforgue, except that he calls his Reality *L'Inconscient*, manufactured in Germany, and art a small sector of cosmic evolution, the
coming to consciousness of the Unconscious. And yet such an
account of the origin of aesthetic values is nowhere to be found in
the annals of the symbolists: and little wonder. Relegating the artist
to a position where in the exercise of his highest function he became
the least free of men, unable to make even an improvement in his own
work[1] was not an action calculated to appeal to a generation that had
embraced artistic freedom in every shape or form as its chief war-
cry, and mortgaged itself to a rickety 'idealism' for the privilege of
doing as it pleased.[2] To go so far towards clearing the road of art of
obstacles to freedom, merely to arrive at a goal where initiative no
longer exists, is a paradox that few stomachs would have absorbed
in 1885.

   The idea of an irrational cognition in which aesthetic value was
equivalent to mystical truth cannot therefore be maintained if we
recognize two undisputed features of art—the artist's freedom in the
exercise of his imaginative activity, and the fact that there can be
better or worse, brilliant or shoddy. That is not to say that art has
nothing to do with truth; on the contrary, Saint-Pol-Roux is well
within his rights when he says:

'La Beauté, c'est l'exaltation de la vérité';[3]

but we see immediately what this means when he goes on:

'Le génie m'apparaît le don privilégié de porter au cube les sensations et les idées,
ou encore de les hausser à une millième puissance ... (les Poètes) sont comme des
êtres divins, pensant, voyant, et créant grand, en un mot, magnifiant.'[4]

That does not mean that poets are shaken by wilder passions, conceive

---

[1] See below, p. 122 n., precisely this position cheerfully accepted by Francis Jammes—but
Jammes shows here a Christian humility not typical of the symbolists at large.
[2] Cf. Morice, in *La Littérature de tout à l'heure*, p. 368, for a stirring account of the artist
winning freedom for himself, and so becoming an exceptional being in a world otherwise void
of liberty. The same story crops up everywhere: 'Le *Moi* émancipé, audacieux, pourra fonder,
sur la ruine des Ecoles défuntes, l'Individualisme' (E. Goudeau, *Entretiens*, t. I, No. 5, p. 141,
viii/1890); 'Le lyrisme est *exclusivement* d'allure intuitive et personnelle, et la poésie va dans ce
sens depuis conquante ans' (Kahn, *Revue Indépendante*, ii/1889); 'Le symbolisme pourra (et
même devra) être considéré par nous comme le libre et personnel développement de l'individu
esthétique' (Rémy de Gourmont, *Le Chemin de Velours*, p. 210), etc., etc.
[3] Quoted in *La Littérature contemporaine*, 1905, p. 305.   [4] ibid.

more grandiose or phantastic ideas as such than ordinary people, or talk longer or louder or simply more violently; it means that they *imagine* them a thousand times more fully, more adequately, more vividly, that they make themselves a thousand times more aware; and this they do through their art. *Eureka* can be approached in two ways: either as a correct account of the natural history of the universe, in which case Poe is on very shaky ground; or it can be taken, as Poe asks us to take it, as a poem, and admired not for its cognitive value but for its imaginative—as Poe's attempt to say for his own satisfaction what he feels, not so much about rigorous universal astronomy, but about the larger problems of man's deepest feelings, his place in the universe, and his relations with God. We do not ascribe a cognitive value to the *Divina Commedia*,[1] though certainly some of its early readers did so; nor do we to-day treasure the *De Rerum Natura* for its physics—or even the account it gives of Lucretius' physics; Poe's *Eureka* might aspire to stand midway between, as a symbol, perhaps even as an allegory or a myth. Yet one or two among the younger symbolists would have been prepared to say that its aesthetic adequacy answered to a cognitive truthfulness, not of the same verifiable sort, but one which could be known intuitively, or by entering into the spirit of its author.[2] 'Entering into the spirit of the author' tells us nothing objective other than what Poe felt and what we can feel; its truth is imaginative, a knowledge of the individual experience; and the experience is prized not because it was once Poe's but because, recreated in the reader's consciousness, it can be judged by standards of aesthetic consistency and structure.

This point is of considerable importance, and one on which we may do well to insist at this stage; for on it hangs the whole critique of the theory of symbols. *Eureka*, assuming for the moment that we credit it with artistic value (we cannot at any rate refuse it a valuation, if only as indifferent prose), can be one of two things; it can be a true expression of what Poe feels about man, destiny, God, and the Universe, in which case its truth is imaginative, the truth of art; its structure stands or falls by its self-consistency: or it can be an assertion

---

[1] In the same sense that it does not seriously impair the value of the Inferno if we no longer believe in the fire-and-brimstone Hell.

[2] Valéry writes: 'Dans le système de Poe, le *consistency* est à la fois le moyen de la découverte et la découverte elle-même. C'est là un admirable dessein, exemple et mise en œuvre de la réciprocité d'appropriation. L'univers est construit sur un plan dont la symétrie profonde est en quelque sorte présente dans l'intime structure de notre esprit. L'instinct poétique doit nous conduire aveuglément à la vérité' (Quoted by Mauclair, *Le Genie de Poe*, p. 211). This casual equation opens the gates to some strange propositions.

about not merely Poe's experience, but all possible experience, scientific, religious, artistic, philosophical; an assertion that there is a structure underlying all experience which is truthfully recorded in the account given. To make such an assertion involves rising above the moment of utterance: of standing over and against it, and judging its conformity with other experiences; in short, making it into an explicit *object*, to be argued and reasoned over. This however goes against the very condition whereby the work of art entirely fills the attention as a concrete experience. *Eureka* can be true as art (i.e. more or less adequate) at the same time as it is false as theory (i.e. inconsistent with other aspects of reasoned experience). You can, in short, call it an extended metaphor. And this is a state in which we can find even the slightest poem; every work of art, judged by artistic standards, is different from itself judged by historical standards.

In the gap between these two standards there falls the symbolism of religion, of myth, of ritual, which on the one hand is constructed from imaginative elements which may have greater or lesser artistic value, but treated as assertions of fact, in which role they are almost always false. As metaphors they may well be true—and the interpreter, whether theologian or psycho-analyst, can always hope to discover their true meaning and their relations with the remainder of the structure of experience. But as metaphors they are also artistic structures; and if they are imbued with formal elements reminiscent of religious or mythical symbolism[1] these enter into their overall structure on the same terms as any other ingredients of art—colour, musical form, vocabulary, rhythm, or the like—and not as any privileged class. The problem is examined in a later chapter; it may be sufficient to say here that to 'assert' what should only be 'imagined' or entertained can come about in any person—Rimbaud's seeing mosques in place of factories is a good instance—but in point of fact is always naturally guarded against. Indeed it must of necessity accompany any imaginative act of any complexity; and metaphor, allegory, myth, looked on as imaginative entities are always the occasion of a complex mental act of 'imagination plus renunciation of simple assertion'. The language of myth and ritual is thick with

---

[1] In this context it is worth remarking that Symbolism, as a stage in literary history, is inconceivable except as coming on the heels of Wagner, the Parnassians, and the nineteenth century's enormous researches into ancient myth and culture patterns: without these, it would have had neither the incentive nor the means to steer poetry into some of the highly specialized channels in which it has run in the present century.

metaphor from start to finish; metaphor chosen in the first place, perhaps, for imaginative value, but soon crystallized into assertion; and an age interested in linguistic experiment of all kinds is only too likely to feel the inclination to make the same passage to assertion. But there is one important fact connected with the emergence of myth—it is a corporate and social creation; it demands a large measure of abnegation from its devotees; and with the symbolist poet this side of the bargain is not to be expected. By this standard, symbolism has enriched the repertory of modern civilization by only one myth, and that a renovated one—Narcissus; nor is it seriously contended anywhere that this myth has any serious hold over any society. Evidently, from the viewpoint of religious or mystic symbolism, the generation of 1885 is feeble; from the less ambitious viewpoint of poetic imagination, its symbols may still be examined. For as art, the symbol is necessarily apprehended as imagination; and the formal structures of the symbol are the structures of imagination. The last coincidence is responsible for the remarkable history of the vagaries of the concept of the literary symbol, which we shall pursue in a later chapter.

5. THE UNCONSCIOUS AND ART

We pass now to the third and last of the terms as it were thrown up by the symbolists in their search for a new and distinctive foundation for art. The Unconscious, which began to make a name for itself at the end of the last century as a field for independent inquiry, is an exceptionally vague term: properly speaking, it is that part of the mind and its activities which is exclusive of all we call conscious, consciousness. But there are two respects in which this statement is useless to the aesthetician. First, we do not know that there is only one sort of mental activity (if there is any at all) below the level of consciousness: if there were, it would be in the realm of sensation, passivity; it would be simply a series of nervous phenomena, sensuous and motor responses; it would, in short, not be mental activity in any sense that we know of. It would leave no trace on the memory, since it would never have reached consciousness; it would afford no work for psycho-therapy, for we cannot psycho-analyse an animal's mind. Secondly, because we do not know at precisely what stage the workings of unconscious mind (whatever that might be) are supposed to affect the creation of art.

Dealing with the first problem first, it is plain that the psycho-analyst cannot recall into the mind what has never been committed to it; therefore '*un*-conscious' elements in the mind are not pre-conscious; they are partly conscious pieces of imagination which for one reason or another are no longer thought. They are part-sensation, part-knowledge: that is why they can at one moment act as relentlessly as a scourge of nature and at the next moment be scotched. But these perspectives are opened up long after the decline of symbolist aesthetic: and there is certainly no trace of any nineteenth-century writer giving his attention to the recurrence in his work of any symbolist obsessions.

(*a*) It is, in fact, very hard so to strip our minds of modern psycho-logical perspectives as to come to a fair understanding of what the term 'unconscious' (*Inconscient*) signified around 1885. Clinical research was already under way; but not along lines calculated to encourage enthusiasm or even interest among poets; the early popular exponent of the Unconscious was in fact Edouard von Hartmann in Germany with his *Philosophie der Unbewussten* (1869). It is enough to say that in this writer's work the Unconscious is not primarily an integral part of the individual mind-body structure, but a metaphysical entity—a transcendental principle, in the succession of Fichte's Ego, Hegel's Idea, or Schopenhauer's Will. Laforgue at any rate did not often make the confusion, popular in later times, between a metaphysical principle and a psychological entity;[1] but as a result, his views on the relation between art and the Unconscious are marred even more by their extreme theoretical frailty than by the frag-mentary nature of their presentation to the world. The Unconscious, we learn, is the '... raison explicative, suffisante, unique, intestine, dynamique, adéquate, de l'histoire universelle de la vie'.[2] It is 'L'Afrique intérieure de notre inconscient domaine';[3] that is to say, it enters into every individual, as part of the cosmos. It is in constant evolution;[4] therefore art, which aspires continuously to its 'expres-sion' (how, in this respect, it is distinct from other human activities we are not told), must evolve—must overcome the temptation to become static, in the shape of convention, rule, cliché,

---

[1] *L'Inconscient* for Laforgue reconciles idealists and determinists: 'Voilà le grand point reconquis, l'Idéal au-dessus des hommes et des œuvres, expliquant le génie comme d'essence divine, pressenti par les Platoniciens et repoussé par les partisans de l'Evolution. Il (L'Incon-scient) sera accepté des uns et des autres, qu'il concilie, attaché qu'il est au substratum de la vie universelle, en indéfini devenir dans le jeu de ses lois, tout en restant transcendant et dynamique' (Ms. inédit., quoted Ruchon, *Laforgue*, 1924, p. 53).

[2] *Revue Blanche*, t. x (the fragment was written in 1881–2).   [3] *Entretiens*, p. 49, t. iv.

[4] Towards consciousness. Art helps by exploring its own particular fields of human feelings and thought (*Mélanges posthumes*, p. 205). Art has, in this task, no more than an 'importance secondaire'.

genre; these latter, besides, lead to 'ennui', or loss of fresh emotional spontaneity. Every work of art must continually also pass out of circulation, for the same reason.[1]

Laforgue's aesthetic is from the outset both anti-intellectualist and anti-formalist. Intellectualism in art (personified for him by Taine) is pernicious because it distracts the artist's energies from bringing the Unconscious to consciousness—in other words, from attending to his feelings:

'Aujourd'hui, tout préconiser ... la culture excessive de la raison, de la logique, de la conscience. La culture bénie de l'avenir est la déculture, la mise en jachère. Nous allons à la dessication: squelettes de cuir, à lunettes, rationalistes, anatomiques. Retournons, mes frères, vers les grandes eaux de l'Inconscient.'[2]

Formalism in art is pernicious because art aspires to hold up the mirror to the Unconscious, which is constantly evolving, constantly changing: the classical ideals:

'... posent d'abord que l'art est chargé de corriger la nature, comme s'il pouvait être d'autres lois d'harmonie que celles du *tel quel* de la vie.'[3]

No art 'forms' as such are genuine:

'... Il n'y a pas de type (de beauté), il y a la vie.'[4]
'... Tout m'intéresse, car je m'incline pieusement devant l'Inconscient.'[5]
'... Chaque homme est, selon son moment dans le temps, son milieu de race et de condition sociale, un moment d'évolution individuelle, un certain clavier sur lequel le monde extérieur joue d'une certaine façon. Mon clavier est perpétuellement changeant, il n'y en a pas un autre identique au mien, *tous les claviers sont légitimes.*'[6]

The Unconscious, however, slips down from its transcendental throne to become sensation, that which is given:

'L'homme de génie reçoit ses impressions ou plutôt les subit sans les avoir voulues';[7]

and this gives us the clue both to what place the Unconscious occupies in art for him, and in a measure what sort of activity art is: on the one hand:

'... la production esthétique a sa source dans l'Inconscient';[8]

and on the other hand:

'L'invention et la réalisation du Beau dérivent de processus inconscients, dont le résultat se traduit dans la conscience par le sentiment et l'invention du Beau.'[9]

---

[1] Which can only lead us to suppose that Laforgue valued his Hamlet above Shakespeare's. To judge from his frequent reference to Hamlet, however, theory and practice parted company on this point.

[2] *Entretiens*, t. iv. Inédits de Laforgue.   [3] *Mélanges posthumes*, p. 297.
[4] ibid., p. 159.   [5] ibid., p. 154.   [6] ibid., p. 141.
[7] Hartmann, *Philosophie der Unbewussten*, French trans., I, p. 307.   [8] ibid., p. 306.
[9] ibid., p. 321.

Is this a theory of inspiration? Laforgue's biographer Ruchon thinks so: the Unconscious implants somehow or other greater and more valuable sensations in the inspired artist for him to spy out: his task is simply to appreciate this fact and transcribe them. Art *reflects* 'l'anarchie même de la vie'. But if what it reflects is the Unconscious, or as it would be more expedient to say, the pre-conscious, art itself is undeniably conscious; and this is something which some of Laforgue's exponents in the twentieth century would do well to ponder. The fact does not seem to have been always clear in his own mind either: but he never allowed theory to interfere so radically with practice as to prevent him composing *deliberately*: how else could he have come to *choose vers libre*?

Laforgue's premature juxtaposition of conscious and unconscious in the definition of art brings in its train some curious consequences. First, the famous paradox, put into his mind by reflections on the contemporary novel and its laborious psychological dissections and analysis:

'Epier les instincts avec autant que possible absence de calcul, de volonté, de peur de les faire dévier de leur nature, de les influencer.'[1]

This is, of course, pure delight to the surrealist, who claims to have found the means of putting into practice an ideal enunciated by the great predecessor. But he wilfully misunderstands Laforgue's intention. To spy out something is to become conscious of it, not to reproduce it unconsciously for future inspection by one's self or someone else. Laforgue wants his art to reproduce on the conscious level the 'feelings' in the Unconscious level of the mind. The Bergsonian, realizing this, shrugs his shoulders pityingly: Laforgue evidently did not realize that the pure intuition to which he was plainly referring cannot be attended to and given verbal equivalents without the inevitable distortions arising from the use of language. The matter is not as simple as that, however; and if the surrealist is brazen, the Bergsonian is disingenuous. Laforgue supposed that there are in the dim recesses of the mind certain instincts accessible, though not easily accessible, to careful introspection; and that they can readily be incorporated into conscious knowledge. But, in fact, these 'instincts' which occupy so much of Hartmann's book are of the realm of physiology: they are a class of event which, if a prerequisite of knowledge, are not themselves knowledge. We know what we imagine about them; we observe and interpret the phenomena associated with them; but we cannot re-live them. Knowledge

[1] *Entretiens*, t. iv. Inédits de Laforgue.

descends no further than imagination will take it; and Laforgue i
asking for something that does not exist when he asks for intuitiv
knowledge of instincts—complexes on the level of sensation. T
'know' sensation is to transform it. (nb *feeling* →)

The second curious consequence is somewhat more practical
There is no doubt that the aesthetic outlined above, for all its am
biguity, demands the scrapping of all rigid formulae for the attain
ment of 'Beauty', and puts in its place some sort of standard according
to which the artist finds within himself the ideal of excellence: a
Beaunier observes, 'Laforgue a conçu l'art comme un moyen d'expression'.[1] But the ideal of expression is nowhere enlarged on by him
in any positive statements, and it is difficult to see how it could be
less still is it ever linked with that process by which sensation is
turned into knowledge; 'expression' in Laforgue's context means
jettisoning all rules for beauty's attainment, and then embodying
in language sensations which have never been expressed before
Originality is thus one limiting feature of expression, indeed, a hall-
mark of genius: but sensation is from an impersonal realm, the 'Unconscious', and is having to be turned into *personal* art. Laforgue
speaks at times as if the personality of the artist was beneath attention
and only the broad stream of art down the ages, not its individua
members, worthy of attention, as reflecting the evolution of the
Unconscious. The poet must, in fact, be free, simply because not to be
free would frustrate the Unconscious, seat of genius. The artist is
not an individual living in a historical context which influences his
work: he is torchbearer to a biological continuity which is sited
beneath the levels on which it can be discussed:

'Qui veut expliquer génie par les deux seuls facteurs visibles et palpables, la
créature, ses conditions de vie, son milieu, ignore le vrai et fécond milieu de chaqu
être, l'invisible atmosphère d'une conscience dans laquelle il vit et se développe.'[2]

And again, the artist is not concerned with Taine's search for essentia
characteristics: on the contrary;

'Pas de milieu. Se hausser jusqu'au génie fatal et imperturbable — ou être intéres
sant comme la mode, c'est-à-dire *chercheur* pour l'évolution.'[3]

So that, if asked about 'expression', Laforgue would say his aim to be
the expression of a moment in the self-development of the Unconscious—the moment embodied on this occasion in the artist's sensations. There is therefore a sort of condominion on sensation; and

[1] Beaunier, *La poésie nouvelle*, 1902, p. 81.   [2] *Mélanges posthumes*, p. 203.
[3] *Revue Blanche*, t. x, No. 84, 1/xii/1896, pp. 483–4.

though Laforgue nowhere says as much, the artist's satisfaction with *his own* presentation of an experience can be the only guarantee that he is doing justice to the rights of his great co-partner. This consideration is missing from Laforgue's aesthetic, just as Taine's 'caractère essentiel', though apparent to the eye of the historian, is absent from the mind of the working artist. Had it been present it must have led to modification of other parts of the theory. As it is, the glaring deficiency in Laforgue's views is that every time he wants to judge a work of art bad, he can do no more than allege that it reflects inadequately the Unconscious in its latest phase of evolution.

This brings us to the third result of Hartmann's system in Laforgue's hands. We have seen that the artist must be original on pain of falsifying the processes of the Unconscious; but what are the limits of originality? With this question we are trespassing on problems dealt with in the following chapter, and we can at this point do no more than answer briefly: the limits are simply whatever Laforgue cares to propose to himself. *Vers libre*, a few delicious monstrosities of vocabulary, a new *Schadenfreude* of specially sophisticated tone— these are the main signs in his poetry of faithfulness to the Unconscious. But surely many forms in his writing are unoriginal? For every new word he coins (and he coins them always from old) there are ten thousand that he takes. meekly from the accepted language; and a one-sided claim for the artist to be original tails off into ridicule when we reflect that the painter's colours are unoriginal; that the musician uses an accepted chromatic scale of twelve semitones; that the poet uses at least some of the language his mother teaches him; and so on.

By now it should be becoming plain what position *L'Inconscient* occupies in these fragments of an aesthetic. As regards the actual operations of creating a poem or a picture the grand principle is as helpless as a flounder; it could be forgotten, and the artist's sensation remains; its dynamic evolution can be denied outright and there would still remain good grounds for freeing the artist from convention and imitative restrictions; it is asserted that the artist is a servant, but by the very nature of things there is no means to support this claim. With one hand it takes the scale of aesthetic value away from the artist and places it in an inaccessible region of sensation, but with the other it returns his responsibility to him by allowing that he can embody the aspirations of the Unconscious with more or less efficiency; and so at the end leaves us very much where we started in our quest for aesthetic judgements of value. Evidently, then, when we look for

reasons why Laforgue should take so fervently to Hartmann's metaphysic, the same answer comes up that suggests itself in the case of
solipsism: he was looking for a reasoned justification of licence, a
counter to the traditional arguments of formalism. Almost as
important, Laforgue was conscious of the need to attack Taine's
historical-determinist and intellectualist aesthetic, to place the artist
in a position where he can do good work and bad work and be praised
or blamed for it; and for this he deemed the Philosophy of the
Unconscious a proper weapon.

But the leading question of what sort of consciousness art gives,
this philosophy is obviously not fitted to answer; Hartmann's early
ventures specifically into aesthetic were in fact conducted in a heavy
beer-garden atmosphere of hedonism. Laforgue ignores them, and
dies before Hartmann's *Aesthetik* is published; the consequent lacunae
in his theories can only be filled conjecturally.[1]

(b) Laforgue's doctrine of the Unconscious, while ascribing each
artist to a unique position in the cosmic process, have been seen to
link him very loosely with its underlying principle; so loosely,
indeed, that there is some doubt in our minds how far he can rightly
be called a 'poet of the Unconscious' at all. The same goes even more
strongly for a writer like Georges Rodenbach, who celebrates its
mysteries in measured and eloquent quatrains, but makes evidently
no effort to bring about any more intimate relationship with the object
of his veneration; if Laforgue is the prophet of the Unconscious,
Rodenbach is its chief ritualist: neither ventures into the holy of
holies.

There is another way of discussing the conscious poet's business
with non-conscious entities; and that is by questioning how conscious
activity can jump the last wall that separates it from the material it
wishes to bring into the sphere of knowledge. The chief discussion
of this problem, and to my knowledge the only one in nineteenth-
century symbolist letters, is in the work of Rémy de Gourmont,
whose erratic allegiances, here as elsewhere, lead us to wonder what
arguments he is trying to further. As his theme in an important article
he chooses the fact that we cannot summon 'inspiration' (as we call it)
just whenever we like; that the poet (Goethe, Vigny, Hugo) no less
than the scientist (Burdach) must wait until the solution of a problem

---

[1] There are numerous eulogies of Laforgue's theories, and some imitations, by symbolists.
They are mostly inept; e.g. the manifesto which claims that Decadence is part of the great law
of progress, and engaged in the continual conquest of new psychological ground: 'Les décadents ont, en effet, acquis au conscient une bonne somme d'Inconscient. Ils ont entrepris résolu-
ment la conquête du Moi, ils ont défriché des terrains nouveaux...' etc., etc. (*Le Décadent*, 4e
année, No. 29, 15/ii/1889).

offers itself almost, as it would seem, of its own accord, to the thinking mind:

'C'est parmi le petit nombre des élus de la conscience qu'il faut chercher les
exemplaires véritablement supérieurs d'une humanité dont ils sont, non les conduc-
teurs, ce qui serait fâcheux et contredirait trop l'instinct, mais les juges. Cependant,
grave sujet de méditation, ces hommes surélevés n'atteignent toute leur valeur
qu'aux moments où la conscience, devenant subconsciente, ouvre les écluses du
cerveau et laisse se précipiter vers le monde les flots rénovés des sensations qu'ils
doivent au monde. Ils sont de magnifiques instruments, dont le subconscient seul
joue avec génie. Lui aussi, le génie est subconscient.'[1]

A few pages earlier, too, he writes, 'La Conscience, qui est le principe
de la liberté, n'est pas le principe de l'art',[2] which would seem to be in
flat contradiction with what he has claimed in the past on the subject
of freedom and idealism.[3]

Here, again, we are not in the presence of surrealism. Gourmont
does not pretend that the whole process of production, which
mutatis mutandis applies to his parallel theory of how the scientist
thinks, is this. The artist is aware of a problem—to find adequate
embodiment for a feeling, a vague half-recognized impulse. This
problem is not one that can be solved by inference from another
solution, for it is unique: no two artistic problems are alike. There are
no recipes in art. In this sense, Gourmont thinks, consciousness fails
the artist: consciousness being identified with reasoning intellect.
Therefore the artist, at any important moment, falls back on some
more primitive activity. This summary dismissal of the lengthy
preparations and discipline through which any great creative artist
passes on his way to the achievement of these uncanny results is
surely unsatisfactory. It ignores moreover the fact that in normal
circumstances the poet is constantly on the watch against false steps—
i.e. making intense use of conscious mental processes. In short Rémy
de Gourmont is genuinely on a slippery path (though not far down
yet) which leads to the negation of all sense of aesthetic value. Of
such tendencies it has been well said:

'Any theory of art should be required to show, if it wishes to be taken seriously,
how an artist in pursuing his artistic labour, is able to tell whether he is pursuing it
successfully or unsuccessfully—how, for example, it is possible for him to say,
"I am not satisfied with that line; let us try it this way . . . and this way . . . and
this way . . . there! that will do". A theory which pushes the artistic experiences

[1] R. de Gourmont, 'Notes sur l'Inconscient' (*Mercure de France*, t. xxvi, p. 54, 1/iv/1898).
[2] ibid., p. 52.
[3] Cf. Valéry's dictum: 'Le poète en fonction est une attente. Nous attendons le mot in-
attendu — et qui ne peut être prévu mais attendu. Nous sommes le premier à l'entendre'
('Calepin d'un poète,' *Œuvres*, NRF, p. 183). But Valéry does not dream of suggesting that this
is the whole story.

too far down the scale (*sc.* of consciousness) to a point below the region where experience has the character of knowledge, is unable to meet this demand. It can only evade it by pretending that the artist in such cases is acting not as an artist but as a critic and even (if criticism is identified with the philosophy of art), as philosopher. But this pretence should deceive nobody. The watching of his own work with a vigilant and discriminating eye, which decides at every moment of the process whether it is being successful or not, is not a critical activity subsequent to, and reflective upon, the artistic work, it is an integral part of that work.'[1]

But when all is said, a problem does remain. How does the material for the artist's imaginative criticism come to be projected before the artist's consciousness? If imagination is (to use Coleridge's term) 'esemplastic', if it raises the poetic operation above the reach of sheer laws of association, yet nevertheless at some low stage in the operations of this faculty, some phase at which language is still so ill assimilated as to be highly general and ill-fitting, association must be found to operate in greater or lesser measure. Its products indeed are what we call linguistic commonplaces or clichés. At this low level, imagination has little individuality, and art is not usually called art at all; the artist's achievement is to have risen so far towards individualizing his conscious experience that he habitually misses out these low stages as successive precisions of his feelings. One might almost say that he creates in some measure his own associations, were it not that this process is infinitely flexible and not rigid, that the 'style' which emerges from a certain habitual 'turn of phrase' has none of the appearance of stiltedness: the phenomena of association have never this quality. It is to Gourmont's credit that he perceived a genuine problem for the philosophy of art to solve, even if his own formulation and solution are riddled with confusion. The problem is simply, Why, with practice, does the poet acquire a greater command over his medium; why does the successful solution of a number of artistic

---

[1] R. G. Collingwood, *The Principles of Art*, 1937, p. 281. Cf. the following—'Il y a bien là ces deux vers, me disait-il (Francis Jammes) en me montrant une longue pièce qu'il avait écrite dans la nuit ... qui ne me semblent pas très bons.
— Eh bien, corrigez-les.
— Je n'ose pas. Je crois que je n'en ai plus le droit. Et si j'avais eu la naïveté de demander: Pourquoi?
— Parce que hier soir, m'eût-il répondu, s'ils m'ont paru bons alors que j'étais inspiré, à present je suis par conséquent moins bon juge' (André Gide, *Feuillets Retrouvés*, in *Journal*, 1941 ed., p. 724).
Gide's comment on this stand of Jammes is so succinctly efficient as to be worth quoting here: 'Il y a une sincérité qui consiste à tâcher de *voir vrai*, et celle-là Jammes ne la connaîtra jamais. Pour être poète il faut croire à son génie; pour devenir artiste il faut *le mettre en doute*. L'homme vraiment fort est celui chez qui *ceci* augmente *cela*' (ibid., p. 288). 'Nature to advantage dressed?" No doubt, if we are careful how to read 'Nature'; but this old truth emerges only slowly through symbolist controversy. Gide's position is that of the end-product, in our age, of the train of thought pursued in earlier discussion of *Le Rêve*; it is also highly relevant to our study of symbolist theories of language in the next chapter.

problems make *more likely* the successful solution of the next; or in any single case of poetic endeavour, how can a poet reasonably hope to *improve* on a phrase or passage with which he is not yet satisfied? In other words, what is meant by the accumulation of experience? Any satisfactory answer to this question must re-open the long-standing controversy on the implications of the difference between 'fancy' and 'imagination'.

(c) If Rémy de Gourmont must be credited with having sensed an important problem in aesthetics, no similar recognition can be accorded to related views of a writer very much more closely linked with the symbolist movement from its earliest days: Edouard Dujardin. Writing at the start of the surrealist craze, and anxious to reflect a little glory on the deeds of earlier days, his apology for symbolism claims (though without much supporting evidence) that the procedures of the 1920's had been invented unknowingly thirty or forty years previously.

'Nous no nous rendîmes compte que plus tardivement (!) de ce qui devait être l'apport décisif du symbolisme. Cette réalité essentielle, cette vie intérieure, les classiques l'auraient cherchée dans la direction de ce qu'ils appelaient la raison; nous la cherchâmes dans la direction jusque-là méprisée, on dirait aujourd'hui refoulée, de l'inconscient. C'était une considérable nouveauté. Robert de Souza a fort bien dit dans l'enquête ouverte l'année dernière par la *Muse Française*, que la gloire du symbolisme était "d'avoir ramené la poésie à sa source mobile, au plus près possible de ses origines subconscientes mystérieuses.'[1]

He further quotes Jacques Poisson[2] as claiming that:

'Les jeunes écrivains de notre époque sentant la richesse du plan où les avaient conduits leurs grands devanciers, Mallarmé, Rimbaud, Laforgue, ont basé toute une esthétique sur l'association sans logique apparente.'[3]

What are we to make of these judgements, having seen for ourselves the scope and restrictions placed by just these three writers on the voluntary and involuntary factors in art? The rhythm of his prose apart, what can have induced Dujardin to speak of 'la raison' and 'l'inconscient' as opposed terms in the search for a 'réalité essentielle'? What (*pace* André Breton) is a 'réalité essentielle' in a world of poetic aspiration? Is all that we can find in these remarks a vague notion that whereas 'classical' art was ruled over by a criterion of naturalism conformability in its material with the experience of everyday life—if you like, imitation), 'symbolist' art allowed itself the luxury of unicorns, knowing them to be fabulous? If this is what is intended,

---

[1] Dujardin, 'La vivante continuité du symbolisme,' *Mercure de France*, 1/vii/1924, p. 60.
[2] In 'Littérature moderne et psychanalyse' (*La Vie des lettres*, No. XIV).
[3] Dujardin, 'La vivante continuité du symbolisme,' p. 72.

then it is undoubtedly true, though hardly 'une considérable nou veauté'. But to judge by the quotation from Souza that follows Dujardin has something else in his mind. And perhaps that whic he has in his mind can only be understood when we take note of th date of his statement (1924) and of the course of French Philosophy–and French writing—between the heyday of symbolism and that yea: Can it be that the name of Bergson has cast its shadow across th memory of the critic; that his historical judgement has been deflecte by that doctrine of art which postulates:

'Cet élément confus, infiniment mobile, inappréciable, sans saison, délicat fugitif, que la langue ne saurait saisir sans en fixer la mobilité, ni l'adapter à sa form banale... Sous les joies et les tristesses qui peuvent à la rigueur se traduire en parol (le poète), saisit quelque chose qui n'a plus rien de commun avec la parole, certai rythmes de vie et de respiration qui sont plus intérieurs à l'homme que ses sentimen les plus intérieurs.'[1]

If so, and if we are content to defer to these opinions, we must revis our opinion not only of the poetry of Rimbaud, Mallarmé, and th symbolists, but of their utterances too.[2] Why do we find no over consciousness of this aim of poetry, or its legatee in literature, th 'surreal' reality—why do Mallarmé, Gide, and a hundred othe struggle to explain the vital interest of 'symbols', 'audition colorée and similar affairs, which on this showing are no more tha irrelevancies of communicative technique?

Dujardin's third contention, expressed in the quotation fro Jacques Poisson, stands on other ground. The idea of an a completely cut off from all normal conceptions of order and struc ture, is only made explicit in the twenties; but for a much longe time than that it has never been very far round the corner; and th (possibly) erroneous constructions placed by critics on the Berg sonian attitude to language did no more than hasten its growth Once the ideal of a realist art is gone, it springs forward to fill a gap and is taken up wrongly when there is no longer any trace of th principle demanding that the artist remain subservient to the patter of everyday life. What his new freedom means in terms of a aesthetic is a question we can defer treating until we come to talk c language and its symbolism. We see in the work of all the gre poetry of modern France—one might say of the post-symboli

---

[1] Bergson, quoted by Paulhan, *Fleurs de Tarbes*, pp. 66–7.
[2] This has been attempted (Fiser, *Le Symbole Littéraire*, 1945); the net result being to show th the only true symbolist author is Marcel Proust. Baudelaire, Rimbaud, Mallarmé, prov despite persuasion to be all too tactlessly recalcitrant; and no gain results from heavy pressu to distort the notion of 'literary symbol' into a distressing hybrid of realist linguistic and Berg sonian intuitionism.

European tradition—a use of poetic imagery, of language, in which the surface structure is no longer the logic of discursive reason, but rather, if we must give it a term, 'the logic of the imagination'. An Apollinaire would explain it by appeal to cubism, another by the laws of association in the service of emotionalism, and so on; but the discipline, whatever it is, that replaces the logic of naturalist technique is common to all art, and refuses to force some techniques (e.g. that of music) into a strait-jacket with the representative arts at the same time as it refuses to throw overboard all the experience of structure.

6. CONCLUSION

We are now in a position to survey the land we have traversed in this first detailed section of symbolist doctrine; namely, as it looked on '*le rêve*', '*rêverie*' and '*l'inconscient*'. The last first: from our study of the symbolist attitude to dreams it emerges that the conception of a totally involuntary art-creation was entirely alien to their intentions; it is not simply that to father on them the first implicit stirrings of surrealist notions (as Dujardin attempts) is unwarranted by the facts, but that such an attempt wilfully misrepresents the movement's inmost intentions. The non-conscious lurks round the corner, in odd suggestions and assaults on the problem of art; but these are in no way typical of the age, except as part of a web of diversified strands and scraps of theory whose emphasis lies elsewhere.

By the same token Rousseau's '*rêverie*' provides nothing of importance in the movement: it is an allied state of mind to that which interests the 'typical symbolist'; but implicit in the latter's view of art is the relegation of '*rêverie*' to one of two possible positions: as an activity it is below the poet's dignity, though not essentially opposed to poetry, and as anything else it is merely an empirical genre not much in favour.

It is when we come to the idea of dream that we find among its multiple connotations one which is of significance. The dream provides material suggestions to the poetic fancy which are new and exciting. So much so, in fact, that even organized within the work of art certain imaginative elements exercise a compulsion which, taken with a number of anti-positivist, irrational prepossessions, suggests a special form of cognition, one which we may call mystic for want of a better term. This cognitive theorem is gratuitous and irrelevant to the strict study of aesthetic problems; but it imposes itself in the course of comparison between aesthetic problems (poetic knowledge) and non-aesthetic problems (other forms of knowledge). As it was introduced to literature on the strength of an outside influence, only the removal of that influence could lead to its renunciation; by the time 'symbolisme' had been replaced by 'naturisme', Schopenhauer was a forgotten name.

These three entities suffice as vehicles for the discussion of poetic knowledge, a field in which the symbolists recorded evidence of value over the long term. In their own age, however, the most notable or notorious aspects of their work was—to use a term of the most general application—linguistic; and they perhaps conceived themselves quite as much reformers of poetic language as innovators of poetic knowledge. Moreover, in the course of our discussion we have frequently been brought up short by the fact that our inquiry leads to a problem connected with the theory of language: Mallarmé's views on structure, for example, are obviously incomplete in the shape in which they have been presented. Everything points, therefore, to the need for a fresh detailed cross-section, to survey the symbolists' conception of language.

PART II

CHAPTER IV

THE SYMBOLIST VIEW OF LANGUAGE

Un désir indéniable à mon temps est de séparer comme
en vue d'attributions différentes le double état de la
parole, brut ou immédiat ici, là essentiel.—MALLARMÉ

Sentir avec génie, et être incapable d'exprimer, paraît
aussi incompatible que d'exprimer avec force ce qu'on
ne sent pas.—SENANCOUR

1. The field of language defined. 2. Edgar Allan Poe and the 'emotive' theories.
3. Partial revolts from the 'symbolic' theory. 4. Mallarmé and the 'music' of
poetry. 5. 'Musicality', the symbolists, and Wagner. 6. The symbolist approach
to form. 7. The disruption of forms. 8. *Vers libre*. 9. The lyric drama; transition
to chapter V.

I. THE FIELD OF LANGUAGE DEFINED

IT is possible to hold one of two views concerning language, in the
philosophy of art: on the one hand, that whatever its nature may
be, it cannot materially affect the remainder of aesthetic theory;
or on the other hand, that it occupies a position of central importance,
and cannot be wrongly or carelessly determined without bringing
distortion, paradox, and falsehood into adjoining parts of the field
of study.

For the first view, the way we normally think of language will be
adequate. That is to say, it will be claimed that we all know what
it is; namely, a way to communicate what is in our minds to other
people, making use of words arranged according to the laws of
grammar, with meanings assigned by convention. In such a language,
the units, the words, out of which it is made, will be *symbols*—that
is to say, signs of reference arrived at by agreement between the two
parties to the communication.[1] Within this general definition, the
theory will discern two specific types of symbolic language: the one

[1] In this chapter the meaning ascribed here to the words symbol, symbolic, will be held to
throughout. In chapter VI, however, we shall be talking of symbols and symbolism in quite a
different sense. This embarrassment, unfortunately, cannot be avoided. On the one hand, long
established usage has sanctified the philosopher's claim to be allowed to use the word in the
way he wants. On the other hand, literary criticism has gone beyond the point where it
could renounce so popular and widespread a term. The 'Symbolist' movement can never be
rebaptized, hasty and ill-considered as may have been the original christening. The two uses,
we shall try to show, are incompatible; and so far from being a source of pregnant insight
into the poetry in question, this confusion of terms has again and again misled critics and
historians of literature, not excluding those of the contemporary scene in the last century.

explanatory and scientific, the other persuasive and rhetorical. And since it is held that the first species is to all intents and purposes colourless and void of emotion (except accidentally); and since also it is held (from observation recorded in some other part of the aesthetic) that art has at any rate some essential connection with emotion,[1] it is natural to conclude that art, or at least the art of literature, differs from other users of language in that it uses it in its second or emotive way. This was certainly the opinion of most late nineteenth-century official thought, including that interested to modify and expand the more limited position of Taine; in the present day it informs most logicians' remarks about literature.

Several things are noteworthy in this view. First, language is symbolic; it rests on an act of intellect: 'This word shall (or does) *refer* to that thing X'. Whatever follows, in the construction of art, cannot destroy this hard symbolic core; and even when—as with so many epithets in poetry—the sign does not evoke the reference, it may be held nevertheless to produce a resulting attitude which depends on long association with the suppressed reference. The second point is really inseparable from the first. If language is symbolic, then a given word or statement or poem must be the sign of a reference to be conjured up before the listener. This reference, if deliberately evoked, must be foreseeable. The clearer the foresight, the more complete the reference in the mind of the speaker. That is to say, before he utters a word, he will have a complete view in his mind of what he wants to do; namely, what effects to produce; he will have lived through a replica of the effect, more or less completely, according to his thoroughness. On this view again it is reasonable to suppose that the essential public action of the artist is an act of charity; that the 'work of art' is a simple vehicle of communication, by which the listener or spectator is put into a state having aesthetic value; and that the artist is either a soulless craftsman devising means to 'coenaesthesia' with Machiavellian coolness and dexterity, or—a kinder view—a genuinely sensitive being anxious to sell certain valuable experiences which he has already gone through and judged to be valuable, and so having recourse to 'art' in one or another of its forms to put across these experiences to whoever will have them.[2]

If this is so, either way, the questions arise: (*a*) by what aesthetic criteria are experiences judged valuable? (*b*) by what process do they

[1] Whether as object of its imitation, or as desirable end to be produced in the audience, or as the first impulse towards art in the mind, or as any combination of these.

[2] Variations include Dr. Richards' approach to the important point that artistic value and communicability are closely connected.

come to be completed before they are put into communicable form?

For the moment, we need only note that the 'experience' of the artist and the (possibly equivalent) experience of the spectator are, on this view, the object of aesthetic inquiry; and that the inquiry into language, as some kind of communicative symbolism, can be carried on or not as we choose, without materially affecting our findings in this self-contained field.

To those having some familiarity with the kind of operations performed when a poem or sonata or landscape are being made, however, the idea of any such divorce is always repugnant. The central feature of these activities is a struggle with words, sounds, colours, and the like: embodying between the artist and his work not the sort of relationship that exists between the printer and his type, where the appropriate letters are effortlessly summoned to fulfil their entirely pre-arranged purposes, but a relationship that is exemplified, in no matter how small a measure, in an act of searching without precise knowledge of what will be found, an act whose adequacy may be judged when it is completed but cannot be judged by a predetermined standard, since in setting up such a standard the goal of the act would already have been reached.

The idea of such an act, common in the experience of all verbally articulate beings, raises great difficulties. It is an act which, when completed, can be judged in respect of its adequacy to a given need; yet, as has been pointed out, it is an act which cannot be a means to an end, since by proposing an end, the act is already anticipated, already enacted. If I decide to paint a picture exactly *so*, that picture already exists as an imagined work of art in my mind; and we are no further along the road to defining the way in which it came to be there, complete. If the idea of a man painting a picture in his mind seems far-fetched, substitute a piece of music: the sonata is no more a sonata for being played than when it is still fresh in the mind of the composer. Yet it is not easy to see how an aesthetic judgement can be made about anything other than the adequacy of art as means to fulfil an end. To say that a thing is 'successful' usually implies just that. Is art in this sense successful; and if not, how can one ascribe varying degrees of value to it?[1]

---

[1] One way out of the problem is to suppose that the artist says 'I will produce or evoke such-and-such an emotion. What are the best means thereto?' This supposes that art deals with generalized concepts—e.g. Hatred, Terror, and so on. But we know, and the symbolists in their rejection of positivism sensed often enough, that art deals with individual experiences, and not with generalized concepts of experience. Yet this escape, it will be seen, figures constantly, if illogically, in symbolist aesthetics.

This type of question is not firmly grasped in the nineteenth century; as we have seen, the symbolists rejected Taine's yardstick of value without fully replacing it by another. Indeed, it could be argued that in any specific case of a symbolist or near-symbolist writer or critic talking nonsense about art, the fundamental frustration lies in an inability to take advantage of the highly suggestive errors of positivist valuation and the view of language that stems from their correction. For as we shall see, as often as they are brought face to face with the positivist or 'emotive' theory of art and compelled to pay lip-service to it in default of a better, they proceed to undermine their avowed doctrine by isolated observations in flagrant contradiction with it. The dichotomy is present from the very start: plain to be seen in the writings of Baudelaire.

Properly formulated, the alternative to the 'symbolic' theory of language might be stated something after this fashion. The consciousness which we find implied in the conception of 'imagination' or 'art' is not something that develops spontaneously out of the intuitive level of perception. It is, on the contrary, something that arises from a voluntary act. We are normally accustomed to think of activity as something at any rate not so impalpable as to be a pure abstraction; and if we are to mean anything when we speak of imagining a work of art we must somehow describe it in concrete terms. In default of a better word, the concrete act in which we embody our conscious experience may be called language.[1] Admittedly the expression is an awkward one, conjuring up associations which are anything but helpful; on the other hand, quite unambiguous words are hard to come upon in the philosophy of art; and this one serves to state with precision the position of art as language *vis-à-vis* other activities, high and low, of the mind. By language, then, is meant a concrete activity by which experience is brought into the focus of consciousness. The thing known as speech is a highly developed form of language; so specialized that on it has been built the whole edifice of rational thought, and it is difficult to think of the substructure of language without its discursive superstructure. Language, indeed, in addition to comprising the special field of speech, includes all manner of gesture and attitude—no less the gestures of the painter with his brush, the dancer with his legs, the actor with the whole range of movement and speech. To quote from the foremost English exponent of this view:

'Speech is after all only a system of gestures, having the peculiarity that each

[1] 'Le Silence et l'attention sont incompatibles' (Valéry, *Calepin d'un poète*, p. 183).

gesture produces a characteristic sound, so that it can be perceived through the ear as well as through the eye. Listening to a speaker instead of looking at him tends to make us think of speech as essentially a system of sounds; but it is not; essentially it is a system of gestures made with the lungs and the larynx, and the cavities of the mouth and nose. We get still further away from the fundamental facts about speech when we think of it as something that can be written and read, forgetting that what writing, in our clumsy notations, can represent is only a small part of the spoken sound, where pitch and stress, tempo and rhythm, are almost entirely ignored. But even a writer or reader, unless the words are to fall flat and meaningless, must speak them soundlessly to himself. The written or printed book is only a system of hints, as elliptical as the neumes of Byzantine music, from which the reader thus works out for himself the speech gestures which alone have the gift of expression.'[1]

Among the many arguments in favour of this approach to the problem of language, it may be urged that in no other way can we describe in theory the essential community in kind of all the arts which we know from experience:

'All the different kinds of language have a relation of this kind to bodily gesture. The art of painting is intimately bound up with the expressiveness of the gestures made by the hand in drawing, and of the imaginary gestures through which a spectator of painting appreciates its tactile values. . . . Every kind of language is in this way a specialized form of bodily gesture, and in this sense it may be said that the dance is the mother of all languages.'[2]

A number of important considerations follow from this initial view of language. We shall do no more than list those immediately relevant to our study of the symbolist aesthetic.

(i) On this view, language is the general name for the whole business of what, following Croce and others, one may call Expression. This is an activity continuous throughout consciousness. It may be carried on well or ill. For normal ends, a low degree of expressiveness is well enough. The higher levels are what we usually recognize as works of art: acts of becoming aware carried to the point of extreme and dazzling lucidity. Art, therefore, is not the strange exercise which a Schopenhauer would have us believe it to be; on the contrary, it is something grounded in the simplest and most widespread form of human activity—something whose lower limits are not ordinarily called art at all, and whose highest and more specialized

---

[1] R. G. Collingwood, *The Principles of Art*, 1937, p. 243.
[2] R. G. Collingwood, *The Principles of Art*, 1937, p. 243. The astonishing relevance of this argument will become apparent when we come to discuss Mallarmé's views on language. An underlying confusion on the nature of artistic value led him to weave fantasies around the printed page and the relation of poetry to dance; yet it is plain that even the confusion of the *Divagations* is an attempt to express an acute awareness of the essential relations brought out by Collingwood.
Cf. 'Without this actual physical embodiment, even if actual embodiment be only imagined, the artistic experience does not exist' (S. Alexander, *Art and the Material*, 1925, p. 9).

ranges, pursued for their own sakes, are a kind of experience open in principle to anyone who desires to scale them.

(ii) Symbolism, in the sense in which we have been using this word, is not prior to language, but subsequent: in speech it draws its material from language, by cutting it up into symbols. Nevertheless, the art of speech, including of course poetry, can be defined as neither language alone nor symbolism alone but a combination of each; in which, however, the aesthetic valuation rests in no way on the symbolic element but on the expressiveness of the whole.[1]

(iii) The valuation of art, therefore, is concerned with the adequacy with which language (in no matter which of its forms) brings into conscious focus the artist's attitude or reaction in the face of experience. This adequacy is judged not by an inspection in terms of ends and means, but from within, by recreation of the experience in the mind of the valuer—that is, the critic, the reader, the audience, or even the poet himself revising the work at a later date.

(iv) The problem of communication does not therefore arise, so far as the language is common to poet and reader: given a sharing of language, the recreation can be undertaken. (By language, though, is meant here a range of elements on which we shall have in the sequel to become more precise.) This being so, we should, if we were extending our study to the inheritors of Symbolism, be forced to examine rather carefully Valéry's notions of 'creative misunderstanding', which indeed are already latent in Mallarmé.

(v) The expression of an attitude cannot take place in a void: nor does each act of expression create its own appropriate snatch of language. The painter operates not only within the range of the colours of the spectrum, and the range of forms familiar in our experience of the external world, but within a tradition as well. The poet may sometimes devise 'new' words and images; but always out of old ones: novelty in art is always a function of formal elements, and it is hard to see how it could be otherwise. There is a given state of language at any time, on which the language user exercises himself.

(vi) But poetry, and indeed most highly perfected art, is specially rich in linguistic resources by reason of its associations with every field of experience. And so far as the poet uses these deliberately as forms

---

[1] Cf. Alexander's point that 'in art the word or marble or drawing has welded into its being the thing which it means' (*Art and the Material*, 1925, p. 24). That this semantic side of speech is not itself a source of aesthetic value is plain from the instance of music—a language *almost* without 'reference' in the ordinary sense. It may be argued that to say language is 'symbolic' means no more than that it always embodies an attitude *towards something*; and on this view symbolism enters into the essence of language. But this is not what is usually meant when it is urged that language is a symbolism.

of expressiveness, his audience will tend to be narrowed down to those people of similar culture who can draw on the same background of experience. The symbolists, when they claimed that art was the affair of a few privileged people, were mistakenly drawing a general law from the peculiar circumstances of their generation.[1]

(vii) Expressiveness is present in all language whatever; and for this reason we cannot draw a hard distinction between poetry and prose; we are accustomed to refer to writing which has the trappings of poetry and the expressiveness of prose as 'verse'; and we are also accustomed to talk of poetic prose; but in point of fact there is no radical distinction between the two fields of speech; nothing but a graduation of the degree of care in expressiveness: casual in Byron, for example, or Lamartine; intense in Flaubert's novels or Racine's verse; or so extreme as to be obsessional—Mallarmé's later sonnets, and the work of Valéry.

(viii) Expressiveness is often, but not always, closely related to the degree of intensity of the struggle between the poet and his medium. This struggle has as its product what we normally call the formal element in art; that is to say, the result when a creative activity is applied to producing an embodiment of individual experience out of language. Formal elements exist at every point in the gamut of artistic utterance: in the simplest metaphor or zeugma as well as in the hugest design—the tetralogical form of Wagner's *Ring* or the sustained balance of Proust's *A la recherche du temps perdu*—and at all intermediate stages; alexandrine, sonnet, rime, five-act tragedy, are merely formal elements of language (in its widest sense as the material of expression) which convention has crystallized around points of natural or aesthetic convenience. At bottom, these formal distinctions are empirical, and have in themselves no binding validity or absolute aesthetic importance. To suppose they had would be to suppose them sufficient means to given ends; and the relation of means and ends has no place in the activity we call art. In the sphere of versification, the symbolists were not slow to perceive this; though it would be an exaggeration to say that they were absolute innovators or revolutionaries, here as elsewhere.

Such a theory of language is far from resolving all the problems of

[1] Typical instances of this, though poles apart in other respects, are T. S. Eliot's *Waste Land*, with its wealth of allusion and quotation, and Valéry's *Jeune Parque*, with its persistent appeal to a subtlety of language inflection far beyond most people's wont and many people's power to follow. The idea of language—i.e. something in which the artist casts his attitudes—must embrace both these extremes of expressiveness, and all intermediate stages as well.

the philosophy of art which the present day forces upon our attention; but it can provide an account of aesthetic valuation, in terms of expressiveness, and of the relation of art with other human activities; and it offers a fair starting-point for the solution of a great many problems of historical perspective. Although its roots are as much in the past as those of any other venture of philosophical analysis, its explicit presentation is largely the work of twentieth-century aesthetic discussion. What, then, we might ask, is its relevance to a study of literary theories in the 1890's? This: that if the above is a possible account of art based at least on an observation of the facts of what poets and painters and composers try to do, then for it to be formulated at all we must have genuine fields of art on which to make our observations. In France it so happens that a weakening sense of artistic values in poetry was amazingly revived at the end of the nineteenth century. This renaissance (it was nothing less) provoked, as always, an extensive discussion among amateur philosophers of what they were doing; and distorted though it was by the circumstances of the time (both ideological and social) it was yet able to reveal that the positivists' account of language simply was not relevant to the field of art *qua* art. There was among the symbolists no mind powerful enough to penetrate step by step to the false initial assumptions of the accepted theory of art [1] If anything, this gives added fascination to the study of their objections at one stage or another to all the presumed facts and features of artistic production on which the positivist aesthetic relies; and our presentation at the start of two theories of poetic language will be justified if it allows us to see with greater ease where the symbolists stand in the history of the theory of language.

2. EDGAR ALLAN POE AND THE 'EMOTIVE' THEORIES

The *Genesis of a Poem* for all the tendencies its author may have shown in other sides of his work, is a classic illustration of the 'emotive' theory.[2] The poet chooses a theme: the horror of final

---

[1] 'Elles' (theoretical tenets of symbolism) 'étaient toutes en germe, mais leur liaison échappait. Je crois que le seul Mallarmé eut assez de compréhension synthétique pour prévoir leur mécanisme... Il a manqué aux symbolistes, quant au fond même de leur esthétique, une relation logique entre la conception et l'expression, et une direction d'ensemble' (Mauclair, *L'Art en Silence*, pp. 198, 203). Mallarmé's critics and exegetes in the present day are finding that the truth of this statement far exceeds what its author could have supposed.

[2] I am aware that Poe subsequently confessed his account a fraud; but Mallarmé's reaction to this information is typical of the age of symbolism: 'Ce qui est pensé, l'est; et une idée prodigieuse s'échappe des pages qui écrites après coup (et sans fondement anécdotique voilà tout) n'en demeurent pas moins congéniales à Poe, sincères' (Letter quoted in Noulet, *L'Œuvre de Mallarmé*, p. 155).

separation by death. The task is then to provide it with a 'form', to clothe it in language. Reacting against the romantic myth that poetry springs fully-formed from its maker's fancy, Poe dilates on the various technical considerations that are present in his mind as he writes: problems of rhythm, of the emotional shades and colours of words, of 'symbols' and images—in a word the whole range of language. So far so good. Why, then, is 'The Raven', or 'Annabel Lee', or nearly every poem of Poe that one can call to mind, such a tawdry affair, at the end of so much careful and undoubtedly skilled labour? Why, if such meticulous attention has been paid to the choice of every word, is not the result an example of that transcendent lucidity which is the stamp of all art of the highest quality? The answer is not hard to find: we probably all feel, to a greater or lesser degree, that Poe is not wholly honest, that indeed he is hardly ever sincere and genuine at all; his poems—for that matter the *Tales* too—strike one as not simply affected, but as posed, artificial. And this is merely another way of saying that in them Poe is not really performing an act of self-expression at all, but an exercise of rhetoric; that to some extent at least he looks ahead at a predetermined 'emotion' to be aroused, and then considers the means to it. In another set of terms, he is not constantly working on an individual feeling—'*this* feeling at the thought of death'—but a generalized one—the abstraction 'the terror of death'—from which all, or nearly all individuality has been drained; he is looking not at himself but at others; not exploring his own feelings in an act which makes them accessible to others, but trying to impose on an audience feelings which are not present (or only partially so) in his own experience. The result we know.

It is all the more regrettable, then, that Baudelaire, in his enthusiastic championing of Poe, should have swallowed whole a doctrine whose latent implications he gives the lie to in almost every line of *Les Fleurs du Mal*. Evidently Poe's debunking of the 'fine frenzy' myth was a leading consideration; but it has been seen that the conception of verbal technique means two very different things according as we speak of art or of the craft of language,[1] according as we are talking of language *qua* language or language as an emotive instrument; and this distinction, though sensed by Baudelaire, as by any writer worth his salt, was never completely brought to light by him. So far as personal experience compelled him to ignore Poe's *Philosophy of Composition*, it was to other explanations that he had recourse in his

---

[1] Verlaine calls this latter 'éloquence' and 'littérature'; Paulhan calls it 'rhétorique' (*Fleurs de Tarbes*).

circumvention of the 'symbolic' theory of language (and of course
its pendent the 'emotive' theory of art). In symbolist times, lip-
service was paid by all[1] to the *Genesis of a Poem* and its author; partly
on the strength of Baudelaire's advocacy, partly on the strength of the
Tales, with their rare and macabre atmosphere, and partly for the
avowed mysticism of its author. But the further implications were
not often recognized. Where they were, and when they found
favour, positivism followed with all its train of argument: a train
that could only be broken off by a flight into mysticism. We shall
look at a few examples.

(a) Hennequin

A good example of the thorough-going attitude to Poe is found in
the young critic Émile Hennequin, who has some interesting remarks
to make on his account. In the first place, his attention is drawn to
Poe's defence of craftsmanship; and the emotive theory is explicitly
stated:

> 'Poe perçoit le rapport défini de cause à effet entre les moyens littéraires à employer
> et l'effet émotionnel fictif à produire.[2] ... Dans la plénitude de ses hautes facultés
> d'analyste, Poe médite son effet final...'[3]

And Hennequin quite lucidly and correctly draws the conclusion
that Poe is dealing not with individual elements of experience, or
imagination, but with concepts of experience—with generalized
concepts like 'fear', 'gloom', and the rest:

> 'Cette aptitude à connaître clairement et à observer habituellement certains
> rapports que les artistes ordinaires se bornent à sentir d'instinct, se résume en une
> particularité de constitution cérébrale que l'on peut exprimer comme suit: Chez
> Poe, les émotions se transforment constamment en pensées.'[4]

Hennequin evidently thinks in terms of two 'stages', so to speak,
in the process of knowledge: the humble, 'intuitive' passive reception
of data such as emotions or sensations, and the higher activity whereby
such data are transmuted into the constituent parts of rational thought.
Faced with the alternative of siting art on one or the other of these
two stages, Hennequin (like Taine) chooses the latter, quoting as
authority for his arguments Herbert Spencer. It is hard not to be
surprised at this irruption of the arch-enemy into the symbolist
camp, and the welcome accorded him;[5] until we take into account

---

[1] Verlaine would seem to have been an exception, here as in much else.
[2] Émile Hennequin, 'E. A. Poe', *Revue Contemporaine*, t. i, p. 50, 25/i/1885.
[3] ibid.   [4] ibid.
[5] Even allowing for the early date of the article. Hennequin remains *persona grata* with the
symbolists right up to his death a few years later.

the enormous weight of contemporary tradition represented by
Spencer and his views, and the virtual non-existence of any alternative
respectable philosophy on which the symbolists might ground their
discussion of this type of problem. But equally interesting is Hennequin's apparent inconsistency three years later, when he pushes his
analysis of language a stage further—again under the auspices of
symbolist journalism, this time, indeed, in a symbolist review. With
his important and prominent article 'Le Poétique et le Prosaïque'[1] he
sets out the emotive theory in a new guise, and in terms which appear
to contradict those used in the article on Poe.

Whereas, in the earlier essay he suggests that the true poet turns his
emotion into a thought, now he asserts the familiar duality between
scientific and artistic language: the rational, logical use of the former
is irrelevant to the latter. Of logical discourse he says:

'Absolument parlant, les mots dans cet emploi sont un moyen de science, et les
œuvres qui sont ainsi conçues ne sont littéraires, si elles le sont, que lorsqu'elles
traitent d'objets fictifs[2] inventés ou dénaturés spécialement en vue d'émouvoir
malgré le mode par lequel ils sont représentés.'[3]

This is the emotive theory in its simplest form. Lions are frighten-
ing; confront the hero of your novel with a terrifyingly described
lion, and you frighten the reader. The latter will then thank you
for providing him with an excitement (fictitious, of course), which
the streets he lives in ordinarily cannot afford him. But we do not
usually give the name of art to stuff purveyed to meet this sort of
demand.

He goes on:

'Mais le verbe a d'autres vertus encore que de décrire. Il idéalise, et c'est là son
caractère propre. Que l'on reprenne le substantif chêne' (the example in question):
'seul ce vocable, exprimant un genre, l'exprime par ses caractères génériques saillants
de force, de hauteur, d'ombre, de végétation vigoureuse; l'esprit en le prononçant,
aperçoit vaguement un arbre magnifique, *idéal*... En expressions plus précises,
un mot générique de la sorte qui présente une image trop grande, trop indéfinie
pour être conçue clairement, qui nécessite donc un effort, une tendance insatisfaite
à l'image, provoque dans le mécanisme cérébral comme une décharge suffuse, une
tension croissante; il y a dans l'esprit un mouvement d'expansion, et une description
conçue en termes généraux pareils, qui se limitent le moins possible, sera une description poétique.'

---

[1] *Revue Indépendante*, t. vi, p. 19, i/1888.
[2] Hennequin's perverse insistence on the fictitious grounding of art stems directly from
the conception of art as a means of *arousing* emotion. If in that operation fiction and non-fiction
(so-called) are equally effective, it is plain that 'art' does not benefit from the truth of a representation. And, of course, the resources of fiction are infinitely greater than those of non-fiction.
See, too, Hennequin's *La Critique Scientifique* (1888), *Analyse Esthétique*, for the 'fiction' of art,
set forth as a principle.
[3] 'Le Poétique et le Prosaïque', *Revue Indépendante*, t. vi, p. 19, i/1888.

Comparing the 'scientific' and the 'emotive' uses of language, therefore, in the first case,

'Les mots sont employés à donner des choses une image la plus précise possible, une image intellectuelle qui laisse dans l'esprit peu de place aux sentiments associés';

while in the second case,

'L'image est vague, lointaine, grandie, à peine aperçue, et mystérieusement belle; de l'émotion qu'elle suggère, toute intelligence est exclue ... on peut dire en somme que tout spectacle, toute scène passionnelle et spirituelle qui peut être et qui est exactement décrite, analysée par le menu, cessera d'être poétique; qu'au contraire, tout spectacle qui reste obscur et diffus, étrange et lointain, dont la représentation toute générale et suggestive, mais cohérente cependant, laisse le champ libre aux émotions qui lui sont associées et à celles même qui résultent de son idéalisation, sera poétique.'[1]

Are we to assume that there is a contradiction between the views of 1885 and 1888? For in the earlier position, Poe was an 'analyst' and praised for it; here it is roundly stated that the more exact and analytic a description, the less poetic. In the earlier position, the poet was to use emotive language with the completest foresight of its effect: here he is counselled to use emotive language, but of such a sort that its effect on the reader can in no way be exactly forecast. In the earlier position, good poetry came from emotion translated into thought; here 'toute intelligence est exclue'. Nothing, of course, is more likely than that Hennequin between 1885 and 1888 has had his tastes profoundly modified by the poetry of Verlaine and Mallarmé; has been struck by the attention paid all around him to the importance of a 'suggestive' side to poetry; and has accordingly been forced to reckon with more than was presented to him by the poems of Edgar Allan Poe and the philosophy of Spencer. But the essential problem is one of theory and argument. Does the positivist abandon the symbolic view of language and all that follows from it?

The answer, I think, is No. The 'analysis' ascribed at the earlier date to Poe is not what is eventually present in the poem (i.e. detailed inventory of the raven, feather by feather) but what leads up to the raven being chosen as an image and the poem written: an entirely different application of the term. Similarly, the intellectual element in Poe precedes the poem—is said to be the means by which emotions are turned into thoughts more easily handled by the writer; whereas the 'intelligence' subsequently banished from the sphere of art refers to the exclusion of argument and didactic features. Only on one

[1] op. cit., p. 20. The whole argument is set out at greater length in *La Critique Scientifique* but along substantially the same lines.

point can there be said to be a shift of opinion; namely, the notion of mapping out in advance the emotive force of language. Even this change is not radical. The full effect of a poem may not be entirely predictable, says Hennequin, but that is mainly because of the complexity and richness of the associations invoked; generalizing words like oak (and presumably perching ravens too) are a kind of blank tablet on which the reader shapes his own reaction, but they are none the less emotive ones, and chosen for their emotivity. Nor are they any the less elements in symbolic language, each expressing 'genre' by 'caractères génériques'; that is to say, they are ambiguous (as he now confesses) in their association because as generalizing terms they refer to a multitude of individual possible images and representations; and because of this fact, they are in the truest sense of the word 'descriptions' (just as Hennequin says). The only difference between the descriptive language of science and the descriptive language of poetry is an empirical one—the degree of vagueness; another way of saying that just as scientific (or prosaic) language is symbolic, so, too, is poetic. There is no break between the emotive language of Poe, as Poe and Hennequin describe it, and the allegedly emotive language of symbolism (Verlaine in particular) as Hennequin analyses it three years later. The same theory, the same implications: only set out with some more sophistication and from a slightly different angle (attention is directed on the finished poem instead of on the initial labours of the poet).

(b) *Jules de Gaultier*

Another young critic, this time less closely associated with the movement of literature around Mallarmé, and writing at a slightly later date, has much the same view of the emotive purpose of language in art, and uses it to bring into more prominence a neglected aspect of Taine's *Philosophie de l'art*:

'Le propre de la poésie est d'exprimer tous les entours passionnels du concept, de faire revivre autour du signe verbal toutes les sensations ensevelies dans les termes généraux du langage.'[1]

In this light the poetry of Verlaine, which is here under discussion, is to be looked at as discourse not in essence different from the discourse of science. Poetry is not the simple exteriorization of emotion suggested by the romantic tradition, but on the contrary an activity of *working-back* from a stored-up abstraction to a group of 'phenomenal qualities' in which it may be embodied; and so obviously

[1] Jules de Gaultier, *Revue Blanche*, t. vi, no. 31, p. 402, v/1894.

superior to music. This last conclusion is of more than passing interest in view of the constant analogies which the symbolists made between their art and the music-drama of Wagner: in Jules de Gaultier's approach, rime, rhythm, indeed all the practices and devices of poetry are no more than trappings to give 'stability' to language. Whatever this may mean, one thing is certain; Gaultier's theory of language does not differ materially from Taine's; and as a result his whole aesthetic, laboriously set out in numerous review articles, is open to the objection that it fails to distinguish between art and not-art.

Thus far, views of positivist tendency which reduce art either to sugar-coating or to gratuitous emotional excitation, can scarcely be said to harmonize with the symbolist poet's own awareness of the value of what he was doing.

(c) *Mauclair*

Nearer home, however, the mandarins of symbolist criticism were by no means innocent of taking a few steps down the road to emotionalism. Mauclair, indeed, seems hardly to be aware of the difficulties that lie at the end of the path, and does not usually distinguish between all the possible relations of emotion to poetry; at one moment he takes the emotivist position for granted:

'Il y a deux choses; faire voir et faire sentir. Le premier don est encore de la littérature' (*sc.* in Verlaine's sense). 'Des esprits tres inférieurs y parviennent. Maupassant, par exemple. Mais faire sentir! ce n'est plus le mot qui peut cela, c'est le chant, c'est le grand pouvoir... Or éveiller les sens, c'est tout ensemble montrer, avec une clarté supérieure.'[1]

Here, indeed, the ambiguity allows us to suppose that Mauclair is accurately describing a quality of good art—namely, high expressiveness—in terms recognized through many centuries. But we might equally say that he has in mind nothing more than the emotive account given by Poe (to whom, indeed, he makes frequent and highly flattering references in nearly all his writings on art, aside from a whole book devoted to that writer). Elsewhere again he claims, or seems to claim, that the way in which a poet is understood by his reader is different from the way in which we interpret the symbolic discourse of an argument.[2] 'Un poète n'est pas fait pour être compris, mais pour être senti'; and again, 'Tout naît de l'intuition'.[3] This sounds rather as if Mauclair means that the poet is writing to express himself, as we

---

[1] *Eleusis*, p. 173.   [2] ibid., pp. 149–51.   [3] ibid.

say, and that the reader is overhearing what he says, and recreating the poem for himself. In which case the purely symbolic account of language can be put by, and the way laid open for a more rational one. But in case we should be tempted to make this assumption too easily, it is well to remind ourselves that the book in which these remarks occur is also largely concerned with the poet's function as a priest in a cult, as a 'seer' who uses language as a symbolism of the 'knowledge' disclosed in the ineffable moments of mystical experience. Language is a symbolism for the situations that the poet sees before him or finds himself experiencing; and these in turn are 'symbols' for the experiences of a superior world which simpler beings are not privileged to wander in; so that when Mauclair affirms that 'tout naît de l'intuition', his argument elsewhere compels us to assume this to mean, that the reader of a poem recognizes in it not discursively but immediately the original mystical experience of the poet. Mauclair is silent when it comes to discussing how the language, how the 'symbols', are marshalled; in other words, we have no conclusive grounds for supposing that he ever questioned the symbolic account of language. Yet in this theory there is little enough room for 'intuition'. So here we are brought face to face with what we have already noted as one of the most persistent features of symbolist theory: rejection in part of those aspects of 'uncompromising realism'[1] which clash blatantly with what the artist knows to be the facts of aesthetic experience, side by side with a casual, but inevitable, acceptance of the underlying tenets of the theory.

The result, as we have suggested, is to cast about for some means to evade acknowledging a glaring contradiction in aesthetic analysis. If language is a conventional system of signs and nothing more, how can the sign gain more value (aesthetically) than the signified thing? How can two plus two be made to equal five? The answer given by Mauclair, in common with most of the posterity of Baudelaire, is to appeal to the arithmetic of mysticism in which one of the twos is really a three; in plain speech, to claim that a chair is not a chair, but a 'symbol' of a transcendental Idea of a chair, the contemplation of which is aesthetically valuable.[2]

---

[1] So Professor A. N. Whitehead termed the symbolic theory of language (in *Symbolism, its meaning and uses*, 1926).

[2] 'De la langue et de l'écriture, prises comme opérations magiques, sorcellerie évocatoire' (Baudelaire, *Fusées*, p. 82). Is there anything to indicate that by this Baudelaire wishes us to suppose the operation of writing poetry to *add* anything of value to the objects evoked? Baudelaire's aesthetic, with its essentially mystic twist, positively *requires* the symbolic theory of language as a basis on which to build the doctrine of literary symbols.

There are other examples besides Mauclair's of the dilemma of symbolists not fully able to escape from the positivist net; a few widely differing examples will suffice to illustrate the tension. In each one, however, there may be discerned the same fundamental assumption regarding the symbolic foundation if not of language in principle, at least of language in poetry.

3. PARTIAL REVOLTS FROM THE 'SYMBOLIC' THEORY

(a) Kahn

In the case of Kahn, the most fanciful notions on the correlation between writing and thought down the ages rests on the assumption that language exists at base to subserve intellectual needs: the upshot is that contemporary thought tends to 'ramener à un plus petit nombre de principes une plus grande multiplicité'; that this in turn must lead to changes in current modes of expression; and that in the interests of 'flexibility' the old grammatical distinctions must be broken down: 'il n'y a pas de terme exactement adjectif ou substantif'.[1]

The modifications that are to be introduced into speech under the auspices of the new poetry are thus justified as following new needs in logical—or at least intellectual—discourse. No more eloquent testimony could be found to Kahn's essential adherence to the 'symbolic theory'. (What is so curious is his assumption that poetry is to be the advance-guard of language reform; when the 'developments' brought about are justified simply on the grounds that they are required by new levels and new techniques of intellectual discourse).

(b) Wyzéwa

So too with Téodor de Wyzéwa, who speaks of 'les notions, groupes de sensations fixés dans l'esprit par des noms', and concludes therefrom—or rather assumes no demonstration to be necessary—that literature is the 'art des notions'; thence that it had (formerly)[2] words as 'signs'; and that also 'par les mots des langages, la littérature recrée les notions'.[3] Again, no suggestion that language has any function more primitive than the already highly intellectual one of expressing 'notions', or in other words establishing relations: that is, acting as a symbolism. The slight modification of this view to suit the case of poetry will be noted later in this chapter.

---

[1] Cf. Beaunier, *La Poésie Nouvelle*, p. 105, and *L'Art Symboliste*, 1889, ed. Vanor.
[2] Written signs having now replaced spoken ones.
[3] *Revue Wagnérienne*, vi/1886. Reproduced in *Nos Maîtres*, p. 31.

(c) Gaultier

If we return for a moment to Jules de Gaultier, we find, expressed almost as an afterthought to the views noted above, an hypothesis which on first sight appears to come much closer to the type of expressive theory which might be of service to the new poetic:

> 'L'hypothèse serait séduisante d'imaginer que, par une analogue évolution, la poésie fut la forme primitive du langage, que les hommes lui substituèrent par la suite un idiome plus abstrait, à l'aide duquel ils édifièrent les idées générales, les systèmes scientifiques et philosophiques, puis que, ce truchement nouveau ne répondant plus qu'aux besoins les plus arides de leur intelligence, ils essayèrent désespérément de retrouver la langue du passé qui savait exprimer la totalité de leur émotion. La poésie, celle des bons poètes, serait le résultat de cet effort pour faire revivre l'ancien sens.'[1]

Evidently the writer of such a paragraph has moved a great way from the naïve conception of language of a Kahn or a Wyzéwa. The salient feature here is that the language of poetry is not a more intellectualized language than that of rational discourse (as Mallarmé seems sometimes to be claiming) or even in principle an equally intellectualized one (as Kahn thinks), but something logically antecedent; an activity without which logical discourse could not come into existence, but which in itself does not suppose the existence of this latter. In speaking of 'la totalité de leur émotion' and an expressive function, indeed, we are in the presence of something on the face of it quite modern in its way of looking at primitive language. But the movement of thought in Jules de Gaultier's time should put us on our guard against identifying him as an anticipator of Croce. For Lévy-Bruhl and Durkheim have also analysed primitive language with an eye to its 'total' aspect, or the 'conscience collective' which seems to be implied in it, without in any way concluding that language was an integral part in *all* imaginative activity: and more recently, developing these perspectives, critics have professed to see in the symbolist movement as a whole a faithful return to the *conscience collective* such as had not been seen before in European art and letters. In each of these cases, despite professions to the contrary, language has been assumed to be a symbolism; and palpable departures from this assumption, when detected, have been virtually shut off in a separate field, as 'magic', 'ritual hypnotism,' or the like. So here, Gaultier soon involves himself in contradictions. In the passage already quoted, it it significant that he should call good poetry

---

[1] *Revue Blanche*, t. vi, no. 31, p. 396, v/1894.

the result of an effort 'pour faire revivre l'ancien sens'—he too, as later Lévy-Bruhl and Cailliet, assumes that this 'ancien sens' has been lost in modern times; this being the result of a *substitution* of an abstract discourse for a concrete one. Here the assumption reaps its own reward instantly:

'Le mot fut antérieurement un signe phonétique, c'est-à-dire, un cri modulé, et un simple cri ... en tant que cri il exprima directement l'émotion physiologique ressentie par notre ancêtre...'[1]

In what sense can one talk of the expression of a physiological emotion being 'modulated'—that is to say, deliberately controlled by some sort of conscious activity? The tingling sensation in our spine when we are gripped by an uncontrollable fear, or the cry we utter when we fall downstairs certainly 'expresses' what Gaultier calls a 'physiological emotion'; but if someone steps on our foot the equivalent expression is an inarticulate reflex movement of some kind or other, and not the remarks we pass 'to relieve our feelings'. Indeed, if poetry were of the order of expression represented by such reflex actions—vocal or otherwise—it is hard to see how we could ever make comparisons of aesthetic value between different cries (we could merely measure cries as quantities in different ways); whereas it is a well-known fact that some people are capable of relieving their feelings a lot more expressively (as we say) than others—and that not through any accident or for any purely 'physiological' reasons. Plainly, it is not enough to talk of an evolution of language from a merely uncontrolled, animal stage straight to a conceptualized and abstract vehicle of discourse: if the latter stage is already too abstract to provide a full account of the language of poetry, the former is not yet human at all. Gaultier is right to say of music that 'elle note un état d'âme antérieur à la formation du concept';[2] but it is interesting to see him conclude that 'le modèle qu'elle imite est la vibration nerveuse elle-même'. Why is it that he cannot find an adequate place for art in his table of the forms of human activity? The answer must be looked for in the assumptions of a positivist theory of knowledge, which it never occurred to him to question, and in which we have already observed the lack of suitable accommodation for an account of imagination. The two cases are not only parallel but connected; on the positivist model there is no stage in knowledge intermediate between intuition and conception, to the latter of which art

[1] op. cit., p. 397.   [2] op. cit., p. 401.

is therefore assigned; for Taine, therefore, the language of art was purely symbolic, as befits its conceptual language; now Gaultier ventures the hypothesis that as this seems to be contradicted by experience (and particularly by the experience of the symbolist movement) the alternative might be looked for in a form of language corresponding to the needs of intuition. The result is to furnish a passive function of experience with a (necessarily) involuntary form of expression. Such involuntary expression does exist, in animals and men alike, but it is not art; and Gaultier, in a reasonable effort to ascribe art to a fairly primitive level of experience, has overshot the mark.

The example is instructive; like greater thinkers than himself, at a later date, Gaultier feels the inadequacy of the 'symbolic' theory of language; he attempts to correct it, and fails; the positivist anthropologists, with a more seductive and refined hypothesis, seem to fare better; but do not in the end succeed in showing how art is anything more than a primitive survival in an intellectualized age.

(d) Gourmont

Much the same thing happens to Rémy de Gourmont, under not very different circumstances. In an essay entitled 'Une loi de constance intellectuelle'[1] he writes:

'Le langage a dû être d'abord purement musical, sans aucun accord avec la réalité' (i.e. presumably not symbolizing conceptually abstracted elements of experience) 'mais ponctué de signes de joie, de peur, d'appel' (this last is surely an inappropriate example) '... Comme l'oiseau, comme le singe, l'homme a d'abord parlé pour lui-même, c'est-à-dire sans intention ... mouvement de langue et de gorge analogues à tous les autres mouvements musculaires, signes de vie... '

Very likely; but the acid test of an aesthetic is whether it allows art to occupy a position superior to this activity (in the sense of being deliberate, and not involuntary) yet 'inferior' to that of rationalized discourse (in the sense of not being yet cut up into purely arbitrary signs); and it is notorious that Rémy de Gourmont was never able to strike this mean; one writer[2] describes him as oscillating between the extremes of 'idealism' and 'materialism', and his view of the nature of the language of art oscillates similarly between the intellectualism of Taine and the virtual automatism of Gaultier's hypothesis. But in the main, Rémy de Gourmont as an aesthetician is concerned with combating in divers ways the logical conclusions

---

[1] *Promenades Philosophiques*, II, 1908, pp. 72–3.
[2] Bencze. His description is not a happy one, but it conforms with Gourmont's own terminology.

of the former, rather than advancing views similar to those of the latter; and invariably we find some interruption of logical continuity to show us that the analysis of direct observation on the one boundary of his aesthetic is never extended to the point where it could overturn on the other the assumption of a primarily symbolic theory of language.

For, ironical though it may seem, the generation which brought the symbolist movement into being was solid on one point of aesthetic doctrine; namely, on this assumption which much of their individual detailed speculation and study tended to undermine. Some among their number give no sign of recognizing any conflict of doctrine such as we are about to survey; but by and large, they appear to have allowed this one fatal error to take root in their minds, at a point below the level to which they were accustomed to pursue their enquiry: the assumption that an intellectual element, an element of reference, was the fundamental mark of language under all circumstances whatever. This element once noted, the interesting and important thing in each individual case is to see at what point a contradiction arises between the implications of the 'symbolic theory' and the data provided by personal experience and introspection.

In so far as the points of intersection and conflict are largely grouped around three or four main issues as slogans, it has been the custom to define the symbolist movement in literature in terms of these convenient slogans; thus we say that the symbolists were preoccupied by the nature of music and its relation to poetry; that they were anti-intellectualists or mystics; that they thought art was in some sense symbolical or symbolist (as opposed here to 'representative'); that they popularized *vers libre*, and by implication attacked all rigid formalism in art,[1] and so on. Such a system of labels has the advantages of an introduction—simplicity, hence opportunity for elegant exposition and misleading lucidity—but it falls (as all histories of literature must fall) between two stools: on the one hand, it sacrifices exactitude of detail to generalization; on the other, it renounces all claim to more extensive generalization and comparison than its ill-defined labels allow. Of the four slogans instanced, we have already examined 'anti-intellectualism'; in a subsequent chapter we shall deal at length with the enormous and tangled issue of 'symbols' (in the literary sense); for the rest of the present chapter we shall attend to two simpler cruxes that follow on from the general dis-

---

[1] And formal distinctions between the arts as well.

cussion of language; 'musicality' and anti-formalism, and the various topics of controversy that attach to them.

4. MALLARMÉ AND THE 'MUSIC' OF POETRY

It would be well, in setting out to examine the position of music in the symbolist aesthetic, to start with an important dissociation of ideas. The word Music has, in our inquiry, two references. In the first place, it may lead us to compare the empirical character of poetry with that of music as a separate art. This involves mainly an examination of the part played in poetry by assonance and dissonance, alliteration, onomatopoea, rhythm and rime, seen as rough equivalents to the much more clear-cut and systematic harmony, counterpoint, and musical form generally. Such comparisons, in moderation, are always interesting, or at least diverting; in excess, they produce the monstrosities of the 'école instrumentiste' which, except as freaks, have little interest: such aberrations result from a too literal acceptance of the dictum that all art aspires to the condition of music. In the second place, it may lead us to examine what it is in music that has an essentially aesthetic value (and music was in some ways a more accessible field for this inquiry than poetry or painting in an age reared on a more or less positivist approach to art); and with the insight so obtained to attempt a new formulation of the aesthetically valuable in poetry. These two connotations of 'music' as (*a*) a gamut of sounds, and (*b*) the heightened quality of poetic language, are in practice inseparable, but in principle entirely distinct. It is sufficient to quote, with Henri Bremond, the line of Malherbe:

'Et les fruits passeront la promesse des fleurs'

to see that the specially poetic quality of verse depends on more than a mere arrangement of sounds in an autonomous pattern; the repeated 'p's and 'f's in this example, an intricate vowel pattern, and so forth: these sounds are indeed part of the charm; but taken in abstraction they are not the achievement of poetry; a man knowing no French would not find beauty in such a line. Any group of sounds at all must exhibit some sort of order or pattern; but that is not to suggest that *appropriateness* plays no part in determining the beauty of verse, any more than in music mere concord or discord is in itself valuable.

Poetry makes deliberate use of certain combinations of sound in its language to which prose is ordinarily indifferent; but for all that, valuation of poetry does not—even for the symbolist—rest on any intrinsic quality of such combinations. This said, we can proceed to see how the two connotations of 'music' were associated and dissociated in the minds of the later nineteenth-century writers.

As our principal example we cannot do better than choose Mallarmé, for it is around his work and under the influence of his ideas that the controversy on music took shape in its most lively and intelligent form. In him, too, our dissociation takes on an added point: for it was not until relatively late in life that Mallarmé began to take an interest in music, at the instance of Dujardin; and even then it is open to doubt whether what he attended to at the Lamoureux concerts was really Wagner's *music* at all. From the way in which he talks and writes, it appears almost certain that like so many other great users of speech, Mallarmé is under the necessity of translating music into a succession of associated visual and other images before he can discuss it: very much as for Goethe the music of Bach suggested nobly dressed figures walking up and down a grand staircase.[1] What is more, the poetry of Mallarmé does not often display an ostentatious attention to heavy alliteration or assonance: a contemporary, discussing his earlier works, remarked:

'Ils montrent que M. Mallarmé n'a apporté dans l'Art ni la vision naturelle et précise d'images, ni une disposition naturelle à la musique des mots... M. Mallarmé ne s'attarde pas aux menues variations musicales: il n'a point l'instinctif besoin de recherches formelles: il n'est point le naïf guitariste que nous révèlent par exemple les œuvres de M. Verlaine... '[2]

Making allowance for the youthfulness of the critic, and the measure of error in the judgement, we can see quite plainly the sense in which Mallarmé was not thought to be a typically 'musical' poet, as opposed to Verlaine—say the Verlaine of the *Romances sans Paroles*. But the same writer, in the same article, eight pages further on, appears first to succumb to the temptation of musical metaphor (extraordinarily common in the symbolist era!) and then to go on in good earnest to the second connotation of the word:

'Le sujet apparaît clairement, sous les modulations environnantes des syllabes musicales, comme apparaît, dans une figure' (*sic*: 'fugue'?) 'le thème fondamental, malgré le conflit incessant des contre-sujets. Parfois le poète doit, pour les besoins de la musique — n'est-elle pas le but essentiel? — employer des métaphores et des périphrases.'[3]

Evidently Wyzéwa is not contradicting his previous denial of 'musical' qualities to Mallarmé's verse, but using the word to mean

---

[1] Wagner shared this failing; that does not prevent musicians from enjoying his music who are entirely free from it.

[2] Wyzéwa, 'Mallarmé:Notes', *Vogue*, 5/vii/1886, p. 366.   [3] ibid., pp. 374–5.

something different, something essentially similar to the 'music' of Malherbe's line; something which is perhaps shown in greater complexity in Mallarmé than in earlier writers, but which runs through all poetry. Having said which, it is perhaps best to have this something described in Mallarmé's own words:

'Toute âme est une mélodie, qu'il s'agit de renouer; et pour cela, sont la flûte ou la viole de chacun.'[1]

Poetry involves the exteriorization, or even the construction, of a state. A state of what? 'Âme' is an extraordinarily vague word; even if we take it in its usual literary sense of the seat of the emotions, we still do not know quite what sort of emotion is implied; whether the purely 'physiological' emotion suggested by Gaultier, or the studied and artificial emotion of a soap-box orator, or some other kind of emotion yet. It is likely that Mallarmé, if faced with the choice, would have rejected the first two of these alternatives without hesitation; it is certain that he never deeply explored the possibilities or implications of a third; we have seen already (pt. I, 60 f.) that the theory of 'Ideas', which led him equally to base art on the treatment in some form of feeling and emotion, was not the account most fitted to a satisfactory development. So that the information conveyed by this elegant remark takes us not a great way. Nor does the parallel remark of Wyzéwa (in connection with *L'Après-midi d'un Faune*):

'Desireux d'exprimer un sujet par la musique des mots, il devait adopter d'abord un sujet musical, c'est-à-dire, un état émotionnel de l'âme, ensemble homogène et complexe.'[2]

This would suggest that the emotional state *was* the 'musical subject'; if the 'musical subject' or 'emotional state' expresses 'the subject', it is hard to see what there is left for this 'subject' to be. The *état d'âme*, however, might very well be assumed to be the subject in question, standing in some sort of relation, other than simple equivalence, to the 'sujet musical', which *expresses* it, this last being obviously the theme or topic—e.g. the Faun and his musings. Such a correction certainly corresponds with the example Mallarmé elsewhere gives (in *La Musique et les Lettres*, see above, pt. I, p. 65) of the essential being the *horror* of the forest, and not the exact delineation of its trees and branches.[3] It seems, when he speaks of the great

[1] *Divagations*, p. 241. The phrase is precious, but the meaning is clear.
[2] 'Les Livres', *Revue Indépendante*, t. ii, p. 337, iii/1887. The earlier affirmation of Mallarmé's lack of musical sense (quoted above, p. 150) makes an instructive contrast with this.
[3] Cf., too, the much cruder and less mature remark: 'Une poétique très nouvelle, que je pourrais définir en ces deux mots: peindre non la chose, mais l'effet qu'elle produit' (Letter to Cazalis, x/1864, in *Propos sur la Poésie*, ed. Mondor, 1945, p. 43).

work which it is his ambition to write, 'le Livre', and of its contents
'qui n'a que faire de rien outre la musicalité de tout', that this is indeed
the sense which music has for him; that as a system of fixed notes,
music proper has no advantage over poetry, and that its pre-eminence
is rather negative—i.e. a relative freedom from the intellectualist
misinterpretations under which poetry is so liable to suffer. This
impression is further strengthened when we consider his observations
on the lyrical plays of Maeterlinck, which are voided of representative
and purely descriptive elements—

> '... Au point que dans cet art où tout devient musique dans le sens propre' (!)
> 'la partie d'un instrument, même pensif, violon, nuirait par inutilité.'[1]

How else, too, in the famous description of Ideas in art (pt. I, p. 62
above) can we take 'musicalement', save as referring to this particular
element which in music is so much more obviously present than in
much speech, even much verse—namely, its expressiveness of an
attitude, an 'emotional' attitude in the widest sense of the words?

In this perspective, of course, all language whatever, not only al
speech, but the language of gesture, of painting, of sculpture, is in
some degree musical. Musical here means simply 'expressive'.
Mallarmé sees this clearly in the case of ballet, which in fact he
appears to have appreciated and enjoyed far more than opera or
music-drama; and we have noted how for him the Idea could be
expressed as well by a dancer's gesture as by a phrase of poetry
(pt. I, p. 65 above).[3] When it comes to speech and its symbolized
form, writing, he was misled by habitual over-simplification into
supposing that two mutually exclusive provinces existed, the one
poetical, musical, the other prosaic, 'commercial', destitute of
aesthetic value. The division, at first sight, appears to be the same as
that enunciated by positivism and much other aesthetic philosophy

[1] *Divagations*, p. 221. His reactions to Debussy's *Pelléas et Mélisande* would have been
interesting. It may be remembered that in this setting the orchestra is several times silent at
moments of ~~moments of~~ significance.

[2] The same ambiguity occurs between the larger sense of 'musical' poetry (i.e. highly
expressive) and the smaller (i.e. full of alliteration, assonance, or onomatopoeia) as between
the larger sense of beauty (i.e. great expressiveness) and the smaller (i.e. debased sentimental-
ism). See Bosanquet, *Three Lectures on Aesthetic*, 1915, ch. III.

[3] This, incidentally, should demonstrate once for all that Mallarmé's 'Idea', if it could be
formulated, was in no way at all related with Plato's. For Plato an Idea is a Universal: e.g.
whiteness; something irrevocably intelligible; the result of abstraction. Even Mallarmé would
not have claimed that the dancer's step could ever refer to a Universal, or be intended to;
indeed, it can hardly refer to anything at all, except by an arbitrary symbolism which is in
principle absent from pure ballet. As a poet, his anxiety to avoid the intellectual realism of
much of Parnasse, led him to suppose that if a word or phrase in a poem did not refer to a speci-
fied historical individual, it must refer to a Universal. But when he speaks in terms of music
he assumes that a word is not aesthetically valuable for its reference at all; words used for their
references are 'reportage'.

down the ages: namely, between the scientific and the emotive use of
language; but this is by no means proven, and we shall have shortly
to state the evidence for and against such an identification. For the
instant it does not concern us except in one of its implications: that
there is no poetry in prose, or at any rate that a piece of prose could
be found which would be completely outside the realm of aesthetic
valuation.

This thesis is explicitly stated in the *Divagations*:

'Parler n'a trait à la réalité des choses que commercialement: en littérature cela
se contente d'y faire une allusion ou de distraire leur qualité qu'incorporera quelque
idée.'[1]

'Un désir indéniable à mon temps est de séparer comme en vue d'attributions
différentes le double état de la parole, brut ou immédiat ici, là essentiel.

'Narrer, enseigner, même décrire, cela va et encore qu'à chacun suffirait peut-
être pour échanger la pensée humaine, de prendre ou de mettre dans la main d'autrui
en silence une pièce de monnaie, l'emploi élémentaire du discours dessert l'universel
reportage, dont, la littérature exceptée, participe tout entre les genres d'écrit contemporains.'[2]

Mallarmé scarcely deigns to give his attention to these non-
literary 'genres d'écrit contemporains'; but he has said enough to
make it clear that he sees in them one thing only: their adaptation of
language as a *symbolic* medium of communication. Each word or
unit of reference is a coin; and the essential thing about coins is that
they represent an arbitrary money value: they are to that extent
the creatures of reason, and the convention of their symbolic value
gives them their currency. That this is a feature of rational discourse,
whether it be journalistic 'reportage', commercial letters, or philosophic speculation, will hardly be challenged. Thought and its communication plainly depend on fixed, or relatively fixed, symbolic
language, however we care to analyse such symbolism. But it
has been asked, more than once, if symbolic language requires prior
agreement on the symbols, by the use of what language was this
agreement reached in the first place? To look at the same problem
from a slightly different angle, can we say that 'reportage' is ever
entirely destitute of any quality which might bring it into the same
perspective of aesthetic judgement as poetry? What of the *Divagations* themselves, with their amazingly tortuous but often brilliantly
effective style of writing? Would they have done as well, in the eyes
of their maker, translated into, say, the prose of Mendès' *Rapport*?
Does what is vulgarly called the *style* of a prose writer, even the bad
style of a bad journalist, fall outside the scope of the aesthetic judge-

[1] *Divagations*, p. 246.   [2] ibid., p. 250.

ment? Obviously not; if it did, we should not even be able to say that it is a 'bad' (i.e. aesthetically bad) style; and it is surprising that with his polite interest in *vers libre* and his prose poems, not to mention the challenging *Un Coup de Dés*, Mallarmé should have been content to renounce so easily the general problem of language in its less obvious fields of application, and erect instead a wall between what one might call 'pure' and 'applied' literature, where, in principle, and indeed in the day-to-day practice of criticism, no such division can ever be interposed.

For one part of his analysis of language, then, we must admit with regret that Mallarmé did not see his way round the impasse of the positivist account which dominated his age—an impasse which has, of course, no inconvenience for the logician or the practical man of science, even though it is awkward for the literary critic and fatal to the aesthetician. Perhaps it is the less important part of the analysis; Mallarmé at least held it to have nothing to do with aesthetic proper; but it cannot for all that be overlooked, for his position on 'reportage' if it did nothing else, forced him to advance theories on poetry which had *ex hypothesi* to be contrasted or opposed,[1] and from this there follow the inevitable distortions. One of these is the theory of Ideas which has already been discussed. Another is the support which his position lent to an already obtrusive tendency to preciosity of all kinds.

When we examine the other side of the picture, Mallarmé's account of language subserving the needs of poetry, no such fallacious simplicity is to be found. On the contrary, we see a man possessing the most acute powers of aesthetic observation, and the most scrupulous attention to the findings of introspection, obliged at almost every moment to think and reason against the stream of accepted beliefs; challenging all the major canons of realist aesthetic, reaching out desperately for help to every artist of the century that promised some sort of guidance—Baudelaire, Poe, Wagner, Manet; snatching at fragments of theory that seemed to support and express what he himself intuitively felt; turning from one set of terms to another in an effort to formulate his discoveries clearly; never coming within reach of a unified and consecutively arranged account of art, but acutely conscious that his experience of writing could in principle, and should in practice, be described in a coherent aesthetic;

[1] Cf. 'Tout ce que vous faites en ce moment illustre cette donnée exacte qu'il faut, si l'on fait de la littérature, parler autrement que les journaux' (Letter to Moréas, 28/x/1886). In such ways are very simple concrete issues—the escapism and preciosity of a sensitive intelligentsia, for example—mirrored in the *emphasis* of quite abstract theory.

and only at the last, baffled by an apparently fruitless task, simplifying his problems by an appeal to the mysterious and the irreducable, by a capitulation of reason to mysticism. In the *Divagations*, the occasional articles and addresses, the correspondence with fellow-poets, there is evidence of an attitude both inspiring and depressing: inspiring when he destroys or attacks, depressing when his own alternatives are confused or obscurantist. Were we confronted by a lesser figure such feelings would probably not arise.

Let it be repeated at the outset that whatever Mallarmé says about poetry is intended to be applicable, *mutatis mutandis*, to the other arts, and that when he speaks of poetry he means something wider than the mere outward forms of verse and prosody; this, indeed, he characterizes as one of the main 'discoveries' of symbolism:

'Une majestueuse idée inconsciente, à savoir que la forme appelée vers est simplement elle-même la littérature; que vers il y a sitôt que s'accentue la diction, rythme dès que style.'[1]

And he adds, significantly for our argument,

'Toute la langue, ajustée à la métrique, y recouvrant ses coupes vitales, s'évade, selon une libre disjonction aux mille éléments simples; et je l'indiquerai, pas sans similitude avec la multiplicité des cris d'une orchestration, qui reste verbale.'

The metaphor of the musician and of the dancer is never far away from his pen. The (logically) first attack on the positivist account of art deals with the relation of the creative writer with his audience. If this were the same as that of a shopkeeper, or newspaper-man, it would follow that the most important thing about writing a poem should be the fact that it was intended to satisfy a specific demand. This is the assumption that lurks at the back of the *Genesis of a Poem*; but it is quite remote from Mallarmé: on the contrary, in *Quant au livre* he has some unusually bitter words for the commercial press and market for books, ending with the whimsical remark: 'A quoi bon trafiquer de ce qui, peut-être, ne se doit vendre, surtout quand cela ne se vend pas'.[2] Of all gestures, those of singing seem to him the most free from degrading ulterior purposes.

The relation of supply and demand, then, has no bearing on the aesthetic problem of communication; the artist does not write with premeditation to arouse this or that specific required feeling. Rather it is suggested that the artist is simply 'L'homme chargé de voir divinement';[3] a whole Divagation is devoted ('Solitude') to the advan-

---

[1] Apropos of Hugo's metrical innovations. *Divagations*, pp. 236-7.
[2] ibid., p. 271.　　　[3] ibid., p. 273.

tages of not giving to the world that which is clear in one's own mind
but is certain to become twisted and distorted by other people of
different views; and for that matter, Mallarmé's neglect of the idea
of writing for an audience is notorious.[1]

But it is properly in his reflection on the 'musical' quality of poetry,
that, as we should expect, the self-sufficiency of creation is brought
home to him most clearly:

'Au contraire d'une fonction de numéraire facile et représentatif, comme le trait
d'abord la foule, le dire, avant tout, rêve et chant, retrouve chez le poète, par
nécessité constitutive d'un art consacré aux fictions, sa virtualité.'[2]

Dreams and song are not naturally the objects of commercial interchange; a poet 'sings' not for someone else but for himself. Others
are free to hear, but have no business to call the tune. The maid-
of-all-work, 'musicality', is now equivalent to nothing less than
lyricism. But 'lyricism' is a term not exhausted by the romantic
formula; and the paragraph that follows this statement, which we
shall notice in another context, makes clear that Mallarmé is not
lapsing into crude emotionalism. Although Mallarmé never comes to
give a more explicit statement of his view of the artist as essentially
a *doer* and not a *communicator* of deeds, there can be no reasonable
doubt but that he was firmly committed to it: despite its appearance
of paradox to the nineteenth-century approach, it follows logically
from the conception of musicality as the value-concept in poetry.

If the replacement of 'communicator' by 'creator' is the first
correction in the theory of language, the second surely deals with
the way these two theoretical figures operate on language. Here
Mallarmé is extremely explicit; so much so, in fact, that the preceding conjecture might almost be inferred from his position here.
In the paragraph just referred to, in *Crise de Vers*, he writes:

'Le vers qui de plusieurs vocables refait un mot total, neuf, étranger à la langue
et comme incantatoire, achève cet isolement de la parole: niant d'un trait souverain
le hasard demeuré aux termes malgré l'artifice de leur retrempe alternée en le sens e
la sonorité, et vous cause cette surprise de n'avoir ouï jamais tel fragment ordinaire
d'élocution, en même temps que la réminiscence de l'object nommé baigne dans une
atmosphère neuve.'[3]

The great question-mark in this statement is contained in the word
'hasard', surely the most frequently misunderstood and most consistently abused jargon term that is to be found in all writing on the
poetry of Mallarmé and Valéry. Yet it stands for a very important

---

[1] Thibaudet's treatment of this side of Mallarmé's aesthetic is excellent (*La poésie de Stéphane Mallarmé*).
[2] *Divagations*, p. 251.　　　[3] ibid.

aesthetic concept. So far from being obscure, or in the least degree perverse, I think that any aesthetic worth the name must introduce it under one name or another.

Its significance is perhaps best illustrated by the use Mallarmé makes of it at an early date, in a letter to Coppée. On one of these typical occasions when he gives his fellow-writers an opinion on their work, with an exquisite tact that all but dissimulates an adverse criticism, we find:

'Le hasard n'entraîne pas un vers, c'est la grande chose. Nous avons, plusieurs, atteint cela, et je crois que, les lignes si parfaitement délimitées, ce à quoi nous devons viser surtout est que, dans le poème, les mots, qui déjà sont assez eux pour ne plus recevoir d'impression du dehors — se reflètent les uns sur les autres jusqu'à paraître ne plus avoir leur couleur propre, mais n'être que les transitions d'une gamme. Sans qu'il y ait d'espace entre eux, et quoiqu'ils se touchent à merveille, je crois que quelquefois vos mots vivent un peu trop de leur propre vie, comme les pierreries d'une mosaïque de joyaux.'[1]

And a parallel remark, couched in curiously similar terms, recurs twenty-four years later in Mallarmé's contribution to Huret's *Enquête*:

'L'enfantillage de la littérature jusqu'ici a été de croire par exemple que choisir un certain nombre de pierres précieuses et en mettre les noms sur le papier, même très bien, c'était *faire* des pierres précieuses. Eh bien, non ... si véritablement les pierres précieuses dont on se pare ne manifestent pas un état d'âme, c'est indûment qu'on s'en pare.'[2]

These two statements taken together constitute not only Mallarmé's approach to the poet's creative use of language but a fair account of what any artist does with his medium. A few words of explanation will sharpen the outlines of the doctrine.

The single word is a jewel, inescapably in some sort the unit of construction in poetry—though not simply by virtue of there being a space left on either side of it on the printed page: no one, ordinarily, would call pronouns, articles, prepositions, conjunctions, and so forth jewels' of speech. Evidently the only sense in which a word has the value of a jewel is the sense in which it is poetical, evocative, in some way striking. Already in Plato's *Cratylus* some words were observed to seem specially fit and appropriate to their tasks; Mallarmé has considerable familiarity with this fact, and also with the opposite phenomenon:

'Mon sens regrette que le discours défaille à exprimer les objets par des touches y répondant en coloris ou en allure, lesquelles existent dans l'instrument de la voix, parmi les langages et quelquefois chez un. A côté d'*ombre*, opaque, *ténèbres* se fonce

---

[1] *Propos sur la Poésie*, p. 75, letter of 5/xii/1866.   [2] Huret's *Enquête*, 1891, p. 62.

peu; quelle déception, devant la perversité conférant à *jour* comme à *nuit*, contradic-
toirement, des timbres obscurs ici, là clairs. Le souhait d'un terme de splendeur
brillant, ou qu'il s'éteigne, inverse; quant à des alternatives lumineuses, simples —
'*Seulement, sachons, n'existerait pas le vers*: lui, philosophiquement, rémunère le
défaut des langues, complément supérieur.'[1]

And he bases the whole existence of poetry on the insufficiency of
words, as words, to strike the right note—the note required by the
poet's *état d'âme*, his *attitude*. In a sense, of course, words are logical
abstractions; but in their concrete use they can only be 'jewels' on
condition that the 'effect' of the experience they refer to is more or
less adequately expressed; and in this perspective there are very few
poems in existence made out of one word. Mallarmé assumes in
any case that the effect to be depicted (I use his own term) is more
complex than anything that a single word could ever hope to cover;
and hence a larger-scale construct, the *verse*, is called for. By an
earlier definition we know that this can be of virtually any formal
pattern, loose or strict (though he himself usually preferred the
latter);[2] the simile of the jewelled decoration is a good one to describe
how the language of poetry must be fused together, so that the verse
is as indissolubly one as a poem of a single word, and any obtrusive
construction of sentences quite obliterated. It is a commonplace,
in talking of Mallarmé's poetry, to remark that all suggestion of
'reportage' is excluded by a quite remarkable distortion of the
normal forms of sentence construction; this in the field of composition is the direct illustration of the principle he sets out, that the
longest verse should have as much musical unity, as much emotional
and stylistic coherence, as the smallest, or as any evocative *word*.

In this task, which the ancients referred to indirectly in another
plane of composition when they spoke of the unity of action in drama,
the poet cannot logically ever fully satisfy himself: a fact clearly seen
by Valéry.[3] As the poem nears completion on one level of adequacy,
unevennesses on another and more exacting level come into view.

---

[1] *Divagations*, p. 242.
[2] As he admitted: 'Oh, plus nous étendons la somme de nos impressions et les raréfions,
que d'autre part avec une vigoureuse synthèse d'esprit, nous groupions tout cela dans des vers
marqués fort, tangibles, inoubliables' (Letter in Ghil, *Les Dates et les Oeuvres*, p. 17). The
precaution was, for him, a wise one—one can hardly think of him without recalling the perfection of many famous lines; but what would his extreme preciosity have turned to in *vers
libre*?
[3] The argument that the poet cannot write at all if he sets himself a transcendentally high
standard is, I suppose, one way of setting a limit to frail human genius. A sterility of this
kind, it is widely known, dogged Mallarmé from a very early date. Valéry, more rationally,
did not identify his intentions with the limiting ideal of poetic beauty; cf. 'La conception de
poésie pure est celle d'un type inaccessible, d'une limite idéale des désirs, des efforts et des
puissances d'un poète' (*Calephin d'un poète*).

Mallarmé did not deliver himself openly and clearly on this question of whether artistic perfection is conceivable in theory or in practice; like all poets, he set himself an empirical standard, and considered a poem more or less complete when it conformed or seemed to him to conform with the requirements of this standard; until it did, he remained unsatisfied and worked on. Starting with brute language, where palpably unsatisfactory expressions abound on all sides and go unnoticed in ordinary discourse, he held it to be the poet's task to eliminate the disorder and replace it by language in the highest degree 'musical'; that is to say, knit together, flowing, the 'words' interacting to the point where they are comparable to a melody in which the alteration of a single note would destroy the effectiveness of the whole sentence.[1] From the point of view of the poet, the one quality that runs through all language in its amorphous brute state is randomness, lack of complete appropriateness; or as Mallarmé calls it, 'Le Hasard'.[2] As compared with what Valéry and Thibaudet later baptized 'la chance', this 'hasard' marks the unsuccessful attempt, or even the lack of attempt, to command language—to the reader the two failings are indistinguishable, and amount to the same thing.

Thus when Mallarmé speaks of verse overcoming 'le hasard demeuré aux termes' despite 'L'artifice de leur retrempe alternée en le sens et la sonorité', he is describing the effort by which the poet overcomes the brute unpoetical quality of unorganized language (which is, of course, perfectly satisfactory as the symbol of a reference) and reaches that standard of expressiveness which we call poetry: in which the sonority or musicality of the finished version simply denotes that the style is more or less appropriate, that the emotional tone is neither wanting nor discordantly inflated, but matched to the occasion. In a certain setting 'ombre' will have a flavour in which the deep vowel sound can make its contribution to the total effect; while in another, where 'ombre' might be impossible on grounds of rhythm, dissonance, and the like, 'ténèbres', though passable on these same grounds, would not be able to make such a contribution of sound to the total impression. Evidently, then, in one respect, 'le hasard' would remain unconquered.[3] The result of a highly adequate

---

[1] The comparison is Bergson's.

[2] Cf. 'Il y a dans ... le *verbe* quelque chose de sacré qui nous défend d'en faire un jeu de hasard' (Baudelaire, *Art Romantique*, 'Théophile Gautier').

[3] It must not be thought from this example that I am equating 'musicality' with vowel pitch simply. Examples could be provided to illustrate exactly the same point in the case of consonant alliteration, or rhythm, or rhyme, or associative effects, etc. Mallarmé optimistically expounds the principle to the possible readers of his *Petite Philologie: les Mots Anglais*:

'Au poète, ou mieux, au prosateur savant, il appartiendra, par un instinct supérieur et libre,

use of language is exactly as Mallarmé describes it (see above, ch. II, 2): any truly poetic piece of literature has *ipso facto* an aura of novelty, 'une neuve atmosphère', the novelty of the individual experience, as opposed to the generalized; and though novelty as such, abstracted from all other considerations, is not a yardstick of aesthetic value, yet it is always present when 'le hasard' is overcome, as a characteristic of genuine art.

An insincerity, the use of a high-sounding phrase when the situation and tone of the whole demand something else, must inevitably wreck the organic unity of any piece of art, however attractive the phrase may appear on its own merits. The failing against which Mallarmé warns Coppée would have its equivalent in music, say, if we were to smuggle into a Mozart symphony an elaborate chromatic progression from Wagner's *Tristan und Isolde*: in each case 'le hasard', that old Adam, would find concrete embodiment in what is usually called an incongruity, the result of an error of taste. On the other hand, the overcoming of 'le hasard' can take place only when the artist is sincere; that is to say, tests his achievement at each state in its growth by reference to his own consciousness. He cannot deceive himself on this point: nor can he deceive his audience; any amount of technical skill cannot construct a truly 'musical' piece of poetry out of a formula. 'Si véritablement les pierres précieuses dont on se pare ne manifestent pas un état d'âme, c'est indûment qu'on s'en pare.' This statement, so obvious for lyric poetry (though there have been those who held out against it—among them Poe) is applicable to all art whatsoever; we can always sense the attitude of the novelist, the playwright, the painter, the composer, through his work: even the presentation of detached superiority, of aloofness, is an attitude, 'un état d'âme', and a false aloofness is one likewise; and there is nothing more destructive in art than pretence, which may at first escape detection but is always revealed in the end. Mallarmé might have gone on from this penetrating observation to formulate an opinion on aesthetic truth; he did not; in an age in which art was looked on even more widely than to-day as something on a level with play,[1] and poetic imagination mainly as the invention of untruths

de rapprocher des termes unis avec d'autant plus de bonheur pour concourir au charme et à la musique du langage qu'ils arrivent comme de lointains plus fortuits: c'est là ce procédé, inhérent au génie septentrional et dont tant de vers célèbres nous montrent tant d'exemples, *l'allitération.* Pareil effort magistral de l'Imagination désireuse, non seulement de se satisfaire par le symbole éclatant dans les spectacles du monde, mais d'établir un lien entre ceux-ci et la parole chargée de les exprimer, touche à l'un des mystères sacrés ou périlleux du langage' (Mallarmé, *Petite Philologie: les Mots Anglais*, 1870).

[1] The German theory of 'Spiel' found its way into Ribot's digressions on art, as into Spencer (*Psychology*, bk. VIII, ch. 9), and all positivist aesthetic of the nineteenth century.

for a pastime (what the modern psychologist, in more serious paths, calls 'fantasy'), such a theory as Mallarmé could have deduced would have seemed at best fanciful, but more probably perverse. As it is, when he talks of the 'fictitious' nature of art, we must understand this term in a limited sense; in the sense that opposes art to history, and not in the sense that opposes the insincere artist to the sincere seeker after truth.[1] To profess fear of a unicorn is not necessarily untruthful in both senses.

There remains one problem to resolve: how did Mallarmé conceive of the activity by which the poet came by 'le vers', and rejected 'le hasard'? What was the process—was it the exercise of logical inference, was it the business of copying or modifying other writers' experiments, or what? To this question the last poem published during his lifetime provides a veiled but final answer: 'Un coup de dés jamais n'abolira le hasard'. We know already what 'le hasard' is, and through the sombre imagery of this magnificent testament of art (for such it is) we come to see that the 'coup de dés' is that effort by which the poet strives to overcome chance. Every single act of composition is a throw of the dice: a throw which even if it wins cannot banish failure from subsequent throws, or influence them in any manner whatever. The throw of the dice is a blind action: blind in that the poet when he says to himself, 'Let's try such-and-such a word—or rime—or metre—' does not work from a ready-made specification. We are all familiar with the sensation of searching for a word: the first phrase that comes to mind may be ridiculous, and we very often give up trying even when we have found something only very approximately answering to our needs; the poet's vocation is to throw the dice again, knowing all the while that the second throw may be no luckier than the first, nor the third—and, indeed, that the number of times he throws has no direct relationship with the measure of his eventual success. The poet can never finally break through the hostile tyranny of the dice-box.

For Mallarmé, coming at the end of a long search for truth on the philosophy of art, this conclusion stands as the symbol of an un-redeemable disaster; and through the long and grandiose series of interwoven images in *Un Coup de Dés* he pours out with an intensity surpassing perhaps anything he had achieved before, what seemed to him the tragic dilemma of a creative spirit, aspiring to an Absolute

---

[1] To call art 'fictitious' is, of course, to commit the error noted above, ch. IV *passim*, of claiming that images are 'illusory'; an exactly parallel but opposite error is to think them (*as images*) 'real'.

but possessing only the means to a relative mastery of expression. When we trace the growth of his thought from the earliest utterances down to his death, and see his immense ambitions topple one by one into a limbo of disappointment, we cannot escape the suspicion that this meticulous observation of the processes of art proceeded from a mind which, in the violence of its reaction from the irrelevant and sterilizing attitudes of the positivist aesthetic, had committed him to doctrines frankly beyond the sanction of common sense. In a man who dreamed of writing 'le plus grand livre qui ait été fait sur la Poésie'[1] and ended by collecting under one cover ten or a dozen prose poems, a couple of literary sketches, and a handful of miscellaneous theatre reviews and occasional articles; who set out to write *L'Œuvre*, over five years, in five volumes[2] 'pour que l'univers retrouve en ce moi son identité',[3] and gave the world one volume of poems and a fragment—*Igitur*; who embarked on a gigantic dramatic work—'Hérodiade' being its first section only—'d'un effet inouï',[4] and left no more than three short snatches; in such a man, how can one fail to suspect a fanatic mysticism at bottom, driving him to an extreme of fastidiousness and to unheard-of demands upon his talents? Fanaticism is a strange charge to bring against so evidently mild and retiring a figure; yet Mallarmé throughout his literary career was not only never satisfied with anything he achieved—a normal and healthy condition—but refused to recognize any lasting value in the work to which he knew human limitation bound him. In his early speculations on existence and 'le néant', common sense set no limits; in his lifelong meditations on the lot of the artist at grips with his medium, prudence again failed to warn him that the snark he was hunting would very likely turn out to be a boojum.

This same *Coup de Dés*, remarkable for the state of mind it discloses in its author, and the unusual despair with which the aesthetic doctrines of a lifetime are brought to a close, is also noteworthy as the application of another of its author's cherished theories on the nature of language. In turning aside to take note of this, we leave, strictly speaking, the examination of symbolist aesthetic; for so far as I am aware, neither in Mallarmé's own time nor subsequently did this side of his work find any noteworthy adherence. Which is hardly surprising; for the view involved savours more than somewhat of idiosyncracy, and would probably appear grotesque coming from any other quarter than this subtle aesthete.

[1] Letter to Cazalis, 12/v/1866.   [2] Letter to Aubanel, 28/vii/1866.
[3] Letter to Cazalis, 14/v/1867.   [4] Letter to Cazalis, iii/1866.

At bottom Mallarmé compared himself as poet more with the dancer than with the composer. Describing the act by which the artist expresses himself, he writes,

'L'écrivain de ses maux, dragons qu'il a choyés, ou d'une allégresse, doit s'instituer, au texte, le spirituel histrion.'[1]

As a metaphor, implying the essential aesthetic unity of language as one or another specialized form of gesture, the passage is striking; but there is evidence to suggest that Mallarmé intended it, even at a comparatively early date, as more than a simple metaphor—as rather the statement of close parallelism in the sphere of movement and formal patterns. For the symbolists, the fundamental unity of all aesthetic activity, something felt and known by experience, gave rise to a wide diversity of theories of a superior form of art to be attained by the combination of some or all of them. This subject we shall return to in a later chapter; for the present it is sufficient to say that Mallarmé, at first attracted by such theories, both strictly Wagnerian and other, soon wearied of them, and even ended by claiming that poetry alone could fill the demand for a synthetic art form of the future. But this sober judgement is qualified by one reservation, which almost certainly arose out of his personal habits of life and work. Mallarmé was not by inclination an orator, despite the fact that regularly on Tuesday evenings at his flat in the Rue de Rome he put a small and select audience under the spell of his eloquence; further, as his views on poetry develop, it becomes more and more evident that in his experience 'poetry' signifies poetry written and read, poetry through the medium of the printed page, and not of the audible voice; where by the printed page is meant not merely a symbolism of human speech, relatively ambiguous at times and in itself aesthetically null, but on the contrary a positive element in art, a field as proper to the poet's attention as the theatrical set is to the producer's. In his early years, we find Mallarmé showing himself as no more than a lover of rare editions; in *Un coup de Dés* he dictates to the printer the fount and exact position of every word on the page. The *book* is now as much an object of his attention as the *poem*.[2] The Introduction to this strange experiment declares that the poem should be read 'like an orchestral score'; but the simile is misleading. Granted that a page of full score is read, so far as possible, from side to side, the eye attempting to embrace the whole vertical range of staves. On this fact Mallarmé doubtless bases his analogy;

---

[1] *Divagations*, p. 257. [2] See *Divagations*: 'Quant au livre'.

each page of *Un coup de Dés* is to be seen as a simultaneous whole, as not a string of words in succession, indeed, but as a single necklace. But in a score the disposition of the various marks on paper contributes nothing to our listening to the sounds, imaginary or actual; they are in the purest sense symbolic, and nothing more. Mallarmé, on the contrary, intended his disposition of the print to occupy an important place in the creation of the poem's total effect.

As a new adjunct to the symbolism of printing, the device has its points; not only do the streams of print wandering across the page replace the normal punctuated sentence (and it has been more than once pointed out that punctuation tends to interfere with our attention to the music of the verse),[1] but it is conceivable that they may draw our attention to the musical unity of the language. Even this has its limitations, though: for example, the title, as it appears in the course of the text, is printed in letters whose great size could hardly have reference to an intended weight of intonation.[2] But Mallarmé is not concerned with this utilitarian aspect of the *mise en page*; he has the ballet explicitly in his mind's eye. The continuity of the dancer's movement, even through the pauses, is for him exactly matched by the spacing, margins, and, as it were, unbroken sweep down the open pages of the book. Yet the movement of the eye as it follows the stream of print across the double page cannot itself be the gesture in which the 'histrion' expresses himself—there has never been an art formed simply from the movement of the eyes, and if there were, either the text would become superfluous, replaceable by rows of different-sized dots, or Mallarmé would have to accommodate himself to the Wagnerian doctrine of a synthetic art, and go back on his considered condemnation of this venture. There can be no justification along this path for the *mise en page* of *Un coup de Dés*.

In actual fact, the only possible explanation why Mallarmé thought it necessary to modify the usual symbolism of the printed page is that the impulse stemmed from a lifelong obsession with the act of reading, and the sensuous pleasure associated with it: a pleasure that most people feel at one time or another, but distinguish from the aesthetic experience it attends on. As well say that the comfort of

[1] E.g. Mockel, 'Mallarmé: un Héros,' *Mercure de France*, t. xxviii, p. 376, xi/1898; Taupin, *Quatre Essais*, 1932, p. 187, etc.

[2] It will be remembered that the paragraphs of later sections of the *Divagations* are also set out in a somewhat curious way, on the express command of the author. But this is no more than an eccentric form of punctuation. *Un Coup de Dés* is a single huge sentence, in which clauses of varying degrees of subordination are characterized by different types.

the theatre seat is an integral part of the play's appeal. Mallarmé tries in the case of poetry to bring about some such graft.

The importance of such an attempt seems to have been correctly judged by the neglect of posterity. The fields it opens up are not lacking in interest, and involve our asking the question, at what point can a range of technical possibilities be said to offer scope for expression or become material for a language of a new art, genre? We have no evidence for supposing that Mallarmé ever considered such a question in a general way; and outside this single eccentricity, his views on the classification of the arts are severe enough—more so than those of most of his contemporaries.[1] But the brief digression will have served its end if it puts us upon the track of an irrationality in his views beneath which hides a sinister confusion of aesthetic and non-aesthetic factors in art. Mallarmé's theory of language, obscurely as it may be couched, affected as it certainly is by an obsession with *perfect* poetry, is lucid and coherent so long as it can be taken for granted that the process of writing is no more than a rather unsatisfactory series of hints to people out of earshot as to the poet's intentions. Speech is the same kind of activity at bottom as dancing or singing; never the perfect embodiment of the poet's aspirations, but a process in which the poem stands in a close and mutual relationship with the writer's consciousness; a mutual dependency, indeed. The poet is certainly 'histrion'. But to justify this view requires the assumption that poetry is essentially a spoken act; and a little superficially perhaps Mallarmé allows his personal habits to lead him to deny this. But what, after all, is the special virtue of the written word? Mallarmé must have known perfectly well that to improve a poem sometimes involves striking out a word and writing another over it; this means disfiguring the page, but no one would suggest that the poem is thereby damaged. Again, by itself the analogy of the page with the stage across which the dancer weaves patterns of motion is too trivial to bear the weight of so determined a theory as that underlying *Un Coup de Dés*; and the same applies to any obsession with elegant editions and subtle *mise en page*. Whatever explanation there may be must lie far deeper; and there is, as has already been hinted, already one point from which an explanation may be initiated.

For all the accuracy with which Mallarmé analyses the act of making a poem, there is one matter on which he is not lucid at all:

---

[1] His greater age and more settled outlook on art is one obvious reason why he was less affected than the young symbolists by the impact of Wagner in the eighties.

namely, why aesthetic pleasure should arise at all from the completed poem, either for the poet ('chargé de voir divinement') or anyone else. A natural conclusion to his argument would be, that what is normally called aesthetic pleasure is not in any sense a peculiar and unaccountable emotion, but simply the feeling that results from the attainment of extreme clarity and lucidity by the imaginative consciousness; i.e. aesthetic pleasure is not a specific and unique kind of pleasure at all, but is present at and enters into more or less every instant of conscious experience, if not always in the heightened form which great art gives us. But such a conception is alien to the thought of the nineteenth century, and Mallarmé adheres to the view that aesthetic pleasure is a highly specialized experience, which arises only when the mind is engaged in contemplating 'Ideas'. We have seen already how ambiguous this latter term can be in the context of symbolist aesthetics; and it is not surprising that a dependent notion such as 'the pleasure derived from contemplating Ideas' should be equally ambiguous. No doubt it has its value: its very elusiveness serves to distinguish such pleasures from the more prosaic gratifications of the senses with which the positivist and physiological philosophers sought to couple the rewards of art. But the vagueness of its definition made it liable to break down as a test for deciding what was art and what was not, or what was pleasure attributable to art and what was pleasure attributable to things other than art; and in the case before us it not so much misled as failed entirely to correct or challenge a latent tendency to confusion in Mallarmé's mind. If the mark of an Idea was simply a rather vague 'disinterested' pleasure, who was to tell Mallarmé as he pursued his Ideas down the page that a certain element in his pleasure was irrelevant and had no integral place in his aesthetic activity? Who, for that matter, would have dared to make any such suggestion to so suave and obstinate an individual? Who even would have *thought* of doing so, in a circle where the enjoyment of art was commonly equated with a mystical and quite inscrutable experience?

It is hard at this distance of time to withhold a smile at the spectacle of so universally held a creed. But to reject it and at the same time remain devoted to the pursuit of a 'symbolist' aesthetic would have demanded a far-sightedness such as no writer in the heat of those controversies could have possessed. In the field in which, almost alone, Mallarmé worked out a partial theory of language, he is already exceptional. We may urge against him his partial misunderstanding (in theory) of the relations between poetry and prose; his notions about 'reportage'; his curious estimate of the importance of the printed page; his aestheticism; and much else besides: when all is said, it remains true that more brilliantly than any writer of his age, he sketched out a theory of composition, and exposed the connection between the experience of the poet and the act of formal creation. For this achievement Mallarmé stands head and shoulders above his fellow-symbolists, as well as somewhat apart from them; and if the *Divagations* fall short of his youthful ambitions for them, at least they represent the most significant contribution of the movement to the discussion of poetic language. Moreover, and perhaps most important of all, they provide an unambiguous illustration of what Mallarmé means by 'music' in the context of literature; it is a meaning that owes nothing to the influence of Wagner in France.

5. 'MUSICALITY', THE SYMBOLISTS, AND WAGNER

On the connection between music and poetry, Mallarmé succeeded in erecting very nearly a complete account of the nature of poetic composition. Of those who, in the nineteenth century, confined themselves to a more limited exposition of the way in which poetry is suggestive of music, few perhaps have given so interesting a description of the essentials as Thomas Carlyle. His views were first drawn attention to by Brunetière, in a famous article on symbolism in the *Revue des Deux Mondes*, so far as they might be said directly to concern the symbolist movement.

'La poésie est métrique, a une musique, est un chant... Musical! que de choses tiennent en cela!... Voyez profondément et vous verrez musicalement.'[1]

Once put on the trail, the symbolist critics were not slow to follow and see what Carlyle could tell them; and at a somewhat advanced stage in the day, Edmond Barthélémy came upon, and passed on to the readers of the *Mercure de France*, the following:

'Si votre description est authentiquement *musicale*, musicale non dans ses mots seulement mais dans son cœur et sa substance, dans toutes ses pensées et expressions, dans sa conception tout entière, alors elle sera poétique; sinon, non. — Musicale, que de mots tiennent dans cela! une pensée parlée par un esprit qui a pénétré dans le cœur le plus intime de la chose; qui en a découvert le plus intime mystère, c'est-à-dire la mélodie qui gît cachée en elle; l'intérieur harmonie de cohérence qui est son âme, par qui elle existe, et a droit d'être ici en ce monde.

'... Toute parole, même la plus commune des paroles, a quelque chose du chant

[1] Brunetière, *Revue des Deux Mondes*, 1/xi/1888; re-quoted by Achille Delaroche, in *La Plume*, 1/i/1891, 'Les Annales du Symbolisme'.

en elle:... Observez aussi comme tout langage passionné devient réellement de lui-
même musical — avec une musique plus belle que le pur accent; la parole d'un
homme même dans l'ardeur de la colère devient une musique, un chant.'[1]

It will be seen that while—in other respects hardly differing—
Carlyle is more emphatic than Mallarmé on the essential similarity
in kind of all uses of speech—the most extempore occasions of prose
usage are not debarred from having their 'intérieure harmonie de
cohérence'—but that he is prepared less even than the French poet
to attempt to define the gift of musicality in rational terms; insight,
the power to come to grips with Mystery, an inexplicable Gift,
Genius, is all he can call the ability to create this coherence of word
and thought, and in this respect he is close to the French symbolists
with their nebulous revulsion from the facile explanations of a Taine
or a Guyau.

But if Carlyle and Mallarmé are at least clear on what it is they
mean by 'musicality' in poetry, the same cannot be said of a great
mass of the symbolist movement—the critics, aestheticians, dogma-
tizing *vers libristes*, and hangers-on. Some plainly had no idea at all
of what was at issue. From Ghil's 'School', for instance, comes a
curious doctrine, which may be summed up in the following brief
credo by the second-in-command of the Instrumentists:

'L'ultime avatar du vers était indiqué: expression d'une Idée philosophique
synthétisée, avec la musique comme moyen d'expression, la musique latente dans les
mots, rendue sensible.'[2]

There can be little interest in the details of the sterile and arbitrary
formulae which Ghil laid down for his disciples, and which amount
in the long run to nothing more than a picturesque glossary of
assonance. His little circle seems to have set out to make itself the
repository of every misconception that could be formed about
word-music, just as it did for the game of 'audition colorée' and
Mallarmé's doctrine of 'Ideas'.

(a) Wyzéwa

But setting aside such freaks as these, it is interesting to find
how surprisingly little the symbolists did think clearly about
'musicality'—or even realize the ambiguities they were involved in.
If we examine the views of Téodor de Wyzéwa, one of the most
prolific Wagnerian doctrinaires of all time, we find that the idea of
musicality in verse evidently exists only in the first of the two senses

[1] Carlyle, 'Heroes: Dante', quoted *Mercure de France*, no. 15, pp. viii/1895, pp. 167–8.
[2] Eugene Thébault, in *Écrits pour l'Art*, t. ii, p. 197, xii/1889.

detailed at the beginning of the last section: that is to say, it refers to the sounds of words alone, and not to the juxtaposition or fusing of sound with the other elements in speech. The fact that poetry is so much less euphonious than music is indeed the reason why it has to have a 'subject' at all:

'La poésie, art des rythmes et des syllabes, devait, étant une musique, créer des émotions. Or les émotions, dans notre âme, sont inséparables de leurs causes, des idées qui les provoquent. Le plaisir, la douleur abstraits n'existent point: il y a seulement des idées joyeuses ou pénibles. Une sonate peut bien nous procurer des émotions sans le secours d'un texte, scénario ou programme; mais d'abord la langue de la musique instrumentale est plus précise que la langue émotionnelle des syllabes; puis cette musique même crée une vie moins pleine que la musique dramatique, où l'auteur nous donne avec les émotions l'énoncé de leurs causes. Et cette nécessité est plus vive pour la Poésie: les émotions que les syllabes évoquent sont tellement délicates et ténues, qu'elles requièrent absolument l'adjonction à elles d'idées précises.'[1]

He concludes from this that

'La poésie devait s'unir à la littérature qui traduit les Idées par des mots précis',

and that for Mallarmé, whose work and ideas he is discussing, 'littérature' refers to what we ordinarily mean by the word 'subject-matter', and 'poésie' is the coeval element of sound—e.g. what might in principle be recorded in some new sort of musical notation. Thus the relation between 'poetry' and 'literature' in this perspective has a direct analogy with that between Wagner's music and the libretto that accompanies it. In each case it is claimed that the non-explanatory ingredient is the aesthetically valuable, and in each case, too, the value of this ingredient cannot be properly brought to the listener without the intervention of an aesthetically insignificant ingredient (the libretto or running commentary).

It is hard to say which of two things this doctrine distorts the most: the poetry of Mallarmé to which it is supposed to be applicable, or the aesthetic of Wagner, of which it pretends to be a faithful reproduction. Ridiculous though it may seem, there is ample evidence to show that we are not misinterpreting a solitary passage from Wyzéwa's writings, and that some such views as these run through his theorizing on art from the very earliest times:

'Traduire l'émotion par des mots précis était évidemment impossible; c'était décomposer l'émotion, donc la détruire. L'émotion, moins encore que les autres modes vitaux, ne peut être traduite directement; elle peut seulement nous être suggérée. Et pour suggérer les émotions, mode subtil et dernier de la vie, un signe spécial a été inventé: le son musical.'[2]

[1] Wyzéwa, 'Mallarmé, Notes', *Vogue*, No. 11, p. 368, 5/vii/1886.
[2] Wyzéwa, *Nos Maîtres*, p. 58 ('L'Art Wagnérien,' IV, *Revue Wagnérienne*, 1886).

From which it would appear *first* that Wyzéwa thinks 'language' (meaning, of course, speech) can exist only in what might be called its 'scientific' aspect; *secondly*, that what might be called the 'emotive' use of language-references Wyzéwa suppresses entirely, replacing it by the idea of music; *thirdly*, that music does not operate by means of references; though the word 'suggestion' is silent as a description of how it *does* operate. As corollaries of these points, two further remarks are called for; in the first place, since 'musicality' is now limited entirely to the crudest notion of sound-play, Wyzéwa's view-point on what is musical in poetry is necessarily biased in favour of the most obvious and blatant at the expense of the more unobtrusive and subtle appropriateness of sound for which there is also room in poetry. And in the second place, just as we have already seen that Wyzéwa's view of speech is crudely symbolic—i.e. language is concerned solely with references—so we find that the musical or emotional-suggestive element must of necessity be emotive rather than expressive. The unfortunate truth is that Wyzéwa took his whole view of how musicality finds its place in poetry from an impression of music-drama, in which the orchestra provided the 'emotional tone', so to speak, and the actors the 'subject'. Wyzéwa sincerely thought Mallarmé to represent the Wagnerian ideal in poetry; it is not surprising that the latter had serious misgivings as to how far this designation appealed to him.

(b) Mauclair

Similar to Wyzéwa's theory of musical speech is Mauclair's.

'De même que la juxtaposition de trois tons fait plaisir sans qu'on la comprenne dans un costume ou un tableau, de même la juxtaposition de mots prétendus sans suite à tel endroit d'une composition poétique fait plaisir et a une influence sur la sensibilité sans commentaire intellectuel et analytique. Car le moyen fondamental d'élire une langue individuelle dans la langue usuelle et commune, c'est, pour le poète, d'attribuer aux timbres et aux sonorités des mots leur valeur ordinairement négligée. Un mot est fait pour être écrit et parlé, et l'émission sonore double le sens. Nous comprenons par l'oreille autant que par la réflexion... La gît le secret du vers dans ce choix musical et ce perpétuel accompagnement du sens.'[1]

He too effects a complete divorce between the 'sense' and the 'sound' of the word. There is, of course, no reason at all why he should not do so, if he is only interested in language as a system of intellectual communication open to embellishments from time to time; on the other hand, if he is at pains to give an account of what we mean when we say that poetical language is 'musical', his ends are not

[1] Mauclair, *Eleusis*, p. 155.

served by dividing the poet's medium into two elements, one of which, symbolic, might be written out in x and y beneath a stave bearing a musical notation of the other. If the 'sense' is insignificant (though he does not say that) poetry would be served by a series of carefully modulated sounds, not necessarily arranged as words or speech at all; if the 'sound' is of no aesthetic importance, once the abstraction has been made (though he does not say that either), it is a waste of time attending to it; if both are important together, in combination, it is Mauclair's duty to analyse and explain why such a combination produces poetry; and this he does not do. He assumes that his task is finished when he says the one element 'doubles' the other. We are reminded[1] of the three-fold division which Wyzéwa sets forth between the human faculties of sensation, emotion, and intellection, with their appropriate arts of painting, music, and poetry; though this time we cannot plead in defence of the critic that his judgement was unsettled by the impact of Bayreuth. We are accustomed, and rightly, to laugh at Max Nordau's ridiculous survey of French symbolism; but leaving aside the rich harvest of poetry which he was so patently incapable of appreciating, we might imagine a more intelligent man than he studying the manifestos of these symbolist apologists and being driven in all good faith to write something after this fashion:

'Ramener le mot lourd d'idées au sens émotionnel, c'est vouloir renoncer à tous les résultats de l'évolution organique et rabaisser l'homme, heureux de posséder le langage, au rang de grillon qui grésillone, ou de grenouille qui croasse; aussi bien les efforts des symbolists conduisent à un radotage dépourvu de sens, mais nullement à la musique des mots cherchée, car celle-ci n'existe tout simplement pas. Nul mot humain de n'importe quelle langue n'est musical en soi.'[2]

(c) *Later approaches*

We shall have more to say on the relations between poetry and music (in the wider sense) in a later chapter; and at this stage we shall do no more than remark that given the enormous prestige of Wagner in the eighties and nineties it is hardly surprising that the urge to wed music to poetry at Bayreuth should arouse an answering impulse to see in poetry itself something answering to the orchestral element in music-drama. Such an influence on the literary mind might be likened to the rise of tide in an island lagoon, answering the larger movement of the distant ocean. Since tides of this sort not only rise but fall as well, such motions can hardly be relied

---

[1] See ch. V.   [2] Nordau, *Entartung* (*Dégénérescence*) I, p. 246. French translation.

upon to raise the inland water-level; and in the same way, the influence of Wagner had no lasting effect, at least in this section of aesthetic analysis. The attempt to describe poetic language in terms of simple sound-phenomena was too naïve to have any effect on the poet in his study; and too rigid to lead to any suggestive *aperçus* in the discussion of language. It is a fact that in the nineteenth century in France, certain possibilities in assonance, alliteration, and the like were developed beyond all former limits; but this owed nothing to Wagner unless anyone would care to prove that a writer like Verlaine—or in England Hopkins, say—were Wagnerites.[1] French aesthetic speculation first took hold of these facts of poetry from a standpoint tinged with Wagnerism—implicit or explicit—at any rate so far as the bulk of the young critics are concerned; and it follows that with the decline of Bayreuth's hold on the imagination, the false start was gradually effaced. The latter analysis by symbolists and near-symbolists of the 'musicality' of verse tends to swing back to the standpoint of Carlyle or Mallarmé, as we have set this out, with its closer adherence to the facts of linguistic phenomena.

Thus long after the 'mêlée symboliste' had subsided, André Gide, who in earlier years had had opportunity to observe Mallarmé's attitude in the controversy, delivered himself of a passage which deserves to be known as a classic exposition of the position of sound in poetry. He is defending Baudelaire against criticisms by Faguet—among others the charge of having had little ear for the 'music' of poetry:

'Musical! veuille ce mot, ici, n'exprimer point seulement la caresse fluide ou le choc harmonieux des sonorités verbales par où le vers peut plaire même à l'étranger musicien qui n'en comprendrait pas le sens; mais aussi bien ce choix certain de l'expression, dicté non plus seulement par la logique, et qui échappe à la logique, par quoi le poète-musicien arrive à fixer aussi exactement que le ferait une définition l'émotion essentiellement indéfinissable.'[2]

That is to say, when the poet's utterance stands in no need of the strengthening devices supplied by assonance or any other special pattern of sound, when, for example, the underlying attitude is not so emphatic as to need to call upon such extra resources, the imposition of heavy slabs of unusual sound effect would not have any positive value: so far from improving the utterance under all circumstances, as Wyzéwa, for instance, would be required by his theories to suppose,

---

[1] The initial stage of experiment with these resources in poetry is of course pre-Wagnerian; but even the Parnassian virtuosity does no more than pick on and develop already existing possibilities.

[2] A. Gide, 'Baudelaire et M. Faguet', *NRF*, 1/xi/1910.

t would be an intrusion, a discordant and stultifying distraction. Granted that a Verlaine or a Swinburne can extend the bounds of verbal technique by the development of striking masses of sound within the verse, or a Wagner the range of orchestral virtuosity by the use of enormous masses of brass; we do not think Mozart any the less great for using a smaller orchestral force than Wagner, or Racine any the less a 'musical' poet (that is to say, simply 'a poet') for not developing an enormous gamut of sound-groupings in his verse, or exploring irregular *vers libre*. The measure of poetic mastery lies in a more or less adequate appropriation of speech, not in the sheer development of 'technique'. On Mallarmé's death, it was noted by at least one intelligent observer, himself a poet, that Mallarmé, in so far as he wrote good poetry, had not departed from the essential, the perennial tradition:

'Quant à la musique des vers, depuis les pastourelles du XIIIe siècle, et depuis Rutebœuf, on n'oserait la dire étrangère à la tradition la plus strictement française; et Racine lui-même est témoin qu'elle ne fut pas tout à fait négligée au grand siècle.'[1]

He might truthfully have gone further and said that 'music' is as continually present in all poetry of all tongues and ages as 'form'. To give impressive support to this assertion is the even maturer and doubtless more pondered judgement of two of the last survivors of the group of lyric poets who in their youth felt the influence of Mallarmé's precept and example—Viélé-Griffin analysing the act of expression on the imaginative level:

'Si au lieu d'abstraire on maintient et on invoque pendant le travail de l'expression je ne sais quelle présence de l'être tout entier, de sa vie sensitive et motrice, alors la participation de ce véritable *résonnateur* communique au discours de tout autres puissances, lui restitue des caractères tout primitifs. Le rythme, le geste, la collaboration de la voix, par les timbres des voyelles, les accents, introduisent en quelque sorte le corps vivant, réagissant et agissant — et ajoutent à l'expression *finie* d'une pensée ce qu'il faut pour suggérer ce qu'elle est d'autre part — la réponse, l'acte, et l'instant d'un homme.'[2]

And Paul Valéry, commenting on the quality of Baudelaire's verse, so lacking in the more flamboyant devices of verbal 'music':

'Cette parole extraordinaire se fait connaître et reconnaître par le rythme et les harmonies qui la soutiennent et qui doivent être si intimement, et même si mystérieusement liés à sa génération que le son et le sens ne se puissent plus séparer et se répondent indéfiniment dans la mémoire... La poésie de Baudelaire garde et

[1] Mockel, 'Mallarmé, un Héros', *Mercure de France*, t. xxviii, p. 369, xi/1898.
[2] *Nouvelles Littéraires*, 28/ii/1931. He suggests that speech *adds* something to a thought; would be less misleading to say that this latter is an *abstraction* from speech. The use of the word 'primitive' is a tacit admission of the preferableness of the latter alternative.

développe presque toujours une ligne mélodique admirablement pure et une sonorité parfaitement tenue qui la distinguent de toute prose.'[1]

In these accounts, with which we shall close this section of our inquiry, 'musicality' has at last assumed its natural and due place in the description of language—language, 'l'instant d'un homme,' the total gesture behind the specialized production of speech-sound. Musicality, as a concept derived from speech-sounds, is an indispensable element in all language—like rhythm, for that matter, which is an aspect of it—but it has no exclusive rights to the attention of the poet *in vacuo*. If we return to our first dissociation of terms, music, as sound, is simply part of a total act; music, as that element which defied definition at the hands of the symbolists, is merely what we recognize in an extremely good performance of that act; in proportion as the act is performed well, the former, together with whatever other elements in speech it may please the critic to light upon, rhythmical and so on, need not necessarily become more salient, just as the finest music is not necessarily the most brilliant, or the best pictures those which display the brightest colours; but the latter type of musicality, over which Carlyle rhapsodizes, and whose attempted perfection brought Mallarmé to despair, this music is nothing more nor less than the expressiveness of language—that is to say, its goodness, the thing we value it for.

The symbolist obsession with 'Music' results from the chance encounter of three important events in the history of art: first, Wagner's personal solution of the operatic problem of combining music and libretto in continuous recitative, and the enormous impression it made on the world of letters, then as always relatively ignorant in matters of music;[2] secondly, an extension of verbal experiment, especially marked in the last fifty years of the century; and thirdly, the realization that poetry, for all the interest of these new

---

[1] Valéry, 'Situation de Baudelaire', *Œuvres*, p. 163. The distinction noted between poetry and prose is, of course, one of degree—degree of 'musicality'; but Valéry, following his master sees only a difference in kind. See above, ch. V, 4. Claudel, on the other hand, glorie repeatedly in the 'latent' music of all speech, from the merest chatter of two girls to the most sonorous verse. (See *Positions et propositions*, 4e éd., 1928, p. 60). Gide, Viélé-Griffin, Valéry Claudel—Mallarmé's conservative lessons were not wasted.

[2] I am not forgetting that at the time of Wagner's first irruptions into French literature he was known only by his early operas, in which the continuous recitative of the *Ring* had no yet made its appearance; *Tannhäuser, Lohengrin,* and the lesser-known *Fliegende Holländer* The argument holds good, nevertheless: for what influenced the symbolists was not so much the enormous originality of the music itself (though we cannot quite neglect that) as the professions of aesthetic faith that used them as illustrations, but might equally well have use Lulli, or Rameau—or Massenet—in their place. The technique of Wagner's later works wa claimed to be *better suited* to 'synthetic art'; but there is no reason why it should be: *Carmen* is as much a music-drama as *Tristan*. As Nietzsche found!

verbal resources, is not merely a trick, an arbitrary variation on the normal didactic or informative discourse, but in some sense connected with an emotional activity—either expressive, or emotive, or mystical, but at any rate lyrical—and in that sense closer to music than to social science; in short, that poetry is intent to 'reprendre à la musique son bien'. When the impact of the first two of these factors had worn off, and the attempts to produce hasty normative theories from empirical developments subsided, the world of literature regained its freedom to examine dispassionately the true importance of formal elements of sound in the poetic use of language. The real achievement here of symbolist aesthetic is to have set on foot a movement towards the proper observation of the *distinctive facts* of poetry; the remarks of Gide, Viélé-Griffin, and Valéry cited above may seem to us to-day nothing more than the very accomplished expression of familiar truths; but plain descriptions though they are, aspects of a type of experience common to all art *qua* art, simple statements of fact void of all controversial theorizing, we could hardly imagine them in the mouth of a writer or critic of the early half of the last century;[1] and were we to find them there, or something like them, it is inconceivable that any pre-symbolist critic should dream of treating them as the initial data for an extended aesthetic theory, or as anything more than paradoxes or remarkable phenomena with perhaps a bearing on religious experience. The outstanding exception to the first half of this rule redeems it by his part conformity with the second half.

6. THE SYMBOLIST APPROACH TO FORM

As with the comparatively narrow field of 'musicality', so with the larger one of 'form', the symbolists' definitions stand at an important turning-point in the history of aesthetic consciousness. We shall begin by setting out briefly what this ambiguous term covers.

The acquiescence by a writer in a given 'form'—let us say the sonnet—does not mean that his composition is dominated by a rigid system of rhyming and the dictates of quatrain and sestet. The more he is a poet, the more he is capable of infusing a sense of purpose and deliberateness into the formal pattern; of bringing it to life, as it were, and forcing it to serve his purposes rather than allowing it to tyrannize over him. He stands in a rather special and elastic relation to the abstraction we call 'sonnet'. On the one hand, he accepts at the outset such and such a rhyme scheme and balance of emphasis, and in that

[1] Always excepting Baudelaire.

measure is accepting for use a formal element in his art which has been used before him, developed and explored, and will doubtless continue to be used long after he is dead. On the other hand, his poem is not simply 'a sonnet': it is 'this sonnet'—that is to say, this and only this combination of rhyming and rhythmic pattern with certain sound effects, attitudes and interests, which is its author's contribution to poetry and to the development of the sonnet form.

Exactly the same thing can be said about much simpler weapons in the poet's arsenal: rhythmic effects within the line of verse; assonance or dissonance, in its most trivial detail, and the like. Metaphor, too, is, in itself, a formal concept; just as a line of iambic blank verse beginning with a trochee offers the example of a particular formal device, so also the juxtaposition of two representations embodies a formal element; so for that matter does any combination of ideas, and that not simply images, visual images in the mind's eye. Even single words offer the opportunity for use as formal constructs, through individual modification in speech by accent and intonation, though this is something commonly obscured by the inability of writing to symbolize more than a small part of speech-sound.

In short, when we begin to consider what we can reasonably include under the name of 'form', it becomes more and more plain that if the five acts of a tragedy are part of a formal pattern, so, too, is the most insignificant relation between parts of a brief utterance; if we can talk of a formal element, balance, or what you like, between tragic and comic scenes in a Shakespearian tragedy, we have no right to withhold the same term from the relation between any one word and the next in those scenes. Moreover, when we consider a play or poem or phrase as art, we find we are considering as one created work not only the former of these two sorts of formal elements but the latter as well; a poem or play constitutes the sum of all the formal elements that go to make it. Just as matter is at bottom nothing other than movement, so art is at bottom nothing more than form—form in a very wide sense. And in this perspective, what more simple than to conclude that on the plane of art subject (theme) and form are one and the same thing—a fact long observed in the case of music, albeit confusedly and incompletely.

Before this view is condemned as a monstrous paradox, or as an unwarranted abuse of terms, we must return to the word 'form' and define its relations to our earlier observations on language. It has been suggested that art is language, and that that is the conclusion at any

rate of certain chains of thought pursued by Mallarmé.[1] Now it is
asserted that art is form. Thus language must be equivalent to form
and both to art. Why have so many words for the one thing?
The answer is that when we talk of 'language' we ordinarily refer
not to language in use, but to language as an abstraction: language
imagined as standing over and beyond every individual use of it;
and when we talk of 'form' we ordinarily refer not to form (or
language again) in use, but to form as abstraction: form or forms
standing over and beyond every individual use of them, the 'genres'
of Brunetière, the rigid (because abstract) concepts of Renaissance
aesthetic. When we talk in abstract terms, these two concepts are not
interchangeable; but when we examine the concrete use of speech,
they are indissolubly wedded.

To put this in other terms: we have already suggested that if the
distinctive work of the poet is simply one of developing a more
acute consciousness ('voir divinement') this desirable frame of mind
is not brought about prior to the activity of producing art to
communicate it, but by the very act and at the very instant of clothing
one's inchoate attitude in the shapes of language; and by language
we cannot here mean gestures, sounds, and the like invented *de novo*
for each situation to be expressed (for this would of course destroy
the very idea of language, and incidentally make art incommunicable),
but language learnt and appropriated (and in that measure modified)
from a complex tradition into which the language-user is born.
In language in use, therefore, there are always present a given element,
a solid body of usage upon which the artist works and struggles to
bring about his art, and with it an individual modification, great or
little, which is referred to when people talk about a writer's (or a
musician's, etc.) 'style': the way he appropriates language. Now it is
inconceivable that any human being in the world as we know it
should so use language that every vestige of the traditional residuum
disappears from it: such a phenomenon would imply among other
things, that he had completely invented a language for himself, that
there was nothing in common between his experience as shaped by it
and those of his fellow-humans; and furthermore that we, the rest of
mankind, were incapable of ever recognizing what he was doing as
utterance or art—except perhaps by inference. Just as one man, in
his personal modifications of language, creates expressions, personal
touches of style, 'idioms' in the fullest sense, which are the formal

---

[1] With the corollary that other symbolist critics whose opinions ran counter to Mallarmé's
landed themselves either in nonsense or else in a description of something other than art and
poetry.

embodiments of his effort to express himself, so, far more profoundly and powerfully, a tradition passing down many generations creates general formal patterns in language (some of the more detailed of these are also called idioms) which represent the requirements of the Average Expressive Man. When these formal concretions are of the relatively large dimensions represented by the five-act tragedy, the detective novel, the symphony, the altar triptych, or the like, there is a tendency to regard them as having swum beyond the control of the individuals that use them, and become autonomous and self-justifying; though at the same time, we most of us talk of such-and-such a writer's individual 'treatment' of this or that form, thereby tacitly admitting that these forms are no more fixed and obligatory than idiomatic speech is confined to the use of phrases in the lexicon. There is no reason why the one sort of linguistic complexes should be glorified with the title of 'forms' (or 'genres', etc.) and treated as sacred, when the other is not: there is no radical difference between them, and the aesthetic problems they present are identical. Traditional forms or genres in art stand in exactly the same relation to the poet's activities as does idiom or 'good usage' in the choice and use of words in everyday speech. From this it follows that there must be something on the larger scale which corresponds to that petrified and inexpressive phrase got out of the dictionary which we call a cliché or *lieu-commun*. And this everyone's experience must tell him is true. Voltaire's tragedies are 'clichés' when set against Racine's.

In any *isolated* element of form there is no aesthetic worth. Ernest Hello, neither a poet nor a philosopher, succeeds oddly enough in expressing this fact very well; and because he is in some sort an outrider of the symbolist movement, we quote a few of his remarks on this subject as casting light on the temper of a new age in French writing. He distinguishes between 'la formule' or 'la règle', the lifeless and improperly assimilated formal element in art, and 'la loi', which he darkly speaks of as 'organic', but which it is less ambiguous (if less concise) to say represents a more adequate appropriation of formal elements to an expressive activity:

'La loi résulte de la nature des choses. La loi de l'art est l'expression de l'ordre dans le domaine de l'art.

'La règle résulte d'une convention.[1] Elle est l'expression des habitudes substituées à la vie, des modes substituées aux lois... Pour apprécier les unités mécaniques de Boileau, il suffit de savoir compter jusqu'à trois. Pour sentir l'unité vivante et

---

[1] Cf. 'La convention est une horloge qui marque une autre heure que le soleil et qui, devant les hommes, a raison contre lui' (Hello, *L'Homme*, etc., p. 306).

organique dont elles sont la parodie, il n'y a pas de procédé: il faut la sentir; il ne faut savoir compter que jusqu'à Un.'[1]

And side by side with this trenchant and rather pompous assertion, he gives a detailed consequence of such a way of looking at form. If the exact satisfaction of an arbitrary formula is no guarantee of artistic perfection, what is? There is, he answers, anticipating Mallarmé, no guarantee possible in the nature of things:

'Tout chef-d'œuvre est une ébauche. L'inachevé est la marque du génie qui peint à grands traits, ne comptant rien terminer... Et plus l'exécution approche de l'idéal, plus l'abîme qui les sépare apparaît large et profond à l'artiste; plus le nombre des côtés du polygone inscrit augmente, plus l'impossibilité de toucher le cercle devient sensible... Pour l'artiste ordinaire, qu'il le sache ou non, la loi est formule. Voilà pourquoi il peut se satisfaire: son programme peut être rempli.'[2]

We are far from wishing to justify some of the extravagant and obscurantist positions towards which Hello bends his observations; but the outsider to a controversy is sometimes well placed to distinguish matters of fact. Not that Hello distinguishes all matters of aesthetic fact with equal clarity; when he says that 'au lieu d'oublier simplement les arts poétiques, l'école de 1830 a eu la faiblesse de les exécrer',[3] it is plain that he has no more clear understanding of form and the nature of 'genres' than did the writers whom he is abusing; for if the major forms go by the board, and all tradition connected with them whatever, why should we discriminate in favour of minor forms? The whole body of language is wiped out; the poet is invited to start right from the beginning again—a fantastic invitation.

Above all this, and irrespective of how we choose to interpret its significance in the philosophy of art, one fact stands out, and may be stated with confidence: the seventeenth and eighteenth-century respect for established 'forms', which proceeded in some measure from the Renaissance's reading of Aristotle, were becoming rapidly and continuously weakened throughout the nineteenth century; and this trend was powerfully assisted in symbolism.

'La forme semble s'anéantir et disparaître; j'ose dire que c'est le grand trait de la poésie moderne,'[4]

writes Taine, with more than a trace of disapproval, and it would be

---

[1] ibid., p. 303.

[2] ibid., p. 302. Plainly Hello speaks here with one eye on the romantic tradition, and its bias towards the sublime, the careless sweep of a grand conception, that does not stop for details. As Benda says, 'L'incommensurabilité entre le langage et la vie est une pièce éternelle de l'arsenal romantique' (*La France Byzantine, ad fin.*). But it is more than that; and Hello's remarks are as true of the author of *La Jeune Parque* as of the poet of *Jocelyn*.

[3] Hello, *L'Homme*, etc., p. 312.

[4] Quoted gleefully by Ch. Morice, *La Littérature de toute à l'heure*, p. 235.

almost a work of supererogation to illustrate and support this statement with a list of examples. In such a list, however, one item would be conspicuously absent; with only some qualifications furnished by the romantic movement, the distinctive foundations of French verse, or at least the framework of its prosody, remain formally unchanged down to the 1880s. It is with more than a theatrical touch of pride that Mallarmé, discoursing on French poetry before a foreign audience, announced late in the century that this exception has now been removed:

'J'apporte en effet des nouvelles. Les plus surprenantes. Même cas ne se vit encore.
      On a touché au vers.'[1]

We shall attend presently to the implications of this sacrilege for the symbolist generation; before doing so, we shall attempt to put Taine's view in a perspective in which it means something for aesthetic.

On the account offered above of the essentially linguistic context of all form in art, even the most developed, it is plain that if we say 'Form in art is on the decline' we are in effect saying 'Art is getting worse' or, at any rate, 'Artists are not succeeding in using such expressive language'—not that they are not trying, but that they are not succeeding. The mark of such failure, as we know, is that the resulting art—be it a symphony or a remark—bears far fewer signs of the individual's conquest over and appropriation of his language material: in an unsuccessful sonnet we are painfully aware that the rhyme-scheme and rhythmic pattern have proved too much for the writer, that he has not used his resources successfully, that different language elements are not harmoniously combined. At such a time the fact that the poem is a sonnet—almost against its will—becomes very obtrusive: the awkward rhymes demand our attention to the fact that they are conforming with such-and-such a scheme; the quatrains, standing woodenly side by side in embarrassed isolation shout out their 'formal' identities; the worse the attempt, the more obviously it calls on us to notice the pattern as something distinct, standing outside it.

'Les chefs-d'œuvre ont une marque, ils font toujours oublier l'artifex. On ne pense au métier que devant les choses de métier.'[2]

Neither Péladan nor any of his rosicrucean disciples achieved eminence as poets by neglecting the hard discipline of words and trusting to grace or inspiration, but the first part of the observation is just.

We do not, then, conclude either that the decline in apparent formal

---

[1] *La Musique et les Lettres*, 1894.   [2] Sâr Joséphin Péladan, *L'Art Idéaliste*, p. 93.

organization in French nineteenth-century literature marks either an 'improvement' or a 'deterioration' in the level of artistic achievement; nor even that it comes properly within the scope of the philosophy of art to discuss such a change. A change there is, and its nature can be analysed more easily when we know along what lines to examine it; an appeal to aesthetic discloses that art remains art whatever the change in taste and custom, and that an increased emphasis on one aspect of composition at the expense of another proves merely the unlimited scope for variety in the act of self-expression. Blank verse is no 'better' and no 'worse' than rhyming couplets; it is different.

The event that took place in the nineteenth century and gave rise to changes exactly parallel to a hypothetical change of fashion from rhyming to blank verse, was called by some a development of individualism; by others, less tender, the growth of anarchy;[1] such phrases tell us little. We want them translated into something sufficiently precise for us to see how they relate to (a) art and (b) the theory of art. Looked at as less irksome restrictions placed in the way of the poet, it must have benefited poetry; looked at as less scope or less challenge to his use of language, it might have harmed it; looked at as simply the exchange of one set of formal materials for alternative ones, it signifies nothing. Nor is it relevant to speculate on the reasons for this change in the higher levels of language: whether it resulted from a general deterioration in the general standards of speech in the language tradition the writer was born into (a function of social change), or whether it was that the breakdown of aristocratic patronage allowed the artist to take the bit between his teeth—these are all problems which, though interesting, fall beyond the scope of our inquiry, and concern the literary historian rather than the aesthetician. We must simply state that the continued disintegration of large literary conventions is a central feature of the nineteenth century, as compared with the opposite trend of the seventeenth. The disruption of such moulds as the classical tragedy; the enormous development in all directions of the scope of the novel (a much 'looser' form than the play); the revival and exploration of lyric poetry; the breakdown of barriers between prose and distinctively 'poetic' language from before Chateaubriand to after Proust—these are the broad movements of French literature, in the context of which we must set the symbolists. In point of fact,

---

[1] '... L'anarchie est évidente. Elle est logique aussi. Elle a ses causes, dont les deux principales sont: *la rupture avec la tradition et l'individualisme*' (Recolin, *Anarchie Littéraire*, 1898, p. xii). This writer styles himself the apologist of 'le vieux bon sens français'. Brunetière and Lemaître (among many others) are of the same opinion.

'form', in the sense of something whose break-up Taine noted, dwells at one and the same time in the living substrata of language and the dead hand of custom.

The disappearance of certain conventions as part of the external linguistic challenge to the poet does not imply that he has less of a task before him, less self-imposed demands to satisfy: on the contrary, the bad, the slipshod writer is far more apt to profess a venial piety in that direction, while the more conscientious or scrupulous artist if he destroys some formal canons, does so because he has set up others. One cannot renounce form: one can develop one's own, by modifying to a greater extent than usual some formal element which tradition hands us, and which we learn as we learn language; the modifications may be either relatively slight—like Hugo's modification of the alexandrine—or drastic—like Claudel's disfigurement of the ode. But whatever happens, there is form: art abhors a formal vacuum as ardently as Nature abhors a material one. And if the inherited traditional element is greatly mistreated, or if, for example, the formal construction is of a sort that we are not accustomed to find (say the overall balance in Mallarmé's *Après-midi d'un Faune* or Debussy's) there is still form, though here Taine's narrow application of the word—and the idea—would not allow us to recognize it.

Moreover, if we consider 'subject-matter' to be merely one of the enumerations of the forms of art, then it follows that any tendency towards a diffusion of subject-matters, a flowering-out into new and unconventional fields, will, if the art be living art, have its part in the distintegration of established forms ('moulds' would be a better word in this context).

'To create a form is not merely to invent a shape, a rhyme, or rhythm. It is also the realization of the whole appropriate content of this rhyme or rhythm. The sonnet of Shakespeare is not merely such-and-such a pattern, but a precise way of thinking and feeling.'[1]

And vice versa: the whole appropriate content of a poem is inevitably the creation of a new form—new to however small an extent. Here, then, is another aspect of the impact of 'individualism'.

7. THE DISRUPTION OF FORMS

The young men who set out to overturn literary history in the eighties had nothing so much in their minds as the desire for novelty,

[1] T. S. Eliot, 'The possibility of a Poetic Drama' (*The Sacred Wood*, 5th ed., 1945, p. 63).

in all its varied guises and with its gratifications. Novelty and originality (in its vulgar sense) plainly have something to do with the problem of formal change; their relation with formal excellence, which implies a harmony of all formal ingredients, is not so obvious.

Jules Laforgue is an example ready to hand; and it is in this respect perhaps rather than any other that we can agree with Fagus' dictum that he is truly 'le Symbole du Symbolisme'.[1] For although in his poems we may be tempted to see an undercurrent of yearning for stable tradition, as when he casts a sidelong glance at the Middle Ages with the 'Complaintes', or anchors himself to the themes of earlier literatures in the *Moralités Légendaires*, there is no doubt that Laforgue held adherence to tradition—for its own sake—to be entirely pernicious. In the particular case of the 'Complaintes', indeed, he writes:

> 'J'ai insisté sur le caractère empirique de la Complainte.'[2]

The form is not so much a prescription for success as (in his phrase) a laboratory in which he searches for a new style. In point of fact he condemns all art-forms (which is, of course, only a small range of what we have called forms):

> 'Le Beau Idéal et les œuvres belles en littérature, philosophie (systèmes), poésie, peinture, sculpture, et la hiérarchie des genres, tout cela est une légende d'esprits médiocres et perpétuée par l'autorité des médiocres.'[3]

from which he infers that not only must the work of genius be 'new'[4] and above all else interesting[5] (*sc.*, in its novelty)—which no art, however slavish, can avoid to some trifling degree—but that there are absolutely no 'laws' on whose satisfaction the success of artistic endeavour depends:

> 'Son principe (celui de l'art) est l'anarchie même de la vie; laissez faire, laissez passer.'[6]

And he passes the responsibility for formal consistency (i.e. poetic excellence) out of the sphere of consciousness to the world of dreams, which presumably will never repeat themselves. It is strange that his poetry, and his imaginative prose, should belie this trust in the 'Inconscient', and that successive collections of his verse, from *Le Sanglot de la Terre* down to the *Derniers Vers*, should put before our eyes a style, a constructiveness, that was gaining continually greater confidence, and conscious confidence at that, down to the time

---

[1] In the *Revue Blanche*, 1903, p. 395.
[2] *Inédits de Laforgue*, 1920, letter to Charles Henry, I, 3, 155.
[3] Laforgue, *Mélanges Posthumes*, p. 155.   [4] ibid., p. 206.
[5] ibid., p. 152.   [6] ibid., p. 208.

of his death. As we have suggested elsewhere, the appeal to 'dreams' is here no more than an attempt to find justifications for technical—i.e. formal—developments which a rigid system of 'rules' for composition can hardly tolerate.

Rémy de Gourmont, too, expels the notion of 'le Beau' as a criterion from the artist's horizons; to hear him speak, one would suppose that 'le Beau' is taken as part of a hedonistic theory of the agreeable, including formulae for its realization:

'L'essence de l'Art est la liberté. L'art ne peut admettre aucun code, ni même se soumettre à l'obligatoire expression du Beau.'[1]

We may fairly say that the attack on outworn rhetoric and clichés comes within the movement for the renovation of form; and in this direction, the efforts of the symbolists have been noted in every text-book and history of literature. Too often their renovations have been dismissed as nothing more than attempts to create a stir, to be different, to live up to a bohemian reputation, to shock the bourgeois; a final estimate on the admixture of dross and fine gold rests, of course, with the critic, studying the whole field of poetry in the eighties and nineties. The history of aesthetic has an easier and humbler task; and among the numerous writers whom time has pitilessly unmasked, there are to be found statements from not a few who are plainly sincere in their distrust of 'Rhetoric' and clear on the reasons for their mistrust. Edgar Allan Poe, I suppose, stood godfather to the movement with his statement that

'La *nouveauté*, l'*originalité*, l'*invention*, l'*imagination*, ou enfin la *création* de la *beauté* (car les termes sont ici employés comme synonymes) constituent l'essence de toute Poésie'[2]

—a plain call to novelty for its own sake. More considered is Ernest Raynaud, who from the pages of *Le Décadent*, before he joins Moréas, fulminates against the results of popular education on speech:

'Dès le collège on nous apprend à mentir à nous-mêmes, à nous vêtir d'une personalité d'emprunt, à taire ce que nous éprouvons, et à exprimer dans des discours fictifs, des sentiments que nous ne connaissons pas.

'L'élève s'habitue ainsi à se payer de mots plutôt que d'idées...

'Il faut restituer aux impressions leur originalité, leur valeur primitive, il faut répudier les idées et les formules toutes agencées ... il faut s'apprendre à voir, à juger par soi-même, et à rendre sincèrement ce qu'on sent sincèrement.

'La littérature dénommée *décadente* est surtout une littérature vraie et consciente.'[3]

---

[1] Rémy de Gourmont, 'L'Idéalisme', in *Le Chemin de Velours*, 1903. Cf. his subsequent (and less 'idealist') view, quoted above, p. 121.
[2] Quoted in the *Mercure de France*, t. x, p. 296, iv/1894.
[3] *Le Décadent*, 'Un Point de Doctrine,' 4e. année, no. 29, 15/ii/1889.

A more irresponsible, but far more imposing denunciation had come eighteen years before, though it passed unnoticed at the time: Rimbaud, feeling his way towards a doctrine of form, had rejected almost all prosody of all time as a game,[1] and even blamed the venerated Baudelaire for indulging his taste for elegant form.[2] What he did not realize was that a certain element of novelty attaches to even the feeblest imitativeness; just as the condition of being a 'voyant' is not something absolutely new and unique in the greatest poets, but only a many-fold magnification of something present if unnoticed in all articulate persons, so also 'originality' in writing is not an ingredient used by the great and neglected by the little, but something necessarily attached to the idea of language. A sonnet by Baudelaire is an original form inasmuch as no such sonnet exists either prior or subsequent to it; an exact copy of it is not a new poem but the same one. Rimbaud, in short, has the same attitude to form and content as Taine; and so long as this attitude persists, there is no end to the sterile quarrel between those people on the one hand who want more subservience to poetic 'tradition' and those on the other who want less: falsely arrived at differences of principle are the hardest to reconcile. By the same token, when Ernest Hello produces an aphorism to which Rimbaud would certainly have assented—

'Le plus grand malheur qui puisse arriver au style, c'est de se faire admirer, indé-pendamment de l'idée qu'il exprime'[3]

—he is suggesting something which is in fact impossible, except for discursive writing, judged as something other than art: in poetry the distinction does not exist.

Another feature of this quest for originality—disguised sometimes under the name of rarity—is that it brings in its train illogical distinctions. Language is a tradition formed from many individual usages; but into that tradition must be reckoned not only the past but the present around the writer. This fact is ignored whenever a symbolist sees salvation in a return to Byzantium,[4] or the poet's

---

[1] Cf. 'D'Ennius à Theroldus, de Theroldus à Casimir Delavigne, tout est prose rimée, un jeu... Racine est le pur, le fort, le grand... Après Racine le jeu moisit' (Lettre à Demeney, 15/iv/1871, in Carré, *Lettres de la Vie Littéraire*).

[2] 'Les seconds romantiques sont très *voyants*: Th. Gautier, Leconte de Lisle, Th. de Banville. Mais inspecter l'invisible et entendre l'inouï étant autre chose que reprendre l'esprit des choses mortes, Baudelaire est le premier voyant, roi des poètes, un *vrai Dieu*. Encore a-t-il vécu dans un milieu trop artiste; et la forme si vantée en lui est mesquine' (Lettre à Demeney, 15/v/1871, in Carré, *Lettres*, p. 68). Unmistakeably the utterance of a child in his teens. But what a child !

[3] Hello, *L'Homme*, etc., p. 313.

[4] E.g. Paul Radiot, 'Notre Byzantinisme' (*Revue Blanche*, t. vi, p. 28, ii/1894).

withdrawal from the corrupting influence of popular speech. Charles Morice at one moment writes:

'Le Public corrompt tout ce qu'il touche. Il déprave la langue tellement qu'on peut défier un orateur de se faire entendre en France aujourd'hui s'il parle français, et la lecture des journaux est instructive à ce point de vue.'[1]

But it is instructive for us in our turn to read in the same book:

'Il est impossible de rien dire de neuf dans une langue neuve: elle est ou elle serait barbare, inapte aux flexions, aux modulations ... en vieillissant, les langues acquièrent avec cette phosphorescence de la matière qui se décompose, cette ductilité subtile qui permet de mieux induire l'idée dans les intelligences moins brutalement ouvertes.'[2]

Evidently Morice is attempting (like all his generation) to do two things at once: cut the poet off from the bulk of contemporary tradition of language, and yet retain ties with tradition in another direction—the direction of the past (cf. Moreas' eulogy of 'la bonne et luxuriante et fringante langue française d'avant les Vaugelas et les Boileau-Despréaux' — *Premières armes*). It is clear to him that language is more, in practice, than a system of intellectual symbols and references: that the poet *learns* his language at the same time as he develops it, and does not simply invent it or take it over ready for use. And in this wish to do two things at once, we see an almost imperceptible trace of Mallarmé, sitting sphinx-like behind the scenes, and exercising an immeasurable influence on the rising generations of poets: the idea of withdrawal from the language of 'commerce' is at the very core of his attitude to art; so is his reliance on a long and rich tradition of spoken and written French, in which the poet, searching through the past history of the tongue in an attempt to make it do more and more for him, shall 'donner un sens plus pur aux mots de la tribu'.[3]

The reputation for Byzantinism, everything that is epitomized in *A Rebours* and parodied in *Les Déliquescences*, is one side of the breakdown of strong outward conventions in the formal composition of symbolist poetry: the dissolution of 'definite subjects' held to be the most fit for writing about, the rejection of a 'poetic vocabulary' as against a prose one, and so forth. It is not our intention to enter in detail into the contours of the history of language—the symbolists

---

[1] *La Littérature de tout à l'heure*, 1889, p. 3.   [2] ibid., p. 363.

[3] What T. S. Eliot calls 'developing or procuring the consciousness of the past', which is the way the poet may develop or procure command over the language of the present. The symbolists were not concerned by the sort of weaknesses which exclusive cultivation of the past might lead to. Their general unwillingness to face the problems set by contemporary usage is what specially marks them off from the succeeding generation.

or many of them) had their own momentary preferences for certain
words, certain phrases, certain constructions, themes even, but the
net result of their work was to reduce the influence of artificial
tradition in all these things.

The other principal sector of the language of art in which the
symbolists achieved notoriety is *vers libre*.

8. 'VERS LIBRE'

The case of *vers libre* is a little different from that of the other
formal components of art in the symbolist perspective. Although
in general they thought of it as quite distinct from orthodox rhythmic
patterns, no fantastic theories were produced to account specially
for the escape from conventional restrictions, despite intense
provocation from the deriders of the 'scolopendres' of Moréas' *Le
Pélerin Passionné*. Two obvious and simple facts present themselves
in explanation of this. The aesthetic principle involved is a negative
one; the symbolists were merely carrying to its logical conclusion
that demolition of arbitrary rules for attaining beauty which the
romantic age had long since inaugurated. Symbolism was in the
romantic tradition here, and on familiar ground. But more important,
literary practice of the second half of the nineteenth century had
undermined the authority of conventional verse patterns from other
directions which were not ignored. Baudelaire had written his
petits poèmes en prose; Rimbaud's *Illuminations*, which appeared in
Vogue, were many of them not in any recognizable sort of verse
at all, yet without being *vers libre* were none the less poetry and
recognized as such without difficulty. So it was not hard to bring
one's self to allow that if poetry could be satisfactorily written in
not only the most conventional patterns (e.g. Mallarmé), but in the
most unconventional as well, there was from the practical point of
view no objection to trying out verse patterns intermediate between
the two extremes. And the slightly self-conscious attitude of experiment did not develop into any one-sided account of poetry. Nor,
on the other hand, did it develop into a positive contribution to the
nature of form.

As usual, Mallarmé saw further than the young writers around him,
and announced that there is

'style, versification s'il y a cadence et c'est pourquoi toute prose d'écrivain
fastueux, soustraite à ce laisser-aller en usage, ornementale, vaut en tant qu'un vers

rompu, jouant avec ses timbres et encore les rimes dissimulés; selon un thyrse plu complexe. Bien l'épanouissement de ce qui naguères obtint le titre de *poème e prose.*'[1]

That is to say, in part repairing his erroneous distinction in kin between prose and verse as such by allowing a Chateaubriand or Flaubert to rank as poets. Even the cautious suggestion that some pros is fragmentary poetry, or, to translate into the context of our presen discussion, has partial formal organization,[2] is extraordinarily pene trating, and anticipates in a curious way more recent treatments o the same subject: e.g.—

'Formal patterns are always emerging in the structure of prose, only to be lo again; they emerge because without them the language would be wholly non poetical and would therefore cease to be language; they are lost again because form is here subordinate to matter, and the poetry inherent in language is therefor scattered into an infinity of inchoate poems.'[3]

It would be hardly possible that with this starting-point Mallarm should fail to take up a position in the matter of *vers libre* somewha more lucid than that of his fellow-poets. They saw no further tha the idea of added liberty; he attempted to define the nature of th liberty and disengage some of its implications. So it is that when he i asked his opinion of *vers libre* he answers:

'La Poésie n'est que l'expression musicale et suraiguë, émotionnante, d'un ét d'âme; le vers libre est cela. En résumé peu mais bon.'[4]

At the same time he is not blind to the implications of empirica differences between the long-standing forms, with their rich associa tions in the past, and the new. He expresses these implications i terms of personality and impersonality, of audience therefore; h claims that the new range of subtleties made available are suitabl only for poetry reaching out to an intimate audience, and that th personal touch is not certain of wide communicability. In the sam *Enquête* he expands this view:

'Pour moi le vers classique — que j'appelle le vers officiel — est la grande nef d cette basilique "la Poésie française"; le vers libre, lui, édifie les bas-côtés pleins d'atti ance, de mystère, de somptuosités rares. Le vers officiel doit demeurer, car il est n de l'âme populaire, il jaillit du sol d'autrefois, il sut s'épanouir en sublimes efflores cences. Mais le vers libre est une belle conquête, il a surgi en révolte de l'Idée contr la banalité du "convenu", seulement, pour être qu'il ne s'érige pas en église dissident en chapelle solitaire et rivale! Sachons écouter les grands orgues du vers officiel . puis n'oublions pas que l'art est infini.'[5]

---

[1] *La Musique et les Lettres* (*Revue Blanche*, 1894, p. 298).
[2] That which is lacking being of course the higher formal element such as makes a poe one poem and not a string of exquisite but isolated rhyming lines.
[3] R. G. Collingwood, *An Essay on Philosophical Method*, 1933, p. 201.
[4] *Enquête*, Figaro, 3/viii/1895.   [5] ibid.

'he same view had already been stated by him in a letter to the soi-
isant 'inventor' of *vers libre* on the occasion of the latter's *Palais
Nomades* being published:

'Il en ressort cè point de vue neuf que quiconque musicalement organisé peut, en
coutant l'arabesque spéciale qu'il commande et s'il arrive à la noter, se faire une
nétrique à part soi et hors du type général (devenu monument public quant à
otre ville). Quel délicieux affranchissement! Car notez bien que je ne vous
onsidère point comme ayant mis le doigt sur une forme nouvelle devant qui
'éffacera l'ancienne: cette dernière restera, impersonnelle, à tous et quiconque voudra
'isoler différemment, libre à lui. Vous ouvrez l'un des sentiers, le vôtre: et faites
eci de non moins important qu'il peut en être mille... Il y a en dehors des musiques
onvenues quelque chose comme de très rajeuni dans le mot qui se présente moins
ppuyé et sans apprêts, comme peut-être aussi perd-il du feu compliqué de ses facettes
bsentes à ne pas s'incruster dans un monde mélodique séculaire et ne faisant qu'un
vec le lecteur déjà.'[1]

Iis apprehensions, justifiable perhaps in the single case of Kahn, are
urely unfounded on the general view. As formal constructs, *vers
ibre* bears the same relation to the alexandrine—*le vers officiel*—as
his latter organized loosely in successive pairs does to the sonnet, or
ny less rigid to a more rigidly organized form: moreover, the
hythmic patterns of *vers libre* are not independent of the entire body
)f language, not at the whim of the user, but on the contrary stem
rom it, and are contained within the limits of its rhythmic pos-
ibilities; so that even in *vers libre* there is something of the 'musiques
:onvenues' acting as a link between poet and reader. The dangers are
-ather that the poet of few scruples will not pay sufficient attention in
ers libre to the equivalent 'feu compliqué de ses facettes'; but that is
n objection to the poet, not the form. An added difficulty is rather
n historical than an aesthetic one: at the time of Mallarmé's writing,
ers libre had not yet acquired the weight of traditional use enjoyed
by 'le vers officiel': it was therefore open to the same objections as
Morice raised against a new language; but against that it provided
with astonishing flexibility every sort of reminiscence of different
orthodox rhythms.

The same attitude of tolerance, or rather of veneration, for the
alexandrine is maintained by Mallarmé when he advances in his later
years to the very boundaries of *vers libre*, and devises *Un Coup de Dés*
with its visual accompaniment. Only this time he seems to be trying
to find some special aptitudes in the various forms that he admits:

'Le genre, que c'en devienne un comme la symphonie, peu à peu, à côté du chant
personnel, laisse intacte l'antique vers auquel je garde un culte et attribue l'empire

[1] Letter to Kahn, 8/vi/1887.

de la passion et des rêveries; tandis que ce serait le cas de traiter, de préférence (ains
qu'il suit) tels sujets d'imagination pure et complexe ou intellect: que ne reste aucun
raison d'exclure de la poésie — unique source.'[1]

It must be confessed that the special fitness of the new verse fo
'tels sujets d'imagination pure et complexe ou intellect' is inexplicable
in view of Mallarmé's professed intention when writing *Un Coup d*
Dés: unless we can be content with some such banal reason as that ;
poem designed (as this one was) to be read and not listened to offer
greater help to attention and the understanding, and is thus bette
suited to matter of 'intellect'. The suggestion is feeble, yet there seem
to be no other. But who would dare to see a rigid distinction i
subject between *Un Coup de Dés* and Mallarmé's other metaphysica
poetry?[2]

Against this rather pedantic relegation of *vers libre* to 'auto
biographical' verse, one contemporary at least protested vigorously—
no less a man than the soi-disant inventor himself. Writing in th
Revue Blanche,[3] Gustave Kahn, after reaffirming the novelty of *ver
libre* against detractors who clumsily cited La Fontaine against him
laboriously denies, point by point, the validity of Mallarmé'
reservations. It is perhaps the one occasion on which posterity ca
support so mean and conceited a figure against so penetrating ;
critic.

Nevertheless, Mallarmé's general position on *vers libre* (l'art es
infini') holds; and in the broad context of his philosophy of art ther
is little that can be added to his meticulous and precise descriptions
The distinction between commercial prose and literary poetry is
we have noted, greatly softened by his pronouncements on rhythm
verse, and form generally; with the result that the tense and formalize
speech of *Pelléas et Mélisande* is not excluded from poetry, and bal
clumsy verse can be relegated to its proper station through its failur
to overcome 'le hasard'. This rearrangement of the relative position
of prose and verse as species of poetry answers, of course, to the pro-

---

[1] *Un Coup de Dés*, Préface.

[2] In any case, T. S. Eliot makes an important point when he says, of philosophical poetry
'Donne, Poe et Mallarmé ont la passion de la spéculation métaphysique, mais il est éviden
qu'ils ne croient pas aux théories auxquelles ils s'intéressent ou qu'ils inventent, à la façon don
Dante et Lucrèce affirment les leurs. Ils se servent de leurs théories pour atteindre un but plu
limité et plus exclusif: pour raffiner et pour développer leur puissance de sensibilité et d'émotion
Leur œuvre était une expansion de leur sensibilité *au-delà des limites du monde normal*, une décou
verte de nouveaux objets propres à susciter de nouvelles émotions' ('Note sur Mallarmé e
Poe,' *NRF*, xi/1926, p. 525). The first part of this statement is open to question; but the latte
half is certainly true; and implies, among other things, that metaphysical poetry offers n
special aesthetic problems: metaphysics being as much material for expressive utterance as ;
day in the country. Why then Mallarmé's special scruples?

[3] 'La Vie Mentale,' *Revue Blanche*, t. x, p. 62, 1/i/1896.

gressive decline of what Taine calls 'form' throughout the nineteenth century, and is the aesthetician's answer to the problems of classification in literature that arise from it.

One direct result, attributable in the first place to Baudelaire, is that verse form as such is no longer accepted as sufficient justification for the use of the word 'poetry'; and very long poems are for the first time open to criticism on the grounds that much of them is no longer properly speaking poetry at all. The view finds its classic expression in Baudelaire's prefaces to the translations from Poe; but the less famous remarks on Hugo's epic work are quite as interesting:

'D'abord les poèmes qui constituent l'ouvrage sont généralement courts, et même la briéveté de quelques-uns n'est pas moins extraordinaire que leur énergie. Ceci est déjà une considération importante, qui témoigne d'une connaissance absolue de tout le possible de la poésie moderne.'[1]

A heavily embellished enunciation of the same point appears at the outset of the symbolist wave:

'La vie moderne est trop complexe pour être embrassée tout entière: nous n'en prendrons que l'élixir. Nous fuirons les ouvrages de longue haleine pour de plus courts, de plus variés, et contenant l'essence des premiers. On n'écrira plus de romans parce que personne n'aura plus le temps de les lire. Les nouvelles succéderont à ce genre de productions littéraires, et le sonnet deviendra la limite la plus reculée de l'étendue des poèmes.'[2]

The effect of this announcement is unfortunately spoilt when we find in the very next column Verlaine's 'Prière du Matin'—a poem of ninety-six lines, which has evidently suffered little from being stretched over so large a canvas.[3] It is difficult to tell, here as in so much else connected with the 'decadent' group, how much is serious and how much is window-dressing. The writers in whose company editor Baju formed his opinions may well have been incapable in the main of constructing 'un ouvrage de longue haleine'.

But the principal result of the rearrangement of the respective positions of verse and prose is precisely the great scope given to writers to range freely from powerful to weak effects and back again: a freedom that has stayed with French prose ever since:

'Quant à la forme, j'ai tenté de marquer la supériorité du rythme sur l'artifice de la prosodie. Exactement j'ai cherché un style pouvant passer, au gré de l'émotion,

---

[1] Baudelaire, *Art Romantique*, 'Victor Hugo,' p. 316.   [2] Baju, *Le Décadent*, 16/x/1886.
[3] Verlaine had only recently begun to be accepted by the Decadents: even in 1882 Charles Morice, under the name of Karl Mohr, had compared him for obscurity with Lycophron and Maurice Scève, and expressed the hope 'qu'il n'aura pas de disciples et que cette poésie n'est pas celle de l'avenir' (*Nouvelle Rive Gauche*, 1–8/xii/1882).

de la prose au vers, et du vers à la prose: la prose rythmée fournit la transition. Le vers suit les élisions naturelles du langage. Il se présente comme prose, toute gêne d'élision disparaissant sous cette forme. La prose, la prose rythmée, le vers, ne sont plus qu'un seul instrument gradué.'[1]

Nevertheless, this new freedom in practice does not immediately break down the traditional view of poetry and prose, as witness Dujardin's attempt[2] to retain a distinction between prose poems (derived from prose) and *vers libre* (derived from verse), when it is plain that any difference, other than that of layout on the printed page, is not an ultimate division. The same writer, however, draws an important conclusion from literary practice in the nineties—namely, that this breaking-down of stylistic barriers brought new possibilities into *lyrical drama*:

'Le propre du drame est précisément de passer successivement du ton le plus lyrique au plus terre à terre... le verset est la forme la plus susceptible de s'adapter instantanément à l'un et à l'autre... En réalité, le but était, consciemment ou inconsciemment, pour les symbolistes, d'élaborer un mode d'expression qui permît de passer de la poésie à la non-poésie au fur et à mesure du mouvement de la pensée, et ainsi la poésie put-elle faire son entrée dans les œuvres qui, au premier abord, y auraient semblé les plus réfractaires: articles de critique, histoire, roman.'[3]

9. LYRIC DRAMA. TRANSITION TO THE NEXT CHAPTER

Out of the disintegrating structural traditions—lyrical, dramatic, narrative (novel)—the lyric drama emerges perhaps the one great artistic contribution, not of symbolism but of symbolists, to French literature. The revival of this tradition, in the hands of Maeterlinck, Claudel, Saint-Pol-Roux, Giraudoux, Supervielle, Cocteau, to mention only names well known, could not have taken place without two important moves from the symbolist era: one being the Wagnerian cult which focused attention on the stage as the setting of a great literary-religious *cultus*, and infused life into an independent, non-naturalist dramatic impulse; the other being the upheaval of prosody which opened new possibilities of dramatic diction outside those of Sardou or Dumas in prose and Rostand (or for that matter the Moréas of *Iphigénie*) in verse. Both these moves were essential:

---

[1] Paul Fort, Préface to *Le Roman de Louis XI*, 1898.

[2] 'Quelque rythmés, quelqu'assonancés, quelqu'allitérés que soient les "pieds rythmiques" du poème en prose, il manque à celui-ci l'unité du vers, cette unité respiratoire qui est à la base de la poésie comme de la musique.

Le poème en prose était la tentative de libérer la poésie en prenant la prose pour point de départ; le vers libre et le verset représentent la même tentative en partant du vers... ' (Dujardin, *Mallarmé*, p. 188).

[3] Dujardin, *Mallarmé*, 1936, p. 190.

without an almost religious veneration for some form of 'total art' which demanded dramatic presentation but did not impossibly curb poetic invention, writers would never have approached a sphere so degraded by commercialism, snobbery, and 'bourgeois values' generally; without new precedents and an exciting increase in flexibility of language resources, they could never have succeeded in their venture. Claudel's writing owes much to the dominant style of liturgy and Bible; but it would not have been attempted without the example of Rimbaud.

The formal trends which opened the way to the lyric drama have been examined in the foregoing chapter. The discussion there polarized itself around the twin problems of form and musicality. The first one explains itself: by removing traditional bulkheads, prose and verse became equal contestants for the dignity of poetry. The second is a little more complicated: for in a work of 'total art' the musical element might be present *either* in its own right (music, either vocal or accompaniment), *or* as assonance and alliteration in poetry, *or* as sheer poetic excellence. But in combination with other arts poetry loses its self-sufficiency, since the total unity of structure is conceived no longer on the plane of speech but on a higher plane altogether (as when we judge an *opera* as opposed to music or libretto alone); and accordingly 'musicality' less frequently means simple poetic beauty. The problem is also linked with that of 'audition colorée', and the alleged correspondence between the arts. As longed for by the symbolists, the total work of art (*L'Œuvre*) is primarily Wagnerian, a music drama; and this formula was hoped to embrace all the diverse aspirations of the age. That it was never realized, in any form at all, may be due to causes outside the power of any single person to alter; the greatest art answers the greatest demand for it; and the demand around 1890 for a successor to Aeschylus, or Shakespeare, or Wagner, was a mere trickle: the voices of a few coteries and their magazines. The mountain laboured, and brought forth a fragmented *Hérodiade*: Mallarmé was no Goethe to repeat the miracle of *Faust*, begun in youth and finished in old age. Maeterlinck's range was successful, but limited; Vincent d'Indy was not Wagner the poet; Dujardin was not Wagner the musician, the producer, the conductor, the unscrupulous promoter; there were no kings of Bavaria in Paris, ready to support the costs of a great venture —and there were no great ventures. In place of *Parsifal*, the experimental stage was given *Pelléas et Mélisande*.

CHAPTER V

THE CLASSIFICATION OF THE ARTS

1. Wagner in France. 2. Baudelaire and Synesthesia. 3. Analogies. 4. Music as an exceptional art. 5. The Wagnerian art-synthesis and myth. 6. The status of music in symbolist aesthetic. 7. Total Art.

1. WAGNER IN FRANCE

THE symbolist movement's interest in and insistency on the 'musicality' of poetry has been repeatedly and confidently linked by critics with the cult of Wagnerism.[1] Examination of the ambiguities contained within the word 'musicality' should have by this time have established the fact that all sweeping uses of it lead to danger, that a loose affiliation of this sort lands us in trouble in the long run; but the dangers of glibly relating the symbolists with Wagner have never been fully revealed. If we apply a simple test by asking how many Wagnerites became symbolists for every symbolist that professed himself a Wagnerite, and examine the conditions of these conversions, some curious things come to light, but none of them confirms the legend of Wagner's 'influence'. In point of fact, neither of the two possible conversions could ever have been genuinely possible, and this for a number of reasons: first, because a wholesale conversion to Wagnerism is only conceivable in an artist prepared to imitate Wagner to the point of only writing music-dramas; secondly, because Wagner's theories were so inaccurately propagated and imperfectly understood that the symbolists of 1885–95 were able—indeed forced—to make up a great part of them; thirdly, because the Wagnerian theory was from start to finish hostile to the whole conception of art that the symbolists were endeavouring to formulate. These claims will be made good in the course of the

[1] E.g. 'C'est Wagner qui a été la grande révélation en musique pour Baudelaire, Mallarmé, et pour la génération symboliste. Ce ne sont pas les simples mélodies d'autrefois, ce sont les polyphonies wagnériennes qui les attirent, et qu'ils rêvent de reproduire par des efforts d'orchestration écrite' (Duthie, *L'Influence du Symbolisme*, etc., p. 149). And (surprisingly) Thibaudet, speaking of Mallarmé: 'Un idéalisme partant des correspondances de Baudelaire, qui se rencontre avec le wagnérisme' (*La Poesie de Stéphane Mallarmé*). Dujardin, a prime mover in this matter, makes even more extravagant claims for Wagnerism as the vessel by which Schopenhauer was made known to the symbolists: '(*La Revue Wagnérienne*) a été le trait d'union entre Wagner et Mallarmé, entre Schopenhauer et le symbolisme; elle a aidé les symbolistes à prendre conscience de la profonde nécessite musicale qui s'imposait à eux' (*Mallarmé par nos siens*, p. 234).

present chapter. To some extent, Mallarmé might be cited as an example of a poet seeking in the works of Wagner confirmation for views already formed;[1] seeking, indeed, but not finding; his disappointment leads to us being given unique glimpses of his general conception of art. For most of the younger writers, however, Wagnerism and symbolism were two simultaneous discoveries; both were novel, to some extent exciting, and so far as could be seen, not incompatible. Many went on to the assumption that both were therefore integral parts of a new general aesthetic. We shall examine in some detail the work of Téodor de Wyzéwa as a representative of this class.

The first stone of Bayreuth was laid in 1872; the opening performance of the theatre was given in 1876. Wagner died in 1883, shortly after the completion of his most characteristic and Wagnerian music-drama (the 'Bühnenweihfestspiel' *Parsifal*). In 1885 the *Revue Wagnérienne* was founded in Paris for the discussion and appreciation of his work.[2] The review was patronized and supported financially by wealthy music-lovers; but its editor Dujardin and most of its collaborators were closely linked with the advance-guard of literature, and admirers of Mallarmé. Wyzéwa was a frequent contributor to the review; and it was at least to a large extent from his articles (reputedly authoritative) that the symbolist movement seems to have taken its ideas on the German musician.[3] In addition, it might be remarked that political and personal factors combined to keep Wagner off the Paris stage until the nineties. All that Mallarmé ever heard of Wagner was performed in excerpts at the Lamoureux concerts; the alternative for those days was to make the Bayreuth pilgrimage. This no doubt sharpened the intellectuals' support for a genius spurned by 'bourgeois' society; and the servile copying of Wagnerian themes by Dujardin (*Antonia* is the French Kundry) and Villiers (*Axel*, etc.) passed unnoticed. In a sense, Wagner's reputation throve on the absence rather than on the presence of his works in France.

[1] 'C'est la *Revue Wagnérienne* enfin, qui, en la personne de son directeur — et je m'en glorifie — a conduit Mallarmé aux Concerts Lamoureux' (Dujardin, *Mallarmé*, p. 40). The event took place on Good Friday, 1885; we do not know what opinions Mallarmé might already have formed of an artist whom Baudelaire had so passionately admired.

[2] For a survey of its career, see I. Wyzewska, *La Revue Wagnérienne*, 1934. Mlle Wyzewska examines Wyzéwa's articles, but fails to pin down many of their inaccuracies.

[3] Schuré's *Le Drame Musical* (1886) is contemporary, and has the advantage of being a hotch-potch of Wagner's own arguments and phrases; but it is not designed to catch the symbolist fancy. For an authoritative account of Wagner's doctrines, H. S. Chamberlain's article in the *Revue des Deux Mondes* (1895) appeared somewhat late in the day. There was no shortage of garbled and confused literature on the matter. [Few took account of the important but awkward changes that took place in Wagner's aesthetic speculations between 1851 and 1870: his earlier writing is untouched by Schopenhauer's influence, and this accounts for some of the confusions recorded in the following pages.]

Wyzéwa's articles are a good illustration of the claim that the symbolists did not really follow—did not really want to follow—the gist of Wagner's theories. In a series of articles ('L'Art Wagnérien'[1]) he sets out to show that Wagner's aesthetic rests on a solipsism attributable to Schopenhauer's influence, sketches out a classification of the arts according to a curious division of the faculties of the mind, and redefines literature in the light of his findings. The whole process is intended to reconcile or rather prove the identity of Wagnerian and symbolist aesthetic. The first part of the programme need not keep us long. Wyzéwa's contributions to 'idealism' have been noted in their place (ch. II, 5); he claims that Wagner is not content to stop in the position of Fichte or Schopenhauer, but makes some unspecified advance on these; notably in overcoming radical pessimism, finding lasting satisfaction in art, and becoming 'le mage divin'.

'Cette ascension fut-elle par lui nettement perçue? Et l'explication que j'en ai tenté, l'eût-il approuvé? cela n'importe en vérité. Et si Wagner a cru, plus modeste que son maître, reprendre seulement la doctrine de Schopenhauer, qui de nous le pourra blâmer de n'avoir pas compris les Parerga?'[2]

Who indeed! Whether or not Wagner would have approved of these condescending analyses, whether they truly reflected subconscious trends in his thought, is something we shall be concerned with for much of this chapter. Wagner's three main contributions to aesthetic, *Art and Revolution*, *The Art of the Future*, and *Opera and Drama* are an unknown world to French letters in the symbolist era. None of the literary Wagnerians, except perhaps Chamberlain,[3] had the necessary mental or linguistic equipment to grasp the thorny dogmas of Bayreuth and translate them to the French scene, even if, so translated, they had continued to mean anything at all. However, it has been well pointed out that what was wanted in the *Revue Wagnérienne* was less Wagner's doctrines set out accurately, than

---

[1] *La Revue Wagnérienne*, 'L'Art Wagnérien': I. 'Le péssimisme de Richard Wagner,' vii/1885; II. 'La Peinture wagnérienne,' v/1886; III. 'La Littérature wagnérienne,' vi/1886; IV. 'La Musique wagnérienne,' vii and ix/1886. The articles are republished in *Nos Maîtres*.

[2] 'Le Pessimisme de Richard Wagner,' *Revue Wagnérienne*, 8/vii/1885. In similar terms Dujardin writes: 'Je suis sûr que Wagner eût été le premier à encourager les disciples qui, à la lumière de son œuvre, non seulement le cherchaient, mais se cherchaient eux-mêmes *au lieu de se contenter de le suivre*' (*Mallarmé*, p. 214). My italics. This from the editor himself!

[3] Cf. Dujardin's remark, for the rest a little theatrical: 'Chamberlain était sans doute un peu mieux instruit que nous, et seul il connaissait vraiment l'allemand. "L'Anneau des Nibelung" en particulier était pour nous un abîme quasi insondable' (*Mallarmé*, p. 199). But Wyzéwa knew German, and Chamberlain translated most of the *Ring* into French for the *Revue Wagnérienne*.

arguments to reinforce symbolist tendencies with the prestige of his name.[1]

As regards the classification of the arts in Wagner's system, Wyzéwa is open to the charge not so much of distortion as of invention. Wagner, to begin with, talks in his works mainly of the relations between speech and music (*Wortsprache* and *Tonsprache*); of the other arts he has nothing directly constructive to say. Wyzéwa is more ambitious:

'Les vrais Wagnériens ne bornent pas à la musique leurs curiosités; ils s'inquiètent encore des progrès de l'esprit wagnérien dans les œuvres des littérateurs, des poètes, des peintres.'[2]

He observes of painting, as Mallarmé observes of the more servile kind of writing, that it is largely 'commercial'; imitative, in this case, tarnished with the habit of never departing from set traditions, and emasculated by its severance from the other arts:

'La peinture, étant une forme de l'art, doit se rattacher à la destination totale de l'art.'[3]

So far so good. Wagner says the same. But the agreement is no better than verbal: Wagner means to ban painting, or poetry, in isolation, altogether: Wyzéwa means to make painting musical, poetical; the difference is not one to overlook. This leads into an analysis of the factors which go to make up artistic creation. They are the same as those which constitute all experience: what Wyzéwa calls sensation, emotion, and intellection or forming notions. The plastic arts are accorded the sphere of sensation, and by reason of this one-sidedness normal painting is stigmatized as an abstraction from reality; statuary, with its omission of colour, is even a stage further from 'reality' than polychrome painting (Wagner did not share his error of supposing that the Greeks did not paint their statues and are therefore condemned to inferiority in this field). Literature, equally, is the art of notions; music, as might be expected, of emotions. Thus painting, music, and poetry are held each to represent one 'mode' of life:

'Or la vie est dans l'union de ses trois modes.'[4]

---

[1] Wyzewska, op. cit., p. 133.
[2] Wyzéwa, 'L'Art Wagnérien, La Peinture,' *Revue Wagnérienne*, v/1886.   [3] ibid.
[4] op. cit. Wyzéwa has some typical gloses of 'la vie'.
'La Vie que nous avions créée, créée afin de nous donner la joie créatrice, a perdu son caractère premier. Il faut donc la recréer; il faut — au-dessus de ce monde des apparences habituelles profanées — bâtir le monde saint d'une meilleure vie: meilleure, parce que nous la pouvons créer volontairement, et savoir que nous la créons. C'est la tâche même de l'art.' ('Art Wagnérien,' II.)
'L'art, dit Wagner, doit créer la vie. Pourquoi? Parce qu'il doit poursuivre volontairement

Therefore, in so far as each art acquires real worth, its practitioner enlarges his field of action to include rudimentary traces of the others —not, as Wagner has it, combines the arts, each developed in its own rights. In poetry, 'musicality' is added to the language of notion (see above, ch. IV, 5(*a*)); in painting, line and colour become 'signes de nos émotions'—therefore musical too; in music Wagner has introduced representative elements (painting) and even logical elements (poetry) by means of *leit-motif.*

In separation, each art tends to become more and more abstractive, more and more self-stultifying. Literature, the art of notion, becomes more and more detailed, and ends finally in the naturalist novel; its communication becomes less and less 'immediate'. The narration of the epic poem gives way to the vicarious acting of persons on a stage; and this in turn to the quite impersonal medium of the printed novel.[1] The only way to avoid such stultification—for it goes without saying that the naturalist novel no less than the 'commercial' portrait are repugnant to the symbolist or Wagnerian artist—is to have recourse, as Wagner does, to 'total' or 'synthetic' art, in which a true balance is restored between the different aspects of human experience; or, what Wyzéwa seems to think the same thing, to poetry or painting of the symbolist or impressionist schools.[2] We must remember that we are dealing with the first efforts of a young and ambitious critic; and that in any case Wagner's own writings bristle with contradictions. But Wyzéwa does not remain within the limits of Wagnerian contradictions; in particular the doctrine of 'sensation' (to bring in the plastic arts) is his own invention. It is not an easily managed one. At every point the elements in art attributable to 'sensation' appear to overlap with those attributable to 'emotion'; on the one hand, sensations are

'phénomènes de plaisir ou de peine ... uniquement des états intérieurs de l'esprit'[3]

la fonction naturelle de toute activité de l'esprit. C'est que le monde où nous vivons, et que nous dénommons réel, est une pure création de notre âme. L'esprit ne peut sortir de lui-même; et les choses qu'il croit extérieures à lui sont uniquement ses idées. Voir, entendre, *c'est créer en soi des apparences,* donc créer la vie' (ibid.). Or again,

'Nous voyons autour de nous des arbres, des animaux, des hommes, et nous les supposons vivants; mais ils ne sont, ainsi perçus, que des ombres vaines, tapissant le décor mobile de notre vision: et ils vivront seulement lorsque l'artiste, dans l'âme privilégiée duquel ils ont une réalité plus intense, leur insufflera cette vie supérieure, les *recréera* devant nous... L'art doit donc recréer, dans une pleine conscience, et par le moyen de signes, la vie totale de l'univers, c'est-à-dire de l'Âme, où se joue le drame varié que nous appelons l'Univers' (ibid.).

[1] 'L'Art Wagnérien: Littérature,' *Revue Wagnérienne*, vi/1886.
[2] Wyzéwa finds in Impressionism an absolutely new artistic principle; namely, an 'emotional' factor.
[3] 'L'Art Wagnérien,' II: 'La Peinture.'

—what any plain man would call emotions; while at the same time, emotions are described as

'un tourbillon confus de couleurs, de sonorités, et de pensées';[1]

or again,

'L'émotion est ainsi un état très instable et très rare de l'esprit; elle est un rapide afflux d'images, de notions, un afflux si dense et si vif que l'âme n'en peut discerner les éléments, toute à sentir l'impression totale.'[2]

—evidently at least in part 'sensations'. It is impossible to distinguish a dividing-line. Sensation, at any rate, is homogeneous throughout all the senses;[3] the painter on canvas can evoke sensations other than visual; but he can also stray into the field of 'emotion', and there are at least two sorts of painting—'la peinture émotionnelle' and 'la peinture descriptive':

'Chacun des éléments de la peinture a ici' (in Rembrandt) 'la valeur d'un accord harmonique: et ces peintres, pour ne pas représenter une vision réelle, n'en sont pas moins puissamment réalistes en ce qu'ils recréent une émotion totale, réelle et vivante. Mais ne sent-on pas combien cette émotion est spéciale, combien différente de l'émotion que nous suggère une œuvre de musique?

'Aussi la *peinture émotionnelle*, à côté de la *peinture descriptive*, a-t-elle un droit légitime à exister, et la valeur d'un art également précieux.'[4]

It is hard to see why Wyzéwa refrains from noticing a category of 'peinture conceptuelle', for which equally good—if not better—justification exists: Baudelaire had filled his *Salons* with invective against it.

The relation between 'sensation' and 'notion' is more straight-forward; but again, answers to nothing in Wagner:

'Nos sensations s'agrègent, et par leur répétition se limitent; des groupes s'organisent, abstraits de l'ensemble initial: des mots les fixent. Les *sensations* deviennent alors des *notions*; l'âme pense après avoir *senti*.'[5]

Literature takes its origin from this faculty, and starts as a purely intellectual activity, each word a symbol for a single concept:

'Le mot est une image: à chaque mot doit répondre une image, une notion nette, unique.'[6]

---

[1] ibid.   [2] 'L'Art Wagnérien,' IV.
[3] 'Sous l'effet d'une lente habitude, nos sensations visuelles sont devenues capables d'évoquer en nous, par leur seule présence, toute la grappe des autres sensations. Il a suffi désormais à l'homme de voir des couleurs pour percevoir, sans autre secours, le relief et la résistance, et aussi la température, et l'odeur, et le son des objets' ('L'Art Wagnérien,' II). Why then trouble to accompany words with music? This is the Baudelairean dilemma; and the argument whereby Mallarmé expressed his differences with Wagner.
[4] 'L'Art Wagnérien,' II.
[5] ibid. For Wagner, words are slowly coagulated out of musical utterance.
[6] 'L'Art Wagnérien,' III: 'Littérature.'

Wyzéwa infers from this that so long as literature remained within this strict discipline, it could not become art; its acquisition of artistic status, indeed, dates hardly from before the nineteenth century; it becomes art only when it acquires the many-sided conformity to life conferred by musicality. In contrast to Wagner, who set great store by the mere presence of rhyme, verse as such is no more art than prose:

'Ainsi entendu, la Poésie fut très postérieure à la forme du vers — qu'elle n'implique pas nécessairement — et aux écrivains qu'on nomme les poètes. Le vers avait été d'abord un appareil mnémonique: exigé aussi par les premières convenances du chant, en raison de sa coupe régulière favorable aux retours de la mélodie.'[1]

Likewise:

'La musique des mots peut en effet être aussi clairement et plus entièrement exprimée par une prose: une prose toute musicale et émotionnelle, une libre alliance, une alliance harmonieuse de sons et de rythmes, indéfiniment variée suivant l'indéfini mouvement des nuances d'émotion.'[2]

To be sure, a good many secure reputations must be knocked down by this new reckoning:

'Dois-je dire que ni Corneille ni Molière ni la plupart des écrivains en vers de notre siècle ne furent vraiment des poètes? Une convention les forçait à déformer leurs pensées pour les soumettre à un rythme fixe et inintelligent, à des rimes superflues.'[3]

Since Wagner, writing in the German tradition of letters, was not confronted by a situation in prosody resembling that of the French symbolists, we need not expect to find that Wyzéwa has been transcribing from his writings any of these arguments in defence of *vers libre*!

Literature only becomes art, then, by grafting upon itself a musicality quite alien to its essential, intellectual, nature.[4] This process can never entirely succeed: musicality—i.e. elements springing from emotional aspects of experience—is at best a temporary interruption, and necessarily dislocates the sense of the narrative

---

[1] ibid.   [2] ibid.   [3] ibid.

[4] The writers responsible for this remarkable operation 'aperçurent que les mots, en plus de leur signification notionnelle précise, avaient revêtu pour l'oreille des sonorités spéciales, et que les syllabes étaient devenues des sonorités musicales, et aussi les rythmes de la phrase. Alors ils tentèrent un art nouveau, la *poésie*. Ils employèrent les mots non plus pour leur valeur notionnelle, mais commes des syllabes sonores, évoquant dans l'âme des alliances harmoniques ('L'Art Wagnérien,' II). Or again, 'La Littérature, art des notions, comme la peinture, art des sensations, ont, sous le développement et la liaison des idées, produit des arts nouveaux, spéciale-ment émotionnels... La littérature a produit un art symphonique, la Poésie, évoquant l'émotion par l'agencement musical des rythmes et des syllabes' ('L'Art Wagnérien,' III). Utterances such as these, which have misled the more gullible critic of present times into supposing the symbolists devoted their energies to stringing together vowel-sounds, neverthe-less reveal a very definite obsession with certain language resources on the part of Wyzéwa and his friends, for which it would not be hard to find an overwhelming quantity of illustrations.

thread;[1] and this perhaps a Wagnerian would point out as a reason why the 'musical' technique of a Mallarmé or a Monet can never make painting or poetry entirely self-sufficing. Though this would allow Wyzéwa, if he chose, to move on to common ground with Wagner in demanding music-drama, or some form of combined art-performance, he hardly takes advantage of his opportunity. Cautiously he draws the Wagnerian conclusion that the separate arts gain by being brought together in a synthetic form:

'[Wagner] a vu que les peintres et les littérateurs, et les musiciens, exerçaient avec un droit égal les modes diverses d'une tâche commune. Désormais, et par lui, l'Art n'est plus dans la peinture, ni dans la littérature, ni dans la musique, mais dans l'union étroite de ces genres et dans la vie totale qui en naît.'[2]

If this is so, Wyzéwa is logically bound to adopt the view, defiantly flaunted by Wagner, that all simple playwrights, simple composers, and simple painters, were wasting their time, and that the only good to nineteenth-century art could come from the adoption of his (Wagner's) practice of combining all in music-drama. Wagnerian doctrine, in point of fact, always over-reaches itself and proves that Wagner was the only true artist history has ever seen. Not surprisingly, Wyzéwa does not persist in the attempt to convince the Parisian world that it contains no true artists; instead, in the course of his remarks on 'musicality' of line and colour in painting, he exclaims:

'Mais à quoi bon cette musique nouvelle? La musique des sons ne suffirait-elle pas à traduire toute l'émotion? Elle n'y suffirait nullement. Les poètes, les peintres symphonistes, créent bien des émotions, comme les musiciens, mais ils créent des émotions tout autres, dont la différence, d'ailleurs, ne peut se définir, l'émotion étant, par sa nature même, indéfinissable.'[3]

The conclusion is rank heresy, from the Wagnerian point of view; and it may sound unsatisfactory and negative; but it would have been important enough had Wyzéwa cared to pause and consider what its

[1] Cf. his remarks, a propos of novels, in 'L'Art Wagnérien', III: 'La vie que peuvent recréer les littératures est une vie où les émotions interrompent, par places, la série des notions. Le romancier devra donc mêler à la forme du récit la forme musicale de la poésie. Il exprimera les douleurs et les joies par des agencements sonores et rythmiques des syllabes, *insoucieux*—dans ces rares passages—du sens notionnel des *mots*: *puisque* aussi bien nuls mots ne peuvent traduire l'émotion.' (My italics.) A curious fancy! He expands it in his next article: 'Traduire l'émotion par des mots précis était évidemment impossible; c'était décomposer l'émotion, donc la détruire. L'émotion, moins encore que les autres modes vitaux, ne peut être traduite directement; elle peut seulement nous être *suggérée*. Et pour suggérer les émotions, mode subtil et dernier de la vie, un signe special a été inventé: le son musical' ('L'Art Wagnérien,' IV).

[2] 'L'Art Wagnérien,' II: 'La Peinture'. Cf. also: 'Comme la vie n'est point des sensations, ni des notions, ni des émotions, mais une série enchêvetrée de ces modes divers, les divers arts doivent tendre à un Art total, unissant tous les signes artistiques pour recréer toute la Vie' (Wyzéwa, 'Une Critique,' *Revue Indépendante*, t. i, p. 66, xi/1886). Even here, Wyzéwa is still tactful: a Mallarmeen sonnet may very well 'tend' towards total art, by virtue of the 'music' in its language.

[3] ibid.

implications were: for if each art has its own (distinct) range of emotional expression, even though the differences are not definable, there is an end to Wagner's (and Wyzéwa's) division of labour for producing 'total art'; what is more, there is an end, once and for all, to any systematic classification of the arts. Each branch of 'musical' art reveals itself as an independent realm, with its own particular connections with 'emotion', and presumably with intellection too.

This line of reasoning is steadfastly refused by Wyzéwa, and the flash of common sense is lost again in a welter of pseudo-Wagnerianism, never to be recovered. It is to some extent a tribute to the young critic that he can so far contradict himself as to come nearer the truth on artistic fact than the aesthetic theory he champions logically allows; when all is said, the theory he returns to is a woeful piece of private apologetic. It is not even what it claims to be—Wagnerian; from the articles in the Revue Wagnérienne it would be possible to infer that he had never so much as set eyes upon a single word from Wagner's pen, nor heard at second hand a reliable account of the Master's philosophy of art.

Wagner makes no such triple distinction as Wyzéwa does between sensation, emotion, and intellection, to correspond with the three main arts. He makes two: on the one hand he classes feeling with the predominant aspect of music and abstract thought with the predominant aspect of speech. If that were all, we might reasonably suppose that Wyzéwa added the third ingredient as a simple pretext for airing his appreciation of modern painters; but it is not all. Wyzéwa places the origin of speech quite outside the sphere of feeling, as a symbolical activity having for its ingredient references the data of perfectly sterile, un-emotionalized sensation; and music is roundly contrasted as the expression of emotion. Speech becomes partly artistic through imitating music. Wagner, on the other hand, declares that music has its origin in the modulated cry of emotion: man singing is not to be distinguished—except as regards the complexity of his song—from the baboon or the parrot; music is the primordial art. Speech, so far from being a fresh stem of utterance, is music, after the latter has been subjected to a process of direction to enable it to particularize reference. As vowel sounds, speech is still musical: Wagner is careful to note that Greek tragedy was sung, not declaimed in a flat voice;[1] consonants are only one of many ingredients that turn it into an instrument of symbolic reference. It is

[1] As compared with our present-day impression of Greek tragedy, he declares, the old drama stands in the same relation as do the painted buildings of mediaeval architecture to its colourless survivals.

inconceivable that Wyzéwa, had he known of Wagner's theory of the emergence of speech from music and emotional expression, should have ignored it in favour of a makeshift so palpably less suited even to pressing the claims for 'musical' poetry as a new artistic development;[1] especially as Wagner had devoted quite an elaborate and lengthy section of *Oper und Drama* (his longest and most important theoretical work) to showing how speech evolves out of musical utterance.

Ignorance of Wagner the theoretician's classification of the arts goes hand in hand with very precise contradiction of certain other, less central, opinions of Wagner the composer. In his fourth article, Wyzéwa is evidently at sea when he claims first that the greatest music is essentially 'melodic', and yet at the same time that Wagner transcends melody with polyphony.[2] Polyphony, after all, is only the juxtaposition of melody—rendered inevitable in Wagner's case not only by musical considerations, but by the complicated and often subtle use of *leit-motif* themes, but not in any sense as an epoch-making elaboration. From Weber to Berlioz, no doubt, polyphonic writing had gone through a thin time: but what of before Weber? Had Wyzéwa studied Wagner's account of the nature of opera, he would have learnt that the basic aria form must be taken as something so general, so all-embracing, that polyphonic elaboration is a mere detail on its surface. Wyzéwa, it must be presumed, is drawing on personal impressions of Wagnerian music-drama to cover ignorance of Wagnerian music-theory; and they are the impressions of one not versed in music. In any case, the denigration of harmony as 'precious' is not only silly, but in contradiction with Wagner's own very sound view of it as an aspect of melody—as a subordinate aspect devoted to developing and refining the implications of melodic line.

More flagrantly anti-Wagnerian still is the suggestion that as

[1] This aspect of Wagner's theory leaves plenty of scope for poetry to exist as a 'musical' art alongside music, music-drama, or anything else. For if speech contains a kernel of musicality, no very radical operations are necessary to restore this to view: certainly nothing so drastic as a 'grafting'.

[2] There is an ugly display of false erudition. E.g. 'Le romantisme est un résultat précieux: il crée l'*harmonie*. Les musiciens antérieurs, et Beethoven lui-même, connaissent seulement la mélodie.' To test the argument, we need hardly trouble which of Bach's organ toccatas we call into instance. Wyzéwa also invents a dialectic for the emergence of polyphony, corresponding to a shift in social emphasis: 'Aux simples âmes incultes, la mélodie, la chanson; à beaucoup la mélodie plus parfaite de l'opéra; à quelques-unes les complexes langages des contrepoints, les nuances des accents et des timbres' ('L'Art Wagnérien', IV). Wagner was not so ignorant—or at least not so incautious

melody becomes more refined—eventually polyphonic—it appeals to a more and more limited audience; finally to an *élite*, indeed, which as described can be none other than the intellectual aristocracy of the Rue de Rome, of the *Revue Wagnérienne*, and its adherents. It may be true that polyphonic music is not the chosen field of art for those 'simples âmes incultes' who maintain the continuity of folk-music; but it was certainly not Wagner's intention to write for an *élite*. To try to fit Wagner into any known brand of ivory tower would have disastrous effects on the tower; no one whose pockets were so bulging with revolutionary, anarchist, religious, and other tracts would stand much chance of getting far in through the door. Wagner saw himself as a liberator of humanity, destined like any other of the great prophets to have an immeasurable effect on the lives of men, in his lifetime as well as in the future; it is not likely that he would be shy of disclosing the wonders of his art to the world outside his immediate supporters—even in Paris, of which he kept bitter memories. We may see in Wyzéwa's false step here the attempt to cut Wagner to fit Mallarmé's suits, rather than to reflect even faintly the intention of Wagnerian art; and this is all the more surprising for the fact that in not one but all of his writings Wagner insists on the mass regeneration of society which cannot be separated from the development of 'Art of the Future'. Revolution and anarchy in the 'Zürich' period; the gospel of love at Bayreuth; invariably Wagner's message is a call to action to all humanity, not a refined whisper to chosen friends.

An equally egregious misrepresentation must close our list of deviations by Wyézwa from Wagner's aesthetic doctrines; again a flat contradiction of a quite basic ingredient.

'Les sons de la musique' (declares Wyzéwa) 'ne doivent pas nous intéresser en tant que sons, mais comme les représentants d'émotions artistiques. Mais un jour vient où, pour les âmes très délicates, les signes de l'art apparaissent trop sensibles, incapables désormais d'être négligés. La perception de l'œuvre est ainsi gênée, un intermédiaire s'est dressé, non senti auparavant, entre ces âmes et l'âme de l'artiste créateur. Alors l'artiste doit employer des signes moins matériels, plus différents, par leur aspect sensible, des choses qu'ils signifient... La musique, art postérieur,' (this is hardly Wagner's opinion) 'et plus constamment modifiée dans ses langages, a subi moins vivement l'influence de cette loi. Mais déjà l'heure approche où les sons musicaux ne pourront plus produire l'émotion s'ils sont directement entendus; leur caractère propre de sons empêchera l'âme de les considérer comme de purs signes d'émotions. Une musique nouvelle deviendra nécessaire, écrite, non jouée, suggérant l'émotion sans l'intermédiaire de sons entendus, la suggérant ainsi meilleure et plus intime.'[1]

[1] 'L'Art Wagnérien,' IV.

This, as anyone will know who has so much as dipped into **Wagner's** writings or formed an impression of their tone, is mere invention. A large section of *Das Kunstwerk der Zukunft* is devoted to showing that drama is only drama on the condition that it is acted on the stage: 'literary-drama', as Wagner derisively calls it, is an innovation of modern times, a mere ghost of drama, condemned to its shadowy existence by the modern playwright's lack of theatre-sense and technique. Wagner himself had a flair for the effective theatrical stroke, and was not ashamed of the fact.[1] The same outraged condemnation of art not intended for performance appears in *Oper und Drama*, with additional blame, this time not for Goethe but for Shakespeare.[2] Wagner makes it quite plain that all the arts, not only drama, are directed to the senses, on pain of not being art; that their full impact can only come about by flesh-and-blood performance. Wagner's motives for this determined stand are obvious; there are plenty of people who will read a play in their armchairs at home; but not many who will—or can—read an operatic score in the same way. If opera (or music-drama) is already defined as a form of art superior to spoken drama, because more complete, then it stands to reason that in default of score-readers there must be flesh-and-blood audiences; especially since art is to become a corporate act of social cohesion. Two explanations offer themselves for Wyzéwa's strange invention: partly he may have wished to give his readers the impression that the critic of the *Revue Wagnérienne* could read a full score (which he quite certainly could not); partly—and more decisively—he was adapting to the case of music what Mallarmé already professed regarding poetry: the very distillation of refined preciosity. It appears that Wagner was having fathered on him a tenet more characteristic of symbolist fashion than of Wagnerian aesthetic.

To settle at this point the conflict of opinion between the flesh-and-blood school of Wagner and the etherializing school of Mallarmé would be anticipating the further course of argument of this chapter; but it may be remarked that if art is an imaginative activity, no basic distinction can be drawn between hearing a piece of music and reading it off the score, between reading a poem silently and reciting it aloud. The armchair drama-reader need not have a stage before him, nor spring up at intervals to gesticulate.

[1] See *Das Kunstwerk der Zukunft*, 1851, *Werke*, 3rd ed., 1897, vol. III, p. 111.
[2] Nineteenth-century playwrights, he declares, seeing how much trouble and expense attended the frequent changes of scene in Shakespeare, despaired of ever solving their stage problems (*Oper und Drama*, 'Das Schauspiel und das Wesen der dramatischen Dichtkunst,' 1.)

The printed page with its imagined speech is often more ambiguous than the spoken word; but that is no basis for a distinction in kind. Wagner and Mallarmé have preferences which exclude one another in practice; but to elevate these preferences into contradictory principles is to fall into self-contradiction. Wagner's 'principle' would involve the claim that no one could remember *Parsifal* the day after he had seen it, or memorize the music: to do these things is difficult, but it is what Wagner himself did, and what every subsequent producer and conductor must do too, if he is to master his work.

Wyzéwa's account of Wagnerianism is not a fair example of the symbolist's reaction to the music-drama; it is much too protracted and, in its way, systematic to be that: but it is a fair example of what the symbolist would have written had he attempted such a task of exposition. The kernel of the whole account lies in the claim that all the arts are to some extent musical, or must become so: where musicality is equated roundly with emotivity. Wyzéwa's attitude is not far different from that of René Ghil when the latter writes, of symbolism:

'... Une expression que nous dirions émotive émane pourtant de tout l'évertuement et permet de le voir sous un aspect d'unité rendant distincte et délimitant historiquement cette Epoque — qui logiquement ne peut être comprise sous une appellation unique... '[1]

Wyzéwa's approach to art is not so simple as that; but it contains the 'emotive' idea as an integral element. The question of emotivity in relation to poetic language has already been treated, and Wyzéwa's position plotted out; from it the interpretation of Wagner follows inevitably. It makes no difference that Wagner's own aesthetic is in this matter relatively anodyne: although he does claim that speech is no more than a vehicle for conveying information, a relatively small modification of his doctrine of the *origin* of speech would lead to his allowing poetry to stand independently, with its own inherent sources of 'musicality' or expressiveness. But Wyzéwa is wedged between the 'emotive' theory of Poe and Ghil and the 'intellectualist' theory of Wagner; and his solution has neither the simplicity of the one nor the ruthlessness of the other, though it combines unacceptable elements from each. All in all, a very fair example of the hesitancy and confusion which marks the period of transition in aesthetic which we are agreeing to call symbolism.

[1] Ghil, *Les Dates et les Œuvres*, 1923, p. viii.

2. BAUDELAIRE AND SYNESTHESIA

It has not frequently been recognized that the doctrine of 'correspondences' which made its way into symbolist tradition via Baudelaire from the romantic movement has nothing to do with the Wagnerian doctrine of synthetic art; less frequently still, that the two are not merely distinct, but incompatible.

The fact has long been obscured by Baudelaire's presuming the contrary (in his long article on Richard Wagner[1]), and going so far as to illustrate the 'theory of universal analogies' from programme notes of the Prelude to *Lohengrin*. His argument is simple. Three critics (one of them, Liszt, a close friend of the composer at the time) give a written account of a piece of music. These accounts tally (roughly); and since there has been no collusion among the authors, it can be assumed that the similarities arise from each critic having correctly interpreted the 'meaning' of the Prelude. This argues that sounds and groups of sounds are as fitted to have definite 'meanings' as speech and words; and this in turn suggests, since music has no dictionary of accepted meanings, that (i) sounds, and all other classes of sensa, images, emotions, notions, can suggest, or even be substituted for one another in communication—'correspondences' on terms of equality—and (ii) all these diverse elements of artistic language,[2] as well as answering to one another, are all symbols in a universal hierarchy, in which that which is symbolized is some aspect of an ultimate transcendent reality. We are here concerned only with the relationship between this doctrine and Wagnerianism; how it relates to the definition of art-values must be held over till the next chapter.

On Baudelaire's theory, every colour, sound, odour, conceptualized emotion (love, hate), every visual image, even if complex (a ship, a carcass), is in some way bound up with an equivalent in each of the other fields: one only, we may infer. This view, in one form or another, is common enough in the early nineteenth century; not only, as Pommier neatly shows, were literary men in France keenly interested in its possibilities (Baudelaire was seriously con-

---

[1] In his *Art Romantique*. The article on Delacroix is equally relevant in this connection: 'C'est du reste un desdiagnosticsde l'état spirituel de notre siècle que les arts aspirent, sinon à se suppléer l'un l'autre, du moins à se prêter réciproquement des Forces nouvelles' (*Art Romantique*, *Œuvres*, ed. Crépet, 1925, p. 5). The ambiguity is apparent.

[2] It is impossible to find a term to describe less loosely this vast range of entities which, in fact, do constitute the sum total of the artist's resources. It includes not only the simplest elements, like patches of red, a note on the violin, but all elements of subsequent levels of elaboration and complexity.

cerned from 1846 onwards at the failure to draw up complete lists of 'corresponding' simple sensa, and asks 'si quelque analogiste a établi solidement une gamme complète des couleurs et des sentiments');[1] it appears in Germany with the Jena school and after;[2] in England, with the generation of Shelley.[3] In Hoffmann and Nerval, outstandingly, the succession of 'correspondences' is carried on. Baudelaire moves in a literary world where table talk turns to drawing up new analogies;[4] and this early outburst is sustained by the symbolists without much critical consideration until the turn of the century, when psychologists conduct statistical inquiries as to how many people have the gift of 'audition colorée'. A thinker as remote from symbolism as Guyau can write, in all complacency:

'Il est probable qu'à tous les états physiologiques correspondent des odeurs déterminées, et comme à tout état physiologique correspond un état psychologique, il n'est pas étrange de supposer que toute émotion, tout sentiment et bien des idées mêmes pourraient avoir leur traduction en langage d'odeurs.'[5]

So far we are in the presence of a decided stand, by romantic poets and by Guyau, on the claim that correspondence between the analogies is grounded not in the whim of a moment but in some necessity beyond our control. For Baudelaire a mystical necessity, for Guyau a physiological one. On this issue the symbolists were divided into two camps, one agreeing, the other disagreeing with the hypothesis of an outer necessity. It is of some interest to note that the former camp came more and more to be dominated by eccentrics and—not to put too fine a point upon it—literary curiosities; and that the latter camp was unable to put forward a satisfactory alternative to account for the facts.

The unbending apostle of 'analogies' is, of course, René Ghil. As if in answer to Baudelaire's call for a *complete* list of correspondences, he set out to note relations between vowel sounds and colours, and vowel sounds and instrumental textures. Hence the title 'école instrumentiste' taken by his 'school'. Psychological science had lately 'proved' that 'audition colorée' existed: it had actually

[1] Pommier, *La Mystique de Baudelaire*, p. 73. He himself offered a few suggestions in the *Salon* for 1859, in *Fusées*, and in *L'Art Romantique*. The 'meaning' of the three primary colours is presumed 'su de tout le monde'.

[2] Novalis' *Heinrich von Ofterdingen* springs to mind. Cf., too, Cœuroy, on the subject of Eichendorff: 'Pour lui déjà les sensations se correspondent; les couleurs ne sont-elles pas des sons, et les sons des vibrations colorées? dit-il dans "Sehnsucht". Ainsi se fortifie l'empire artistique ou tous les arts sont unis sous l'hégémonie musicale' (*Musique et Littérature*, 1933, p. 26).

[3] See W. B. Yeats, *The Symbolism of Poetry*, 'Works,' VI.

[4] Even Musset seems to have lent a hand at this game. See Pommier, op. cit., p. 9.

[5] *L'Art au point de vue sociologique*, p. 5 n.

made statements of historical fact to that effect;[1] the Instrumentists were satisfied with it as a conclusive vindication of their 'theories' and of anything they might care to say in the future. The result is the *Traité du Verbe*, and Ghil's subsequent writings; it comes as a shock to find that Merrill and Viélé-Griffin made their poetic débuts in the *Écrits pour l'Art*, and that the latter could write an article of praise on the Master, in which the following is typical:

'Il chercha la couleur des Voyelles: et s'il reconnut que le sonnet de M. Rimbaud contenait des vérités (par hasard, dit-on) il releva des erreurs choquantes: sous l'une des voyelles, son simple, M. Rimbaud par exemple, plaçait une couleur composée.

'Dès lors le poète n'avait plus qu'à voir à quel instrument correspondait par sa couleur (c'est-à-dire par son nombre le plus approchant de vibrations), chaque Voyelle; et il pouvait conclure: "C'est en allant quérir selon l'ordre de ma vision chantante les mots où le plus souvent se nombre la Voyelle maîtresse demandée que l'immatérielle obéissance vibrera de l'Instrument au timbre qui sied." '[2]

A somewhat ponderous way of saying that alliteration has come into its own—with a vengeance. No wonder if Verlaine's summing-up:

'... Ghil
Est un imbécile'

has an appealing freshness that we find difficult to resist; though in fact Ghil's verses, allegedly constructed on this system, are by no means as bad as one might fear. Robert de Souza is near the truth when he writes of Ghil:

'Tout était faussé par un tempérament de fanatique abstrait et obtus, et son tempérament l'emportant de beaucoup sur sa sensibilité poétique, il fabriqua un système non pour qu'il dépendît de la poésie, mais pour que la poésie lui fût soumise.

'C'était exactement le contraire de tout ce que rêvaient les symbolistes.

'Dans la liberté de forme demandée à la poésie, ils entendaient, pour le raffinement même et suprême de l'expression, retrouver l'ingénuité première. Ils n'avaient pas rejetés des conventions historiques donc extérieures pour adopter des conventions pseudo-scientifiques non moins arbitraires.'[3]

[1] If the psychologists of 'audition colorée' would realize they were historians of language, they might perhaps be induced to discard their terrifying pseudo-scientific terminology, and save the student of symbolism much needless worry and toil.

[2] Viélé-Griffin, 'Trois Portraits,' *Écrits pour l'art*, 7/i/1887. Though the instrumentist school has died long ago, a parallel movement survived in music. We may note the essay of one M. L. Favre, agronomist, entitled 'La Musique des Couleurs' (1900). M. Favre is not interested in art—'ce que je cherche à réaliser c'est l'*agréable* et non le *beau*'; he proposed, by the joint presentation of music and colours, scientifically blended, to give his audiences a sort of emotive joy-ride. 'D'une façon nette ou d'une façon obscure, fortement ou faiblement, toutes les vibrations (celles que nous connaissons et celles que nous ne connaissons pas) et en général tous les contacts, doivent agir sur l'organisme humain, et préparer ce qu'on appelle "l'émotion" ou, si l'on veut, l'état émotif' (op. cit., p. 6). An echo of the project is to be found in Scriabin's colour music. See, too, A. B. Klein, *Colour-music—The Art of Light* (1926); this writer also produced a Colour-organ, to project 'a sequence of tones arranged in logarithmic order'. Mr. Aldous Huxley (*Brave New World*) goes one better with his 'Feelies'. For a concise survey of 'colour-music', going back to Louis Castel's 'ocular clavessin' (1734), see V. J. Clancey, 'Colour Music' (*The Realist*, vii/1929).

[3] *Mercure de France*, t. cclix, p. 401, 15/iv/1935.

This brings us to the opposing camp, where a majority of symbolists are to be found, and to which most of Ghil's more outstanding supporters sooner or later went over. Morice attacks the rigidity of Instrumentisme:

'Non pas qu'en effet les sons (puisque toute la Nature lui est soumise) échappent aux prises d'une loi de coloration, sons et couleurs n'étant qu'une double et symmétrique émanation de la lumière; mais cette loi, sans rien d'absolu, est nécessairement individuelle.'[1]

Mauclair equally condemns pedantry over the 'Sonnet des Voyelles':

'Il était trop aisé de voir que le célèbre "Sonnet des *Voyelles*" de Rimbaud n'était ni une théorie ni une plaisanterie, mais la notation d'une impression momentanée, aussi sincère qu'exclusive de tout dogmatique.'[2]

Wyzéwa says that his generation of poets calls the use of analogy symbolism, 'une simple substitution d'une idée à l'autre'.

'Ainsi, voulant exprimer la sensation odorante d'une fleur, et ne trouvant aucun mot propre pour l'exprimer directement, je me résoudrais à la qualifier symboliquement de "gris perle".'[3]

But if he avoids the idea of a necessary link between smell and colour, or smell and words denoting colour, he suggests no good reason why the reader should be able to penetrate the poet's intention. No doubt he would concur with Mauclair in grounding the analogy in a common emotional denominator—to do which Mauclair has to contradict the 'anti-dogmatic' thesis noted above: in his authorized biographical novel on Mallarmé (*Le Soleil des Morts*) he makes Calixte Armel talk an almost Baudelairean language:

'Tout est réciprocité, allusion et allégorie, dans la vie et dans l'art. Celui qui posséderait la faculté de saisir immédiatement toutes les analogies, celui-là serait l'artiste immortel, et du même coup le psychologue par excellence; car une âme n'est que le dedans d'une forme. Le musique n'exprime jamais une forme, orage, plaine crépusculaire, arrivée d'un héros — mais elle transpose tout cela et n'en donne que le résultat émotionnel. La description qui alourdit la littérature lui est inconnue.'[4]

But this raises a very important point; if, as claimed by Morice, Kahn, Laforgue, and many others, poetic language with its emotional attachments is at the beck and call of individual whim, what happens to the reader? One answer is, let him fend for himself;[5] but that is

[1] *La Littérature de tout à l'heure*, p. 321.   [2] Mauclair, *Eleusis*, p. 137.
[3] 'Le Symbolisme de M. Mallarmé,' *Revue Indépendante*, ii/1887.
[4] Mauclair, *Le Soleil des Morts*.
[5] This is Kahn's view. 'Le lyrisme est exclusivement d'allure intuitive et personnelle, et la poésie va dans ce sens depuis cinquante ans ... et rien d'étonnant à ce qu'un nouveau pas en avant fasse paraître le poète comme chantant pour lui-même' (*Revue Indépendante*, ii/1888). Or Lucien Muhlfeldt: 'Alors pour qui écrira-t-on? Pour soi d'abord. "J'ai assez de quelques

hardly good enough. Besides, on many occasions the 'analogies' present no difficulty at all: white stands for purity, as everyone knows, and from this obvious example we can trace instances of growing ambiguity all the way to Wyzéwa's 'gris perle'. There is plainly a lacuna in symbolist doctrine at this point, which can only be filled by a satisfactory theory of the underlying general medium of poet and reader: namely, language. But the symbolists, we saw in the last chapter, were largely without a satisfactory theory of language, or at least dependent to a large degree on notions taken over from positivism.

The problem is not, in fact, an insoluble one, nor even specially difficult to formulate. If we keep a hold on the idea of tradition in language, with the concomitant idea of language as a totality of interpenetrating contexts (the phrase is Dr. Richards') there is no reason why the facts of these analogies should appear any more recondite than those of the exactly parallel case of *morphemes*.[1] The concept of the 'interanimation of words' can be matched with the wider one of the 'interanimation of linguistic elements'; when 'linguistic elements' are taken in a wide sense to include all the imagery of poetry (of course, not simply *visual* imagery), and indeed all the material drawn on by Imagination. Seen in this light, the too 'personal' poet—the lyrist of *Les Palais Nomades*—simply punishes himself by not paying sufficient attention to language tradition, which naturally includes other people's use of language—the uses of as many other people as are going to understand his poems anyway. The would-be poet whose roots fail to go deep enough into his language is cut off from the springs of true expressiveness, and withers as naturally as a plant in summer. The problem of communication illustrates its own solution with the corpses of bad poetry.

Synesthesia, as it is technically called, embraces two distinct notions: (*a*) the spontaneous feeling such as that E flat 'is' green, white 'is' pure, the rose's perfume sad, or any like coupling of sensa or feelings; and (*b*) the deliberate trading on these couplings by artists—

ecteurs," dit à peu près Montaigne, "j'en ai assez de trois ou deux, j'en ai assez d'un, j'en ai assez de pas un." Il y a des natures sensibles et communicatives qui ne se résoudront pas à perdre le plaisir, même pris seul, de l'épanchement littéraire. Il arrive bien qu'on parle tout haut sans interlocuteur. Et l'illusion de la postérité est naïve mais licite' ('Sur la Clarté,' *Revue Blanche*, t. xi, no. 75, 15/vii/1896). But a theory of language will show how something taken up and constructed from a tradition will be accessible to others enjoying that tradition; with the corollary that an incommunicable utterance is a bad utterance and not worth troubling about anyway.

[1] See I. A. Richards, *The Philosophy of Rhetoric*, 1936, ch. III. [The term coined in this context has, of course, nothing to do with the morphemes of linguistic science.]

e.g. writing 'white' with intent to suggest 'pure', and so forth. Thi
latter provides the symbolists with their stock illustration of 'sugges
tion' as opposed to 'description'; though with little reason, for i
white means 'pure', to use 'white' once this meaning is recognized i
quite as explicit as to blurt 'pure' straight out.[1] But however we car
to look at any of the phenomena of synesthesia, one feature remain
common to all: they are phenomena of *substitution*. It may be tha
outstanding cases of synesthesia arise with people who are experience
in only *one* art, and think of others in terms of it;[2] such an hypothesi
encourages the suspicion that the symbolists were interested in musi
less for its own sake than as a possible embellishment for poetry an
the use of speech; or it may be, on the other hand, that there ar
artists whose creative experience is so many-sided as to force nove
conjunctions of language into their writing.[3] Whatever the occasio
or its psychological explanation, however, synesthesia involves th
idea of substituting for one element of (artistic) material an alternativ
element which, on its own or in conjunction with its tenor[4] appeal
more strongly to the artist (or spectator) or at least forms an apte
vehicle for expressing an artistic intention. In point of fact, the sub
stitution can hardly be conceived of as a total replacement; and i
speech, where different sense elements exist ideally side by side, a
shadows of words, the conception of *metaphor* takes for granted th
survival of original meaning in the new metaphorical form.

Against this background of a possible resolution to the aestheti
problem presented by synesthesia, we can return to Baudelaire, an
examine what the 'correspondence' theory implies for a classificatio
of the arts; then relate our findings with the Wagnerian doctrines
It will be remembered that we have claimed to find the two incompatible; since to multiply examples from different arts woul
needlessly lengthen the inquiry, we shall limit ourselves to poetr
and music, and we can cover the ground by asking and answerin
three questions in turn. As between two artistic fragments, is th
relationship of analogy anything other than that which holds betweer
two symbols with the same reference? Following on from this, doe.
music contain referential symbolism? Lastly, how do our finding

---

[1] In point of fact, the 'allusiveness' in either word springs from other (partly suppressed
parallel couplings to vestals, lambs, snow, and so forth.
[2] See Ségalen, 'La Synesthésie,' *Mercure de France*, iv/1902, p. 77. Goethe is a clear case i
point.
[3] Hoffmann would be an example; but hardly Baudelaire, for all his interest in music an
painting; less still a Rimbaud, a Mallarmé.
[4] 'The course of meaning which holds on through something written or spoken' (*O.E.D.*)
I borrow this useful term from Richards, who contrasts it in metaphor with the 'vehicle'.

on these questions tally with those of Wagner on the one hand
and Baudelaire on the other?

3. ANALOGIES

In Baudelaire's theory of universal analogies, any material used by
the artist is considered in two lights. First, it is assumed to be related
to all possible substitutes in the other arts—a phrase of speech to a
musical sound of given pitch and texture, a patch of colour, and so
on—and in this horizontal relation we shall speak of it as an *analogue*.
Secondly, it is held to be related to some transcendental reality,
from which it derives in the last resort the relation with other musical
sounds, odours, etc. This vertical relation causes it to become what we
shall term the Baudelairean *symbol*, and confers on it its specifically
aesthetic value.[1] We are concerned with it only as analogue.

If we go back to the article on Wagner, we find implicit the view
that the Prelude to *Lohengrin* and the independent verbal transcriptions
are analogues of one another and symbols of a transcendental vision
enjoyed by the composer. That at least must be assumed if the
Prelude is to be allowed as evidence for the correspondence theory:
if it is a 'mystic analogy' that enables Baudelaire to understand the
meaning of the music (i.e. in this case translate it into speech) this
analogy is a cousinship that exists only through a common grand-
parent—a transcendental entity—'symbolized' by each cousin. But
this symbolic relationship involves a transfer of artistic value to the
'symbol'. Therefore if Baudelaire's résumé of the music is a true
analogue, it must possess artistic value, must be a poem of some
stature. But is it? Looked at as well-written prose, Baudelaire's
criticism has always a certain distinction; but no one could seriously
claim that the résumé stands or is meant to stand comparison with
Wagner's music in matter of artistic worth. Competent, yes;
beautiful, no. At the first approach, the doctrine of universal analogies
disappoints.

What is worse, if we go closer, it seems as though this doctrinal
fantasy is leading us straight into the intellectualist camp. We have
seen (above, ch. II, 2) that for Taine there could be no proper
distinction of merit between a Dutch old master and a programme-
blurb; the one was a synonym of the other, and nothing more.
So long as the idea of artistic content was allowed to stand away from
artistic form, no redress could be found for the injustice. If artistic

---

[1] For a discussion of this theory of value, see below, ch. VI, 3 (*b*).

value resided simply in the 'meaning' (the intellectual reference)—pointed no doubt by clarity, wit, and so forth—any synonym for that reference must have equal artistic worth. Suppose now that in the course of one of his *Salons*, Baudelaire chances to describe at some length one of Delacroix' paintings: as indeed he was frequently in the habit of doing. Could one fairly describe such a description as an analogue of the picture, and hence by definition as valuable artistically as the picture? To do so is to endorse some of the more vicious implications of intellectualist aesthetic. It would mean we must acclaim as a poet any school-child with access to a picture-gallery and a modicum of common sense; one could become a poet of high repute by acting the parasite on a universally acclaimed painter. Or the most servile hack-translation from a foreign language would have the right to be acknowledged as great a work as the original. The argument for analogies leads to a whole range of paradox; the grand dogma of the universal hierarchy shrinks into a humdrum assertion that synonyms can exist, not only within a given language but also between any pair of languages that can be brought together. Or in other words, there is no need to postulate a heaven of forms when attempting to classify the arts: languages as symbolisms can have their common references here on earth.

Two counter-objections must be heard in Baudelaire's defence. In the first place, it may be urged that Baudelaire nowhere claimed his résumé of Wagner's music as a literary masterpiece. To that the answer is simple: had he been consistent he must have done so, or renounced the claim that the résumé was an analogue of the music.

The second counter-objection is more serious. Granted that the résumé of a painting or the translation of a poem may be a mere synonym of its abstracted symbolic or intellectual content, it might yet be that *some* material element of art might escape from the reproach of being pure synonyms of their analogues—some elements so small and simple that they pass freely through the trawl-net of intellectual relationships. Unmixed colours, for instance, appear to be void of any elements of reference—sometimes. We shall see in the next chapter that the Baudelairean symbol may be defined as a contradiction in terms from this point of view: an attempt to claim a relationship (e.g. between white and purity) which enjoys the functions of an intellectual relationship (stability, universality, and so forth) without, in fact, being a simple reference grounded in an agreed use of language. Baudelaire could deny that white is associated with purity because the vestals wore white robes, and claim that on the contrary their robes were white because white is a natural symbol of purity;[1] he would justify this view with the universal analogy theory, according to which its symbolism is grasped 'intuitively'. Now in the ordinary sense of the term 'symbol' (i.e. as defined and used in ch. IV) such intuitive grasp is inadmissible. What may be claimed for whiteness[2] may very well be claimed for single notes in music—even granting exception for controversial cases like trumpet fanfares—and since music is evidently not in any way an 'imitative' art, why not press the claim for more complex organizations like a chord, a whole melody, a progression of harmonies ... or even a symphonic structure like *Lohengrin*, always with reservations for 'programme' music and so forth? This second counter-objection brings into focus as a sort of test-case the whole position of music in the several nineteenth-century hierarchies of the arts: a problem that attracted—and defied—all aestheticians without exception from Schopenhauer to Mallarmé. The next two sections will be devoted to the problem of music, first as a general problem for aesthetic, and subsequently as a specific problem for Wagner.

4. MUSIC AS AN EXCEPTIONAL ART

The choice is broadly between a rational and irrational aesthetic; specifically between an account of musical utterance which amplifies the concept of music as expressive language, and an account which impounds it in a mystic enclosure with all the representative arts and writes over the gates: 'These representations are inexplicables'.

In speech, as we have claimed, symbolic elements take (or are given) shape on a substrate of logically anterior expressive utterance, and can be resorbed into the mass of language treated as simple utterance. This same process of resorption is also a feature of painting: a still-life from nature is not merely an arrangement of shapes, masses, colours, though it is that certainly; in addition, it can be the candle, the saucepan, the table cloth that these shapes and colours refer to, and this element of organization necessarily grafts itself on our attention to the design. So, too, with a major section of the plastic arts, though 'abstract' art would seem to show that explicit symbolic

---

[1] The controversy, unless solved by an adequate theory of language, never rises above the level of the hen-and-egg argument.

[2] *Sc.* by Baudelaire. In the present study it follows from the central argument of ch. IV that if 'white' acquires a purely symbolic reference (e.g. the royalist faction) it does so by artificial agreement, and this reference is no source of artistic worth; and if the symbolic reference is arrived at by the inter-animation of language elements (like a morpheme), even so, no artistic worth could conceivably reside in it, in its own rights—i.e. regardless of context.

elements can be considerably curtailed in certain circumstances.[1] So, too, with architecture; in this or that building we may call attention to a reminiscence of the Gothic cathedral, with all that attaches to it; architectural shapes and masses are continually grouping themselves into stubborn 'meanings' of that kind.

We have mentioned architecture: no two arts are more repeatedly linked together in the classification of the arts than architecture and music. For Taine, they are the two exceptional arts which are not imitative; Schopenhauer illustrates his aesthetic predominantly from them, and if music has a specially privileged and unique position *vis-à-vis* the Will, all the same his treatment of the two fields shows similarities. Valéry was doing more than point a metaphor when he spoke of architecture as 'musical'.[2] We have to ask, then, whether music is void of such resorbed symbolism as is undoubtedly present in its sister-arts. The whole energy of nineteenth-century aesthetic, when it deals with music, is given to answering this question one way or the other. Among the band of writers who defended the anti-representative thesis, there are some imposing names. For Schelling, whom some of the symbolists claimed to have read, 'music is the archetypal rhythm of Nature and the Universe'; for Schopenhauer, music stands outside all other arts, as 'not a copy of the Ideas but the copy of the Will itself whose objectivation they (the Ideas) are'—an essentially mystic expression, as has often been noted.[3] In another perspective, for Lamennais,

'Ce que la musique représente, ce qu'elle tend à reproduire, ce ne sont pas les choses telles qu'elles sont, mais leur type éternel,'[4]

which is as good as a denial of a representative element. We need not speak here of the Hanslick notion of 'pure form'. On the other hand, come the romantic musicians of the nineteenth century themselves; the general public; and a good number of theorists unable to stomach the paradoxes of Hanslick.[5] Combarieu's *Rapports de la musique et*

---

[1] Even so, something in principle very like 'red for rage', 'white for purity', and so on can hardly be ignored by even the most determinedly 'abstract' artists: reduced to a minimum, but still present.

[2] (Cette âme de l'architecte) 'Je la devine musicienne et longtemps recluse dans la pure solitude de son rêve. D'abord elle aura puisé l'exacte harmonie et les magiques infinis où les rythmes aboutissent, dans les ondes frissonnantes et profondes que les grands symphonistes ont épandues, Beethoven ou Wagner. Car de subtiles analogies unissent l'irréelle et fugitive édification des sons, à l'art solide, par qui des formes imaginaires sont immobilisées au soleil, dans le porphyre' (*Paradoxe sur l'architecture, Œuvres*, 195).

[3] E.g. by Bosanquet, *History of Aesthetic*, 2nd ed., p. 367.

[4] *Esquisse d'une philosophie*, t. iii, p. 310 f.

[5] I suppose that pieces like Mendelssohn's 'Songs without Words' contributed as much as anything to the musical education of the nineteenth-century middle classes. They are certainly not innocent of reference.

de la poésie (1894) gives a fair account of this side of the picture. It is significant that in speaking of Schopenhauer and Schelling's philosophy of music, he says:

'Ils ne nous donnent aucun critérium pour distinguer la bonne musique de la mauvaise'[1]—

a frequent objection, and one hard to refute. For this side, it seemed to stand to reason that music stood in some relation or other to states of emotion at the least; without being imitative—how can you imitate a feeling?—it *represented* that feeling. Moreover, it was a *concrete* object of representation; not as Schopenhauer in an unwary moment claimed, a purely abstract one.[2]

If, as we should say, music is a language and expressive of concrete emotion, it will follow that it must display features proper to a tradition. And so it does. Slow time and a minor key do not constitute a funeral march, the stylized expression of a certain realm of grief; yet we all recognize a funeral march when we hear one, if we know anything of the tradition of Western music (and we can hardly escape that). Just as the elegiac poet is not expected to carol like the skylark, so the funeral march composer is not expected to write a piece in three-time. We recognize the march as such not by any single feature in abstraction, but by the quite complex taking-up of a tradition which may defy our efforts to define it exhaustively. Our familiarity with a tradition is formed by our acquaintance with this and previous pieces of music: it is a question of interpretation, not simply one of association; and least of all an intuitive awareness of 'analogy' between the music and a feeling of grief, or more properly, a *description* of a feeling of grief. If we are non-musicians, again, we recognize church music crudely by the singing and the organ, and other such aspects of its language; if musicians, we recognize further its participation in one part or another of the tradition of church music, again by an act of interpretation. And let no one say that this account is vitiated by a circular argument, that we cannot both know the language by its instances, and the instances by their language: for it is out of this circular argument that every growing child breaks as it learns to speak.

It is characteristic of a tradition that it momentarily fossilizes out-

[1] op. cit., p. 12.
[2] See Bourdeau, *Pensées et fragments de Schopenhauer*, p. 163. A curious middle position on the whole controversy was taken up by the psychologist Ribot (in *La Logique des Sentiments*, p. 131 ff.); he resolved the difficulty by allowing the parallel existence of what he called 'la musique pleine' and 'la musique vide'. It remains to determine into which class any given piece of music must fall: and this exercise makes plain that the division attempted by Ribot is by no means easy to effect.

standing parts of itself; so that in a musical language certain phrases, or turns, say, of orchestration, become fixed in a quasi-symbolical reference. For example, the 'ominous' lower notes of reed instruments that Wagner is so fond of; or the harp-arpeggios of the Rhine music. These are 'morphemes', and nothing else. Inasmuch as they are simply accepted and hashed-up with the minimum of formative modification, they become, in Dr. Richards' fullest sense, musical phrases evoking attitudes. But they are not without references: they become in the last resort parasites, parasites of abstraction, preying on the original expressive worth which attended their creation. In this sense Combarieu can study fossils in the operatic tradition of the nineteenth century as though they were permanent recipes, on a par with what many people think they find in the speech of their own time and locality.

This allows us a new approach to the Prelude to *Lohengrin*. Granted the originality and brilliance of Wagner's dramatic music, which most certainly dazzled Baudelaire as it dazzled the generation of 1886 at the Lamoureux concerts: what we must remember is that it takes its place in a powerful tradition of dramatic and to a large extent representative music. Baudelaire's world of music contained not so much Mozart and Beethoven, acclaimed though the latter was, but rather Bellini and Spontini, Meyerbeer and Donizetti, Weber and Berlioz; the Mayerbeer of *Robert les Diable* and *Le Huguenots*, the Weber of *Oberon* and *Der Freyschütz*, the Berlioz of numerous literary friendships and of regular music criticism on the *Journal des Débats* between 1838 and 1846. The romantic tradition existed; it was a tradition one of whose features was the exploration of everything between rhetoric and descriptive music; and it is no exaggeration to say that Wagner's greatness lies in his having absorbed it completely and entirely into his language, developing to an unprecedented degree its representative and dramatic scope. In this tradition it would be as absurd to say that the revelation of the Graal was not an integral part of the language of the upper strings of the orchestra as that the bowl of flowers is not an integral part of the language when the artist paints his still-life: and equally gratuitous to say that the embedding of the one and the other idea in the music and the painting springs from an association between a supernatural essence and a shape, or a sound.

So far, then, as there is a relation between music and the programme note, it is a relation between synonyms. Such a relation is suited to the abstract and general, not to the concrete and individual. The programme note can no more exhaust the individuality of the music than the scientist can exhaust the individuality of the universe; all it can do is abstract one important element of the music, and record a synonym in its own language. It is a commonplace that synonyms are never exact equivalents, interchangeables.

Baudelaire's doctrine of 'universal analogies' implies among other things an absolute equality, not to say interchangeability, between the arts. There is no hierarchy of 'more' and 'less' artistic art-media, no barrier between poetry and music save one of convenience or personal aptitude in the use of language. The one covers the same ground as the other. This was not the opinion of Wagner, nor is it what an examination of the facts would suggest. When we listen to a certain piece of music by Debussy, it is the title and our knowledge of literature that eggs us on to read into the orchestra's inflexions the picture of a somnolent Faun. Evidently, no other piece of music would be so favourable to this 'interpretation'; but that merely shows that Debussy had an extraordinarily keen insight into the representational corners of the nineteenth-century tradition, and in modifying its potentialities created new (possible) music references. Yet the music is not the poem; at most, it is a very approximate transliteration of mood, without the point and inflexion of every line of Mallarmé's poem—how could it be more, since Mallarmé's imaginative consciousness is *built* at its clearest levels out of speech and Debussy's out of music?[1] Or take another example, slightly different: *Pelléas et Mélisande*. Debussy's setting is acknowledged to fit Maeterlinck's play like a glove (little as either playwright or composer may afterwards have liked the effect). On Baudelaire's theory, this glove should either be transparent, or else a simple mirror image, projected alongside the play: to drop the metaphor, the music, if it is not to distort wrongfully the effect of the words and action must, if entirely appropriate, merely reduplicate them—double the material used without modifying the effect. Now it can hardly be claimed that a musical setting 'spoils' a poem *ipso facto*, for it makes it into something else, not in fact comparable, and not necessarily the worse for the change.[2] And it is similarly ridiculous to deny that a song is more than *and different from* either the poem or

[1] Cf. 'Still more clearly is it true that the emotions which we express in music can never be expressed in speech, and vice versa. Music is one order of languages, and speech is another; each expresses what it does express with absolute clarity and precision; but what they express is two different types of emotion, each proper to itself' (R. G. Collingwood, *The Principles of Art*, p. 245). 'Emotion' is a misleading word here.

[2] Mallarmé's 'nuirait par inutilité' is in the context of the musicality of *poetry*, it will be remembered: not of opera.

the melody that are wedded in it. So that while Baudelaire usefully combats the idea that any one art is intrinsically superior to the rest, he does so only by showing that there is a needless redundancy of effort in the world, since each art can do what all the others can. He postulates the equivalence of languages; whereas, if language is the form of concrete imagination, no two languages can ever have more in common than synonyms—i.e. abstracted elements from them.

Although the fact escaped the attention of his immediate successors, Baudelaire's aesthetic stands fairly and squarely against the pre-eminence of music. And in this respect it is a useful support for what was eventually to be the symbolists' replacement of music as supreme art by poetry. But, opposing implicitly Schopenhauer's classification, and what was later assumed to be Wagner's adaptation of it, Baudelaire is also committed to saying that there can be no valid hierarchy of the arts at all: that each art is itself and nothing else, that only empirical classifications can be made in terms of senses, or in terms of the arts as they are observed to exist in their most notable representatives—both positivist procedures, whose rigidity distorts one's whole vision of language as an activity. This second Baude-lairean negative to the project of constructing a hierarchy also escaped the notice of the symbolists; for they were intent on developing the more spectacular parts of the analogy theory to suit their taste in metaphor, and they overlooked its less direct implications.

5. THE WAGNERIAN ART-SYNTHESIS AND MYTH

For Wagner, song is the parent of speech; music accordingly occupies, in this relation at least, a favoured position. In his *Oper und Drama* he is at pains to show that the poet's 'sounds' are scattered and rendered musically incoherent by his duty to sense; the musician's 'musikalisches Ton' alone remains fully organized. Sound is an 'embodied inner feeling'; the—

> 'original exteriorizing medium of the inner being is *Sound-Language*, the involuntary expression of an inner feeling externally evoked'.

By these tokens the barking dog is an artist, even if a rather limited one. But music is not simply a primordial language of art, it is also the universal language which knows no frontiers—'rein menschlich' (purely human); and this is what gives it its pre-eminence for art. A narrative, a picture, a mime, are sited in history, and as such liable to all the misadventures of communication: in a word they are 'contingent'; music rises above all such risks, and moves in the sphere of essences.[1] As a result, however, of this superior nature, music can never stand alone: the purely human must invariably be associated with one of the lower arts—or rather, with all of them.[2] Wagner considered, for example, that Beethoven's symphonies are dramas— works not simply dramatic in any loose sense of the word, but running commentaries on a theatrical action—programme music. How plainly he reveals himself here in the true romantic musical tradition! No more eloquent testimony could be found to the strength of this tradition than the claim that Beethoven could not even be 'understood' as non-theatrical music. To be sure, it is only the wild exaggeration of a grain of truth. But Wagner uses the argument to show that the proper scope for music is in the music-drama, with its close dependence on coagulations of musical fragments into references, or *leit-motifs*; and so justifies the close union between the arts in which he was specially interested.

At the same time, he left music in a position of unquestioned supremacy. This is natural in view of Wagner's personal aptitudes; whereas his position in the history of music is beyond the reach of detractors, as a poet or dramatist or even producer his non-existence would have made little difference to the course of the nineteenth century.

The claim for the supremacy of music is still further enhanced by his theory of the social function of art. Art is described as at once intuition and interpretation: the interpretation of life; and as man's life is predominantly social, art must interpret social life. Greek drama is the ideal which is to be restored to European civilization; and Greek drama, Wagner reminds his readers, was synthetic art: the chorus supplied a musical element in the performances. One might suppose, then, that with a 'Purely Human' thread running through, the choice of subject for presentation was indifferent, since music could help it to cross all barriers set up by incomprehension; but this is not so. For the interpretation of the life of society, any subject adequately presented must grow to the stature of a myth:

'The tragic poet simply communicated the content and the essence of the myth in the most convincing and comprehensible manner available; and Tragedy is no other than the artistic perfection of myth itself, it being understood that Myth is the poem of a common outlook on life.'[3]

[1] These views, of course, strengthened the conviction that Wagner was the apostle of Schopenhauer. Schuré has a long footnote in *Le Drame Musical* on Schopenhauer and music, in corroboration of the Wagnerian distinction between music and the plastic arts (*Le Drame Musical*, p. 168).

[2] But *this* has no relation with anything that Schopenhauer held.

[3] *Opera and Drama.*

Myth may be defined as an imaginative creation embodying in itself a highly generalized (intellectual) commentary on human experience. Accepted and 'believed' immediately, myth is religion; simply accepted, or accepted after the mediation of interpretation, or not accepted but simply understood, it becomes art: but these polarized extremes are abstractions. Myth may be supposed to come into being by selection from a number of individual imaginative interpretations of life: the one most general, and also effective artistically, being favoured. Among a race of pygmies, the story of Jack the Giant-Killer would certainly improve on its present status as a fairy-tale.

Wagner has a rather laborious dialectic to show the relations of thought and feeling, individuality and generality, man and the state, tyranny and anarchism, Œdipus and Antigone.[1] The upshot is that in the times through which he lives, the artist's prime task is to aim at the destruction of the state, and assist in the evolution of a new humanity where the individual is freed from the slavery of present inhibitions and injustice. For this specific task, which is not expected to last indefinitely, art must appeal not to feeling but to understanding: 'pure human' individuality is an abstract conception of future possibilities, and to give a glimpse of it, the artist must at this stage 'actualize all feeling in thought'. The evolution of the consciousness of 'pure humanity' is something that must emerge with time; it cannot be imposed or even fully preconceived. The drama of the future, freed from this preliminary spade-work, will return 'from understanding to feeling'; we may, if we will, interpret this to mean that the music-drama of the future will be simply musical. But in the meantime, many Siegfrieds will perish, and Wagners go unrewarded,[2] before Wotan's rule is finally broken, before anarchism restores a range of values which have remained lost since the days of Athens.

There is no point in our examining at any length this welter of parochial, vaguely comical, and (it is to be feared) largely self-destructive theories. Three plain features stand out, however, through the advocacy of the music-drama. (*a*) The doctrine that art is an appeal to the whole man, a total work to be performed on a real stage, with music, mime, poetry, and scenery co-ordinated in the light of a total effect (not ballet, however, which for Wagner is tainted with the memory of flippant and inconsequential French and Italian

[1] ibid.
[2] Wagner's theoretical writings largely date from before his adoption by Louis of Bavaria.

Opera).[1] Only in this way can the artist's vision be communicated without distortion, and without being bridled by the 'insufficiency' of the several arts; (*b*) Music occupies a special position as reproducing and communicating the artist's most 'purely human' feeling which is without barriers of race and time; (*c*) Myth is the natural material with which to express collective and social interpretations, accessible to a whole community because having its origin there, and in any case specially suited to the propaganda needs of a revolutionary age. The first of these features speaks for itself, and needs no further amplification; but before leaving Wagner, there are several things to be said about the remaining two.

He is unduly optimistic about the *communicability* of music. Not all the prejudice against him in France was on political grounds; even the early *Tannhäuser* excited the venom of music critics. The 'purely human' element of feeling in art is distinguished on the one hand from an intuition of essences (*à la* Schopenhauer), and on the other from the general intellectual import of myth. But is there room for all three of these basic conceptions in a single aesthetic? Schopenhauer would certainly never have endured the idea of 'pure humanity' nor, on other grounds, 'myth' as indispensable to art. The former is too demonstrably belied in the contemporary 'difficulty' of Wagner's music, and the latter is an open breach of the anti-intellectualist front, to be endured only under special conditions and with numerous reservations.[2] For the myth in Wagner is esteemed entirely for its

---

[1] Wagner distinguishes between (i) the intuitor, (ii) the poet or exterioriser, and (iii) the artist or user of all the arts. Each art finds its highest development only in the work of this last, despite appearances to the contrary. [He knew nothing of Renaissance attempts at 'total art'.]

[2] This alone should serve to show how far Wagner is from being a 'disciple of Schopenhauer'. The latter's position on myth is quite unequivocal, and follows from his outright condemnation of allegory, symbol, and emblem—for him all varying grades of the same intellectual activity, in which the presentation of art is used as a vehicle for an abstract concept. E.g. 'If the irruption of concept is harmful to art, we cannot approve of a work of art being explicitly devoted to the expression of a concept: this is the case in *allegory*. An allegory is a work of art which means something other than it represents. But intuition, and consequently Ideas too, express themselves directly and completely, and need no mediation from any foreign element to indicate them' (*Die Welt als Wille und Vorstellung*, I, 50, p. 279). Now, it may be objected that Schopenhauer is here speaking of allegory and not myth; that allegory can depict a purely impersonal figure (e.g. Caracci's *Genius of Fame*) when myth is always Siegfried, or some other individual in whom the general import is lodged; but we must remember that in either case, as too with colour-symbolism, the conceptual relation is for Schopenhauer separated by an unbridgeable gap from the sensuous representation; that, in fact, the allegorical element which he stigmatizes as 'ein fehlerhaftes, einem der Kunst ganz fremden Zwecke dienendes Streben' (op. cit., p. 281), shades off by imperceptible stages in art into any intellectual ingredients whatever; and so by the strict study of art, Schopenhauer would have been forced into contradictions in the application of his Platonic Ideas theory. It is significant that his principle fields of application are architecture and music—two arts most apparently devoid of any intellectual content, because 'non-imitative'; when he comes on to discuss poetry, which he confesses to consist *entirely* of conceptual elements, he evolves an escape from his dilemma which hardly carries conviction. From the general trend of Schopenhauer's remarks about the sensuous representation of con-

intellectual generality, which retains all its cogency under the un-trained handling of a whole community. Difficulties of this kind might be multiplied—they are the direct outcome of an arbitrary 'division of labour' among the arts, and especially the fictitious distinction of poetry into intellectual and music into emotional utterance.

6. THE STATUS OF MUSIC IN SYMBOLIST AESTHETIC

When we consider the symbolist reaction to all these problems, it must be remembered throughout that the Wagner *cult* among the intelligentsia lasted a bare three years—the lifetime of the *Revue Wagnérienne*—and that it gave way after 1888 or thereabouts to a less partisan, less feverish, appraisal of Wagnerism, or simply to neglect.

(a) *Wagnerians*

The one issue which survived these superficial shifts of topicality is, whether music did or did not occupy a dominating position in the hierarchy of the arts. In answer to this question, there are ranged on the one side all those literary figures—mostly non-poets—whose allegiance to Wagner and Schopenhauer (however ill-comprehended) led them to answer affirmatively. And on the other we find those writers for whom an intimate acquaintance with the resources of speech makes it impossible to concede superiority even to music. In the first class we find, of course, Schuré, the rabid Wagnerite, arguing on vague and metaphysical grounds[1]; the music critic of the *Revue Blanche*, Alfred Ernst, who is nevertheless careful to state that the superiority of music is limited strictly within the Wagnerian scheme for the division of the arts, and therefore rather potential than actual;[2] this class of writer is larger than the number of familiar names among them would at first suggest. And while on this topic,

cepts on the one hand and Ideas on the other, it appears that he has not been able to deal successfully with what we have called the resorption of intellectual elements in artistic imagination. Wagner is more brutal, less scrupulous, and altogether beneath comparison with Schopenhauer as an aesthetician; but he experiences no such difficulties: for he recognized, as a datum of artistic practice, the place occupied by intellect in his own work.

[1] E.g. 'Le sentiment musical est le sentiment idéaliste par excellence, car il tient aux racines de notre être où se confondent le physique et le moral' (*Le Drame musical*, 63).

[2] E.g. 'Les sujets de Wagner, mythologiques ou non, sont musicaux parce que purement humains, et ils sont humains parce que musicaux. Admirable cercle vicieux! Ce caractère d'union, de fusion, de synthèse et de vie est sans doute la marque artistique profonde du drame musical wagnérien. Nous le retrouvons partout, quel que soit l'angle sous lequel nous considérons l'œuvre. Conçus, selon la forte expression du Maître, "dans le sein maternel de la musique," ces drames de pure humanité s'épanouissent tout naturellement en musique...' (*Revue Blanche*, t. vi, no. 27, i/1894, p. 80).

we might recall also the extraordinarily pronounced taste for conducting literary criticism—and even aesthetic discussion on the nature of poetry—in musical terms: a kind of tacit concession, perhaps, that music was the one field of activity which was purely and unequivocally artistic, together with a certain preciosity and ambition to be thought an initiate of many arts at once. Thus Mauclair can speak of Baudelaire's *Bénédiction*, Rimbaud's *Bateau Ivre*, or Mallarmé's *Guignon* and *Hérodiade* as 'symphonies', as if this was the highest possible term of praise.[1] The procedure is systematized in Ghil's *Instrumentism*, of course, where the metaphor of criticism shades off into the pseudo-aesthetic jargon of the analogies; thus (speaking of Merrill's *Les Gammes*—itself a noteworthy title!):

'Généralement ce sont: à des heures d'un jour idéal, des étapes candides ou charnelles ... d'un vague et lointain Amour: tandis que la Flûte innocente et le Hautbois si velouté, et aussi le Basson mélancolique s'effacent peu à peu sous l'angoisse grandissante des Violoncelles et des Violons coupés en vain de Harpes...'[2]

It is when this sort of writing is encountered time after time in far wider circles than Ghil's that we begin to see the true source of Wagner's musical prestige among the French intelligentsia: an immensely impressive orchestration, colouring and commenting on every turn of his dramatic actions. And yet Berlioz, an equally sensitive user of descriptive elements in his music, did not exercise any comparable influence on the poetry of the July Monarchy; it required the symbolist re-appraisal of poetic values before the interchange could take place. Wagner did not simply radiate an 'influence': rather the symbolists looked around for an 'influence' and found Wagner.

(b) Morice

By and large, however, when they found him, they did not go the whole way with his views; even to the limited extent that Wyzéwa did, in his classification of the arts. Their literary innova-

[1] *Eleusis*, p. 133. The habit is, of course, common in all modern criticism; and merely points to the inter-animation of speech, music, painting, within the circle of a culture's whole loosely-integrated 'language'. But Mauclair takes it further: 'La Critique actuelle a grand besoin de se renouveler. Je vois le principe de son renouvellement dans *la fusion des arts*. Il doit y avoir un corps de notions techniques communes à tous les arts. C'est à la critique de montrer que dans un tableau, un poème, un morceau de musique, la matière est la même, qu'il n'y a pas d'art matériel et d'art immatériel, pas plus que dans le monde, il n'y a pas la matière et la non-matière, mais un système de lois cosmiques... Il faut donc qu'un critique connaisse les principes de tous les arts, qu'il sache comment se fait une œuvre. Tantôt il s'adressera à des musiciens, tantôt à des peintres, tantôt à des littérateurs. Il faut, par exemple, qu'en s'adressant à un musicien, il puisse lui dire, en lui montrant un Whistler: c'est du Schumann...' (op. cit.).
[2] René Ghil, *Écrits pour l'art*, iii/1887, p. 47.

tions are too absorbing, their musical knowledge too limited,[1] for
them ever to follow a Schuré in the dethronement of poetry. Charles
Morice, for one, is greatly to be contrasted with Wyzéwa. On the
one hand, he evidently aims to assign music to a very lofty position
when he says:

'Si la Musique nous passionne en effet plus profondément et plus généralement que
la Peinture, c'est que celle-ci est à la fois plus lointaine et plus intime, plus près de
l'origine et de la fin des sentiments et des sensations que celle-là. La ligne et la
couleur se fixent et défient le temps: le son, à peine exhalé, lui cède; il vit de mourir,
c'est un grand symbole! Mais il se dépasse lui-même, il force le silence dans ses
dernières retraites et y réveille l'écho; c'est toujours un appel vers quelque chose
d'inconnu, de mystérieux, une exhalaison, une expansion de l'âme... La Peinture
est un témoignage, la Musique est une aspiration... ';[2]

but when he comes to survey the Wagnerian experiment, music in
turn is made to cede its place:

'Trois regrets — l'union, non pas la synthèse des formes artistiques. Nulle ne
domine et là serait le défaut. Evitons la sempiternelle discussion de la précellence
des arts entre eux: tranchons vite; que celui-ci soit le premier qui s'élève au plus
près de ce point de départ où il faudra que tous reviennent: la Pensée; et celui-ci est
le plus près de la pensée qui parle la plus précise parole. C'est évidemment la Poésie.'

'Precision,' no doubt, might destroy the necessary vagueness of art—
'le transparent et nécessaire voile de la Beauté'—so poetry must
certainly achieve a *fusion* with the vaguest artistic elements, in which
it will yet remain supreme. 'Sinon, il y aura juxtaposition, union
même, synthèse et fusion, point.'[3] He concludes roundly:

'C'est le malheur de l'Art qui a voulu que Wagner fût plus musicien que poète.'[4]

This is no mere personal or chance remark; it is the jumping-off
ground for the symbolist classification of the arts, which reaches its
logical exposition only in Mallarmé. Morice seems to be looking
forward to a new synthesis, a new total art to replace Wagner's, a
poetry whose musicality is more than a question of vowel-sounds,
but is yet not so external to speech as to demand a separate technique,
an independent and 'juxtaposed' language. And that is Mallarmé's
aim also. Before it can justify itself, Morice must also find reason to

---

[1] Cf. Alfred Mortier's diatribe against symbolist dilettantism; music must be pursued for its
own sake, if it is to remain an art: 'Après cela, permis au compositeur, s'il lui convient. de
plaquer un titre plus ou moins suggestif et même tout un programme sur la couverture de la
partition afin de satisfaire les littérateurs et de permettre à leur imagination d'appareiller vers
les Iles du Rêve' ('La Musique et les Dilettantes,' *Mercure de France*, iv/1895). He hints at quite
remarkable voyages of this latter sort. Mortier is frankly a supporter of Hanslick; and his
perspective for 'descriptive' elements in music is not yet satisfactory (see the problems raised by
Debussy's music in this connection). But the attack on 'impressionism' was overdue and
salutary.

[2] *La Littérature de tout à l'heure*, p. 281　　　[3] ibid., p. 197.　　　[4] ibid., p. 197.

isolate music and poetry on one side, away from plastic representations; otherwise there is no hope of taking total art off the stage. Fortunately, this is easy—

'L'espace et le temps scindent fatalement l'Art en deux groupes: le groupe arithmétique de la Poésie et de la Musique, le groupe géométrique de la Peinture, de l'Architecture et de la Sculpture.'[1]

The wording is strangely reminiscent of Hello's classification; and so far as it goes, seems to serve Morice's purpose. Mallarmé went about the same task in a rather more subtle way. Without pursuing the matter, it is worth remarking that within a decade Morice had given up his attempt to 'group' the arts, and returned to the Wagnerian synthesis (*vide infra*, §7): could it be that Mallarmé's decisive failure had convinced him of the impossibility of narrowing the foundations on which total art was to stand?

(c) Mallarmé

More interesting, because more thorough, is the decisive revulsion which Mallarmé shows when confronted by the challenge of Wagnerian music-drama. Mallarmé's interest in the stage is one of the most constant features of his intellectual life; *Hérodiade* was a task that occupied him from the years of Parnasse down to the day of his death; the celebrated *Faune* was conceived 'absolument scénique, non *possible au théâtre*, mais *exigeant le théâtre*';[2] he was an assiduous theatre-goer, and published many of the reviews he wrote for the *Revue Indépendante* in his *Divagations*. Accordingly, it is no light thing for him to say, of Wagner's *rapprochement* of opera and drama, that

'Le concours de tous les arts suscitent le miracle, autrement inerte et nul, de la scène'[3]

—a miracle, moreover, which

'surgit au temps d'un théâtre, le seul qu'on peut appeler caduc, tant la Fiction en est fabriquée d'un élément grossier'.[4]

He develops the theme of the revivifying effect of music:

'Une simple adjonction orchestrale change du tout au tout, annulant son principe même, l'ancien théâtre, et c'est comme strictement allégorique que l'acte scénique maintenant, vide et abstrait en soi, impersonnel, a besoin, pour s'ébranler avec vraisemblance, de l'emploi du vivifiant effluve qu'épand la Musique.'[5]

---

[1] ibid., p. 357.   [2] Lettre à Cazalis (Jean Lahor), vi/1865, in *Propos*, p. 51.
[3] 'Richard Wagner: Rêverie d'un poète français,' *Revue Wagnérienne*, viii/1885, reprinted in *Divagations*, p. 143.
[4] ibid., p. 143.   [5] ibid., p. 144.

'... Un auditoire éprouvera cette impression que si l'orchestre cessait de déverser son influence, le mime resterait, aussitôt, statue.'[1]

'... Des deux éléments de beauté qui s'excluent et tout au moins, l'un l'autre, s'ignorent, le drame personnel et la musique, il effectua l'hymen ... un harmonieux compromis.'[1]

But that is only one side of the question. Through writing for the *Revue Wagnérienne*, Mallarmé's *Rêverie* is not by any means entirely favourable to Wagner. Already in the exposition (the article falls roughly into three sections) occurs the following—

'Le sentiment se complique envers cet étranger, transports, vénération, aussi d'un malaise que tout soit fait, autrement qu'en irradiant, par un jeu direct, du principe littéraire même.'[2]

'Du principe littéraire même!' There is the poet's answer, foreshadowed, or rather reflected in Morice's *Littérature de tout à l'heure*; an answer to the 'singulier défi qu'aux poètes dont il usurpe le devoir avec la plus candide et splendide bravoure, inflige Richard Wagner.' It is an answer big with possibilities, pointing the way to that *Œuvre*, that work of pure literature, in which Mallarmé attempted for twenty years to imprison the languages of the dance and of music— a fabulous project, yet one which the terms of his aesthetic seemed to point to as the goal of art.

After a long development section, from whose ungrudging praises of Wagner we have quoted the leading sentence above, there comes a final renunciation of the Wagnerian ideal. For Wagner's experiment is essentially to harness music with legend, legend made in the last resort from the 'drame personnel', the historical myth: in the path of the Greeks, maybe, but not as he would have it:

'Si l'esprit français, strictement imaginatif et abstrait, donc poétique, jette un éclat, ce ne sera pas ainsi: il répugne, en cela d'accord avec l'Art dans son Intégrité, qui est inventeur, à la Légende.'[3]

We shall pursue this thread in the next section: here it may be remarked that the work of art which is not a legend, embedded in space and time, will require for its 'explication orphique de la terre' not the width of Bayreuth's solid proscenium, but simply the the imagination of the reader; not the music-drama, but the Ode;[4] and the Ode, as imagined poetic speech, contains its own music; a music which Mallarmé long gave attention to.

'Voilà pourquoi, Génie, moi l'humble qu'une logique éternelle asservit, ô Wagner, je souffre et me reproche, aux minutes marquées par la lassitude, de ne pas faire nombre avec ceux qui, ennuyés de tout afin de trouver le salut définitif, vont droit à l'édifice de ton Art, pour eux le Terme du chemin.'[5]

[1] ibid., p. 144-5.   [2] ibid., p. 143.   [3] ibid., p. 147.   [4] ibid., pp. 147-8.   [5] ibid., pp. 149-50.

Wagner's art is only a temple 'à mi-côté de la montagne sainte'; Mallarmé gazes on, upwards, towards

'cette cime menaçante d'absolu, devinée dans le départ des nuées là-haut, fulgurante, nue, seule; au-delà et que personne ne semble devoir atteindre'.[1]

In spite of the 'décadent' tone of the apostrophe, Mallarmé has here outlined what was to be his permanent attitude to Wagner.

7. TOTAL ART

Wagner's music-drama was 'total' art in several senses, which must be distinguished. First, it was 'total' inasmuch as it included elements of three or four separate arts, music, *décor*, poetry, and mime, and was intended by these means to express without any distortion the experience of the artist. Secondly, it was total by virtue of its being both mythical and musical: its 'pure humanity' and its extreme generalization in the hero-legend was intended to give it the widest possible audience—to bring together all humanity, eventually, without regard for race or state. Whether or not it *could* do this is of no account; in principle it was intended to, and the intention was known to the symbolists.

To avoid confusion, we would call the first aspect of art-synthesis its *total* aspect, and the second aspect simply its *universality*; but 'universality' might be misunderstood for yet a *third* aspect of Wagnerian influence. When Villiers de l'Isle Adam wrote his *Axel*, partly on the model of the Nibelung cycle, he assumed Wagner to have intended, and himself to have repeated, a work of art of epic dimensions in which the entire experience of Man is set out, ordered, and subordinated to a general interpretation of Life. Such was the *Divina Commedia*, or *Faust*; Villiers thought the *Ring* more than a straightforward anarchist's allegory of the growth of 'pure humanity'; and he made his own cycle into a sort of repository for what he conceived to be the universal truths of idealism. This vision of the total meaning of life haunted the symbolists; and if *Narcissus* is to be called the myth of symbolism, *l'Œuvre* is certainly its counter-

[1] ibid. Cf., too, 'Certainement, je ne m'assieds jamais aux gradins des concerts sans percevoir parmi l'obscure sublimité telle ébauche de quelqu'un des poèmes immanents à l'humanité en leur originel état. Je me figure, par un indéracinable sans doute préjugé d'écrivain, que rien ne demeurera sans être proféré; que nous en sommes là, précisément à rechercher la transposition au livre de la symphonie ou uniment *reprendre notre bien*, car ce n'est pas de sonorités élémentaires par les cuivres, les cordes, les bois, mais de l'intellectuelle parole à son apogée que doit, avec plénitude et évidence, résulter en tant que l'ensemble des rapports existant dans tout, la Musique' '*La Musique et les Lettres*, 1894, p. 52). This rather later text is even more clearly anti-Wagnerian than the *Rêverie*.

myth, its negative fable: its crowning glory, ever-awaited but (in spite of valiant attempts) never realized. The career of this negative fable makes perhaps one of the most typical chapters in the history of the movement.

We have, then, to distinguish three things: the combination, fusion, or juxtaposition of the various arts; the universal *appeal* of all great works of art; and the universal sweep of all experience to be embodied in one supreme work of art, its all-embracing import.

(a) *The union of the arts*

For Mallarmé the Wagnerian synthesis was out of the question after 1885 (i.e. from the time he first paid any serious attention to the classification of the arts by Wagner), because it argued a 'musical' poverty in poetry which he could not concede to exist (compare ch. IV above, 4, and ch. V, 6, *ad fin.*); for Morice too, even for Ghil, with his tonal qualities of speech, and many like-minded poets, its whole roots in the pure intellectuality of speech made it untenable. From a considerable section of the symbolist movement we need not expect, and shall not find, much sympathy for the idea of a native music-drama.[1] *Pelléas et Mélisande* (1902), with its quite un-Wagnerian idiom, did not revive the idea.[2]

Even so, the Wagnerian Bayreuth festival ideal died hard. Edouard Dujardin, on the collapse of the *Revue Wagnérienne*, bravely announced his next venture in a brochure which contained the following:

'L'idéal dogmatique de la *Revue Indépendante* sera l'union de tous les arts dans un effort commun à recréer la vie.'[3]

It is unlikely that he made the same distinction between 'union' and 'fusion' that we have seen Morice make.

Paul Adam impatiently called for steps to be taken towards the setting-up of a new synthetic art:

'Même, d'aucuns osent prétendre que l'art intégral agira sur les cinq sens, que d'ici à la réunion en un seul cerveau des habilités musicales, plastiques et littéraires,

---

[1] In the world of poetry, at any rate. Wagner's musical adherents were more faithful (Vincent d'Indy, etc.); though already in 1885 the non-literary, non-musical world's majority view had been enunciated by E. Rod: 'Par là même qu'il a réalisé l'idéal intime et profond de la nation à laquelle il appartient Wagner ne sera jamais réellement *populaire* que pour cette nation-là' ('Wagner et l'esthétique allemande,' *Revue Contemporaine*, t. ii, 1885, p. 315).

[2] See Vallas, *Claude Debussy*. Eng. Translation, 1933, ch. VIII.

[3] Brochure bound into the Bibliothèque Nationale's copy of the *Revue Indépendante*. Ten years later, Dujardin denounced this as 'le vice fondamental de l'œuvre wagnérien...' 'L' Œuvre que Wagner a conçue est, telle qu'il l'a conçue, IMPOSSIBLE' ('Les Représentations de Bayreuth,' *Mercure de France*, viii/1896).

deux arts autres se seront créés: l'un pour les odeurs et les saveurs, l'autre pour le tact:... ce ne sont là sans doute que des imaginations, intéressantes parce qu'elles indiquent un état d'esprit assez courant. Il importe seulement de conclure que l'Art intégral se prépare, qu'il se manifestera dans la forme scénique. Aussi appartient-il aux écrivains nouveaux d'instaurer un art scénique afin de hâter, en France, l'avènement de joies esthétiques encore insoupçonnées, seules sensations qui excusent la vie.'[1]

A very young and tentative Paul Valéry ignored the teachings of his mentor, and stepped from Baudelaire to Wagner's side in a perplexing way:

'Les mondes immenses, dont les Fêtes prédestinées sont les habitacles d'élection, apparaissent, résumés en de secrètes suggestions, sous chacune des formes objectives que leur impose la native préférence des créateurs... Ainsi l'effort du siècle a conquis l'intelligence des principes futurs — l'analyse esthétique d'aujourd'hui a prévu la victorieuse synthèse des prochaines œuvres.'[2]

Without the concessions made to music in Wagner's particular art-formula, the idea of a *dramatic* art was considerably more popular: indeed, almost universally acclaimed by a generation that saw little profit and almost no publicity in meagre editions of lyric poetry, and who, in any case, needed for their health as artists some definite, some *resisting* problems to match themselves against. The idea comes undoubtedly from the cult of Wagner,[3] but again, only on demand; and in crossing the frontier it liberates itself somewhat, and shrinks to the stature of the theatres of the coteries. Charles Morice claims to detect

'le courant heureux et fatal qui emporte notre âge à l'apothéose suprême de l'Art intégral',[4]

but it is not quite clear whether this art is to be dramatic or simply lyric in design.

'La *Littérature de tout à l'heure* est synthétique: elle rêve de suggérer *tout l'homme* par *tout l'Art*,'[5]

suggests that 'L'art intégral' is not necessarily lyric drama; and the view is supported by his *Commentaires d'un livre futur*; but in 1905 he writes,

'Le théâtre est un art inférieur, — à moins qu'il ne soit l'art suprême... Je crois que le logique développement de l'esprit moderne nous rendra, *bientôt*, le Théâtre, sous les espèces, qui sont les siennes propres, de l'art social.'[6]

---

[1] 'L'Evolution dramatique,' *Entretiens politiques et littéraires*, x/1891, p. 135.
[2] *Paradoxe sur l'architecte*, 1891 (*Œuvres*, ed. du Sagittaire, 1931, t. i, p. 194).
[3] The chief French antecedents of symbolism have little time for the stage: e.g. 'Mes opinions sur le théâtre. Ce que j'ai toujours trouvé de plus beau dans le théâtre, dans mon enfance, et encore maintenant, c'est le *lustre* — un bel objet lumineux, cristallin, compliqué, circulaire et symétrique' (Baudelaire, 'Mon cœur mis au nu,' *Œuvres posthumes*, p. 97). See, too, Crépet's note, ibid., p. 14.
[4] *La littérature de tout à l'heure*, p. 263.   [5] ibid.   [6] *La Littérature contemporaine*, 1905, p. 62.

Are we to suppose that this is the lyrical drama at last acknowledged? Not quite; there is a reservation, which for not being quite Wagnerian is none the less hostile to the modern dramatic conception:

'La danse détient le secret de cette renaissance [*sc*. de l'art]. C'est entre les pas de la danseuse, divine de s'ignorer, et pareille à la nature elle-même dont elle est un visage, que la poète inscrira son poème.'[1]

It is, indeed, a variation of Wagner's cry, 'Back to the Greeks'. In an astonishing article of some years before Morice has pleaded that advantage be taken of the Exposition Universelle to stage a huge drama festival comprising games and races, performances of drama, literary festivals of Balzac and Wagner, and ending up with a 'Revue de cent ans'—a kind of Cavalcade on a vast scale.[2] He offers these suggestions seriously; it is a massive disregard of historical perspectives that allows him to do so!

Somewhat less wild, but equally hopeful, are the views of two dramatic poets interviewed by Le Cardonnel and Vellay: Saint-Pol-Roux with his revolutionary aims:

'Je dis que les temples futurs, ce seront les théâtres: théâtres n'ayant rien de commun, est-il besoin d'ajouter, avec ces "conventicules de la sottise" que sont la plupart de nos salles de spectacle où le métier entre pour beaucoup et l'art pour rien. Je considère donc le Théâtre de demain comme le plus puissant, peut-être l'unique moyen de rénovation sociale...

'L'art du théâtre est l'art par lequel l'homme s'égale à Dieu. Or Dieu crée. L'œuvre de théâtre qui n'offre d'apports et ne s'affirme création se classe parmi les fausses couches. Il sied au poète dramatique d'être *le poète entier*, au sens grec: créateur';[3]

and the more successful, and therefore perhaps less ambitious Maeterlinck:

'Alors ce sera peut-être l'avènement du drame musical, du drame lyrique. Je crois, pour l'avenir, à la possibilité d'un théâtre du même genre que le théâtre allemand. Le théâtre allemand est peu connu chez nous: mais il est plus sérieux que le nôtre, et il agite des problèmes bien autrement intéressants.'[4]

Somewhat aside, we find (as always) Mallarmé, revolving over a period of decades a conception of a total and dramatic art which owes nothing to his fellow-symbolists, and not a great deal to Wagner.[5] The first stage is the planning of *Hérodiade* as a drama, a task that was plainly uncongenial to the poet, and never completed.

---

[1] op. cit., p. 63.
[2] 'Une restitution du théâtre antique,' *Mercure de France*, ix/1895, p. 268.
[3] *La Littérature contemporaine*, p. 306. (My italics.)   [4] ibid., p. 280.
[5] See Thibaudet, *La Poésie de Stéphane Mallarmé*, 1913, ch. XI. Thibaudet, writing before the rediscovery of *Igitur* and the publication of the bulk of Mallarmé's private documents, unfortunately fails to detect the time succession in his views, and the constant rarification of his ideal. The result is a quite unnecessarily complicated picture.

This would have been a lyric drama certainly;[1] but of Mallarmé's wider intentions we know nothing. The second stage, inspired perhaps by Villiers de l'Isle Adam's 'idealist' teachings, is the conception of a dramatic monologue, the action with one character. This corresponds with Mallarmé's idea of how we should look on *Hamlet*. In this perspective, the hero alone is important: the secondary characters are virtually his dreams, figments for the development of his own nature; the playwright (and audience) identifies himself with the hero, and 'creates' his own world.

'Le pièce [*Hamlet*], un point culminant du Théâtre, est dans l'œuvre de Shakespeare, transitoire entre la vieille action multiple et le Monologue ou drame avec Soi, futur. Le héros; tous comparses; il se promène, pas plus, lisant au livre de lui-même, haut et vivant signe, nie du regard les autres. Il ne se contentera pas d'exprimer la solitude, parmi les gens, de qui pense: il tue indifféremment, ou du moins, on meurt. La noire présence du douteur cause ce poison, que tous les personnages trépassent: sans même que lui prenne toujours la peine de les percer, dans la tapisserie.'[2]

The 'drame avec Soi, futur' was to have been *Igitur*, the strange monologue in studied and highly artificial lyric prose, which Mallarmé declaimed to Villiers de l'Isle Adam and Catulle Mendès at Avignon, in 1870.

The third stage in the conception of *l'Œuvre*, however, takes it off the stage entirely. The attempt to give to the dramatic subject its purest universality seems to Mallarmé incompatible with the mediation of flesh and blood actresses and actors with individual faces and the possible hazards of an inept *décor*.[3] His tastes in language, combined with the doctrine of Ideas, drive him to seek to abolish theatrical images—however allusive and symbolical—in favour of what might perhaps be identified with *schemata of images*. There presently arises the rumour of an *Œuvre*, meditated for long years, and around which the most fantastic stories are woven: that it was to be in twenty volumes, that it was esoteric in the extreme, that it was to be typographically disposed for the uninitiated to read it without cutting the pages, etc., etc.[4] There can be no doubt that Mallarmé traded upon this invisible asset, which he did nothing to destroy; almost certainly, too, he derived a certain amusement from the curiosity of

---

[1] In verse, with a number of personages, and an essentially allegorical plot, if we accept Thibaudet's interpretation, which is reasonable.

[2] Lettre, *Revue Blanche*, t. xi, no. 75, 15/vii/1896, p. 96.

[3] Cf. 'Si notre extérieure imagination choque, en l'écran de feuillets imprimés, à plus forte raison sur les planches, matérialité dressée dans une obstruction gratuite' (*Divagations*, pp. 198-9).

[4] Ghil appears to have been taken in by all rumours. See *Les Dates et les Œuvres*, 1923, p. 234.

his disciples. In his *Autobiographie, Lettre à Verlaine* (16/xi/1885, published in 1924), he speaks tantalisingly of

> 'Un livre, tout bonnement, en maint tomes, un livre qui soit un livre, architectural et prémédité, et non un recueil des inspirations de hasard, fussent-elles merveilleuses...'

'Le Livre' has now replaced 'Le Drame', at the very same time that he is carefully distinguishing his position from that of Wagner; and it is clear that the emphasis of 'totality' in the projected supreme work of symbolist art is now upon the third of the aspects listed at the head of this section. Mallarmé had hinted a few months earlier in his *Rêverie* that this 'livre' is perhaps impossible of achievement; elsewhere he styles it *Le Monstre qui-ne-peut-être*.

The shift of front is, however, greater than this succession of *stages* might let it appear. For, after all, the theatre is in the first place at least envisaged as the setting for synthetic art, as well as, if not rather than, the *summum opus*; now, among the ingredients of this art Mallarmé discerns *gesture* or Dance as being distinct from mimed representation; and in the course of his theatre rounds for the *Revue Indépendante* he formed the view that the two are incapable of coalition:

> 'Un art tient la scène, historique avec le Drame; avec le Ballet, autre, emblématique. Allier mais ne confondre; ce n'est point d'emblée et par traitement commun qu'il faut joindre deux attitudes jalouses de leur silence respectif, le mimique et la danse, tout à coup hostiles si l'on en force le rapprochement.'[1]

In a sense, the contrast between dance and acting is on a par with that between 'pure' and 'dramatic' or 'programme' music, and the distinction no more valid: bodily gesture underlies both the former as more specialized gesture (of song or instrumental playing) underlies the latter. What ballet is ever so 'pure' as not to have resorbed in it some action, some succession from sad to joyous, from sad to despairing; what music so 'pure' that it does not strike some such tone as triumph, determination, energy, tranquillity, embodied so thoroughly in its language—indeed inseparable—that abstraction is an amputation? The distinction, then, is an empirical one, not fundamental as Mallarmé thought; so that in place of the purification of art that he held he was effecting by banishing theatrical mime, there was no more than a voluntary truncation of artistic resources, or decision to explore one set of language possibilities rather than another; the retreat from Wagnerian legend (too close to earthly history) is designed to bring us into the realm of 'pure' art, 'pure'

[1] *Divagations*, p. 176.

poetry, 'pure' Ideas; whereas it simply exchanges one cut of imaginative language for another. The result is called 'preciosity', 'abstraction', 'Allusion', and what not, according to the viewpoint of the judge. But it is still language. Mallarmé thinks that ballet can be innocent of meaning, simply gesture, and pins his faith in it:

'La Danse seule capable, par son écriture sommaire, de traduire le fugace et le soudain jusqu'a l'Idée — pareille vision comprend tout, absolument tout le Spectacle future'[1]

—but fails to see that if this gesture embodies 'un état d'âme', as by his admission it does, then it cannot be but that it has meaning, if only in quite embryonic form. All effort to separate gesture from mime by a radical distinction in kind does violence to elementary facts of art, including the fact that between drama and simple miming, simple miming and the most classically abstract ballet, an infinity of possible gradations exists which makes any hard and fast dividing-line invidious, not to say vicious.

For the final evolution of his theories, however, some such dividing-line is imperative. Mallarmé wishes to embody in his total (book-) art what he finds valuable or exciting upon the stage; and this is expressive gesture, screened off (so far as possible) from mime; but in addition, he would have us do without the flesh-and-blood gesture entirely, and substitute some less distracting medium for arousing our participation in the Idea.

'La Danse seule, du fait de ses évolutions, avec le mime me paraît nécessiter un espace réel, ou la scène.

'A la rigueur, un papier suffit pour évoquer toute pièce: aidé de sa personnalité multiple chacun pouvant se la jouer en dedans, ce qui n'est pas le cas quand il s'agit de pirouettes.'[2]

He prefers, indeed, 'l'immortalité de la brochure'.

It will be remembered that Mallarmé has defined the dance as a language[3] which expresses briefly what speech would take paragraphs to describe. This is a comparatively early judgement; in time he comes to turn it round, though not contradict himself. The dance—as gesture—is to be not described, but transcribed, taken up into poetry. Speech has absorbed music—or at least all that it is fit to take; now it is to absorb dance in its march towards 'total art'. Of course, it is speech rhythm in the widest sense that is to do this;

[1] ibid., p. 142.   [2] ibid., p. 194.
[3] Of the dancer he says, ' "*Elle ne danse pas*" suggérant par le prodige de raccourcis ou d'élans, avec une écriture corporelle ce qu'il faudrait des paragraphes en prose dialoguée autant que descriptive pour exprimer, dans la rédaction: poème dégagé de tout appareil de scribe' (*Divagations*, p. 173).

and to register the refinements of the excessively stretched rhythmical sense, there is the notation of *Un Coup de Dés*. As highly articulated prose may with practical advantage after a certain point be transcribed as *vers libre*, so *vers libre*, when carrying the weight of the most subtle inflexions of emphasis, is re-written in the notation of Mallarmé's last and allegedly most obscure poem. Whether anything is gained has been questioned; what is beyond doubt is the poet's intention in the matter. There is a whole order of delicate expression for which in daily life we use gesture: the shrug of the shoulders, the lift of the eyebrows, the language of the hands, even the ironic wink, are acts which may well accompany but do not replace, and are not replaced, by speech. Such bodily gesture deepens and enriches the specialized gesture of speech. Mallarmé sought to deepen and enrich the already 'musical' utterance *internally* by some similar means; but ignoring that poetry is imagined bodily speech, he conceived the possibility of an 'ideal' language of gesture which might be imported into imagined but *disembodied* speech;[1] with the result that the gesture element claimed to be imported into *Un Coup de Dés* is either no new element at all but simply the fiction of a false aesthetic principle, or else something which was present already, though not recorded by the symbolism of writing—something inherent in all speech as rooted in rhythmical expressive language. The notation of the poem, as we foreshadowed above (ch. IV, 4), adds nothing to the intrinsic force of the language, though it may help the reader to approach near to the author's intended phrasing.

Un Coup de Dés is not Mallarmé's *Œuvre*; nor is *Hérodiade*, nor *Igitur*; indeed, if Thibaudet's sane interpretation is accepted, the first is rather Mallarmé's awakening to the remoteness of *Le Monstre qui-ne-peut-être*.[2] But these works—and others perhaps as well— all bear a certain relation of one kind or another to the central but non-existent work. They are all in some sense studies—abstracts in preparation for the great achievement. *Hérodiade* and *Igitur* trace

---

[1] I.e. poetry which is not only read silently, but is presumed not to have its roots in the custom of uttered words at all.

[2] On the strength of our rendering of 'le hasard' above (ch. V, 4) it might be claimed that our own interpretation of the poem clashes with Thibaudet's. In the one case, 'le hasard' denotes the impossibility of ever mastering language so completely as to make a perfect poem; in the other, the impossibility of ever cutting loose of the limited images and themes of this life in the attainment of the transcendant and universal *Œuvre*. But, in fact, the two things are the same. We have claimed (ch. IV, *passim*) that language includes the widest constructs— myth, images of all kinds, etc.—so that 'le hasard' defined as a hindrance to finding the perfectly appropriate word and 'le hasard' defined as the inherent imperfection of all myth are simply a very small and a very large-scale example respectively of a necessary negative value in all art. And there can be little doubt that Mallarmé himself was fully alive to this wide extension of his term.

the course of successive modifications of the dramatic ideal down to the Ode,[1] then to the pure lyrical monologue, finally impersonal, its myth fragmented more and more in an effort to rise above the 'contingent'; *Un Coup de Dés*, at the moment of renunciation, traces the means by which the element of dance would have been brought into the total art.[2]

One lesson appears to emerge from the case of Mallarmé. The art of poetry cannot be rigidly separated, as Wagner tended to do in principle, from mime or music. This stands to reason. If art or expression is grounded in gesture, then attempts to cut gesture up into various compartments (this is what rigid classifications of the arts involves doing) will be a misleading and dangerous occupation. At all points there is danger of an overlap. Wagner appears to have noticed one such between music and primitive speech; but he overlaid it with an intellectualist formula for speech in the present day. Mallarmé discerned two major cases in his own aesthetic—in which he was no doubt helped rather than hindered by his theory of Ideas. In this respect he stands at the very opposite pole from the school of, say, Taine, or from all aesthetics that classify art according to the two 'higher senses' of ear and eye, or according to some other artificial, because extraneous, rule, or simply according to works of art. The example of poetry in Mallarmé's speculations might serve as a warning that the classification of different sorts of languages—speech and other—is always empirical and often precarious.

(b) Total art and society

Symbolist art set out in the early eighties with a strong leaning towards esotericism, dandyism, and eccentricity; by 1885 this had become a defensive enclusiveness against philistinism and hostile gibing; by 1900 it was no longer symbolism. The problem whether art 'should' be addressed to this number of people or that, is strictly not one for the aesthetician, but for the publisher; yet it is one of the most frequently debated. The aesthetic of expression, however, can state that language as it is learnt is language in use; and that consequently the poet, even in his loneliest utterances, is speaking *as if*

[1] Cf. 'J'imagine que la cause de s'assembler, dorénavant, en vue de fêtes inscrites au programme humain, ne sera pas le théâtre, borné ou incapable tout seul de répondre à de très subtils instincts, ni la musique du reste trop fuyante pour ne pas décevoir la foule: mais à soi fondant ce que ces deux isolent de vague et de brutal, l'Ode, dramatisée ou coupée savamment; ces scènes héroïques une ode à plusieurs voix' (*Divagations*, pp. 229–30).

[2] See also Bonniot, 'Préface,' *Igitur*, 3e. ed., 1925, p. 25, for interesting but not always perhaps meaningful probing into some notes left by Mallarmé on the classification of drama, dance, mime, hymn, and the Hero.

he was addressing an audience. There is no need to think further
than Mallarmé's shadowy audience or companion, a repetition of
himself, with whom he makes his voyage to the enchanted island of
art—

'Nous fûmes deux, je le maintiens.'[1]

The question is not without a wider interest; for if art is viewed as in
any necessary sense persuasive, relation to the audience is an over-
riding consideration for the artist; while, on the other hand, one writer
at least of the generation of 1890—Saint-Pol-Roux[2]—anticipated
more recent views to some extent in his view of the relationship
established by the mere problem of using language, between the poet
and tradition.

The most generally known and accepted fact about French poets
towards the end of the nineteenth century is that they had their
roots deep in a deliberately eccentric, even anti-social, intelligentsia.
Murger's *Vie de Bohème* (if it ever existed) had gone a long way
towards complete transformation by 1885; it was an affair of clubs,
coteries, and reviews, standing on their dignity. A notable fore-
runner, *La Nouvelle Rive Gauche*, proclaims editorially its hostility
to the whole world of letters as it survived from the Second Empire;
the brotherhood of art, withdrawing itself from tasks of public
morality, completes the isolation started by bohemian romanticism.

'Nous ne croyons pas à l'*utilité*. Nous l'avouons ingénument: détruire nous em-
barrasserait, car nous n'avons rien à mettre à la place de ce qui est. Et peut-être
est-il *bon* que les choses aillent *mal*.
   'Vous n'êtes donc pas socialistes?
   'Nous sommes anti-sociaux.
   'Notre désir, notre rêve à nous, serait d'échapper à cette société détestable où
nous sommes. C'est impossible, il n'y a plus de solitudes, et il est défendu de se dés-
intéresser de la chose universelle. La loi est une robe de Nessus dont rien ne peut
nous délivrer.'[3]

A typical utterance for 1882; and the Décadents set off on a rather
similar tack four years later:

'Peu nous importe que les foules ne nous comprennent pas. L'écrivain, soucieux
de son art, doit faire abstraction de leur existence. C'est à elles de s'élever vers lui,
non à lui de s'abaisser vers elles.'[4]

The *Revue Wagnérienne's* attitude to the wide public can be summed

---

[1] *Prose (pour des Esseintes).*
[2] See Rolland de Renéville, *Univers de la Parole* (1944, p. 61), for certain of his views on
language, published for the first time, though written in 1929.
[3] op. cit., 17/xi/1882.   [4] Baju, *Le Décadent,* 16/x/1886.

up in Wyzéwa's remarks about the democratic flood-tide, already
noted; and Charles Morice, at a rather central moment of time,
1889, sums up what he sees around him in the following terms:

> 'L'isolement où les Barbares ont relégué les Poètes, les conduit au triomphe de la
> formule ésotérique — proclamée désormais sans danger, puisqu'il n'y a plus de
> silence — les force à s'enfermer dans les limites providentielles de l'Art et du Génie.'[1]

Mauclair systematizes the formula in a myth which greater writers
than he were to make effective use of:

> 'On meurt de solidarité utilitaire, d'associations à des fins viles et contingentes [!],
> d'absence éthique: on meurt de demeurer au milieu des étrangers. Il faut être
> libéré de son temps.
> 'J'en appelle aux mille hommes qui savent que l'art existe, en France. Les
> meilleurs doivent s'abstraire. Tous se confinent en eux-mêmes, et tous sont des
> Narcisses, par goût, par besoin, par horreur d'autre chose que de leur image.'[2]

Mauclair's 'egoism', like that of Barrès, is founded on an impulsive
reaction from 'utilitarianism', from cant and hollow principles,
Panama Canal scandals, and so on. It is not intended to be a reasoned
position, and so far as it concerns the problem of the artist and his
audience, solves nothing. Narcissus can no doubt study himself;
but he cannot do it except by studying himself as affected by 'la chose
universelle' in different ways; and there, already, is a community
with his audience, if he speaks. To proclaim this sort of egoism is not
to settle anything about your audience: for an audience is everybody
who speaks the same language.

Mallarmé's polite but firm refusal to attend to 'la Foule' is too
well known to require delineation. The attitude is strengthened by a
certain secretiveness that is part of the mystic's typical apparatus.
Art is a religion for an *élite*; it is too abundantly clear that the mob—
or even the professional classes—will have nothing to do with it:
Verlaine alone could command good sales, and Verlaine was almost
a relic of another age.

In the face of this pervasive attitude, it is hard to credit Wagner
with the conversion of the symbolists to the idea of evangelical art.
It is true, that in the very midst of their withdrawal they still awaited
a Work of Art that should unite the whole of society. Mallarmé,
between whom and Leconte de Lisle there is here an unexpected
comparison, looked on his present world as an interregnum, the poet
dethroned from his rightful pontifical chair; he set his hopes back

---

[1] *La Littérature de tout à l'heure*, p. 13.   [2] *Eleusis*, 1894, pp. 29–30.

into a distant future.[1] But even so, the opportunity lies open to the citizen to peer into the heart of the universal mystery:

'La scène est le foyer évident des plaisirs pris en commun, aussi et tout bien réfléchi, la majestueuse overture sur le mystère dont on est au monde pour envisager la grandeur, cela même que le citoyen, qui en aura idée, fond le droit de réclamer à un Etat, comme compensation de l'amoindrissement social.'[2]

Morice, as we have seen, dreamt of new Olympiads not 'some day' but as an immediate programme for the next Exposition, and joins to this a spirited attack on Wagner for not having set up Art as the *successor* of Religion, but simply made it religious art.[3] And so on. Call it what we will—rationalization of guilt consciences, attempt to refute charges of 'cloisonnisme', or simply the wish to be successful, backing the patently anti-social attitude of symbolism—there is a concomitant, almost a necessary, impulse towards an audience, towards the solid block of living tradition for which, and on which, the poet lives. But between Wagner and the symbolists there is this difference, that Wagner not only recognized the possibility of gaining a wide audience, and in some sense at least allying his art to religion, but took steps to achieve this end; while the symbolists spoke much of making art a religion, but in fact made it no more than a private cult. To say, with Dujardin,[4] that there is here a signal instance of Wagner's influence, is to ignore this simple distinction.

'Literature,' said Arthur Symons, 'in speaking to us so intimately, so solemnly, as only religion has hitherto spoken to us, becomes itself a sort of religion, with all the duties and responsibilities of the Sacred Ritual.'[5]

---

[1] 'Notre seule magnificence, la scène, à qui le concours d'arts divers scellés par la poésie attribue selon moi quelque caractère religieux, ou officiel, si l'un de ces mots a un sens, je constate que le siècle finissant n'en a cure, ainsi comprise; et que cet assemblage miraculeux de tout ce qu'il faut pour façonner de la divinité, sauf la clairvoyance de l'homme, sera pour rien' (*Divagations*, p. 191).

[2] ibid., p. 192.

[3] E.g. 'Wagner n'a pas vu le rôle divin de Religion suprême qui incombe à l'Art Suprême. Il limite l'Art dans ses tendances vers la Vérité, à faciliter *L'intelligence de la vérité divine que renferme la religion, par une représentation idéale de ses allégories*' (*La Littérature de tout à l'heure*, p. 199). Morice's arguments against Wagner, and for the 'Religion of Art' are too long to quote in full here (ibid., pp. 199–200, and pp. 67–9, also p. 356); but they are unusually weak. Roughly they are that Criticism has discredited myth from the point of view of truth (David Strauss, etc.), and that religion relies more and more on artistic efficiency to exercise its hold over the faithful. Having thus to his own satisfaction disposed of religion, Morice is at a loss to provide a convincing account of how art (in general) or art (as a supreme work of art or mythology) is to take the place of religion without itself becoming religion in the sense that Morice has condemned.

[4] 'Dans l'œuvre et dans les théories de Wagner, Mallarmé reconnut immédiatement un exemple de ce qu'il rêvait lui-même; au lieu d'être le divertissement d'une soirée, l'Œuvre d'art devenait une sorte de fête religieuse, où la foule prenait conscience du plus profond et du plus véridique d'elle-même (*Mallarmé*, p. 79). Yes, but how wide a gap separated their two conceptions of the cult of art!

[5] *The Symbolist Movement*, p. 9.

Thibaudet tellingly compares Mallarmé with a priest, his art a mass, which requires no more than the priest for its consummation, and for which the congregation is not indispensable. But the comparison is not just; for many chapels are endowed, and only few poets. Moreover, the poet's art does not gain from enforced isolation; on the contrary, it declines from lack of fresh air; like Antaeus, it weakens in proportion as it is cut off from its source, its tradition. No one would claim that the liturgy performed in a chapel is less efficacious than one performed in a cathedral; but poetry knows no such egalitarianism, and the literary chapel produces not many miracles. The symbolists, when they looked to the theatre, to the larger audience, were perhaps instinctively looking to renew their strength in the bracing air of public criticism, their inspiration in contact with the wider contexts of their language; and the modern theatre has always a strong appeal to the poet, as a large and yet firm medium for his effort; but the lyric stage of 1890—even for Maeterlinck—was not ready; and the lyric poet was not ready either. It required another decade, the digestion of symbolist acquisitions, and the rejection of symbolist bric-à-brac, before the two could meet on fruitful terms. The last word on the times rests with Viélé-Griffin—himself not without interest and practical knowledge in lyrical drama:

'Il n'y a pas plus de théâtre sans public qu'il n'y a de haut fait d'armes sans provocation de guerre... Les mœurs bourgeoises (les seules qui important dans l'espèce et pour l'heure) se font de moins en moins favorables au développement d'un théâtre littéraire... Quant à la seule magic évocatrice de l'idée et du mot, elle reste sans effet, et son heure n'est pas. Théâtre de demain? C'est le théâtre en petit comité, le théâtre de coterie, aux promiscuités encore inévitables, duquel il est, peut-être, sage de préférer le tête-à-tête du livre.'[1]

Claudel is already of another moment in the history of literature; and he adheres to a more ancient and more widespread tradition of literature and feeling than the generation before him did. Perhaps *Le Soulier de Satin* is the most truly 'total' work as regards appeal and breadth that has appeared on the modern French lyric stage; yet it could hardly be dubbed *l'Œuvre* to which Mallarmé and his peers looked forward.

(c) 'L'explication orphique de la terre'

Gustave Kahn, speaking of Paul Adam's preface to *Le Mystère des Foules*, has an interesting approach to the third symbolist problem

---

[1] *Revue Blanche*, t. vi, no. 30, iv/1894, p. 333.

of 'total art'—the universality of import of the dreamt-of masterpiece. He writes:

'Evidemment l'œuvre d'art, poème ou roman, doit être la métaphore d'une philosophie.

'Le seul mot de philosophie reste à définir précisément. On sent bien, et l'exemple d'Adam n'y contredit pas par son livre, que le vocable doit être compris élastiquement.

'Cette philosophie ... serait la somme de ses expériences, le fruit d'un regard sur la vie.'[1]

The implications of this position are serious, and, if pursued, lead to the resolution of an irksome dualism that has worried the philosophy of art for many years—the dualism between 'good' and 'great' art, between the Beautiful and the Sublime, the perfect and the grand. Omitting for the moment the reference to philosophy, or rather paraphrasing it as a 'general attitude to life', we obtain a truth which is valid to some extent for even the most trivial utterances that aesthetic may care to take note of: namely, that a partial expression of an attitude contains within itself the germ or implication of his whole attitude. If he develops within the formal scope of a certain utterance the maximum clarity in attitude, we say that the poet has written a poem—'beautiful' in proportion as its limiting point of expressiveness is approached; but there is always a limiting point. Dante's view of life embodied in a sonnet might be a fine sonnet as sonnets go, but it would not be the *Divina Commedia*: to achieve the latter, every line is needed that is there. Now in the structure of a really big poem, the intricate detail, some of the minute reckoning with the subtlest resources of language, might be out of place (though it may well not be); Rimbaud speaks of 'prose rimée' in this context: but it remains true that the structural problems are far greater in all respects to the artist that really faces them. To express a general attitude more fully than a sonnet will allow, a greater span of structural—formal—problems must be taken in hand. Bach's Passion Music is an altogether bigger thing than any of his suites: and not merely in length or complexity of balance, but of course also in profundity of feeling. The correspondence is inevitable. 'Great art' is simply very 'beautiful' art; the achievement in really big structures of really big feelings. There is the most scope for the inter-animation of language. To resolve to write a sonnet is to renounce for the moment the task of exploring the widest and deepest in experience:

[1] 'La Vie Mentale,' *Revue Blanche*, t. x, no. 62, 1/i/1896, pp. 10–11.

not because sonnets are too short but because they present the artist with a firm limit to the problems he can undertake in them.[1]

Good and Great art are thus one and the same thing. That need not force us to abandon a useful and real distinction in literary criticism between the Mallarmé and the Rimbaud, the Watteau and the Van Gogh, the meticulous and the bold. But this is not a distinction in aesthetic: it relates to the use of language by individuals, and also on a larger scale to the movement of tradition; other well-known synonyms for the terms of this distinction are classical and romantic, used in a certain way.

All this is implied in Kahn's remark; and he is evidently aware that it goes somewhat against the grain of symbolist aspiration, for he attempts to deny the fact, claiming that his ideas are developed

'Suivant une évolution indiquée dans nos premiers efforts'.[2]

But this is not true. The symbolists, once again, attempted to draw a demarcation line between simple poetry and *l'Œuvre*, something entirely different in kind; for Mallarmé an absolutely unconditioned masterpiece; for others, a *summum opus* of special and indeed religious attributes. Only with poetry in its actual state, no such achievement. Hours might be spent speculating on the possible claimant to the succession of Dante and Goethe; but they would be wasted hours; for where among the symbolists was the poet with that familiarity with his age, its affairs and problems, to write the poem of industrial and colonizing France? Symbolist tradition, for all its claims to be a new religion, to give unequalled insight into deep truths, was too narrowly-based to carry the weight of an epic. It is an interesting reflection on the age that after the death of Hugo, the most nearly epic poet is Verhaeren.

We have noted Mallarmé's contribution to the negative myth; it was in nearly all respects exceptional, and a more typical effort seems to call for our attention before we leave this chapter. Ghil's ambitious and unreadable effort we shall leave aside, to concentrate on another and lesser-known work. Following no doubt the example of *Les Fleurs du Mal*, whose deliberate arrangement no reader can entirely ignore, G.-A. Aurier projected his *Œuvre* as a collection of poems. Poe's most diligently followed advice in the nineteenth century is brevity, intensity; the epic of the latter half of the century is transformed into the arranged collection of lyric poems; Hugo is

---

[1] Our personifying the sonnet should not be taken as conceding it an existence in its own rights: in literature all thinking people are nominalists.
[2] op. cit.

no exception. In a prefatory notice to Aurier's *Œuvres Posthumes,* Rémy de Gourmont notes, somewhat acidly,

'Les poètes font bien encore des poésies de circonstance, mais ils s'en défendent et, quand ils les assemblent en volume, leur ingéniosité travaille à leur enlever, par des artifices de groupement, l'apparence qu'elle gardent pourtant toujours, de poésies de circonstances... Jamais personne, peut-être, n'a lu, d'affilée, tout un volume de vers, comme on lit un roman dans sa nouveauté, — et le poète, fût-il Baudelaire, s'est livré en vain à un pénible labeur de mosaïste.[1]

He recommends a simple chronological arrangement (quoting Goethe in support). Aurier, however, had other views; and a certain interest attaching to his plan, 'en sa barbarie spontanée,' we make bold to reproduce it integrally.

NOTES POUR LA PREFACE DE MON VOLUME DE VERS

1. Mépris de la société actuelle pour le poète: la poésie est un passe-temps, etc., l'homme sérieux, etc. Il faut en prendre son parti. Nous autres, nous avons la conviction de l'incomparable grandeur de notre œuvre, etc. Cela nous suffit. Donc, que ces lignes ne soient lues que par les dix futiles... etc.

2. Qu'est-ce que *le poème*?
Une synthèse de toutes les idées générales perçues par un moi donné.

	La synthèse des sensations constitue:	les sciences.
,,	sciences ,,	les philosophies.
,,	philosophies ,,	les dogmes.
,,	dogmes ,,	le poème

Le poème est donc, par excellence, la conclusion intellectuelle; le poème est l'essentielle synthèse du moi.

3. Donc composer un poème signifie:
Exprimer dans un langage spécial les ultimes généralisations du moi. Or ces généralisations sont de deux sortes.

(*a*) généralisations centripètes (idées générales se rapportant à des psychies attribuées au moi: conscience, etc.)

(*b*) généralisations centrifuges (idées générales se rapportant à des psychies considérées comme non-moi: métaphysique, esthétique, morale, etc.)

Mon œuvre comprendra donc d'abord deux parties correspondant à ces deux classes de généralisations.

[1] Aurier, *Œuvres Posthumes*, 1896, p. xiii. The epithet 'mosaïste' may be an obvious one; but I find it again in Dr. Richards' *The Philosophy of Rhetoric* (1936) in a context which has interest when juxtaposed with the present one. Gourmont is discussing whole poems, Richards is discussing words, and the vicious doctrine that each has its allotted 'meaning', irrespective of all other elements of the language: 'its evil is that it takes the senses of an author's words to be things we know before we read him, fixed factors with which he has to build up the meaning of his sentences as a *mosaic* is put together of discrete independent tesserae. Instead, they are resultants which we arrive at only through the interplay of the interpretative possibilities of the whole utterance' (p. 55). What is true of the sentence, is true of the work of art, and from the smallest to the largest scale. It is in this perspective that the full advantage of our wide definition of language in chapter IV above becomes apparent. If *Les Fleurs du Mal* were really a poem, with a decisive organization overall, instead of poems loosely strung on a string of predominating attitude, we should find ourselves *unable to avoid* finding more tangible signs of the 'interplay of interpretative possibilities' than in fact we do.

Mais il est un ordre de psychies qui, pour être centripètes, n'en subissent pas moins inéluctablement la force centrifuge du moi, et sont par nous rapportées à ce moi (comparaison avec la force centripète de la terre, modifiée par l'ambiance atmosphérique). Ces psychies seront: l'amour, la haine, en un mot les manifestations proprement dites psychologiques. Donc, mon œuvre comprendra indispensablement une troisième partie, que je placerai, ainsi qu'il est juste, entre les deux parties antérieurement énumérées.

Avec ces trois parties, l'Œuvre serait complète, étant absolument adéquate à toutes les nécessaires généralisations du moi, mais d'un moi tellement *nu* qu'il cesserait d'être humain. Pour lui donner ce caractère, une quatrième partie sera donc nécessaire, partie comprenant toutes les négatives psychiques, telles que: les mensonges, les ironies, les perversités, l'amour de l'extralégal, de l'artificiel, etc.

L'Œuvre, ainsi construite, sera donc complète, adéquate absolument au moi du poète.

PLAN DE L'ŒUVRE

1e. Partie (Titre à déterminer)
Psychies centripétiques: le moi conscient de lui-même, de ses vouloirs, etc.
[These are titles of poems completed or projected]
L'œuvre maudit.
L'agonie des chimères.
Contrition.
Les marais du cœur.
Le rondel des prédestinés.
Ultimus dolor.
Le dire du fou.
La joie du bourreau.
Balzac, ce géant.
Subtile courtisane.

2e. Partie (*Les Intermédiaires*)
Psychies centrifuges, modifiées par l'attraction du moi: amour, haine, passions, morales, sociales, esthétiques, etc.
Les illusions perdues.
Lever de lune.
Duperies de l'amour.
Chanson d'adieu.
Sous des ciels ingénus et mauve d'élégie.

3e. Partie (*Les Cosmogoniques*)
Psychies définitivement centrifuges, extériorisations définitives du moi, généralisations scientifiques, religieuses, métaphysiques, etc.
Pauvre des sequins d'or.
Chrysos
Les Sapins.

4e. Partie (*Les Ironies*)
Quintessence des mensonges, des perversités et des doutes. Le doute et l'ironie sont les dernières fleurs de l'âme cultivée:
Le Sonnet de la fille aux péchés mentis.
Madrigal.
Réminiscences.

From all this, we may make our way to a fairly clear view of the poet as theoretician. His youthful impressionability, with its sincere flattery of Laforgue and Baudelaire, the naïve terminology, tell heavily against him; we should not be so amused, perhaps, if we knew more of the background of similar projects that many of the nineties' aspiring poets drew up as a matter of routine. Aurier's misfortune—or perhaps his fortune?—was never to have faced the problem in practical detail of constructing *l'Œuvre*. Already in this sketch, Rémy de Gourmont notices several 'inanités': in successive drafts poems are shifted around without evident signs of special fitness in any context.

This is no place for going into the for and against of ordered arrangements of lyric poems. The fact that no inevitable and necessary order stares the poet in the face indicates nothing more serious than that the poems are independent and to some extent monadic; there is a difference between the cohesion of movements in a sonata and the cohesion of the sonatas in a composer's life-work. In this context, too, we may repeat of the symbolists at large that 'la veine personnelle est en somme courte'; and there was no wider field for exploration: or if there was, the ivory tower had no windows facing out on it. The aspiration towards *l'Œuvre* is one for the fulfilling of which conditions were, on balance, highly unfavour-able to the symbolists. Great art argues the existence of heroic language resources—always remembering the wide sense 'language' is used in. In place of—say—the solid and immense body of symbolism and experience offered by a mediaeval Christianity, as pressed into service by Dante, the symbolists had nothing but some pseudo-philosophical scraps, some new developments of metaphor, a museum-knowledge of some myth, and a powerful dislike for middle-class life in an industrial state. No place here for 'total art'; the wonder is that the revival of lyric poetry took place at all.

At the same time, they did not realize that every time a poem was written, it was a part achievement of their ideal.[1] In a curious blend of mystic dogma and artistic despair, they enclosed their ideal of a great art-work in the concept of religious myth; but their whole outlook

---

[1] Mallarmé, of course, did, in spite of his forbidding theory of the 'absolute masterpiece'; but who in his time would not have thought the following remarks simply an addition to the repertory of paradox: 'Cette Œuvre existe, tout le monde l'a tentée sans le savoir; il n'est pas un génie ou un pître ayant prononcé une parole, qui n'en ait retrouvé un trait sans le savoir' (in Thibaudet, op. cit., p. 137); again, 'J'irai plus loin, je dirai: Le Livre, persuadé qu'au fond il n'y en a qu'un, tenté à son insu par quiconque a écrit, même les génies. L'explication orphique de la terre, qui est le seul devoir du poète, et le jeu littéraire par excellence' (*Autobiographie*, Lettre à Verlaine, 16/xi/1885, 1924).

was unequal to the task of adapting and developing such myth; their general attitude to the whole of existence was very closely and painfully limited. Indeed, when we run through some of the myths they did produce—*Igitur* the Mallarméen Hamlet, *La Chevauchée d'Yeldis*, *Paludes*, *Narcisse*—we find them all in some way pointing to the voluntary isolation of the poet in search of a distant and difficult ideal, few being called and fewer chosen. Hardly the stuff of Œdipus or Lear, Faust or Satan. Taine, had he lived, would have said that the 'personnage régnant' was missing from the scene. Claudel alone of the poetic generation that followed might be said to have re-discovered a 'personnage régnant'—with the qualification that his 'personnage' is no mortal figure. For a time the custody of myth had passed out of the hands of the poet into those of the novelist. The lyric poem moved inevitably towards Valéry's myth of Narcissus.

The fall of the barriers between poetry and prose, Wagnerism in the guise of various theories of 'musical' language, the rescue of myth from the parnassian refrigerator, the mystery-play—all these are closely linked features of the symbolist ideal, and we have seen in the course of time how some came to life while others died of anaemia. This ideal was the historical flesh-and-blood in which we see the attempt of a generation to classify the arts in a system agreeable to its abilities and hopes; it was not to be expected that any finally satisfactory solution to this problem would be achieved. Wagner's influence in particular has been grossly overrated—in any event it was born of misunderstanding and dilettantism and issued most often into blind alleys. The symbolists use him simply as a name or slogan to place against their own pet theories: indeed, the Wagnerian philosophy of art is grotesquely out of place anywhere but at Bayreuth; there were no Wagners among the symbolists nor Bayreuths in France.

CHAPTER VI

THE SYMBOL IN ART

Un hiérarche, oui, un Pontife du monde sera celui-là, le Poète et l'Inspiré Créateur qui, prométhéen, saura façonner de nouveaux symboles et prendra un nouveau feu au ciel pour nous le livrer à jamais.—CARLYLE, quoted on the flyleaf of *Entretiens*, t. i, no. 1, iv/1890.

Tout objet dont le bois se compose répond
A quelque objet pareil dans la forêt de l'âme.
VICTOR HUGO

1. Preliminary. 2. Some unsuccessful attempts at definition. 3. Symbols in mystic tradition: (a) Carlyle; (b) Baudelaire. 4. Symbolist Successors of Baudelaire: (a) Mauclair; (b) Mallarmé; (c) The Complete Symbolist: an Interlude. 5. Symbol, myth, and allegory. 6. Beyond myth and metaphor. 7. Recapitulation. 8. Conclusion.

I. PRELIMINARY

BEFORE embarking on the last main cross-section of our detailed inquiry, it would be as well to take stock of the position we have now reached.

In chapter III, we determined the nature of the poetic knowledge for whose independent existence the symbolists were in search. Their special leanings towards mystical accounts of reality, sensed dimly through the painted veil of the universe, led many to regard poetry as an exercise in mystical knowledge; but others, and among them Mallarmé, were seriously concerned to describe the act as well as the knowledge, and from this there emerged the view of imagination (not so named) as satisfying two prime demands: the demand for an account of emotion in art and the demand for an account of form.

In chapter IV, accordingly, we plotted out the symbolists' attitude to form, and saw them concerned quite as much with establishing the claims to existence of 'organic' or spontaneous *form* as with destroying the pretensions of 'fossil' or dictatorial *forms*.

In chapter V, we examined their reactions to the challenge of legend and their failure to keep distinct the mystical idea of the Baudelairean Symbol and the strictly intellectualist idea of the Wagnerian Myth.

These inquiries, though woven through each other in respect of the material they treat, are yet in themselves well able to stand alone. Nevertheless, we do not propose to leave them so, and in this final chapter we shall attempt to show how a perfectly basic aesthetic entity, whose identity will emerge as we go along, was used to support the weight of aesthetic speculation in each of these various fields.

The literary symbol, under whose covering aegis alone we are entitled to speak of symbolism at all, will be found to have been described and defined with a view to explaining all these primary aesthetic problems:

1. The problem of poetic knowledge (§3).
2. The problem of emotion in art (§4).
3. The problem of resorbed intellectual contents (§5).
4. The problem of form (§6).

We shall show that the literary symbol, when correctly identified, can provide a solution to each of these problems, and in such fashion that each solution taken alone is consonant with, and even implies, the others.

Being so indiscriminately invoked for dealing with so great a variety of problems, it is not to be supposed that the term 'symbol'[1] is precisely a model of clarity and handiness. In chapter IV, we employed it in a sense that is fairly universally recognized; but this sense, as we noted at the time, must not be allowed to prejudice the present inquiry.

On the count of ambiguity, we need not press its disadvantages. They strike the eye at every turn. But we can distinguish ambiguity on two levels. First, a fairly steady stream of writers have talked of 'symbols' in connection with their art, as characterizing one or another of its features; and such writers have often though by no means always had a consistent idea in their mind of what they intend. 'Symbol' for them denotes one or several combined meanings out of at least half a dozen distinct possibilities. Even within the context of aesthetics, 'Symbol' means one thing to Baudelaire, and his spiritual successors, and quite another to Laforgue; between Baudelaire and the young W. B. Yeats there are many points of contact, but not identity in the use of the term; Mauclair (in *Eleusis*) seems at times to be attempting a synthesis of incompatibles; and so on. We shall have to enumerate each of these different applications, and show for what reasons in their historical contexts and under exhaustive definition each contains elements which prevent them being brought as species

---

[1] 'Symbolism' appears to be first mentioned in *Le XIXe siècle* on 11/viii/1885, by Jean Moréas.

under one single general definition of Symbol as a literary entity:
yet these elements are the historical life and colour of the closing
decades of nineteenth-century French poetry.

The second level of ambiguity arises when well-intentioned
theorists or literary critics set out to perform this impossible task of
developing from one or other of these uses of 'Symbol' a general
notion applicable to all the others. In the attempt to reach a conclusion, they involve themselves in such ambiguity, not to say worse,
that the temptation besets us to dismiss the whole venture, expel the
term 'symbol' from our vocabulary, and abandon any curiosity as to
what successive generations of writers have been trying to get at
when they use it. And this is perhaps what many people have done.
But the persistence of the word in criticism and the sanctions of
common sense are not lightly to be ignored by the aesthetician. In
a majority of cases, unsuccessful attempts to embrace the whole field
of literary symbolism owe their failure to superficiality—incon-
sidered use of words such as 'represent', 'emotion', 'suggestion',
'ideal meaning', and the like. We shall begin our study of the question
'What is a Symbol in art?' by examining some of these attempts; not
simply to add scalps to our belt, but in order to find out what goes
wrong with these definitions, and to see how the mistakes of others
can be pressed into service to help us to a right solution of the problem.
This done, we shall review a fairly large body of data which these
unsuccessful definitions fail to encompass adequately. Lastly, drawing
on the lessons of past failures, and also on pointers from the two
preceding chapters, we shall re-open the original question whether
such a thing as a symbol can exist in the philosophy of art, as an
entity which can embrace all or a large part of the individual
definitions and usages of the symbolist poets; and if we succeed in
answering the question, go on to decide what aspects of the symbol
are matter for aesthetic, and what for literary criticism. That is to
say, two things are to be established: first, what is the aesthetic
datum—the general feature in all art of all time, *qua* art—which is
embodied in the symbolists' conception of symbols; and secondly,
what are the empirical elements in which the aesthetic concept is
embodied for various of the symbolists.

It has repeatedly been stated that the symbolist movement is a
renaissance of poetry pure and simple. It has also been claimed, and
with equal justification, that the art of the symbolists plainly differs
in a great many respects from most literature that went before.
If we can adequately separate and pursue the two distinct inquiries—

the aesthetic and the historically-empirical—we shall have not only reconciled these two claims but gone a long way towards eliminating confusion from the term 'symbol'.

2. SOME UNSUCCESSFUL ATTEMPTS AT DEFINITION

From the last chapter we have fixed in our minds the meaning usually attached to 'symbol' in ordinary usage and in philosophic discourse: namely, a sign, not necessarily a word, accepted as between two or more parties for the limited purpose of making a reference to something else: perhaps another symbol even. A red colour-light is a symbol for the order 'stop'; the word 'stop' is itself a symbol for an injunction laid by the traffic authority upon the users of the street. Words like 'stop' can be used as symbols for a wide variety of purposes: either to impart information, or to evoke a more immediate practical response, as in our example, or in other ways yet. As such, their choice is, in principle, a matter of indifference; to the average English town-dweller, the red colour-light and the police-man's gesture are equally effective symbols, and an infinite number of alternative symbols could be devised, of equal efficacy, provided they were sufficiently advertised beforehand, so that people knew they were symbols, and also what they symbolized. In an earlier chapter we noted that for purely informative purposes a programme blurb is as good as a Dutch Old Master. It was noted at the time, however (page 24, pt. I), that from the viewpoint of art the choice of alternatives is not a matter of indifference. In other words, the simply symbolic function of language is not as such a source of aesthetic value.

If this is true of simple references, it is obviously true also of complex ones—e.g. allegory or parable. There may be practical advantages in the use of these, empirically there may sometimes be artistic advantages; but merely to complicate the symbolism of language by having two symbolic stages (allegory to simple exposi-tion, simple exposition to reference) will not of itself introduce an element of aesthetic value. Other motives must determine the poet who elects to 'use' allegory or, so to speak, second-power symbols.

It remains that a large number of critics (intelligent and otherwise) have started by a ready acceptance of the normal use of the word 'symbol' and attempted to use it unemended to characterize a whole literary movement. We could hardly give a better introduction to the survey of this field of confused opinion than by quoting a short passage from a work of repute:

'The word symbolism has certain historical associations through the various dictionary meanings of "symbol" which are worth noting. In addition to its constant underlying sense of a sign or token (something "put together") the term has already enjoyed two distinct "floruits". The first, traceable to Cyprian, applies to the Creed regarded as the "sign of a Christian" as distinguished from a heathen, as when Henry VIII talks about "the three creeds or Symbols". . . . Secondly there is widespread use of the adjective symbolist in the nineties to characterize those French poets who were in revolt against all forms of literal and descriptive writing, and who attached symbolic or esoteric meanings to particular objects, words and sounds. Similarly art critics loosely refer to painters whose object is suggestion rather than "representation" or "construction" as symbolists.'[1]

There are two possible ways of reading this definition, and each leads to misleading notions about 'the adjective symbolist'. Either the poets are said to be using 'objects, words, and sounds' in the 'constant underlying sense of a sign'; namely, to stand for something less concise than themselves—like the fish symbol in early Christianity—in which case the 'symbolic or esoteric meanings' are as a sheer matter of fact often conspicuous by their absence, and make nonsense of the definition (in any case, this is not necessarily the sequel to a revulsion from 'literal and descriptive writing'); or else, like the painters in the case, the poets 'in revolt' against realism and naturalism are indulging in 'suggestion' rather than 'representation', in which case it is hard to see why suggestion should necessarily be associated with symbolism. In point of fact, we are far from rejecting the suggestive comparison with post-impressionist painting; only it has nothing to do with that aspect of the subject which we are now confronting. What we are examining is symbolism in art; in so far as some post-impressionists' work could be defined as the 'symbols' of their attitudes this inquiry could be extended to embrace them; but we have not yet established this for painting any more than for poetry.

Among the writers of 1885, we can trace quite a large variety of theories all ultimately based on the idea of symbolic reference. Rémy de Gourmont says, for example, of the Chief Symbolist:

'La théorie symboliste, si abstruse pour moi, est cependant claire à quelques-uns. Elle est pour M. Moréas sans mystères: il sait que symbole veut dire métaphore, et s'en contente,'[2]

and the same is noted by Charles Morice:

'Si nous donnons au mot symbole un sens précis, le talent de Moréas s'arrangerait mal de cette définition. Il s'exprime directement ou par des allégories; et il y a une confusion perpétuelle entre l'allégorie et le symbole.'[3]

[1] C. K. Ogden and I. A. Richards, *The Meaning of Meaning*, 4th ed., 1936, p. V.
[2] Huret, *Enquête*, 1891. [3] ibid.

By 1891 it was denied in retrospect that Moréas had ever been a symbolist; and his example serves as an illustration to the view that symbolism as an explicit and determinate description of art has never had any real existence outside the minds of one or two of its theoreticians.

But what can we say when we detect even in the writings of the most loyal and accredited of symbolist critics more than a tendency to explain the whole symbolist experiment as an extended exercise in allegory? Writing of the *Iphigénie* theme, Dujardin warns, it is true, against pastiche *à la* Moréas, but commends a very dubious alternative.

'Un symboliste chercherait quelle signification profonde peut avoir ce sacrifice humain, il tâcherait d'en dégager le sens ésoterique.'[1]

On this showing, one of two things might be responsible for the importance of symbolism. Either the poet using his symbol could produce something aesthetically valuable by the simple fact of not saying what he has to say 'directly', or it might be that he equated aesthetic value with some other form of value—i.e. truth—and measured the poetic qualities of his work by the insight it gave him into the nature of the world he lived in. We have seen this latter belief's appeal for an aesthetic tradition that followed in the wake of early positivism. Something of the same sort is to be seen in the account given by André Beaunier. He, it is true, avoids the allegorical trap and sets up a warning notice by it:

(declaring that fables are not simply allegories) 'Mais le poète symboliste retrouve dans la Fable ancienne l'éternel mystère incarné. Il utilise à sa manière ces symboles consacrés ... il les enrichit de ce qu'il aperçoit lui-même de plus complexe et de plus varié dans l'essence intime de ce qui est. Il invente à son tour de semblables mythologies.'[2]

The sum total of these, and very many other similar instructions, is that symbolists must not ignore myths and fables, but that they must recreate out of them what is further on described as 'le sens du mystère'. The statement implies that fables have some hold already over their audiences in the form of a wealth of affective associations; this to be sure is one stage towards a definition of symbols, but not a long one; and it is not greatly extended by the author's efforts at more precision:

'Il y a deux manières essentiellement en art, dont l'une consiste dans *l'expression directe*, et dont l'autre procède par *symboles*. Un symbole est une image que l'on peut employer pour la répresentation d'une idée, grâce à de secrètes condescendances dont on ne saurait rendre compte analytiquement.'[1]

'... La valeur expressive du symbole est dans une certaine mesure mystérieuse ... l'art est réaliste ou symboliste.'[2]

From this a number of possibilities emerge. A symbol is an image (we will not discuss this very loose term) which represents an idea: we may proceed on the assumption that the poet by some special faculty stumbles upon such images from time to time. But the relation is not symmetrical: we cannot say that an image *per se* is a symbol, but only that *some* images are. This is a more important point than it might appear. The chair I sit on might, if some outstanding dignitary were to sit upon it, acquire temporarily some special symbolic significance; normally it does not. The 'secrètes condescendances' are sparing of their gifts. That is to say, symbols are not the stuff of a philosophical (or rather theosophical) interpretation of reality, drawn on by the poet, but simply certain forms for occasional significant experiences; and Beaunier, whether from fear of appearing ridiculous in an age of unbelievers, or simply from lack of assurance, does not attempt to classify this experience as falling within the scope of experimental psychology, religion, or any other system of views. He recognizes fairly clearly at what point the 'mysteries' cease (in realist art) but that is not much gained.[3]

Along similar lines is the following attempt at a definition of the symbol, undertaken by another sympathetic critic, after the event:

'Pour être un poète symboliste il n'est pas nécessaire de faire proprement ce qu'on appelle des symboles; il suffit d'exprimer les secrètes affinités des choses avec notre âme. Mais une poésie qui a ces affinités pour objet sera le plus souvent symbolique; car dès que nous les suivons avec quelque teneur, elles revêtent la forme du symbole. Qu'est-ce donc que le symbole? Distinguons-le de la comparaison et de l'allégorie...

'Le symbole a pour caractère essentiel d'éclore spontanément, sans réflexion, sans analyse, dans une âme simple qui ne distingue même pas entre les apparences matérielles et leur signification idéale.'[4]

'Les secrètes affinités' is already by 1901 a well-worn phrase, and imply by their nonchalance a whole tradition of adherence to certain notions of Baudelaire; namely, those which relate him to the body of mystic thought. But Pellissier is not himself a convinced mystic— far from it; and his use of this phrase (perhaps deliberately) is ambiguous. He may be referring to the doctrine of Universal

[1] ibid.   [2] ibid.

[3] Indeed, it increases our difficulties by suggesting that 'symbolism' is art in the fullest sense (i.e. something of almost religious importance) while 'realism' is art in a different, and perhaps less important, sense.

[4] G. Pellissier, 'L'Evolution de la poésie dans ce dernier quart de siècle' (*Revue des revues*, 15/iii/1901).

Analogies; or he may perhaps be referring simply to a relationship between objects as material for art and the emotions connected with them in various ways in the artist's mind. He seems to postulate three things of the symbol: (1) that it is a way of noting affinities between some sort of mental function of the artist and some aspect of his material; (2) that they are spontaneous, which in the present context can mean no more than that they cannot be made to a pattern or set procedure; and (3) that they demand no sort of highly abstractive mind. In short, at the basis of this statement is the implication that for symbols to flourish, men must be capable (*a*) of pursuing 'secret affinities', affinities between their minds as subjects and other things as objects, and yet (*b*) too childlike to distinguish between 'natural appearances' and their ideal signification: there appears to be some measure of contradiction between these two requirements. Tentatively we might suggest that this ambiguity springs from the fact that Pellissier is trying to combine two incompatibles in one definition: first the view (held certainly by some symbolists) that symbolist art is based on a mystical cognitive faculty, which relates elements of experience as symbols to real meanings, 'significations idéales'—the references being the 'secret affinities'; and secondly, the view (also held by symbolists) that the relation between the artist and his material—that is to say, his symbols, if he uses them—is too close to admit of his establishing the subject-object relationship with it. For the first view, the subject-object relationship is obviously required: the poet, as subject, perceives a mystic import in his material, as object; for the second it fails to correspond to the facts.

Some writers have provided definitions of the nature and instructions for the use of symbols which fall to pieces on examination, and betray none of the subtle doubts—or scrupulous attempts to reconcile irreconcilables—that characterize the example we have just dealt with. Among the mandarins of the reviews and the literary dinners Moréas was not alone in his inability to satisfy posterity why he had chosen to call the movement symbolist. Gustav Kahn gives the following definition of a symbol:

'La présentation en un livre ou un poème d'une série de faits passionnels ou intellectuels par le plus caractéristique de ces faits,'[1]

which seems, if anything, to revive Taine's 'caractère essentiel ou saillant'.[2] Plainly this will not do—even an empirical test of *Les Palais Nomades* does not show us that in selection of material Kahn

---

[1] *Revue Indépendante*, iv/1888.   [2] Taine, *Philosophie de l'art*, 2nd ed., 1872, p. 63.

the poet is proceeding in a way utterly and radically different from Zola the novelist. All art is selective, as opposed to what we presume reality to be: our experience is selective.

René Ghil's definition is a good deal more opaque; plainly he envisages something a little out of the ordinary:

'J'avais donc [articles in *Basoche* 1885] en admiration pour Mallarmé, consacré quelques pages au "symbole" — non point mallarméen, cependant, mais qui pour moi demandant du Poète une évocation de la vie toute, représentait la leçon philosophique, la vérité essentielle, à amener hors des mille éléments de cette Vie ... une idée de synthèse... '[1]

Already a glimmer of that 'sociocratic' faith which after 1889 was to make of the *Écrits pour l'art* one of the more diverting performances of the nineteenth century.

Ignoring the freakish efforts, we could also multiply examples of attempts to find a common denominator for the art of a Mallarmé and a Moréas, a Laforgue and a Verhaeren, a Marie Krysinska and a Maeterlinck. The search is apparently fruitless on the plane of technique: the assumption is therefore made that it must be carried on at a less concrete level; and most of the results which we have noticed up to the present pass straight from the technical, at which perhaps not all possibilities have been explored, over to a sphere of mystical speculation in which a common denominator could not possibly be found either for distinguishing symbolist literature from earlier traditions or for establishing its general kinship with them. We shall work on the assumption—redundant to attempt to justify at this stage in the argument—that this passage from a possible to an impossible ground of explanation, or, at any rate, from a fruitful to a fruitless, is largely due to the insistence observed throughout all the cases we have explored up to this point, to make the central feature of a literary symbol, and the source of its special aesthetic value, reside in the fact of its making a reference to something else—some transcendental order of experiences or not, as the case may be. If only we can rid ourselves of this obsession, it may be possible to advance beyond the cloud of contradiction and mystification that surrounds the trusting and undiscriminating exegete of symbolist doctrine.

3. SYMBOLS IN MYSTIC TRADITION

The whole literature of mystic evidences abounds with symbols; ranging from the interpretation of the architecture of cathedrals in

---

[1] Ghil, *Les Dates et les Œuvres*, 1923, p. 38.

the Middle Ages down to the generous assertions of Swedenborg that everything in the world is a symbol of something in the supernatural order—and Fourier's conscientious efforts to fill in this ambitious catalogue. But in reality a division may be made in this wide sweep of mystic symbolism; on one side it is possible to group those writers who trace a plain and simple reference (e.g. the rainbow is the symbol of clemency)—the majority—and on the other the more select group asserting that everything in the world is a symbol, or a potential symbol, in a system of 'universal analogies' or something of the sort, but refrain from committing themselves to ridicule by expounding the actual references. For these latter it is sufficient to have the intuition that a certain object of perception is *something more* than just what it appears to be, but they hold themselves unfit (or undisposed) to say precisely what the *something more* is, except that it has an effect on them similar to that which they would feel in the presence of a Sign or Symbol of some specially impressive supernatural entity. Fourier is a good example of the former class; most mystics appear to hover between the two positions, trusting their interpretative judgements on some occasions, but not always; it is with the exponents of the latter position, and more especially those who turned it to the explanation of aesthetic problems, that we have to do.

(a) Carlyle

The *Entretiens politiques et littéraires* devoted the first page of each of its numbers to an epigraph drawn from the works of Emerson, Carlyle, Edgar Allan Poe, Baudelaire, etc. There was nothing exceptional in this, for these writers, and especially Carlyle, were held up generally as the prophets of anti-positivism, and Carlyle in particular was widely-known in this role.[1] All the more important, then, that *Sartor Resartus*, one of the more widely-read of his books, contains a long and important chapter on 'The Symbol', which marks him out as a member of our second class of symbolizing mystics.

Carlyle opens by drawing attention to the pregnant qualities of silence and obscurity.

‘ "The benignant efficacies of Concealment," cries our Professor, "who shall speak or sing? ... Speech is of Time, Silence is of eternity. ... Thought will not work except in silence: neither will Virtue work except in Secrecy." ’

[1] The same ironical fate which made of Ribot's *Schopenhauer* the 'idealist's' handbook, made Taine's *Idéalisme anglais* into an excellent and accessible introduction to Carlyle.

R

The Symbol is thus introduced as something pertaining to the realm of mystery.

'Of kin to the so incalculable influences of Concealment, and connected with still greater things, is the wondrous agency of *Symbols*. In a Symbol there is concealment and yet revelation: here therefore by silence and by Speech acting together, comes a double significance.'[1]

This preliminary discourse may be simply in the spirit of the semi-comic part which Carlyle has taken upon himself in the person of Professor Teufelsdrokh; alternatively the passage may be taken as a genuine profession of faith from a radical mystic. There follows a definition:

'In many a painted device or simple seal-emblem the commonest Truth stands out to us proclaimed with quite new emphasis.' (Carlyle is certainly serious now.) 'For it is here that Fantasy with her mystic wonderland plays into the small prose domain of Sense and becomes incorporated therewith. In the Symbol proper, what we call a symbol, there is ever more or less distinctly and directly, some embodiment and revelation of the Infinite; the Infinite is made to blend itself with the Finite, to stand visible, and as it were attainable thereby. By Symbols therefore is man guided and commanded, made happy and wretched. He everywhere finds himself encompassed with symbols, recognized as such or not recognized: the Universe is but one vast Symbol of God; nay, if thou wilt have it, what is man himself but a symbol of God; is not all that he does symbolical; a revelation to Sense of the mystic god-given force that is in him? . . . '[2]

There is much here that is obscure; and the explanation is not in fact effected by stating that the relation between finite and Infinite summed up in a Symbol is the same as that between man's physical actions and his spiritual processes. But after a short digression to inveigh against James and John Stewart, the 'Motive-*Mill*wrights,' Carlyle returns to the charge in a passage which, if it does not unravel the tangle of rhetoric, assures us at least of how its main strands lie:

'Of Symbols, however, I remark further, that they have both an extrinsic and intrinsic value, oftenest the former only. What, for instance, was in that clouted Shoe, which the Peasants bore aloft with them as ensign in their *Bauernkrieg*? Or in the Wallet-and-Staff round which the Netherland *Gueux*, glorying in that nickname of Beggars, heroically rallied and prevailed, though against King Phillip himself? Intrinsic significance these had none: only extrinsic; as the accidental standards of multitudes more or less sacredly uniting together; in which union itself, as above noted, there is ever something mystical and borrowing of the Godlike.... '[3]

One use of Symbol, then, is plain: it is, in its extrinsic form, simply what common usage takes the word to mean—a sign. Carlyle is careful to point out that as yet these two examples he cites 'have no

---

[1] Carlyle, *Sartor Resartus* (1831).
[2] op. cit., pp. 134–5.   [3] ibid., p. 136.

intrinsic necessary divineness'; it is hardly necessary to note that this 'mystical quality' of a quite simple association for definite worldly ends, shows to what an extent Carlyle's whole energy is turned towards an irrational picture of his world. There is no difficulty in discovering the tendencies which lead him to subsume under one substantive 'Symbols' both extrinsic and intrinsic.

What, then, is the intrinsic variety?

'Another matter it is, however, when your Symbol has intrinsic meaning, and is of itself *fit* that men should unite around it. Let but the Godlike manifest itself to Sense: let but Eternity look, more or less visibly through the Time-Figure. . . . '[1]

'For is not a Symbol ever, to him who has eyes for it, some dimmer or clearer revelation of the Godlike? . . . '[2]

Every age has its share of question-begging terms which serve to absorb shocks between the jarring elements in philosophical systems. Of such terms 'Godlike' and 'Eternity' are fair examples. In these two statements, the vital phrase is 'to him that has eyes for it'—a phrase which rings very like Schopenhauer's doctrine of genius or Rimbaud's view of the poet as seer. To him that has eyes for it, indeed, almost anything may appear; especially as in this particular type of experience Fantasy (see the earlier quotation) with her wonderland is impinging on the normal processes of vision. 'Godlike' and 'eternity' (or, as above, the 'Infinite') stand in our way, and exclude the possibility of exact statement on the type of experience undergone by 'him that has eyes for it'. But it is a mystic experience; who can doubt it, when all things, including man, are seen by its light as 'one vast symbol of God'; when through the barrier of the finite world, eternity is glimpsed?

Anything and everything can be an 'intrinsic' symbol to the visionary; this being so, it is hard to see how we can avoid the conclusion that

'of this latter sort are all true works of Art; in them (if thou know a work of Art from a Daub of Artifice) wilt thou discern Eternity looking through time; the Godlike rendered visible'.[3]

Here is the bridge-passage to a symbolist aesthetic. We may regret, though we cannot be surprised, that Carlyle abandoned the thread of his argument on art at this stage (save for certain remarks to the effect that heroic lives and religious systems present yet more exalted

[1] ibid., pp. 136–7. [2] ibid., p. 136.
[3] ibid., p. 137. Lammenais, *Esquisse d'une philosophie*, III, has much the same statement: 'Le privilège de l'homme est de pénétrer par la pensée jusqu'aux essences que l'œil interne découvre seul, et jusqu'à la source de toutes les essences, l'Etre infini ou le Beau absolu. Le manifester dans les formes émanées de lui et qui le reflètent, tel est l'objet de l'art, son but magnifique.' It was eagerly taken up by Péladan (*L'Art Idéaliste*, p. 94).

symbols); there is no explanation forthcoming why or how works of Art give insight into the 'Godlike'. But again, a resemblance is traceable to Schopenhauer's view of the nature of a work of art: translated into the German philosopher's terms, 'if thou know a Work of Art from a Daub of Artifice' means simply, 'if you partake sufficiently of the nature of genius to distinguish genius from its imitations'; and by implication a work of art is defined as a work capable of promoting certain kinds of mystic exaltations—an interesting glimpse of Carlyle's criteria of art-judgement, and, taken in conjunction with those of Schopenhauer and others of the same generation, a valuable sidelight on certain aspects of romanticism.

(b) Baudelaire

Whatever may have been the influence of Carlyle and other remoter thinkers, however, it must quickly fade into insignificance before that of a man who combined the prestige of original and daring speculation with the persuasive force of great poetry. Baudelaire is all things to symbolism: the model for imitation, by writers finding their first feet in poetry; the critic whose unpopular judgements on Wagner and Delacroix were ratified by time; the translator and exegete of Edgar Allan Poe, a hero whose fame in the eighties, and later, was equalled only by the lack of discrimination and judgement shown by his neophytes; and lastly, the author of *Correspondances*.

For Baudelaire the term 'Symbol' is almost entirely—but not quite[1]—bound up with a theosophical view of the universe. All things whatever—as for Carlyle—are symbols, or at least potential symbols; and they are symbols, if not of God, then at least of a transcendental reality to which the artist has special access. Symbols are phenomena; anything present to any of the senses; and their symbolic value is assured by the fact that the artist—or the artist in any of us—notes certain cross-references between the different orders of sensation. The poet is not so much an inventor as a man discover-

---

[1] See, for instance, his playful references to the pear as Daumier's symbol of Louis-Philippe. Baudelaire suggests that there is 'une analogie complaisante' between the two, which renders the symbol immediately accessible. 'Le symbole dès lors suffisait. Avec cette espèce d'argot plastique on était le maître de dire et faire comprendre au peuple tout ce qu'on voulait' (*Curiosités esthétiques*, p. 408). Baudelaire claims that this symbol is arrived at by means that fall within the scope of the universal analogy; but the claim is thin. More interesting is his sanctioning of the Wagnerian myth: 'il est intéressant que Baudelaire, qui avait condamné le procédé mécanique du symbolisme hiéroglyphique chez un Chenavard, n'ait apparemment pas vu qu'il y a une analogie entre ce système et le système de Wagner' (Woolley, *Richard Wagner et le Symbolisme*, 1931, p. 52). In addition, perhaps it is not otiose to remark that Baudelaire sometimes makes 'symbol' interchangeable with 'allegory', without the vestige of a reference to supernatural analogies; e.g. 'et quelques chants symboliques' (de Pierre Dupont) (*Art Romantique*, art. 'Pierre Dupont').

ing combinations which by their miraculous force compel the view that they are evidence of the overriding order and unity of all created things. Art is a mediation effected by a highly skilled craftsman between the more sluggish members of humanity and this superior reality.

This far at least we may be tolerably sure that we are reproducing faithfully the doctrines implied by *Correspondances*. But a serious question now presents itself: if the universe is an uncompromising system of universal analogies, if symbols of smell, colour, form, sound, etc., can be bracketed together as it were, at what point must the poet stop in his search for new combinations, new metaphors? What is it that imposes the limitations that undoubtedly exist for the poet in his revelatory exercises? For there is a plain antithesis between the universality of the so-called 'correspondances' and the often quite clearly delineated finite field of images and 'symbols' with which a given writer—say Baudelaire even—works. Presumably this limitation is open to a common-sense explanation: the consciousness of symbolical references could hardly be present continually in the mind; it is not an everyday occurrence; it comes rarely, even to poets, and to some people not at all. So at least Baudelaire would have said, if we may judge by other aspects of his work (notably that treating of drugs). Moreover, the awareness that the object of a certain experience is a symbol does not take the form of a clear perception, either of its truth (for how can we say what a symbol defined in this way 'asserts'?) or of its meaning (for the reality it symbolizes is outside direct experience): it is a confused awareness; and yet it is not the confusion of unfamiliarity—on the contrary, there goes with it a feeling of inevitability: Carlyle, it will be recalled, speaks of intrinsic symbols as being 'fit' and 'inevitable'.

But this common-sense explanation, true though it may be, within the context of this particular description of experience, is not sufficient to set the Baudelairean theory of symbols in an unassailable theoretical position. The argument is not consistent with itself. The common-sense doubts which a common-sense explanation can answer are stilled, but not removed. If we repeat the objection in more rigorous way, we shall see that it is very formidable. Compare certain statements in the famous sonnet itself. To begin with, it is claimed that the universe (La Nature) is built out of symbols; that the 'temple' is formed from living and symbolic pillars; the forests are made up of symbolic trees.[1] Everything has a 'symbolic' element. This interpretation may be challenged. It may be asserted that in the sonnet there is no single proposition which a logician could call 'universal', that Baudelaire does not explicitly claim that *all* the trees are symbols, or that *all* perfumes, colours, and sounds 'correspond'. To that we may reply that this is a poem, not a treatise; that what would be an intolerable ambiguity in a reasoned statement is no defect in a poem; and that the first and most natural impression we get from reading the poem is that *all* perfumes, etc., are being referred to. And we shall shortly bring evidence from Baudelaire's critical writings to show that this is indeed what he intended.

The inconsistency, the flaw, or, seen from another angle, the lacuna in the doctrine is this: the interpretation of the preceding paragraph does not fit in with the fact already stated concerning the relative paucity of any given writer's 'insights'. The latter fact is incontrovertible; no man, however much a poet, can feel that everything he sees is a 'symbol'; that every single analogy with which he points his discourse, whether intellectual or fanciful, is a reminder of the underlying system of universal analogy: such a man, were he to be found, would be classified as insane, or at the least looked on as peculiar. Baudelaire was certainly no such man; not even Gérard de Nerval, with whom he was well acquainted, was ever in this condition. Not all metaphors, moreover, awake or exemplify the sense of 'awareness' he cites as evidence for his views; least of all those which have passed into common usage and go almost unnoticed in daily intercourse. And it is a linguistic commonplace that precisely this progression is the ordinary fate of metaphors.

If we accept the first of the alternatives that face us, and declare that any single thing of which we have experience is a symbol, there is no way of distinguishing in theory between the most powerful and striking use of symbol or metaphor and the prosaic and banal examples that are to be found in almost any (artistically) second-rate record of mystical experience. In other words, the groundwork for a philosophy of art has not yet been laid, and the notion of aesthetic value as something variable has not yet come into existence. If we

---

[1] For a penetrating study of *Correspondances* see Pommier, *La Mystique de Baudelaire*, 1932. Baudelaire's sonnet, though occupying an unique place in *Les Fleurs du Mal*, is far from being an isolated phenomenon in the stream of French poetry: indeed, these same images turn out to be almost the stock-in-trade of the later romantic lyricists—Gautier, Hugo, Nerval, and the rest: as indeed the whole topic of 'audition colorée'.

accept the second alternative, and say that a symbol is characterized by the special response which Baudelaire considers so valuable and so peculiar to art, we are no better off; for the quality of the response has yet to be defined, together with its relation to other aesthetic concepts. Were Baudelaire to enter more particularly into an account of when and in what way objects of experience acquire the force of 'symbols' he might have produced an aesthetic, instead of a number of brilliant but disconnected observations on aesthetic experience.[1] But he preferred to concentrate his attention on one particular phenomenon—constellations or groups of 'symbols' found in a certain kind of metaphor: the metaphor of 'transposed sensations', 'audition colorée,' and so on. His Swedenborgian interests suggest to him that there is a special virtue in these metaphors; but treated as linguistic phenomena it is not hard to see that they represent simply a marginal addition to the resources of the late-romantic poet of the forties: between them and all other material of language the differences are only empirical: that is to say, not such as could serve to distinguish art from some other form of non-artistic writing. And in the last resort, Baudelaire's difficulties arise from taking the observation of empirical distinctions of language within art as the starting-point for a theoretical distinction between art and not-art.

His prose criticism, in the light of this view, expands the conclusions already reached. First, a corroboration of the claim that the doctrine of *Correspondances* is universal in scope. In *L'Art romantique*, where Baudelaire introduces the subject more frequently than anywhere else, he enthusiastically ascribes to Gautier if not a direct awareness, at least a general intuition of the system of 'analogies':

'Il possède plus qu'aucun autre, le sentiment d'universelle hiérarchie écrite du haut en bas de la nature, à tous les degrés de l'infini.'[2]

The hierarchy is universal: all nature is comprised within its system. In the same article Baudelaire again refers to its universality and diverse instances of its application:

'Si l'on réfléchit qu'à cette merveilleuse faculté [his style] Gautier unit une immense intelligence innée de la *correspondance* et du symbolisme universels, ce répertoire de toute métaphore... Manier savamment une langue, c'est pratiquer une espèce de sorcellerie évocatoire. C'est alors que la couleur parle, comme une voix profonde et vibrante; que les monuments se dressent et font saillie sur l'espace profond; que

---

[1] He comes close to doing so in a disjointed remark in *Fusées*: 'Dans certains états de l'âme presque surnaturels, la profondeur de la vie se révèle toute entière dans le spectacle, si ordinaire qu'il soit, qu'on a sous les yeux. Il en devient le Symbole' (p. 82).   But what here is supernatural? What is 'la profondeur de la vie'? The mystic may have something he wants to say, but he never becomes clear what it is.

[2] *Art romantique*, 'Théophile Gautier'. *Œuvres* (Conard), II, p. 179.

les animaux et les plantes, représentants du laid et du mal, articulent leur grimace non équivoque; que le parfum provoque la pensée et le souvenir correspondants... '[1]

One may question whether poems such as the *Symphonie en blanc majeur* do in fact lend themselves to this kind of interpretation; whether indeed Baudelaire is not perhaps a little hasty in ascribing to the practitioner of novel metaphors such far-reaching if unconscious insight. In fact, this ascription may be taken as support for the view enunciated above that Baudelaire's attention is wholly taken up with the development of linguistic techniques; in the perspective of language given in the last chapter, Gautier's contributions to metaphor occupy the same position *vis-à-vis* the act of poetic creation as do Baudelaire's 'transposing' metaphors; all of them being empirical extensions to language. So far as Baudelaire is dazzled by the novelty of the one sort in attempting to base a whole aesthetic on it, there is no reason why he should not be similarly impressed by the other sort. We shall presently have further evidence of such attempts.

In extending the theory to the relation between literature and music, Baudelaire is on even more slippery ground; and to-day we may laugh at the fanciful 'programme note' interpretations of the *Lohengrin* Prelude, whose concurrence in various points so intrigued him in the article on Richard Wagner; we are no longer interested in attempts to prove by generalizing from the particular that certain sounds are necessarily bound up with specific sensations of other orders; but the excitement of such notions for Baudelaire in 1851 must not be forgotten. In point of fact, of course, nothing is more natural than that these 'programme notes' should overlap to at least a great extent: as we have seen, musical language is constantly crystallizing around representative notions, though these are purely incidental to its nature. But historical perspective makes it hard to sympathize with Baudelaire's belief that the system of analogies is fixed and permanent:

'Le lecteur sait quel but nous poursuivons: démontrer que la véritable musique suggère des idées analogues dans des cerveaux différents. D'ailleurs il ne serait pas ridicule ici de raisonner *a priori* sans analyse et sans comparaisons; car ce qui serait vraiment surprenant, c'est que le son *ne pût pas* suggérer la couleur, que les couleurs *ne pussent pas* donner l'idée d'une mélodie, et que le son et la couleur fussent impropres à traduire des idées; les choses s'étant toujours exprimées par une analogie réciproque, depuis le jour où Dieu a proféré le monde comme une complexe et indivisible totalité.'[2]

The position is by now tolerably clear; by his presenting the world as an indivisible totality, with infinite ramifications among its

[1] ibid., p. 165.   [2] *Art romantique,* 'Richard Wagner,' p. 207.

analogies, Baudelaire leaves no room for doubt that he is prepared to acknowledge that anything at all—even the desk he sat down at to write his articles—had peculiar to it analogies in other realms of sense which someone or other, some day, might discover. In an ideal world, entities of which desks, perfumes, sounds, were mere symbols, exist as the link in the 'correspondances'; and everything has its link, everything is a symbol. Thus inasmuch as the artist is simply the mystic enjoying insight into supraterrestrial realities, all experience of the outside world is symbolic, therefore aesthetically valuable; and certain sorts of metaphor are specially valuable because they drive home by circumstantial evidence the symbolic nature of symbols. The embarrassments of this position are, as we already know, great; and they are not diminished by giving metaphors a specially privileged position. In fact, only a theory of language could resolve these difficulties.

Of the three great articles which form the backbone of *L'Art Romantique* as we have it, the third, on Victor Hugo, is no less explicit than the others on the subject of the universal analogy. Here even is a glimpse of one of the original protagonists of the doctrine—from whom, indeed, it is lifted almost bodily, though to fulfil a new, aesthetic function.

(Speaking of the inadequacy of Fourier's crude fantasies on the theory of analogie[1]) 'Swedenborg, qui possédait une âme bien plus grande (que celle de Fourier) nous avait déjà enseigné que *le ciel est un très-puissant grand homme*; que tout, forme, mouvement, nombre, couleur, parfum, dans le *spirituel* comme dans le *naturel*, est significatif, réciproque, *converse, correspondant.*'[2]

And further,

'Lavater, limitant au visage de l'homme la démonstration de l'universelle vérité, nous avait traduit le sens spirituel du contour, de la forme, de la dimension... Si nous étendons la démonstration (non-seulement nous en avons le droit, mais il nous serait infiniment difficile de faire autrement) nous arrivons à cette vérité que tout est hiéroglyphique, et nous savons que les symboles ne sont obscurs que d'une manière relative, c'est-à-dire selon la pureté, la bonne volonté, ou la clairvoyance native des âmes. Or qu'est-ce qu'un poète (je prends le mot dans son acceptation la plus large) si ce n'est un traducteur, un déchiffreur? Chez les excellents poètes, il n'y a pas de métaphore, de comparaison, ou d'épithète qui ne soit d'une adaptation mathématiquement exacte dans la circonstance actuelle, parce que ces comparaisons, ces métaphores, et ces épithètes sont puisées dans l'inépuisable fonds de *l'universelle analogie*, et qu'elles ne peuvent être puisées ailleurs...'[3]

The last words of this passage are not without interest, as the logical conclusion of a thorough argument. Every phenomenon in man's environment is (potentially at least) raw material for a metaphor or a

---

[1] In the *Théorie de l'unité universelle.*   [2] *Art romantique*, 'Victor Hugo,' p. 305.   [3] ibid.

poetic image. Baudelaire takes it for granted (one can hardly do otherwise) that a writer cannot go outside the totality of human experience for the material of his art; and as every single element in this totality is covered by the law that it corresponds with some other element or elements, then obviously every comparison or metaphor which is 'fitting', which arouses a response, is necessarily the discovery of a *correspondance*. There is thus a kind of inexorable dividing line between good poetry, where the images and comparisons 'come alive', so to speak, and all other kinds of writing; between art and not-art. A writer who is not a 'déchiffreur', who has not the innate gift of translating and pointing analogies, may use any number of similes, metaphors, and other constructs of language without ever once stirring his reader into the frame of mind which might be called religious if it were not exclusively the product of metaphor. Thus on a close inspection, Baudelaire's aesthetic is a doctrine of metaphor; but a singularly rigid one: for there are only two classes into which metaphors and symbols can be divided: the good and the bad; and within these two classes there can be no further distinction. Not only is the theory rigid, it is misleading; for it takes no account of the passage of this or that metaphor from one class to another; no one in Mr. Bernard Shaw's *Caravan of the Curious* was impressed with the *beauty* of the statement that pepper is hot, or a treble note high—those phrases had become so much part of the language that their transposing nature had come to be entirely ignored on aesthetic grounds, and only discussed as an intellectual curiosity.

We get a fair idea how far Baudelaire was from developing his observations on certain types of metaphor in the direction of a theory of the language of art when we probe further and find him grounding them in the realm of Le Beau, which he defines (like any spiritualist philosopher of his time) as simply a value concept distinct from the true and the good, and entirely 'disinterested':

'C'est cet admirable, cet immortel instinct du Beau qui nous fait considérer la Terre et ses spectacles comme un aperçu, une *correspondance* du Ciel.'[1]

The connection between the two was no doubt simpler to Baudelaire than it is to us to-day: from a distance one might be tempted to think that the relationship was like that of two fellow-countrymen in a hostile land—two notions, unable to fit into a pattern of rational thought, assumed, therefore, to be related by their both belonging to the realm of irrational speculation. And yet, as we may see, it is

[1] *Art romantique*, p. 159; for definitions of Le Beau, see the same work, pp. 155 and 334.

not possible to telescope together a theory of metaphor and a theory of universal 'correspondances'. Hypothesis dictates the form of the latter, but experience governs the practice of the first; and between the two lies an awkward gap to the bridging of which Baudelaire devotes a scanty attention. From his tone, indeed, one might be led to doubt whether he had even noticed the gap. On one occasion later he does glance in its direction—in an appreciation of Victor Hugo, where one might expect to find cautious qualifications. The passage, though lengthy, is sufficiently interesting to be worth quoting in full:

'Victor Hugo était, dès le principe, l'homme le mieux doué, le plus visiblement élu pour exprimer par la poésie ce que j'appellerai le *mystère de la vie*. La nature qui pose devant nous, de quelque côté que nous nous tourniions, et qui nous enveloppe comme un mystère, se présente sous plusieurs états simultanés dont chacun, selon qu'il est plus intelligible, plus sensible pour nous, se reflète plus vivement dans nos cœurs: forme, attitude, et mouvement, lumière et couleur, son et harmonie. La musique des vers de Victor Hugo s'adapte aux profondes harmonies de la nature; sculpteur, il découpe dans ses strophes la forme inoubliable des choses; peintre, il les illumine de leur couleur propre. Et, comme si elles venaient directement de la nature, les trois impressions pénètrent simultanément le cerveau du lecteur. De cette triple impression résulte la *morale des choses*. Aucun artiste n'est plus universel que lui, plus apte à se mettre en contact avec les forces de la vie universelle, plus disposé à prendre sans cesse un bain de nature. Non-seulement il exprime nettement, il traduit littéralement la lettre nette et claire; mais il exprime, avec l'*obscurité indispensable*, ce qui est obscur et confusément révélé. Ses œuvres abondent en traits extraordinaires de cette nature, que nous pourrions appeler des tours de force si nous ne savions pas qu'ils lui sont essentiellement naturels. Le vers de Victor Hugo sait traduire pour l'âme humaine non-seulement les plaisirs les plus directs qu'elle tire de la nature visible, mais encore les sensations les plus fugitives, les plus compliquées, les plus morales (je dis exprès, sensations morales) qui nous sont transmises par l'être visible, par la nature inanimée, ou dite inanimée; non-seulement la figure d'un être extérieur à l'homme, végétal ou minéral, mais aussi sa physionomie, son regard, sa tristesse, sa douceur, sa joie éclatante, sa haine repulsive, son enchantement ou son horreur; enfin en d'autres termes, tout ce qu'il y a d'humain dans n'importe quoi, et aussi tout ce qu'il y a de divin, de sacré, ou de diabolique.'[1]

Here Baudelaire extends in an almost unique effort the theory of universal analogies into the realm of practical criticism; and the difficulties spring up instantly. As some of them originate in part from the nature of the example he is treating, we must be careful to distinguish the more fundamental from the less. In the first place, we may say that a limiting case in the mystic apprehension of the universe would be an omnipresent mind capable of deriving *all* the 'correspondances' between things and events and so forth. Nature

[1] *Art romantique*, 'Victor Hugo,' p. 304.

is, however, apprehended in only a limited degree by finite creatures, and only a varyingly small number of 'correspondances' are practically available to any single individual, according to his innate gifts. Here, then, the opposition noted above between the crude doctrine of 'correspondances' and the obvious facts of creation in poetry is somewhat softened; individuals partake according to their abilities of whatever 'correspondances' they may find ready to hand. But there is a curious corollary to this: Hugo, an outstanding individual (though the concrete illustration is not material to the argument) apprehends nature in at least three of its aspects, corresponding to the arts of painting (colour), sculpture (form), and music ('harmonies of nature,' whatever they may be); *by virtue of this*, Baudelaire says, he is particularly well fitted to mark out the 'correspondances' and fulfil what Baudelaire obviously conceives to be the poet's highest function: the expression 'du mystère de la vie'. Now Baudelaire's statement that different minds develop to different extents their reliance on one or the other of the senses is a commonplace of psychology; equally we have noted, in our discussion of the artistic imagination (p. 79 n., above) that the artist's activity of creation feeds on any or all of these orders of impressions; but it does not follow from this that the best—or even the most advantageously placed—artist is the one whose poetic material is drawn from the widest possible range of experience. To suggest such a thing is to suggest that a man who spreads his butter thinly over a very large slice of bread *necessarily* uses more butter than one who spreads it more thickly over a smaller slice. Anyone can detect the fallacy of such an argument: but Baudelaire fails to detect it here, firstly because Hugo might be described as a poet who not only used a very large slice of bread, but spread his butter extremely thick over the whole of it—whence our caution over the complications introduced by the example; and secondly because in theory (though of course not in his poetic practice) Baudelaire was distorting the conception of language to suit a metaphysical principle: the linguistic resources which he most liked were grouped around a certain type of metaphor, answering to a certain view of religion and art, and he elevated his preferences into a pseudo-aesthetic doctrine. But the fallacy survives into the symbolist era, where it merges with Wagnerian doctrines of synthetic art in a horrid confusion.

A second objection to Baudelaire's position depends on a simple question of matter of fact: it is not true that Hugo's linguistic virtuosity yields up on examination the marks of any special preference for transposing metaphors; Hugo is not the Complete Baudelairean. To be sure, the fitting images are acknowledged to be *literal* translations; the vague and fugitive sensations which he records might be intimations of universal analogy; the matter-of-fact parenthesis 'avec l'obscurité indispensable' throws the reader back to the 'confuses paroles' of *Correspondances*; but when all is done, Hugo's conformity with the analogy theory is limited to one point: he draws analogies between aspects of nature and types of human individuality. In emphasizing this, Baudelaire passes to the natural conclusion of Swedenborgian mysticism and ascribes to the 'symbols' qualities which simply form part of the artist's imaginative creation; and the anthropomorphic view of nature (of which instances abound in Hugo's writing) turns out to be no more than a rather watery doctrine of empathy, in the development of which a certain liberty of detail rather than any 'obscurité indispensable' is the poet's desideratum. Looked at in this light, the inconsistency noted earlier in dealing with Baudelaire's mystical cosmology is transferred into an equivalent inconsistency in his view of language, in particular highly poetic language. In the one case we revealed an antinomy between the universe considered as a collection of phenomena linked together in the ideal sphere and the simple facts of aesthetic experience of ordinary people, and even poets. The same trouble arises now in the field of style and metaphor; on the one hand, it is asserted that all comparisons, metaphors, epithets, have their source in the analogical structure of the universe, and that their fitness and 'mathematical' exactitude is the indication of the right analogy being found; while on the other hand, the example of Victor Hugo as the accredited high god of empathy points to a quite different source of felicity in expression—and one, be it said, which demands a far wider conception of poetic language if we are to describe its nature adequately.

All along we have been trying to see whether the doctrine of *Correspondances* was ever deepened and developed by its author to the point at which it can be linked up with a more specifically aesthetic kind of inquiry. At the only point at which it is capable of such a link—a possible theory of metaphor—we see that the link is unsatisfactory. It might be well, before we take leave of this supremely important precursor of the symbolist movement, to examine briefly the reasons for the check. This should not be difficult; and indeed more than one critic has placed his finger on the crucial failing, without always fully realizing its importance to the philosophy of art.

Already it has been noticed that Baudelaire's theory of universal analogy as the subject-matter of mysticism and the source of poetry rules out the possibility of language being an important part of poetic experience. True, he says 'manier savamment une langue, c'est pratiquer une espèce de sorcellerie évocatoire', etc. (see above, p. 263). But this is an isolated remark; moreover, in its context, it is an extremely ambiguous one, and might be taken to mean that 'manier savamment une langue' consists precisely and solely in expressing 'correspondances'. At any event, Baudelaire never comes to suggesting that the use of language *is* poetry: putting his experiences into words is in his perspective a secondary side of the poet's activity, which is first and foremost mystical, a-linguistic.[1] We might say that for Baudelaire, words are symbolic, in the ordinary acceptation of the word—i.e. they symbolize things or experiences; but that the things and experiences they signify are symbols in the mystic's special sense—a sense which marks out the point where aesthetic value is generated. It has been well said that

'Ni l'un ni l'autre (Baudelaire et Hugo) n'insistaient pour replacer ce phénomène dans la vie de la langue. En parlant de symboles et de symbolisme, Baudelaire ne disait pas que pour le poète "inspiré" ce sont les mots qui sont chargés d'une valeur émotive nouvelle.'[2]

A point not so frequently made, but which also derives from this blind spot in Baudelaire's aesthetic, regards his limitation of the term Symbol. Limitation might seem to be the wrong word, for we have seen that in his view any aspect whatever of the outside world may on occasion become invested with importance to the artist as a symbol: yet it is a limitation, for it excludes words, language, the poet's material, from the realm of symbols. This is understandable, since words obviously have references, whatever may be believed about other things; and Baudelaire would not have wasted time in arguing that words derive beauty from referring to things, so naturally all that is said about *Le Mystère de la Vie* must be taken as not applying to words and their simple references. The point only becomes embarrassing for the historian of symbolism when he finds that other poets of succeeding generations use the word symbol in relation to their verse, but in speaking not of the things referred to by their

---

[1] But see above, p. 175, and below, p. 296, for Baudelaire's claim that poems are the result of formal constructiveness. It is quite certain he never dreamt that this formative act was the essential act of *using language*.

[2] Taupin, *Quatre Essais*, 1932, p. 181.

language, but of the language itself. As they are not only numerous but important, we cannot dismiss their usage as a mere aberration. Two courses are open to us: either we can retreat into the position of allowing that there are, in this field, two separate and distinct meanings of the word 'symbol', according as we refer to the poetic image or the word; or else we can claim that both usages are justifiable, that they are in fact not two references but different sides of one single one, and that the poetic symbol properly comprises not only the image but the word referring to it as well: a view for which the last chapter has prepared us already, and which we may find clearly expressed by Alexander:

'A thing (e.g. a word) *means* the real things or qualities or patterns of things for which it stands. But in art the word or marble or drawing has welded into its being the things which it means. Its meaning is part of it in the same way as in the perception of an orange the round, yellow form does not merely stand for the juiciness of the orange but is actually qualified by it and fused with it into one. In the marble block the Hermes does not merely mean life and divinity but is divine and alive, in so far as we appreciate it as a work of art.... This which is so clear with the statue is true also of language in art. The words are no longer mere sounds, but are alive with the qualities they mean.... '[1]

It will be noted that Alexander does not use the word symbol in this argument, but the word language. It is at least a possibility that the literary symbol we are pursuing is nothing more nor less than a unit of language; such a possibility would reconcile the conflict that already threatens to break out between two views of its nature. It must be left to later to decide whether it will suffice to reconcile all the possible claims to the term. For the moment we may note that such a solution would comfortably bridge the gap between Baudelaire's observations on certain experiences of metaphor and the theory of language whose absence we noticed a few pages back. But it would do so at the cost of the universal analogies and the supernatural 'correspondances'.

4. THE SYMBOLIST SUCCESSORS OF BAUDELAIRE

The view of a 'symbol' as a poetic image distinguished by some special efficacy from the usual images attendant on the use of speech is maintained by a whole succession of writers in the symbolist period in books, articles, treatises, and reviews; and there can be no reasonable doubt that the general aesthetic consciousness of the movement was continually confronted by it. But there was no

[1] Alexander, *Art and the Material*, p. 24.

authoritative pronouncement on symbols such as might rally a whole group of writers and critics to a coherent doctrine; and this becomes less and less surprising in proportion as we come to see more and more how ambiguous the notion of 'symbol' is from the empirical viewpoint of poetic composition, and how inaccessible it was in the given circumstances of the general theories of art. Within the perspectives opened up by Baudelaire, however, it is possible to distinguish a rough grouping of sub-variants, some of which we shall now proceed to examine by turn.

(a) *Mauclair*

As so often, the most characteristic examples of a tendency are to be found not among the loftiest but among the more humble figures that take part in it; and this is particularly true of the field we are engaged upon. We therefore make no apology for turning again to Camille Mauclair, whose earlier years in the world of letters, before the turn of the century, was spent at the feet of Mallarmé, and who, though undistinguished by his creative achievements, is yet conspicuous for a large and steady output of critical and explanatory articles on aesthetic problems of the new poetry (and later of the new painting). At a fairly late stage of the 'symbolist mêlée' he attempted to elucidate for himself in *Eleusis* (1894) the nature of our protean concept. True to one part of Baudelaire's teaching he states roundly,

'Le symbole n'est pas l'allégorie, ni la coïncidence, ni l'analogie, qui ne sont que des procédés littéraires, et non des valeurs métaphysiques.'[1]

Coats of arms, for example, are not symbols; they are

'déductives, *en dehors* de l'intellectualité ... signes d'un langage courant';[2]

and again,

'L'allégorie, l'analogie, la comparaison et la coïncidence étant des procédés d'extériorisation, des déductions, ne peuvent être confondues avec le symbole, qui est essentiellement un prodrome d'intuitivisme.'[3]

What, then, is the symbol?—J'appelle symbole tout ce qui paraît.' This large statement, which indeed called forth comment from reviewers at the time of its appearance,[4] is of course fully in keeping with the doctrine of Baudelaire; though as it stands, it is open to all the complaints of ambiguity that we have noticed in the preceding

---

[1] *Eleusis*, p. 97.   [2] ibid., p. 98.
[3] ibid., p. 99. A few years later, in *L'art en silence*, Mauclair renounces symbolism, because, he says, 'L'Allégorie n'est pas un élément fondamental de création' (op. cit., p. 203), and literary circles persist in identifying symbol with allegory.
[4] It received especially harsh attention at the hands of Lucien Muhlfeldt, in the *Revue Blanche* (t. vi, no. 29, iii/1894).

pages. If we again ask, how is the symbol to be distinguished as a class of things important to literature, Mauclair gives a rather wild answer:

'Mais le symbolisme, c'est-à-dire exactement le fait de considérer l'objet comme distinct de sa notion pure, comme témoignage d'une écriture du monde dont le sens gît en notre sensibilité, le symbolisme n'est pas autre chose qu'un théorème d'idéalisme hégélien, et ne peut donner titre à une tentative d'art que par une impropriété de signification étymologique... On ne "fait pas de l'art avec le symbole," et cela ne veut rien dire; le symbole, c'est l'objet... Tout le monde parle des objets et tout le monde n'est pas symboliste, en admettant que cela signifie quelque chose, car le symbolisme serait de ce fait une banalité presque absurde.'[1]

'En admettant que cela signifie quelque chose': Mauclair's task is to find out in what way a symbolist looks differently on the world from anyone else. His solution is, as we might have suspected all along, a garbled version of Schopenhauer ('Mon Maître'—as he calls him in *Eleusis*, p.80):

'Un objet est distinct de sa notion pure; il s'y résorbe.'[2]

In other words, a rose is a 'symbol' not of love, or of a military faction, but of the Idea of a rose.

'Et je remarque que seule ma conception, étant idéale et non matérielle, est durable et inattaquable, puisqu'ainsi elle échappe à tout danger physique, et que cette rose dont je parlais se peut détruire mille fois sans que la connaissance que j'en ai conservée s'affaiblisse. Si donc quelque chose est réel dans tout ces éléments, ce n'est pas la rose que j'ai regardée, mais c'est la disposition de mon esprit dont elle est cause.'[3]

It is by no means clear that Mauclair properly grasps what Schopenhauer intends by 'Idea': and it might be argued that 'concepts' (so carefully distinguished by the Master) might equally well be under discussion in the passage summarized above; but one thing is clear enough, and that is that the 'symbolist', so far from being a man using words in a special way, is simply a man who feels that the rose in a painting is more than a simple copy of a 'real' rose, and supplies the material for a special kind of contemplation. The word 'disposition' in the quotation is a big question-mark—paper money for which Mauclair will later be seen to try to give hard cash in a currency not at all agreeable to Schopenhauer; but for the moment we have done what we set out to do—namely, establish certain limited similarities between Baudelaire and one theorist of symbolist doctrine—though it might on the surface seem to be set out in rather misleading terms.

---

[1] op. cit., pp. 87–9.　　[2] ibid.　　[3] *Eleusis*, pp. 80–1.

S

There follows from this the same attitude towards the poet's vocation:

'Tout objet est le symbole passager de son idée-même. Le monde n'est qu'un système de symboles subordonné à un système d'idées pures qui sont régies par des lois cosmiques, et dont la réunion constitue la divinité. L'univers est pour ainsi dire une écriture immense dont chaque objet est une lettre et dont le total raconte le divin.'[1]

The doctrine is set out in almost identical terms in the same author's *Notes sur l'idée pure* (1892) where we are told that the artist, looking on life—'la vie, *médiateur plastique*'—

'use de sa plénitude potentielle pour dévoiler sa signification. Ceci se peut formuler que les objets sont des caractères hiéroglyphiques, où s'inscrit complexement l'idée pure, et qu'en cet assemblage de formes, comme en toute géométrie, la connaissance profonde et le soigneux formulaire de l'écriture ou des figures aident à la compréhension et dédient à la lecture plus de clarté. L'esprit tend à la connaissance complète du monde extérieur, d'où souci métaphysique. Cette lecture donne un sens, qui est la notion des idées pures, ou révélation de l'inaltérable dans le modifié, du type dans la descendance, du primordial dans l'évolution.'[2]

And accordingly, 'L'idéaliste donne à l'objet une utilité révélatrice ou symbolique'.[3]

The same doctrine, no doubt, and yet not quite the same. Let us first cut away the rubbish: the confusion between ideas and concepts which would have made Schopenhauer's hair stand up on end; the careless use of 'métaphysique',[4] the mystical passage to the transcendental, the fanciful simile with geometry; the 'idée pure'. What remains? Two points, both of some interest. First, that the artist (or the idealist: for anything but an 'idealist' artist is to Mauclair a 'realist', and *ex hypothesi* no artist) performs a certain act: he tries to form a clearer idea. Of what? Mauclair suggests the 'ideal significance' of 'le monde extérieur'; but as we have seen, by his own confession (page 101 above), this is to be found nowhere but in his own 'disposition'. We may quarrel with the idea that the certain act in question is designed to allow the world around us to 'give off' pure ideas, as it were; but the view that the artist in the exercise of his functions is *becoming aware* of something (and that within himself) is not without importance, and we may have to return to it when we have surveyed other parts of the field of definitions. Secondly, the artist imposes some special task on his 'object': he causes it to be symbolic. Symbolic of what? Of the pure idea, answers Mauclair.

---

[1] *L'Art en silence*, 1900, p. 190.
[2] 'Notes sur l'idée pure,' *Mercure de France*, ix/1892, t. viii, pp. 42–3.   [3] ibid., p. 43.
[4] Cf. 'L'expression symbolique pure, désirée par Hegel (!!) est le rêve d'un métaphysicien plutôt que d'un écrivain' (*L'art en silence*, p. 190).

Setting this aside, however, as an answer (for 'pure ideas' can do nothing but plunge us down once more into an ocean of meaningless and indefinite attitudes), it remains true that the artist does draw his material from the outside world, real or imagined (what other material could he find?) and does present it as something other than an end in itself. For the rose to be a pure end in itself, is the limiting example (unattainable in any case) of realist art:

'L'expression d'art doit se servir de réalités pour exprimer des idées pures, et seulement comme intermédiaires entre la conscience humaine et Dieu. Le réalisme, c'est-à-dire l'étude des symboles *pour eux-mêmes*, est donc une vaine occupation, méconnaissant la destination de l'art.'[1]

The world of objects, therefore, including of course people and events and so forth, can always be looked on, or rather worked with, as a class of *instruments* by the use of which a certain operation (its nature at present unspecified) is performed.

Up to this point we have followed Mauclair in the study of the symbolism of only the simplest of the 'objects' which the poet draws from the world of his experience: and whatever our dislike of his account of pure ideas, there can be no doubt that in its tortuous way it has a certain consistency. But Mauclair does not stop at this point: indeed, by his definition of the symbol ('tout ce qui paraît') it is impossible for him to do so; some paintings, to be sure, limit their material to a few simple objects—still-lifes or landscapes—but a very large number do not; nor can we conceive of drama as composed of anything less complex than human actions and inter-actions. And the concept of art (and therefore of 'pure ideas') can hardly be withheld from this type of creation. There is nothing for it but to extend the concept of symbol to these forms of artistic structures; and Mauclair does so. As example of the simpler kind of symbol he already in *Eleusis* cites Henri de Régnier's use of the Sword; where it is by no means certain that this use should not be more properly called emblematic.[2] In the field of novels, he states confidently that a character in the action can be symbolic (provided always that it be 'construit en vue de fortifier notre contingent d'idéation');[3] in drama, again, he admits characters as symbols—Hamlet or Hedda Gabler. In Wagner, it would appear that Mauclair found myth symbolic:

'Admirable symbole de Siegfried avec le dragon! C'est là que Wagner avec une force incroyable donne la formule nette et triomphante de l'intellectuel.'[4]

---

[1] *Eleusis*, p. 170.   [2] ibid.   [3] ibid., p. 93.   [4] ibid., p. 127.

Gide's *Voyage d'Urien* provides him with a whole scene that is a symbol:

'Admirable et pénétrant symbole qu'Urien parvenu au pôle suprême, au point d'orientation de l'existence, y découvre un cadavre tenant un papier vierge d'écriture... Je pense que vivace auprès de ce cadavre gît une vérité universelle. Nous sommes les gardiens d'un spectre que nous n'avons jamais vu, et de son absence s'épanouit son prestige, il n'est permis à l'esprit de se dévouer qu'à une immatérialité, non point à son témoignage. Ainsi nul symbole ne trouve sa valeur en soi, mais en sa raison d'être... '[1]

Evidently this aspect of composition, if it is symbolic, is also dangerously near to allegory; and is not allegory the enemy of symbolism? No, replies Mauclair,

'Qu'on fasse entrer l'allégorie, l'analogie, la coïncidence en concours d'une composition esthétique, rien de plus naturel';[2]

but symbolism has nothing to do with art as such: it is a 'metaphysical theorem'; that is to say, in the examples quoted, Siegfried and the corpse are symbols in so far as they are distinguished as objects (real or imaginary) from their respective 'pure ideas'. The value of art lies in the presentation of symbols as material for ideation. Presumably, then, the 'vérité éternelle' of Gide's scene is quite irrelevant to the reader's aesthetic activity; at a stretch (though Mauclair does not say so) the reference of the allegory may enter also as part of the symbol; and the pure idea be the pure idea not of the image but of the allegory taken as a whole. But in that case the allegorical nature of the work is, as such, not the source of artistic merit ('... l'allégorie n'est pas un élément fondamental de création...'); in which case, Mauclair's enthusiasm at having found the 'key' to either of these two scenes (and any others like them) is a little disturbing.

More disturbing still is the other defect of the theory of pure ideas, already noted in passing in the case of Schopenhauer (*vide supra*, p. 57, pt. I): namely, it cannot provide of itself an explanation of why we find some art good and some bad. Mauclair's aesthetic, for example, seems to bring him to despise Pissarro *a priori*:

'Cette besogne honnête et médiocre, de copier toute sa vie des fermes, des oies, et des plants de choux, est-ce pour arriver à cela que les maîtres ont existé? Est-ce que cela ne révolte pas l'esprit?'[3]

The answer springs to mind that perhaps these objects, certainly

---

[1] *Mercure de France*, viii/1893, t. viii, pp. 302–3.   [2] *Eleusis*, p. 88.
[3] *Mercure de France*, vii/1894, t. xi, p. 271. Mauclair contradicts himself elsewhere, though: 'Deux prunes et un couteau près d'un verre, de Chardin, c'est plus noble qu'une princesse de Carolus-Duran, infiniment, incomparablement. Le sujet n'est rien du tout' (*Eleusis*, p. 184).

fit to be included among 'tout ce qui paraît', are symbols, and that Mauclair has only to contemplate their 'idées pures' to become aware of their merit. Of course, the situation is ridiculous; but it would have an analogy in literature if Mauclair were asked to comment on a realist novel. He would say it is not art; but the pure ideas theory would not help him to explain why; it would not help him to give expression to his attitude towards realist art; all it would do would be to mislead him into thinking that empirical differences (as between the language of realism and that of symbolism) are the repositories of distinctions between art and not-art: the common critical vice.

Evidently, then, some modification has to be introduced. The situation is exactly similar to that encountered in the case of Baudelaire, where the theory of 'correspondances' and 'symbols' gave no opportunity of variation in aesthetic judgements. Mauclair's problem is to find a criterion which will enable him to say why some images and the like *do* appeal to him as art (or lead him to contemplate their 'pure ideas'), and others do not. With little regard for consistency, he jettisons surreptitiously the aesthetic he has held to up to this stage, and effects a junction with certain views which we saw him holding, or suspected him of holding, in the last chapter.

To the problem, what symbols are fit and confer value on art, he opens his answer by declaring that 'Il n'y a pas de symboles fixes, un langage, un volapük de symboles. La poésie n'est pas une langue chiffrée'—

'Qu'on ne se contraigne point à des symboles inadéquats à soi-même, mais qu'on les choisisse dans sa propre existence intérieure.'[1]

That turns the hunt back towards the poet's own 'disposition'. And since therefore a symbol is not an arbitrary sign in an intellectual volapuk, the ultimate criterion of a symbol's worth is not to be looked for in the same direction as that of the allegory; namely, intelligible clarity.

'Les littérateurs, race de gens qui disent: n'est-ce-pas? devraient bien ne pas tant s'embarrasser de gloses sur ce qui est pensée: y a-t-il émotion? Tout est là, et tout y revient.'[2]

The cat is out of the bag. The poet uses symbols; but the important test of their aesthetic value—and presumably the sign whereby we may know ourselves to be engaged in the contemplation of their

---

[1] *Eleusis*, pp. 169–70.
[2] ibid., p. 125. Cf., too, 'Il n'est qu'un sujet de drame: l'homme et son jeu avec la nature—il ne faut point s'adresses à la mémoire des faits en eux-mêmes, mais de l'émotion qu'ils causèrent' (*Eleusis*, pp. 251–2).

'idées pures'—is an emotional one.[1] This does not yet tell us very much: whether it is an emotion felt at the thought of the symbol (as the memory of the smell of mown hay may arouse emotions), or an emotion fully formed in the mind which chooses one out of a number of possible symbols for purposes of communication (in which case, we still have no answer to the question, 'What determines the choice?'), or an emotion rendered clear and present to the poet's consciousness by being expressed and embodied in a certain symbolic presentation of the original begetter of the emotion—these and a dozen other conflicting possibilities at once spring to the mind. And it is no use trying to guess which possibility is the right one. Mauclair never explores the further implications of this line of inquiry, and there is nothing to show that he had any clear views on the matter. The most we can find is a remark with some bearing on the problem; when he says that poetry is not 'une langue chiffrée', he adds, 'ce que signifie l'Epée pour Henri de Régnier ne répond en rien à mon sentiment'—which would seem to imply that the emotions connected (in one way or another) with the sword-symbol in the poet's mind need in no way correspond with those in the reader's—the last word in aesthetic subjectivism. All we may say is that in poetry (and presumably by extension in all art generally) a certain use of language is marked by emotional force; and that in certain circumstances the material, the symbols, acquire aesthetic value, according to their emotional aura. This attitude is widespread; and we find echoes of it in Ernest Raynaud's résumé of the views of the symbolist critic Edouard Dubus:

'Les formes esthétiques du poème sont *des symboles*. Le symbole étant défini: une figure, une image, qui exprime une chose purement morale... Le poème destiné à reproduire une émotion esthétique sera *symbolique*'.[2]

And indeed in a pronouncement of Mallarmé:

'Tout objet existant n'a de raison que nous le voyons ... sinon de représenter un de nos états intérieurs: l'ensemble des traits communs avec notre âme consacre le symbole.'[3]

The vagueness and hesitancy which mark these slogans and many

---

[1] 'Disons simplement que le symbolisme par son échange continuel de concordances, transpose dans l'art plus de sensibilité' (*Eleusis*, 1894). As a statement of simple fact, this justification of the symbol is shaky. As a distinction of degree, it is insufficient to serve as the basis for an aesthetic principle.

[2] *Le Décadent*, 2e Série, 1888, no. 7, 15/iii/1888.

[3] This is far from representing his whole view; but it was an accessible part of it, and was bowdlerized in the manifesto of Ghil's 'Instrumentist School' ('Notre Ecole,' *La Décadente*, t. i, no. 1, 1/x/1886), and qualified by his pronouncement that the whole trend of the times was 'emotivist' (see *Les Dates et les Œuvres*, 1923, p. viii) and his evident and repeated view of 'le Rêve' as marked by intense emotion.

others of the same kind should not divert our attention from the central fact: namely, that for all the definitions given, a symbol is evidently something with strong affective overtones, and is equivalent to the material, in the widest sense, used by the poet. A symbol is an emotional unity, and it does not appear that from the viewpoint of these successors of Baudelaire it need be limited to comparatively elementary poetic images. Taken in conjunction with a simple theory of the 'emotive' function of the language of poetry, this view could have crystallized into a rather ordinary (and fallacious) aesthetic; but standing in the way of such a conjunction was the concern with a cognitive, mystical element in art, which if it showed the symbolists to be aware of the delicacy of the task of describing what a work of art *is*, at the same time prevented them from ever finding a relatively settled theory.

We have noted in the previous section that Baudelaire's theory of symbols left no room for the part played by language in art. The same objection holds good in the case of Mauclair (and this would incline us to think that the ambiguity noted earlier (page 142) on the place of emotion in language should be resolved in Mauclair's aesthetic in favour of the emotionalists): there is no reason at all to think that he includes in the word Symbol ('tout ce qui paraît') the language in which the poet expresses these symbols. In this connection it would be well to remember that he was at least as much interested in painting as in poetry; and that the language of painting is not made out of words. But neither is it made up out of photographic images of objects: and had he thought of pursuing the analogy between the two arts, Mauclair would have realized that he was condemning himself to ruling out altogether the painter's technique, brush-work, and so forth as contributors to aesthetic worth. And yet Mallarmé had a very clear appreciation of these points (see ch. II, above, page 63); and it is evidently with Mallarmé in his mind that he is forced to go back on some of his distinctions between 'symbolism' and all other art to make place for the awkward intruder, language:

'Le style se ressent d'une vision symbolique, précisément par la nécessité de faire pressentir les correspondances intérieures des phénomènes dont il est écrit. Toutes les qualités de souplesse, de translucidité, de suggestion, toutes les ressources d'harmonie verbale deviennent désirables, alors qu'elles n'étaient que nuisibles dans l'étude déterminée d'un fait en soi.'[1]

With a jump he has bridged the gap between symbols and art, even to the point of entirely overshooting language as such and landing

---

[1] *Eleusis*, p. 107.

on a specification of style. It is only to be assumed that for Mauclair, as for Baudelaire, language is no more than an instrument for recording: for noting down not now the 'analogies' between elements in experience, but rather the quintessential 'idea' of this or that experience. Yet this view, unmodified, would lead to poetry coming to be thought of as something very little better than a kind of haphazard algebra: which is rather what Mauclair's judgement on Mallarmé implies it to be;[1] or at best some system of communication whose nature is quite indifferent to the artist using it. The 'symbolist' operation, properly speaking, would then go forward as the act we have noted above, and be complete already before the artist decided to put it into words.[2] Thus for a symbolist theory of language there is perhaps no need at all; Mauclair, in the argument he develops in *Eleusis*, appears to take it for granted that language is nothing more than a system of 'idées pures' according to certain 'principes abstraits' (whatever these may be) and otherwise in no need of further analysis. Yet as some uses of language seem more suitable for this than others, a decision is taken, empirically, to use such language. And the criterion of suitability, as we have seen, is its 'musicality', when by that is meant the attempt by the poet to arouse emotion by sound-elements in speech, on the supposed analogy of language. Surprisingly, we find ourselves at this point not a long way away from Ghil's definition of 'faire prédominer le Rêve par le Symbole, le Chant par une retrempe alternée des mots en les sens et la sonorité'— at least so far as concerns the lack of fusion between the two efficacious elements in speech.

(b) Mallarmé

The position taken up by Mallarmé on the meaning and use of the literary symbol is not at all explicit, and he seems to prefer not to make too frequent a reference to it; when he does so, it is some-

[1] See above, p. 65 n.

[2] This is suggested by the following: 'A mesure que nous étudions les symboles et trouvons sous leurs aspects variables les principes abstraits qui les constituent, nous nous faisons une idée plus claire de la divinité, notre connaissance la réfléchit plus directement, et l'idéal est que, par une connaissance totale des lois cachées sous les symboles, la conscience et Dieu s'identifient. Tout acte de travail cérébral est donc à ce point de vue, un acte de foi religieuse' ('Esthétique de Stéphane Mallarmé,' *Grande Revue*, xi/1898, p. 197). It would be interesting to know what are these abstract principles. Or again, 'Qu'est-ce-qu'une idée pour un poète, sinon une image? Trouver une image, c'est saisir une relation et en donner un signe, c'est-à-dire constater une idéation. Plus un poète invente des images, plus il établit des relations — c'est tout ce que je vois sous le terme idée, et c'est tout ce qu'on peut lui demander' (*Eleusis*, p. 125). We seem to be back at Baudelaire's theory of metaphors; at any rate, the position of language is the same as in that writer's aesthetic.

times in one sense, sometimes in another. But at least he cannot be accused of ignoring the linguistic element in poetic imagery; Viélé-Griffin speaks of

'le horror sacré que ressent M. Mallarmé en face du *mot* qui, naturellement, pour lui, est le symbole, par lui pénétré, d'un *autre chose* nécessaire'.[1]

And we are reminded of Mallarmé's own quaint remark, in *La Musique et les Lettres,*

'Le tour de telle phrase ou le lacs d'un distique, copiés sur notre conformation, aident l'éclosion, en nous, d'aperçus et de correspondances.'[2]

It would be rash indeed to claim from this and a few other chance remarks that Mallarmé falls into the opposite pitfall to Mauclair and abstracts the word from its meaning as the source of poetic worth; especially in view of his remark (quoted above, p. 278) on the relation between *objects* and *states of mind*; and I do not believe that any writer or thinker in the age of symbolism would have made any such suggestion. But one can claim on the strength of this evidence that Mallarmé has progressed a certain way from Baudelaire's conception of the symbol. Further, too, than many of his contemporaries.

But we cannot find in his writings the evidence that would show us that Mallarmé attempted to provide a *theory* of the symbol sufficiently coherent or sufficiently comprehensive to replace or modify the efforts of Baudelaire and the Baudelairean succession;[3] to reach this we must examine further applications of the term.

(c) The Complete Symbolist: an Interlude

Several of the early writings of W. B. Yeats, written directly under the impact of a visit to Paris and the works of Mallarmé and Maeterlinck, give us an interesting impression of the complex strands that went to make up the broad view of the symbol; and by way of an interlude we make no apology for giving a brief account of them. Yeats starts from the distinction we have already seen in Carlyle:

'At first I tried to distinguish between symbols and symbols, between what I called inherent symbols and arbitrary symbols; but the distinction has come to mean little or nothing. Whether their power has arisen out of themselves, or whether it has an arbitrary origin, matters little, for they act, as I believe, because the Great Memory associates them with certain events and moods and persons. Whatever

[1] *Entretiens politiques et littéraires,* viii/1892, t. ii, p. 71.
[2] *La Musique et les lettres,* 1895, p. 43.
[3] Perhaps because of this, there has often been a tendency to ignore the fact that Mallarmé is one of the boldest experimenters of all time in the realm of symbolism, whose resources he took in his sonnets and—especially—in *Un Coup de Dés* to the most extreme lengths.

the passions of man have gathered about, becomes a symbol in the great memory' (Yeats proposes a universal mind accessible through magic to human minds).... 'The symbols are of all kinds, for everything in heaven or earth has its association, momentous or trivial, in the great memory, and one never knows what forgotten events may have plunged it, like the toadstool and ragwort, into the great passions.'[1]

Here is the starting point, the system of universal analogies, with its justification in a supernatural order—a Baudelairean conception, infused with the typically Celtic interest in magic. The removal of distinctions between symbols leads naturally to the removal of a barrier between symbol and allegory:

'I said that the rose and the lily and the poppy were so married by their colour, and their odour, and their use, to love and purity and sleep, or to other symbols of love and purity and sleep, and had been so long a part of the imagination of the world, that a symbolist might use them to help out his meaning without becoming an allegoricist.... It is hard to say where Allegory and Symbolism melt into one another....'[2]

Yeats' instinct is, of course, right. Put in terms of our discussion of language in the preceding chapter, we could say that language includes not only the construct 'sleep' and the construct 'poppy', but also the construct formed by their frequent associations together. Just as the image of 'poppy' fuses—or can fuse—with the word and its sound in language as art, so, too, the additional meaning of 'sleep' can be fused with the image and the word 'poppy'. Yet there is nothing inevitable about the process, and however much we may think the poppy a 'natural' symbol for sleep, reflection will show that it is nothing but the tradition of language—in the widest sense— which makes us think it so. Consequently there is no reason why the poet should not contribute his new symbols to language, even if these are destined not to survive their first appearance. There is, indeed, no distinction between 'inherent' and 'arbitrary' symbols.

As symbolists Yeats lists a very wide range of artists—all poets and painters who specially appealed to him: Wagner, Keats, Blake, Shelley, Rossetti, Villiers, Beardsley, Whistler, Maeterlinck, Verlaine, and many others. In fact, he identifies great art with symbol, and sees a simply empirical distinction of value between symbol and allegory:

'William Blake was the first writer of modern times to preach the indissoluble marriage of all great art with symbol. There had been allegorists and teachers of

[1] Yeats, *Magic*, 1901; *Works*, vol. VI, pp. 50–1.
[2] 'Symbolism in Painting,' 1898, *Works*, vol. VI, p. 178. The more mature Yeats develops symbolism, in a different climate, to lengths quite as uncompromising as Mallarmé, and does not fail to observe the implications for aesthetic theory. But in this he belongs, like also Paul Valéry, strictly outside that age which we are concerned with here.

allegory in plenty, but the symbolic imagination, or as Blake preferred to call it, 'vision,' is not allegory, being a "representation of what actually exists really and unchangeably."'

Yeats goes on:

'A symbol is indeed the only possible expression of some invisible essence, a transparent lamp about a spiritual flame; while allegory is one of many possible representations of an embodied thing, or familiar principle, and belongs to fancy and not to imagination: the one is a revelation, the other an amusement.'[1]

Less ambitious, but perhaps more revealing is a remark about 'the continuous indefinable symbolism which is the substance of all style':[2] a dangerous assertion, tending to link symbolism and all art by the most risky side of the doctrine—the empirical, historical side— and one which Yeats repeats in the following passage:

'Metaphors are not profound enough to be moving, when they are not symbols, and when they are symbols they are the most perfect, because the most subtle, outside of pure sound, and through them one can the best find out what symbols are.'[3]

The distinction in kind between symbols and non-symbolic metaphor is one which we have already discussed in relation to Baudelaire's theory of metaphor; and there is no need to go over old ground to expose the fallacy involved.

In precisely the same way as Mauclair, Yeats explains the aesthetic value of the symbol in terms of a mystic cognition—'some invisible essence' which it is a delight to contemplate; but when he comes to expounding the signs whereby we recognize some symbols to be artistically good and others less so, he has recourse to an emotional criterion. Yet he goes somewhat further than Mauclair along the route traversed by Mallarmé, when he shows his intuitive grasp of the process of language:

'All sounds, all colours, all forms, either because of their pre-ordained energies or because of long associations, evoke indefinable and yet precise emotions, or, as I prefer to think, call down among us certain disembodied powers, whose footsteps over our hearts we call emotions; and when sound, and colour, and form are in *a musical relation*, a beautiful relation to one another, they become as it were one sound, one colour, one form, and evoke an emotion that is made out of their distinct evocations and yet is one emotion.'[4]

Yeats has still left open the alternative of 'pre-ordained energies' and 'long associations'; yet in another passage he seems to imply— perhaps unconsciously and against his intentions—that the latter course is the aesthetically important one. It is not certain whether

[1] 'William Blake and his Illustrations,' 1897, *Works*, vol. VI, p. 138.
[2] 'The Symbolism of Poetry,' 1900, *Works*, vol. VI, p. 188.
[3] ibid., p. 189.   [4] ibid., p. 190 (my italics).

he ever read a suggestive passage from Charles Morice's *Littérature de tout à l'heure*[1] regarding the need to symbolism of a long prior tradition of language; in any case he would have absorbed the idea in the days when he wrote what Morris called 'my sort of poetry'; certainly in his own experience, it was abundantly plain that the symbolist lived on the stored-up resources of his language:

'It is only by ancient symbols, by symbols that have numberless meanings besides the one or two the writer lays an emphasis upon, or the half-score he knows of, that any highly subjective art can escape from the barrenness and shallowness of a too conscious arrangement, into the abundance and depth of nature. The poet of essences and pure ideas must seek in the half-lights that glimmer from symbol to symbol as if to the ends of the earth, all that the epic and dramatic poet finds of mystery and shadow in the accidental circumstance of life.'[2]

Evidently, Yeats is limiting his use of 'symbol' here to relatively small constructs of language, as opposed to the highly complex ones of the epic poet or the dramatist (though note that he makes a parallel between them); and within this field, he distinguishes two main sorts of symbol, the emotional and the intellectual. The intellectual evoke ideas alone, or ideas mixed with emotions 'and outside the very definite traditions of mysticism and the less definite criticism of certain modern poets, these alone are called symbols'.

'If I say "white" or "purple" in an ordinary line of poetry, they evoke emotions so exclusively that I cannot say why they move me; but if I say them in the same mood, in the same breath with such obvious intellectual symbols as a cross or a crown of thorns, I think of purity or sovereignty.'[3]

The 'emotional' symbols (Yeats' distinction is arbitrary) are far less stable than the others, and at the same time constitute an enormous class: 'in this case all alluring or hateful things are symbols,'[4] and by themselves 'their relations with one another are too subtle to delight us fully, away from rhythm and pattern'.[5]

We have already seen (p. 282) that Yeats has a very clear idea of the organic relationship between sense, rhythm, pattern, sound, and the rest; he calls it a musical relationship; but under attraction from the doctrine of symbols and 'essences and pure ideas', he is drawn into giving another account of the position of rhythm. If in the hurly-burly of our normal consciousness these ephemeral symbols slip

---

[1] 'Il est impossible de rien dire de neuf dans une langue neuve: elle est ou elle serait toute barbare, inapte aux inflexions, avec modulations... En vieillissant, les langues acquièrent, avec cette phosphorescence de la matière qui se décompose, cette ductilité subtile qui permet de mieux induire l'idée dans les intelligences moins brutalement ouvertes' (p. 363).

[2] 'The Philosophy of Shelley's Poetry,' 1900, *Works*, vol. VI, p. 100.

[3] 'The Symbolism of Poetry,' *Works*, vol. VI, p. 193.   [4] ibid.   [5] ibid.

through our fingers and are lost to our enjoyment, rhythm can yet do much to remedy this situation:

'The purpose of rhythm, it has always seemed to me, is to prolong the moment of contemplation, the moment when we are both asleep and awake, which is the one moment of creation, by hushing us with an alluring monotony, while it holds us waking by variety, to keep us in that state of perhaps real trance, in which the mind liberated from the pressure of the Will is unfolded in symbols.'[1]

With the entry of the Will, and the symbolist's escape from it into contemplation, we are back to Schopenhauer and the Ideas, and our tour of Yeats' phase as an early theoretical symbolist is at an end. There is no original contribution to the study of symbolism, except of course the poet's always attractive presentation of his idea; but Yeats has always been remarkable for his quickly receptive mind; and in the essays written at the turn of the century he put to good account, it would appear, the doctrines—or at least a good part of them—which he heard through Symons from the boulevards or Mallarmé's select reunions. Seen through Yeats' lens, the state of symbolist aesthetic in Paris appears in an interesting light, for what it then was—a curious and amorphous conglomeration of notions taken from the most diversified sources, and pressed together into a slightly pretentious, and distinctly mystifying, doctrine of art.

5. MYTH AND ALLEGORY

Already in this chapter we have had occasion to notice cautions against confusing symbolism with allegory. We shall now attempt to see if these cautions are needful, and if so, what the differences are between the two things.

First, we must make an important distinction. Works like *The Pilgrim's Progress* or Melville's *Moby Dick*, both outstanding examples in modern literature of allegory, are also great art. In each, a certain kind of lesson, or general proposition, may be learned from interpreting the plot; but the possibility of this exercise in no way detracts from the artistic merits of the two books. No one would suggest that the biblical Book of Revelations, another allegory, is for that any the less great literature. The allegory is not, *prima facie* and in itself, destructive of artistic worth; and if symbols are not simply big or little allegories, that is not because allegories are incompatible with art.

[1] 'The Symbolism of Poetry,' 1900, *Works*, vol. VI, p. 193.

As a corollary to this, we might repeat what has already been noted earlier (in the quotation from Alexander's *Art and the Material*, *supra*, p. 271) that art is quite capable of swallowing up reference or semantic elements in language; if this holds good for simple pieces of language, it will hold good also for complex ones: if 'words are alive with the qualities they mean', myth can be alive with its allegorical sense. In general, when we find writers contrasting symbol with allegory as incompatibles, it is because they think of allegory as possessing extremely little artistic worth; and it is quite true that a piece of writing can continue to be a meaningful allegory even when stripped of its artistic value (by being badly translated, say, and then badly adapted for the films). What remains constant in the process of deterioration is not an artistic value—an individuality—but an intellectual one—a generality. By bearing this in mind we shall have a straightforward standard against which to set the symbolists' mistrust for—or confidence in—allegory and myth.

Myth is art in so far as it attends to its individuality, as an expression of an attitude; not in so far as it lays claim to general truth. And in this former respect it is open to the symbolist artist. In other words, the 'symbolic' in art is not merely the embodiment of a generalized concept in a representation, but its embodiment in such a way that the representation itself has aesthetic value. That is not to say that the representation (or symbol) is a pure end in itself, a 'thing of beauty' irrespective of its creator or spectator; but rather that it should avoid being merely a dessiccated sign for a concept. Naturalist aesthetic has two terrors for symbolism: either it treats art as a more or less approximative communication of concepts (e.g. Taine's *caractère saillant*) or it makes art into the gratuitous and indifferent exercise of imitative craft.[1] Symbolism attempts to steer between the Scylla and Charybdis of naturalist doctrine. It announces this intention by proclaiming that all objects are signs,[2] and also—though not always—that reading these signs constitutes a species of cognition different from that of ordinary practical discourse. The latter statement is made necessary by the careless presentation of the former.

[1] Cf. Flaubert's ambition to write a book 'about nothing', which is, however, less an exercise in imitation than an exercise in style.

[2] Cf. 'L'œuvre d'art ne doit point, même pour l'œil du populaire bétail, prêter à pareille équivoque [i.e. be taken for other than symbol]. Il faut donc que dans l'œuvre idéiste [Aurier's new variation on 'idéoréaliste'] cette confusion ne puisse de produire, il faut donc que nous soyons mis en état de ne pouvoir douter que les objets, dans le tableau, n'ont aucun valeur en tant qu'objets, qu'ils ne sont que des signes, des verbes, n'ayant en eux-mêmes nulle autre importance' (G.-A. Aurier, on Gauguin, *Mercure de France*, iii/1891, pp. 161–2). The writer concludes from this that art aims at expressing 'les Idées'; and that the man who can avoid the shameful equivoque noted above is a superior being. The doctrine of Mauclair, in short.

The principal influence in bringing myth to the concept of the symbol was, of course, Wagner. Not, indeed, that there existed no other possible quarters from which a whisper of such a *rapprochement* could come: the whole burden of the earlier German Romantic movement at Jena, and some of its successors, had been the renovation of myth; and in an important article Jean Thorel brought the results of this movement before the eyes of the French world of letters,[1] but this was not until 1891; and in any case, the far more topical shock of Wagner's music-drama overshadowed for the younger generation the relatively inaccessible writings of a century earlier. It would be foolish, too, to ignore a steady stream of allegory in French poetry right through the nineteenth century: in Vigny, Hugo, Leconte de Lisle, Baudelaire, and a hundred others.

The most prominent Wagnerite symbolist was Téodor de Wyzéwa, and in his thoroughgoing acceptance of the equivalence of myth and symbol, he goes near to falling on the first horn of the naturalist dilemma. For example, writing of Mallarmé's earlier poems, he says:

'Noterai-je dans les vers anciens quelque autre qualité du poète? Une tendance à voir toutes choses comme des symboles. Un hôpital? c'est notre vie. Le sonneur? c'est le poète invoquant l'idéal. La rose? C'est Hérodiade. Nous sommes bien loin des images de Hugo, rapides et fortuites, tropes scolaires, vite abandonnées:

[1] 'Si tous les phénomènes de la vie physique et de la vie morale ne sont que des manifestations différentes d'un principe unique, chacun de ces phénomènes pourra être appelé à suggérer cette existence supérieure qui est partout présente, et chaque objet de la nature, chaque fait de la vie morale pourra et devra devenir symbole. Et puisque tout dans ce panthéisme, car il faut l'appeler par son nom, aboutit ainsi à l'être absolu, on conçoit tout d'abord l'infinie complexité d'interprétation de toute chose, qui laissera donc aux poètes une source intarissable de symboles, où chacun pourra puiser sans cesse, sans que jamais la source ne tarisse ni soit seulement moins vive. Quant à donner plus de profondeur au symbole, et à faire en sorte qu'il se présente plus capable d'émouvoir profondément, c'est précisément là ce qui constituera le vrai poète et le distinguera des simples manieurs de mots et d'images. Entendu dans ce sens, et tout le monde l'entend ainsi maintenant, le symbolisme date de toujours, puisqu'il est le fond même de toute poésie, et que tout ce qui n'est pas lui ne peut guère être qu'arabesque curieuse ou exercice de rhétorique, ou simple travail d'analyse, qu'il est un peu puéril alors de parer du manteau de la poésie.' Thorel suggests that the superiority of the symbol over allegory and comparison consists in its 'synthetic' character: a false distinction, of course. He goes on to give an example of symbolism: the famous novel *Ondine*.
'Ce petit livre ... donne de manière parfaite l'exemple de ce qu'il faudrait sans doute que présentât tout symbole pour être dédié à l'art. On y découvre en effet une succession, une progression de sens, qui font de lui d'abord un conte populaire, de péripéties fort claires, et accessibles à tous, avec de parfaits tableaux propres à susciter en nous l'image des mille extériorités où se complaisent nos sens; on peut y suivre en même temps le drame émotionnel de sentiments intensément humains, dont moins de lecteurs déjà pourront percevoir toute la grandeur; enfin le poète appelle chacune des forces naturelles qu'il évoque, et chacune des situations émotionnelles qu'il crée, à nous suggérer des idées d'essence générale, qui ne pourront plus être perçues que d'un nombre plus restreint encore de lecteurs, anxieux de se rappeler en chaque instant cet "esprit absolu" qu'ils voient au fond de tout.'
(Jean Thorel, 'Les Romantiques allemands et les Symbolistes français,' *Entretiens politiques et littéraires*, ix/1891, t. iii, no. 18, pp. 101–3). The article reads, as a whole, more like a condensed breviary of symbolism in 1891 than an attempt to characterize the German movement. But at least it reminded the French reading public of the work of Novalis, Friedrich Schlegel, etc.

voici déjà la vie entière considérée sous un double aspect, réel et fictif. L'artiste voit constamment, avec une égale sûreté, les deux mondes: et il transpose dans l'Art toute réalité sensible.'[1]

Not only in the early poems, however: *L'Après-midi d'un faune* is noted by Wyzéwa for the fact that its hero is not only an individual, but in some sort a universal image of man facing a metaphysical topic of reality and illusion (see the passage already quoted above, p. 70); likewise the *Prose pour des Esseintes* is nothing more nor less (in his view) than a picture of an anchorite facing the same metaphysical questions. Indeed, Wyzéwa interprets Mallarmé's poetical works, or at any rate the obscurer ones, as nothing other than variations upon the solipsist theme of *Claire Lenoir*, revealing the eternal secrets of reality: 'il avait aperçu que la source suprême des émotions est la recherche des vérités'.

Evidently, on the terms set out in justification of the 'Faune', there is no reason why this use of 'symbol' should present difficulties to the aesthetician. Roughly speaking, it is a Sign with intrinsic artistic merit. It is in this sense that Rodenbach's recurring image of submarine life (in 'Vies encloses') 'symbolizes' the life of the Unconscious; or that Laforgue's use of the moon or moonlit nights 'symbolizes' the ultimate boudhist void.[2] In the *Moralités Légendaires*, too, Wyzéwa finds a symbolism:

'Dans chacun de ces six contes, Jules Laforgue a voulu réaliser des symboles, c'est-à-dire représenter des mythes anciens sous le vêtement moderne qu'ils peuvent recevoir. Les légendes de la mythologie grecque, les traditions païennes, elles sont sans doute l'expression de la vie telle que la concevaient ces âmes lointaines à travers les qualités spéciales de leur nature et de leurs mœurs. Transporter ces symboles dans notre monde moderne était impossible si on ne les modifiait profondément: car notre vie s'est modifiée: et nous n'agirions plus comme ces hommes d'autrefois dans les mêmes circonstances. Et Jules Laforgue a imaginé dans les circonstances que narrent ces légendes, les actes et sentiments d'hommes modernes.'[3]

A symbol, then, is roundly equated with a myth. It remains to decide what Wyzéwa considers a myth is or does. It is 'l'expression de la vie'; by which we may suppose him to mean that a myth is a work of art in which is expressed its maker's attitude to the more profound problems of his world. It is the profundity or greatness of the theme which causes it to assume the position of a religious work— perhaps even doctrine. And this being so, it is not difficult to see

---

[1] *Vogue*, no. 11, 5/vii/1886, p. 368.　　　　[2] See Ruchon, *Laforgue*, p. 137.

[3] *Revue Indépendante*, no. 14, xii/1887, p. 342. Cf. Rémy de Gourmont, 'Les symboles qu'il (l'artiste) imaginera ou qu'il expliquera seront imaginés ou expliqués selon la conception spéciale du monde morphologiquement possible à chaque cerveau symbolisateur' (*Le chemin de velours*, p. 210).

that in such a context the question of deciding what is fit to be a symbol and what is not may be left to common sense to solve. A symbol is judged by its expressive adequacy; judgement as to that is obviously a prime function of the creative artist, and equally obviously dependent on the general cultural tradition of the moment. Moreover, there is no reason why the concept of myth should not be so reduced, compressed, and simplified, that at its lower extremes it is indistinguishable from the Baudelairean symbol:

'Monticelli nous peint un lion... Monticelli a vu et nous montre l'analogie profonde et certaine qui existe entre le pelage du fauve et sa férocité, et sans prêter à la bête le geste menaçant de la naïve illustration, il a seulement fait rugir les tons terribles de cette robe féroce.'[1]

Here is Charles Morice's contribution to the gallery of symbols; and it will be seen that on the one hand it satisfies Baudelaire's requirements, and on the other could hardly be separated from the idea of allegory, in so far as it is a sign. If the painting were crude, the lion in a naïve attitude of hostility, the whole devoid of artistic worth, it would still be a sign, or emblem, conveying the notion of ferocity, though as bad art we might refuse to call it symbol; but if on the contrary it is a masterpiece, expressive in every inch of the painter's attitude to his subject, or (if allegorical) to his age, it could certainly be called a symbol in Wyzéwa's sense.

By the same tokens, Hamlet (in both Laforgue's and Shakespeare's versions) is a myth; perhaps even more in Laforgue's time than in Shakespeare's; therefore a symbol.[2] In this sense it is hard to see where to draw a limit: all characters in drama appear to partake, be it ever so little, of the nature of myth; or in other words, a 'symbolic' figure is one who sums up in his behaviour a certain attitude of the author as embodied in his character.[3]

Similarly with the novel: Alfred Vallette, writing in the *Mercure de France*, can excuse a preposterous character in a contemporary novel (Lemonnier's *Le Possédé*) on the grounds that she is a symbol. But it is significant that in so doing he topples into the ever-present trap for symbolists—

'Rakma ... se justifie totalement comme abstraction, comme un symbole du vice fatal'[4]

—namely, he treats the representation as a mere convenience:

'le signe en quoi il est possible de condenser le plus de vérité'.[5]

[1] Morice, *La Littérature de tout à l'heure*, 1889, p. 284.
[2] Cf. 'Mêmes certains [myths of Wagner] satisfont à l'esprit par ce fait de ne sembler pas dépourvus de toute accointance avec de hasardeux symboles' (Mallarmé, *Divagations*, p. 146).
[3] This is the line taken by Pierre Valin, 'Le Symbole au théâtre,' *Ermitage*, III, 31/i/1892.
[4] *Mercure de France*, viii/1890. [5] ibid.

A typical mystic novelist seems to have put a variation on the same situation in terms not of Wyzéwa's expressiveness of myth, but of the divine meaningfulness of all things:

'Le symbole, c'est l'homme, qui est le langage de l'inconnaissable. L'homme est un signe'[1]

—a sign in the mystic, not the rational sense, of course: something suggestive, whose value is not given by a definition. The damage done to symbolism, the obfuscation of the issues with which it was trying to deal, by so-called mystics whose professions of faith were loose slogans is a constitutive element of the day which no literary historian can afford to ignore.[2]

We have noted that for Laforgue a myth was something that stood in need of renovation from age to age, even though in effect the theme may be presumed to remain more or less constant (or to put it more accurately perhaps, even though the themes form a fairly clearly recognizable family). This second aspect, the universality of myth, was a conception to which attention was constantly being drawn; and a very large number of symbolists (though by no means all) laid great stress upon it. For Rémy de Gourmont, at a relatively early stage in his opinions, symbolist art

'doit s'enquérir de la signification permanente des faits passagers, et tâcher de la fixer — sans froisser les exigences de sa vision propre — tel qu'un arbre solide émergeant du fouillis des mouvantes broussailles; il doit chercher l'éternel dans la diversité momentanée des formes, la Vérité qui demeure dans le Faux qui passe, la logique pérennelle dans l'Illogique instantanée... '[3]

So too, of course, Mauclair:

'Quiconque fixe avec profondeur un trait de vie crée du même coup un symbole, car tous les phénomènes sont les signes d'une vérité permanente.'[4]

And the following is typical enough of the confusion as to this two-sidedness of symbolism—individuality and universality:

'A. M. Stuart Merril [sic] ... nous voudrions reprocher cependant de ne perdre encore assez méthodiquement sa propre personnalité en le ON humain, par la recherche des quelques éternels lieux-communs symboliques qui régissent la pensée'[5]

—where Viélé-Griffin proposes that the demands of 'universality'

---

[1] Marcel Schwob, *L'homme au masque d'or*, Préface.

[2] Cf. 'Le mysticisme semble s'accorder surtout avec le symbolisme. On peut même sous ces deux noms ne voir qu'une même doctrine et qu'une même tendance. Le mysticisme de nos plus jeunes gens n'est qu'une religiosité aimable et vague, un tendre besoin d'extase et d'épanchement... Cela se satisfait avec un petit nombre de mots vagues et de brochures bleues... Voilà bien le principe du symbolisme: il n'y a de réalité que dans un mystère qui, par définition, est inconnaissable' (Léon Blum, *Revue Blanche*, t. vi, no. 27, i/1894, pp. 38–9).

[3] 'L'Idéalisme,' 1892, in *La Chemin de velours*, 1902, p. 211.   [4] *L'art en silence.*

[5] Viélé-Griffin, 'Trois Portraits,' *Ecrits pour l'art*, 7/ii/1887.

should direct the poet towards certain themes and imageries, without examining in what way a purely theoretical conception (relation between individual and universal in art) can possibly link up with the purely empirical world of poetic activity. If Viélé-Griffin is here putting into critical practice a favourite dictum of his patron Mallarmé, regarding the *impersonality* of myth, he is doing it very ineptly. We are, in fact, in the presence of an attitude to symbolism in which the stress in definition is placed not on art absorbing and neutralizing allegory, but on the allegory serving the purposes of intellectual, communication: in the same way as Vallette's glose of Rakma emphasized the non-artistic side of the symbol: the indifferent side of abstraction.[1]

For essentially, allegory has two sides, the concrete and the abstract; an allegory reduced almost to the latter alone (say the parable of the prodigal son expressed in terms of 'x' and 'y' or in civil service jargon) would be virtually devoid of value as literature—that is to say, as expressive language. That is not to say that the presence of abstract components is damaging to art; for that would be tantamount to saying that thought has no place in poetry, which is ridiculous. What it *does* mean is that in art it is not the 'subject' of the allegory, not the family of themes to which the work belongs (the concept of all the *Hamlets* ever written) that is valuable, but the theme as expressed in a given language; the subject as part of the material, part of the form, of the work of art, presented in such a way that the utmost is (as we commonly say) 'got out of it'. Half a dozen different narrations of the parable of the prodigal son will each have the same didactic use; but no two will have the same value as art: one 'subject'

---

[1] This emphasis is specially to be remarked in symbolist theorizing about drama. Mauclair, for instance, writes:

'Ainsi la condition de simplicité synthétique du drame rejette l'intervention du cas particulier.' (All must make way for) 'la révélation de la foule sous l'apparence du personnage' (*Eleusis*, p. 258). This, linked with Carlyle's views on heroes and their relations to the commonalty, produces the result that the dramatic character is 'un des plus complets exemples du symbole' (ibid., p. 259); in support Mauclair cites approvingly Wagner and Maeterlinck. Wagner, of course, is the principal source of this aesthetic heresy; Schuré, in his *Drame musical*, which does little more than vulgarize Wagner's own remarks, says of the artist:

'Ce n'est qu'à condition de nous offrir de hauts symboles et de nous parler des vérités éternelles par ses types vivants qu'il accomplit sa mission supérieure dans l'humanité' (*Le Drame Musical*, 2e ed., 1886, p. 10).

Thus too the musical critic of the *Revue Blanche*, himself a keen Wagnerian and something of a symbolist:

'... La réalité dramatique y engendre le symbole, y suggère des idées générales, ayant été, dès l'origine, vue, comprise, saisie sous l'impérieuse poussée d'une idée générale, d'un sentiment dominant...' (Alfred Ernst, *Revue Blanche*, t. vi, no. 27, i/1894, p. 80). What is more, M. Ernst attributes the special and outstanding qualities of Richard Wagner to the fact that he, of all artists, has at last penetrated to the true and unique interpretation of his symbols: he is 'cet artiste par qui l'antique Légende est arrivée à la définitive conscience de sa propre signification' (*Revue Blanche*, t. vi, no. 27, i/1894, p. 79).

may be present throughout, but seen as poetry or poetic writing there will be six distinct and individual allegories, or, if you wish, symbols. Moreover, there is no reason to suppose that the clearest from the didactive point of view will necessarily be the best art— the best symbolism; it may well be that the most lucid account would be written with x and y as names for the protagonists, and 'national savings certificates' in place of the fatted calf. This was all very clearly seen by at least one young (non-symbolist) critic of the times:

'Qu'il me soit permis de dire encore du symbolisme dont en somme il s'agit surtout ici, qu'en prétendant négliger "les accidents de temps et d'espace" pour ne nous montrer que des vérités éternelles, il méconnaît une autre loi de la vie, qui est de réaliser l'universel ou l'éternel, mais seulement dans des individus.

'Les œuvres purement symboliques risquent donc de manquer de vie et par là de profondeur. Si, de plus, au lieu de toucher l'esprit leurs "princesses" et leurs "chevaliers" proposent un sens imprécis et difficile à sa perspicacité, les poèmes, qui devraient être de vivants symboles, ne sont plus que de froides allégories.'[1]

Making the necessary adjustment of terms, this appears to be a most adequate general criticism of the dangers inherent in symbolism at this point in our scale of specifications; the poet or playwright (our minds turn, not quite fairly, perhaps, to Maeterlinck) who has his eye fixed on some 'éternel lieu-commun' cannot be confident that he will avoid sacrificing the artistic worth of his writing in favour of 'abstract truths'; though on the other hand, if he feels strongly the wish to write a poem on some philosophical subject that haunts him, there is no reason why his poem should suffer by taking the form of a not immediately obvious symbol. Proust has made a good point; but he has put it to ill use in making it an argument against obscurity as such.[2] And that is why we cannot agree with the judgement of another astute contributor to the *Revue Blanche*, writing three months later on the same topic:

'Le symbole est un signe; encore faut-il qu'il soit le signe de quelque chose, et le meilleur signe possible pour représenter à nos yeux ce quelque chose. Je consens qu'il soit difficile s'il est frappant, mais peu m'importe qu'il soit élégant s'il est vide. Je suis d'ailleurs bien convaincu qu'on peut goûter une œuvre sans rien saisir du sens caché qu'y céla jalousement l'auteur, et c'est un plaisir qui a son prix, comme tous les autres. Mais c'est un contresens esthétique, à mon gré, de ne voir dans le symbolisme que l'évocation poétique et dispersée d'images peut-être agréables; il faut qu'on ait voulu suppléer par ces images à la connaissance discursive, à la connaissance détaillée de l'objet.'[3]

[1] Marcel Proust, 'Contre l'obscurité,' *Revue Blanche*, t. xi, no. 75, p. 72, 15/vii/1896, p. 72.

[2] No one thinks the worse of Dante for introducing recondite allegories; as symbols, as the language of art, they invite us to enjoy them all the time that we are searching for the poet's fuller meaning as expressed in them.

[3] Léon Blum (review of Schwob's *Croisade des enfants*, *Revue Blanche*, t. xi, no. 81, 1/x/1896). The occasion does admittedly offer some provocation.

M. Blum has here ingenuously taken a symbol to be a *sign* for some element of discursive knowledge, clearly conceived and ready to be communicated. Plainly, when the communication of intellectual discourse is in question, one criterion of adequacy, and one only, is applicable to symbols—namely, foolproof lucidity: in which field algebraic notations are commonly found to be the most satisfactory. But as we have seen already (see chapter III) art is not conducted along these lines, and in chapter IV we have set out a view of language which reveals the different criteria applicable to the artistic and the scientific fields of speech. The same distinction is valid when we deal with the constructs of poetry which are called fable, myth, allegory, or symbol; and it may be summed up by saying that in poetry (or painting, for that matter, when heroic fables are in question) the artist has not completely mastered his myth and its full significance for him, and then set out to record this mastery in words or colour: much rather he is making himself conscious of it, and of his feelings towards it, by a process which is none other than artistic activity. The poet dealing with any kind of 'thought', from the simplest ('I am haunted by literary impotence'—Mallarmé *passim*) to the most complex, has the language as the vehicle for expressing his attitude to the thought in question; and it is for him to choose whether he shall think in only a certain part of his available resources (as, for example, language tending towards 'abstractness') or avail himself of its entire range, in which images and the fullest associational play have their part.

The latter, or 'richest' use leads straight to the introduction of myth or allegory, or in (some) symbolists' terms, symbol: where symbol stands not merely for a convenient *sign* but for an expressive concretion of linguistic imagery which is absolutely irreplaceable. In the same way that for some symbolists 'natural affinities', between 'white' and purity, 'green' and jealousy, meant not an arbitrary decision to make this equivalence but the recognition that in certain historical circumstances these words and/or associations offered themselves persuasively to the writer searching for an adequate form for his attitude, so, too, in the slightly more exalted plane where thought demands poetical expression each poet will find, on the basis of his experience, certain 'symbols' or 'myths' which provide as it were an integrated language at a relatively complex level.

There is, then, no obligation laid on the poet to have a perfectly lucid reference for his symbol (such as, for example, Viélé-Griffin offers in the *Chevauchée d'Yeldis*); any more than on certain occasions, admittedly for very special purposes, poets are not tied down to allowing to each word they use a normal and full semantic value (or painters a straightforward representative reference to the shapes they press into use). And this liberation finds expression at two fairly distinct stages. In the first, the artist is freed from any feeling that he is under obligation to make use of traditional myths; a process which in another aspect of his work has its analogy in his liberation from strict traditional metrical forms. But just as in the latter case it is not possible (even if it were desirable) ever to escape from the moulding influence of tradition, so in the former it is simply and formally impossible to 'invent' a myth for one's self entirely out of the blue: one can re-combine fragments of material, one can create a new form, but only out of old pieces. Mallarmé, for example, reproaches Wagner cautiously with using recognized mythical forms for his music-dramas, and says:

'L'esprit français ... répugne, en cela d'accord avec l'art dans son intégrité, qui est inventeur, à la légende';[1]

but the argument is false: Siegfried is no less an original creation than Shakespeare's Hamlet—or Laforgue's—or than Mallarmé's own 'Faune', for that matter.[2] And in a sense, Mallarmé's quest for the material of *l'Œuvre*, the myth 'dégagé de toute personnalité', provides a negative illustration of this point: for the attempt to devoid the myth of all 'contingency' whatsoever resulted in its never being created: all he can do is to take up fragments of potential myth throughout his life (*Hérodiade*, *Igitur*, the shadowy symbols of *Un Coup de Dés*) and leave each one more and more elusive and recondite than the last: the 'explication orphique de la terre' has its feet too securely placed on the ground of tradition for Mallarmé ever to achieve a final conquest.

We may conclude, if only from Mallarmé's peculiar literary career, that within the concept of myth every instance must show both individual and universal characteristics, the former stemming from its form as art, the latter from its representative elements embedded in its formal structure; and however much the ingredients may be varied in proportion to one another, they cannot either of them exist independently. Empirically, *L'Après-midi d'un faune* is different from the *Lohengrin* myth, in so far as it is a theme much less frequently treated, in so far as its author's creative work in assembling its elements is proportionately greater than Wagner's adaptation of a

---

[1] *Divagations*, p. 147.

[2] One might state the same relation between invention and derivation by saying that there can exist no work of art for which, in principle, we cannot find 'sources', either in real experience or in imagined experience, earlier literature, etc.

well-established legend; but not in any other way. In other words, any piece of art formed out of representative material—i.e. an overwhelming preponderance of all art—is myth, in embryo at least, and therefore symbolic, if we care to make those two terms interchangeable.

Thus all drama, for example, would be 'symbolist' drama. This fact was hard for some of the symbolist critics to swallow; they would have preferred to reserve the term for the darlings of the younger generation—Wagner, Ibsen—but such a distinction, while reflecting contemporary taste, did violence to the term 'symbol'. We have already seen Mauclair's admiration for the Siegfried symbol; the same welcome was extended to most of Ibsen's major plays:

'... L'étranger, dont la volonté domine Ellida, *la dame de la mer*, et qui la trouble jusqu'au fond de l'âme, ayant en lui toute la fascination de la grande mer, de la mer lointaine, symbolise la tentation du Rêve et de l'Inconnu qui tourmente parfois notre vie et appelle notre pensée anxieuse.'[1]

Ibsen's scenes have a significance 'à la fois naturel et symbolique':

'sur tous ces détails réels et ces personnages naturels plane un symbolisme supérieur qui magnifie la portée des choses'.[2]

The idea that a myth can be at the same time a work of art, especially in drama, is curiously distorted for another symbolist reviewer, who sees in this fact the basis for a 'dualist' theory of symbols, in which the uninitiated can enjoy the spectacle (as, for example, the 'story' in Poe's *Raven*) and the initiated penetrate to its hidden 'meaning'.[3] In the light of what has already been said on the subject, we need hardly embark on a detailed criticism of this confusion. The segregation of audience into those who 'seront frappés du conte du Corbeau', and those who 'verront sous la fable la figure et les idées philosophiques qu'elle évoque' is a ludicrous one in the nineteenth century of grace, it would be a strange man who sat through the performance of *The Lady of the Sea*, or read the *Raven*, without ever sensing the 'symbolical' or allegorical content. And from the opposite point of view, anyone valuing the *Raven* exclusively for some perennial truth contained therein would hardly gain our respect as a judge of poetry. The distinction, quite simply, cannot be made; the reference of a myth is part of its form, part of what contributes to its aesthetic value; failure to grasp completely the full

---

[1] Henri Bordeaux, on Ibsen, *Mercure de France*, t. xii, p. ix/1894, p. 66.
[2] ibid., p. 59.
[3] Pierre Valin, 'Le Symbole au Théâtre,' *Ermitage*, III, p. 26, 31/i/1892.

significance of a work of art is a much commoner occurrence than might be supposed, and does not destroy the recognition of artistic value in what *is* appreciated, nor alter its nature.

The point at issue here—as at all previous points in our discussion of the nature and scope of the literary symbol—is not simply that a general notion (or a notion capable of becoming general) should be set forth, one way or another, but that it should be set out artistically; that is to say, that a formal constructiveness must occupy the whole field of the poet's practical attentiveness. For that is the sole distinction between art and other processes of mind; between the coherent, 'inevitable' presentation, and the aesthetically disjointed; between the symbolizing poet and the philosopher who wastes less time over his style than over his matter. It is a point capitally made by Baudelaire in talking of the naturalist painters:

> (These painters) 'prennent le dictionnaire de l'art pour l'art lui-même; ils copient un mot du dictionnaire croyant copier un poème. Or un poème ne se copie jamais: il veut être composé';[1]

or again when he says that the external world, the artist's language, is only

> 'un amas incohérent de matériaux que l'artiste est invité à associer et à mettre en ordre',[2]

as though this were not something which every man and woman is doing at every moment of conscious life, save only that the artist does it a great deal better! It is a point made with equal cogency by Téodor de Wyzéwa (though with less clarity):

> 'Nous voyons autour de nous des arbres, des animaux, des hommes, et nous les supposons vivants; mais il ne sont, ainsi perçus, que des ombres vaines, tapissant le décor mobile de notre vision; et ils vivront seulement lorsque l'artiste, dans l'âme privilégiée duquel ils ont une réalité plus intense, leur insufflera cette vie supérieure, les *recréera* devant nous... Mais où l'artiste prendra-t-il les éléments de cette vie supérieure? Il ne les peut prendre nulle part sinon dans notre vie habituelle, dans ce que nous appelons la réalité.'[3]

In short, the symbol is a complex example of that formalizing element of language which, as we have suggested in the former chapter, is indispensable to the poetic activity of expression.

---

[1] Baudelaire, *Curiosités esthétiques* (ed. Calmann-Lévy, s.d.), p. 326.
[2] *L'Art Romantique* (ed. Calmann-Lévy, p. 17).
[3] Wyzéwa, *Revue Wagnérienne*, reproduced in *Nos Maîtres*, p. 14. The reader will notice the 'idealist' twist to the argument, so typical of Wyzéwa in his campaigning days on the *Revue Wagnérienne*. Cf. p. 46.

6. BEYOND MYTH AND METAPHOR: THE SYMBOL AS PURE ARTISTIC FORM

We have already seen that the symbol can be exemplified over a wide range of formal complexity. At the lower end of the scale it designates the smallest language entity that we recognize: the word with its attendant image and emotion. This is the phenomenon which Baudelaire had in mind for his theory of metaphor; which engaged the attention of Shelley, and after him of the symbolist in Yeats, and sometimes (in a disguised terminology) of Mallarmé, not to mention the innumerable critics and hangers-on of the symbolist movement who understood the letter rather than the spirit of the *Correspondances* sonnet and ventured into the sphere of a mystical aesthetic. Higher on the scale, it embraces the myth, in either rudimentary form (that is to say, when a fully-formed tradition has not yet formed about a theme, as in the case of Mallarmé's principal poems) or in the very stable form that Wagner utilized for his music-dramas. But there are also instances of formal artistic construction which ordinarily we should hesitate to call myth for one reason or another. Take the case of Maeterlinck's plays. Treated in the Wagnerian manner, one would assume them to be in some sense allegorical; we would try to extract a general statement from that formal element which we can pick out and isolate by calling it a 'plot'; we would then say that the plot allegorizes a recurring situation in life which a large number of people find important. And yet we cannot do this with *La Princesse Maleine*, or *Pelléas et Mélisande*, despite the deliberate damping-down of all that might detract from attention to the most general and impersonal aspect of the dramatic construction: there simply is no allegorical import. We feel there ought to be one; we feel, from every stroke of the author's pen, that there must be a 'meaning' of some sort, which when we have found it, will illuminate the plot and relieve our anxiety. There is none; or at any rate, nothing such as we expect. The only general statement that emanates from these plays is something such as 'life is a very mysterious thing'; and that not as a proposition but as an attitude. And the presence of this attitude, which is one of the most prominent aspects of the author's style and his work's formal composition, runs through every one of his plays more or less, giving them an extraordinary air of sameness. Maeterlinck is not the only writer of the symbolist era to take advantage of this particular effect (which we might call 'pseudo-myth', and which indeed demands for its success a very long and stable tradition of audiences *succeeding* in finding general statements when they look for them): even more reliant on the device is André Gide—the young Gide of *Paludes* and *Le Voyage d'Urien*. As we read through the numerous sections of the latter, which for a stylized impersonality appropriate to allegory rival even Maeterlinck's, we come to feel with the narrator, as we turn over each page,

'Sera-ce ici que nous trouverons un lieu qui devant nous ne se dérobe, ou s'il demeure enfin ne nous attire coupablement? Ou penchés sur le pont du navire, les regardant se dérouler, devrons-nous toujours errer devant les plages et les plages?'[1]

In point of fact, much of the effect of the work depends on our readiness to pretend to ourselves that there *is* an allegory, if only we can attain to it, or feel sure when we do that we have not got hold of the wrong one. An interesting device, but not one open to indefinite repetition. And, as I have said, one which depends for its success on a tradition of successful detection of general imports.

But these are border-line cases around the symbol as ordinarily understood by Wyzéwa and the Wagnerian wing of symbolism. In each of them there figures at least the shadow of the general proposition, of the 'philosophème', as it has been called.[2] Yet if there is not to be a gap between our provisional definition of the symbol as simply an artistic monad (of whatever scale) and the actual concrete history of its application in the nineteenth century, it must be possible to find a fairly general and established use of the term which does not centre on the fact of an allegorical or pseudo-allegorical element; for such an element is not in any way held to be inevitable in our hypothesis. Equally, were we to find such an explicit or implicit usage, then there would be no need to construct a theory of the symbol which depended on a simple synthesis of the Baudelairean and Wagnerian doctrines (i.e. a definition equally applicable to myth and metaphor), which otherwise would impose itself.

This link, to which we have not yet had occasion to make reference, exists, and blends in the last century (as, indeed, in this) with those uses we have already examined. Implicitly we find it in Mallarmé (though not baptized by the name of symbol, it remains the outstanding aspect of his poetry, rather than myth, and certainly won him the style of 'symbolist').[3]

[1] Gide, 'Le Voyage d'Urien,'1893 (in *Œuvres, NRF*, t. i, p. 303).
[2] Raymond Bayer 'De la méthode en esthétique,' *Revue Philosophique*, i–iii/1947, p. 4.
[3] E.g. at a symbolist banquet a toast was drunk (after many others) 'à la Poésie Symboliste et à son représentant le plus éminent qui nous préside: "Stéphane Mallarmé". Ce toast est souligné d'unanimes applaudissements' (*Entretiens*, ii/1891, p. 60). Strange that to us Mallarmé seems to stand almost apart from his times!

'Nommer un objet, c'est supprimer les trois quarts de la jouissance du poème qui est faite du bonheur de deviner peu à peu; le suggérer, voilà le rêve. C'est le parfait usage de ce mystère qui constitue le symbole: évoquer petit à petit un objet pour montrer un état d'âme.'[1]

Such a passage describes the expressive function not only of the pseudo-myths such as *Hérodiade* or *L'Après-midi d'un faune*, or *Igitur* or *Le vierge, le vivace et le bel aujourd'hui*, but also of such obviously non-mythical poems as *Eventail*.

More explicit even is Edouard Dubus when, in a review of some poems of Marie Krysinska, he writes:

'Tout d'abord, un sens aigu du symbole. Les spectacles de la nature y sont de purs états d'âme, témoin ce féerique soir:
  'C'est l'Heure épanouie comme une large Fleur
  Où le ciel attristé semble prendre en ses bras
  Les monts, les arbres et la mer
  Pour d'intimes communions
  A l'horizon perdu,'[2]

where it would not occur to any reader to suppose an allegorical significance to lurk beneath this modest evocation of a mood. Similarly, writing of Verhaeren, Charles Baudouin notes that

'Un paysage de rêve, obtenu par condensation de plusieurs paysages réels qui évoquent une émotion analogue, est un symbole de cette émotion.'[3]

which is definitely a misinterpretation of the nature of poetic language, but serves well enough to fix the literary phenomenon to which the critic applies the term 'symbol'. Mockel, on the subject of the same poet, has evidently the same idea of the reference of 'symbol' as Baudouin; moreover, for him it seems that this idea is not only independent of an allegorical content, but definitely excludes such an element as *incompatible* with the ideal of expressive art:

'Ce livre, les *Villages Illusoires*, serait un symbole presque parfait s'il n'y avait à quelques endroits des taches déplaisantes d'allégorie... Mais s'il est vrai que "le symbole suppose la recherche intuitive des divers éléments idéaux épars dans les formes," et que "le symbole est créé par la cohésion soudaine des formes lorsqu'elles se montrent désormais *nécessairement* liées et expriment implicitement leur unité idéale," ce geste suprême de l'Art doit être salué ici.'[4]

---

[1] Mallarmé, quoted by Thibaudet, *La Poésie de Stéphane Mallarmé*, 1926, p. 110.
[2] Edouard Dubus, in *Mercure de France*, xii/1890.
[3] Baudouin, *Le Symbole chez Verhaeren*, 1924, p. 17.
[4] Mockel, 'Verhaeren,' *Mercure de France*, t. xiv, p. 203. Compare Raynaud's analysis of Dubus' outline of 'symbolism', in which, mingled with much obscurantism about 'correspondances', we find statements such as the following: 'Le poème destiné à produire une émotion esthétique sera *symbolique*... Le poème symbolique est celui qui, évoquant par le vers des formes esthétiques, logiquement reliées entre elles dans l'unité d'un sujet de composition, a pour objet la réalisation du beau... Le symbole étant défini: une figure, une image, qui exprime une chose purement morale' (*Le Décadent*, 2e Série, no. 7, 15/iii/1888). The date is noteworthy.

The definitions quoted here are not without their force; and they argue varying degrees of insight into the nature of poetic creation; one wonders why it is that Mockel cannot envisage a myth having the same inner cohesion or tension of form; even granted the increased danger of poetic duty being neglected for didactic, and the 'coherence of form' being sacrificed to coherence of argument, cases are to be found of the two coinciding. It would have been interesting to have had Mockel's verdict on Baudelaire's *Albatros* or Mallarmé's *Le vierge, le vivace et le bel aujourd'hui*.

By no one perhaps was this position of the symbol as beyond myth and metaphor stated with more clarity at the time (or rather, shortly afterwards, since wide critical reflection usually follows and seldom runs side by side with the high tide of creative activity) than by André Gide. When we study his earliest works, and particularly his two pieces *Paludes* and *Le Voyage d'Urien*, and the fragmentary *Journal* around the turn of the century, we have the impression of a young man powerfully influenced through Mallarmé by the symbolist adventure, and essaying what he held to be an essentially 'symbolist' technique under the careful eye of a self-critical judgement. The *Voyage* is propped up with introductions and explanatory notes in the *Mercure de France*; the *Journal* contains—admittedly in fragmentary shape—a good deal of aesthetic speculation: one might almost say experiment. It comes as no surprise to us to find Gide using the term symbol' in some of the senses we have examined up to this point;[1] but it seems as though with the passage of a few critical years he cast off the hot-house atmosphere of 'idealist' aesthetic, and came round to

[1] In Mauclair's sense: 'Il (le poète) sait que l'apparence (de chaque chose) n'en est que le prétexte, un vêtement qui la dérobe et où s'arrête l'œil profane, mais qui nous montre qu'elle est là.' (And as a footnote to this: 'A-t-on compris que j'appelle symbole — tout ce qui paraît.') ('Traité du Narcisse,' originally in *Entretiens*, t. iv, iv/1892; i.e. prior to *Eleusis*; also in *Œuvres*, *NRF*, t. i, pp. 216–7.) Again: 'Le poète pieux contemple; il se penche sur les symboles, et silencieux descend profondément au cœur des choses — et quand il a perçu, visionnaire, l'Idée, l'intime Nombre harmonieux de son être, qui soutient la forme imparfaite, il la saisit, puis, insoucieux de cette forme transitoire qui la revêtait dans le temps, il sait, lui, redonner une forme éternelle, *sa* Forme véritable enfin, et fatale...' (ibid., p. 217). And much else in the same vein in the 'Traité', with the symbol always as the phenomenon behind which lurks the form. The 'Traité' has been slightly altered on several occasions, but never varied from this central doctrine; and within the framework of this strange synthesis of Schopenhauer and grey timeless myth, more than one acute observation on the nature of composition peeps through: e.g. 'Tout représentant de l'Idée tend à se préférer à l'Idée qu'il manifeste. Se Préférer — voilà la faute. L'artiste, le savant, ne doit pas se préférer à la Vérité qu'il veut dire: voilà toute sa morale; je dirais presque, que c'est là toute l'esthétique...' (ibid., p. 216). If I understand this aright, Gide is imposing on the artist the modesty of truth of expression; by which alone hollow-sounding and incongruous (and so artistically bad) utterances can be kept at arm's length from the human mind, always prone to play-act. Or again, 'La question morale pour l'artiste n'est pas que l'Idée qu'il manifeste soit plus ou moins morale et utile au grand nombre; la question est qu'il la manifeste bien' (ibid.). Which is simply a demand that art shall be judged, *qua* art, by the standards of art.

something similar to the definition we are at present examining; that is to say, the symbol as coeval with the artistic unity of a work of art, or that of which we say it has unity of form, or, to coin a phrase, the esthetic monad at the highest and most complete level:[1]

'En étudiant la question de la raison d'être de l'œuvre d'art, on arrive à trouver que cette raison suffisante, ce symbole de l'œuvre, c'est sa composition';[2]

and again,

'Une œuvre bien composée est nécessairement symbolique. Autour de quoi viendraient se grouper les parties? qui guiderait leur ordonnance? sinon l'idée de l'œuvre, qui fait cette ordonnance symbolique';[3]

and

'L'œuvre d'art c'est une idée qu'on exagère... Le symbole c'est autour de quoi se compose un livre... La phrase est une excroissance de l'idée';[4]

it would seem that not only has the idea of symbol been here stretched to the limiting case, the case that embraces in principle all others subordinate to it; but that the notion attached to the Schopenhauer term 'Idea' has been similarly stretched, and in the process emptied of its mystical reference, so that it remains like 'symbol' as a superfluous word, a synonym for 'form', 'content', 'art-unity'. Perhaps somewhere in the course of this loosening and emancipation from 1890-vintage theories, Gide touches on an intermediate stage, in which the symbol refers to something essentially similar to that represented above by Marie Krysinska's fragment; an aesthetic concretion, but not yet recognized as a self-contained, independent aesthetic monad. Thus, writing of *Le Voyage d'Urien*, in 1894, he equates the embodiment of an attitude with the attitude itself; each scene in the voyage is a landscape embodying a feeling—

'Emotion et manifeste forment équation; l'un est l'équivalent de l'autre. Qui dit émotion dira donc *paysage*; et qui lit *paysage* devra donc connaître *émotion*.'[5]

and it may well be that the incompleteness of this position is mirrored in the overall patchiness of the 'Voyage'—which in effect is nothing more nor less than a string of fragmentary pseudo-myths which neither stand on their own nor form a strict whole.

Sanctioned by usage, then, one may extract a simplifying definition that can embrace the variety of definitions that we have encountered

---

[1] Highest because within it less complete monads may be distinguished—as isolated tunes in a symphony, metaphors in a poem, or figures in a fresco.
[2] 'Réflexions,' *Œuvres*, NRF, 1933, p. 424 (first publ., 1897, in the *Mercure*).
[3] ibid., p. 424.   [4] ibid., p. 73.   [5] *Mercure de France*, t. xii, pp. xii/1894, pp. 354–5.

along our lengthy, and perhaps rather tedious, but at least all-embracing, survey of the uses of 'symbol' by the symbolists: *namely, the aesthetic unity of created art—which is indifferently unity of form and unity of content.*

Perhaps it would appear that, like Urien, we have arrived at the end of our pilgrimage only to find that the sheet of paper on which we hoped to find so much is entirely void of writing: that we have been presented with a concept so destitute of definite and historical boundaries in space and time that it is no longer possible, by its use, to distinguish the symbolists of the nineteenth century from the artists of any other time known to us; or even from those contemporary writers of the naturalist school against whom they waged such remorseless war. But so far from this conclusion being taken as a defeat, we should much rather welcome it with relief: for it shows us that what we have found below the surface of these numerous explanations is truly a datum of aesthetic; a characteristic of art as such, rather than of this art at this time as opposed to that, in this medium as opposed to that, and so forth. What we have arrived at is, in fact, something so entirely colourless that any specific and historical scena of ideas may be painted upon it without distortion of the colour-scale; so absolutely and flatly general that the interpretation of no artist's creative work can suffer from relation to its terms. It would not be a paradox to say that the various senses in which the word 'symbol' is understood represent so many different ways of grasping the central—indeed, objectively the *only*—aesthetic fact; namely, the unity of an expression.

However, we must not shut our eyes to the fact that much of what the symbolists asserted in discussing the nature of literary symbolism has the air of confusion, mystification, or error when we judge it to-day; and it is this element that we have separated off which serves to put the symbolists in their historical perspective. For as claimed at the start of our inquiry, aesthetic is a branch of philosophy; and by and large, and subject to much halting and misplaced effort, makes a certain secular progress, in which something of what has gone before is retained, purified, and enlarged by the addition of new ideas, and something, too, of the old is discarded as incompatible with the new. This discarded portion of aesthetic theory is precisely what remains when the general idea we have reached of a symbol is subtracted from all the material we have examined in this chapter: and it is this portion which, looking backwards from the present, constitutes the *historical* determination of the symbolist movement. Another way of establishing the historical determination would be in relation to an antecedent period; and it is to be hoped that our study could enable a certain determination to be made in this way too.

Were this examination of aesthetic doctrines to have dealt with clear-thinking and experienced critics, instead of with young and impetuous poets, it is conceivable that the aesthetic doctrines we have been examining would have been adequate, within certain limitations apparent to us to-day, to describe *all* art whatever, and not only that art (namely, the poetry of around 1890 in Paris) from whose impact they arose. For example, Schopenhauer's doctrine of *Ideas* (an advance on some logically earlier views, in as much as it emphasized the 'contemplative' or intuitive aspect of art and the essential identity of creation and enjoyment, yet in our eyes to-day inadequate, since it cannot give an account of gradations of artistic value) is nevertheless capable of application to all art, of whatever period. Equally, though in a sense never penetrated to at the time, the romantic doctrine of the essential lyricism of art is universally applicable, though in the form in which it was expounded in the early nineteenth century it excluded a great body of classical art. The first of these two cases is of a philosopher (and of one, moreover, whose experience of art was not of the widest); the second is of a body of aesthetic opinion closely tied to a generation of artists and writers. It is, accordingly, the latter which should offer the closer analogy to the symbolist movement as regards difficulties of interpretation, and the extraction of an aesthetic theory as opposed to fighting criticism; and we find this is so. The romantics emphasized the lyricism of art, but enclosed this spacious and absolutely sound tenet in a narrow mould characteristic of their historical context: the symbolists emphasized the essentially expressive character of formal unities or, as they preferred to call them, symbols; but did not see that this datum of aesthetic stretched far outside the boundaries of mystic traditions, linguistic novelties, and the German romantic art-myth which for the moment occupied the artistic stage. In each case it has been the laborious and difficult task of succeeding generations to break down these limitations of circumstance and history, and to bring to light the perennial underlying datum of aesthetic which in its historical embodiment may have been distorted beyond the power of the ordinary non-expert to recognize it.

Although we have had much opportunity of seeing this already, we will give here one further example, particularly illuminating for our proposition. Charles Morice, asked what symbolism was, replied:

'Ce que j'appelle symbolisme, ce n'est pas une esthétique précise ... ce que j'appelle symbolisme, c'est la littérature elle-même.'[1]

He goes on to say:

'L'Œuvre littéraire est toujours fondée sur une transposition, c'est faire de la littérature que de ne pas parler directement des choses.'[2]

A truth followed by an error: if the latter statement were true, the *récit de Théramène* would not be literature. Morice, in stating that art does not refer directly to things, that in fact it evokes, or suggests, is giving a pretty good definition of the high-lights of the art of his time—namely, 'transposing metaphors,' allusiveness in all its forms, 'la chanson grise, Où l'Indécis au Précis se joint'. In short, he is not stating an essential fact about art, all art, art as such, but about the artistic media with which he himself was particularly associated: the media, the poetic language resources of 1890, or thereabouts.[3]

Just as in the last chapter we saw that *vers libre* is not a feature of art of such radical novelty as to give rise to an entirely new aesthetic, so in this we may say that the symbol, under the many forms in which it appears in symbolist poetry, is also only empirically different from material forming the stuff of poetry before and since. A historian of language (language always in the widest sense) is concerned with the specific differences of *vers libre* subsequent to Kahn and Laforgue; equally he is concerned with the specific forms of language subsumed under the name of 'symbol'—the language of Baudelaire; the quality and tone of the *Moralités Légendaires,* or of any other of the instances we have noted and many others besides; and with divers empirical characteristics of these trends of language. For example, these units of language appear to be the more powerful of the tools in the poet's

---

[1] *La Littérature contemporaine*, 1905, p. 61.   [2] ibid.

[3] When he goes on to give an example, his grounds change slightly; an ambiguity in the word 'transposition' allows him to give a perfectly universal instance of art: 'Quand Wagner nous donne les *Murmures de la Forêt*, il ne nous apporte pas le vent qui passe dans les feuilles, mais le vent qui passe dans son âme; c'est pourquoi il fait une œuvre d'art' (*La Littérature contemporaine*). For a true example of 'indirect' speech we should have expected, on the contrary, the first alternative: a suggestion of a visual image by a musical. In alluding to the artist's emotional consciousness he introduces a realm of whose attitudes any form of art is the *direct* expression. The confusion is presumably due to the representative character of the 'Wald-weben' and the unforgettable novelty and impressiveness of Wagner's musical technique; perhaps also the fact that in Wagner's 'pictorial' music the representative medium is not a closely imitative one: i.e. does not reproduce the rustle of leaves or the crackle of twigs with slavish exactitude; or in other words, is *indirect* inasmuch as it obeys standards of aesthetic rather than intellectual truth. Taking this instance as a whole, it is evident that Morice is giving utterance to a truth of some consequence in the philosophy of art; equally evident that he has obscured it beneath a presentation of opinions and preferences which are peculiar to his age, and which properly form the object of study of the historian of literature, or of language, rather than of the aesthetician.

armoury; naturally recalcitrant, less mobile and flexible in extended reasoning than their simpler brethren would be; liable, therefore, to broaden the gap between ordinary statement and poetic utterance. The days are far behind when Pope can write an extended treatise on a philosophical topic in much the same style as he devotes to *The Rape of the Lock* (Ghil's valiant efforts notwithstanding). Calling, therefore, for greater application, though not of course guaranteeing 'better' results, the impromptu in poetry disappears. In other words, the poetic symbol is more deep-reaching into the poet's attitude than the general term which classifies his attitude (love, hate, pain) of the ordinary language in which he normally expresses this; but more treacherous too. If we accede to the demands of convenience and agree with custom to the extent of applying the term 'symbol' to certain types of language formation at a certain stage in the history of European literature, we can also say that it is marked off by an empirically drawn line, and not by any inherent and radical difference, from the non-symbolic. In the realm of simple images and simple words, e.g. 'rose', the famous 'géraniums diaphanes', and so on, and all those words or images which seem specially important and 'fitting' on given occasions, the symbol is distinguished as that which in its context most effectively and expressively suits the poet's purposes, so far as these are within the purposes of poetry; so, too, in the realm of metaphor, where there is no sharp division of kind between the fossilized metaphor and the new and poetically forceful combination of images; so, too, at every point in the scale of poetic forms.

That so much concerted attention was paid to the different members of this scale by a whole generation of writers can be laid down to two causes. In the first place, a radical failure to see that the problem of language is the central aesthetic problem for art, rather than some more or less difficult, but easily transcribable, quasi-mystical experience. This we have dealt with in previous chapters; it remains only to recall to what an extent this error resulted in fantastic and wayward notions of the essence of the new art, and persistent inability to do more than glimpse one aspect at a time of the significant nature of symbols. This anarchy of interpretation, and inability on the part of the symbolists themselves to bring their attempted definitions into harmony, should be sufficient evidence of the absolutely central position of the theory of language in any aesthetic.

But this headlong fall into relative incoherence on the part of wise and foolish, young and old, poet and critic, would not have had the impetuous vigour which can hardly escape the notice of any student of the age, were there not some powerful force to drive them so to commit themselves. And this force, far from being at bottom a monstrosity, or making necessarily for obscurantism, was nothing other than a revival of the claims of art against not-art. The perversities and preciosity of some writers, the obscurity of Kahn, the excesses of some vers-librists, and so forth—need not be regarded as in any way essentials in the aesthetic spirit of the age, but rather as excrescences provoked by a number of causes: obsessions with theoretical will-o'-the-wisps (e.g. 'scientific' analysis of composition, 'audition colorée,' artifically sought after in writing, wild experiments in rhythmic forms), and, among the weaker brethren, a surrender to the attractions of *fumisterie*, a challenge to smug philistinism.

7. RECAPITULATION

Let us attempt to gather up the threads of this long chapter.

It has not been possible to limit the 'literary symbol' to one or another of the many formal constructs that appear in art. If we draw up a list not of possible meanings for to-day but of meanings *actually* used in the past, and often embodied also in present use, we get something like the following:

    i. Any isolateable member of the external world or any quality, which bears witness (to the mystic) of a supernatural unity and 'universal analogy' in the world (Baudelaire).[1]

    ii. Any sensible thing or any word so far as it suggests to the Mallarméen poet the Platonic Idea immanent in it (Mauclair).

    iii. Any representation serving as a sign of a general attitude which either tradition or supernatural decree has invested with powerful emotional resources (Yeats).

    iv. An allegory, provided always that the work of art possessed, or tended to possess, a high degree of artistic integration. Hence, also, all myth, and by extension, pseudo-myth (Wyzéwa, etc.).

    v. A single representation abstracted from a complex of experience involving many associated representations, which is intended to do duty for its fellows as the most characteristic (Kahn).

    vi. Any work of art, not being an allegory or myth, whose evident purpose is to express the artist's attitude (Verhaeren).

---

[1] The names are for convenience of reference only, and are not intended to suggest that the definitions they are annexed to are the exclusive property of any single persons.

vii. A formal construct or poetic image of great force which constantly recurs in the poet's work as his mind circles around a certain predominant attitude (Valéry, etc.).

viii. Any work of art at all, considered as a formal unity, or embodying an aspiration to formal unity (Gide).

There are, within these definitions, numerous possible variants; the fourth, for instance, as well as overlapping with the third, in what Schopenhauer calls 'emblems', is of enormous range within itself, embracing Mallarmé's regretful 'Faune' and the cosmological exegesis of Wagner's *Ring*; likewise a symbol can be at once a dramatic figure—*Hamlet*—or a dramatic situation—the theme of an Ibsen play. The second, too, shades off into the first in the murkier passages of Mallarméen philosophy; the seventh might be taken as an extension of the fifth, as an embryonic example of the fourth (myth), or as virtually identical with the third. Worse still, many writers do not properly distinguish, when talking abstractly, between the more widely removed usages—Carlyle speaks of 'Symbols' sometimes in sense (i); sometimes in senses (iii) and (iv); and so on. And there is nothing remarkable about this overlapping: on the contrary, we should be astonished if we found that theory made unbridgeable distinctions between different formal elements in art: for art, as language, is homogeneous.

Nevertheless, a second layer of confusion has been added by writers in the field of literary criticism picking on the word 'symbol' in one or another of these applications, to the exclusion of all others, for the furtherance of their own particular ends and theories. Thus both Bergsonists and amateur enthusiasts of twentieth-century French anthropology have at various times sent their colonists to the continent of Symbolism. Moreover, the definitions listed above are by no means indissolubly wedded to distinctive and mutually exclusive philosophies of art.

Can we from this huge mass save anything at all? Must we, in order to have a definition of literary symbols adequate to our own times and styles, throw overboard everything that has gone before, and start afresh? Or can we still hope to encompass the whole range of literary symbolism in a single theory of its place in art which, if it will not accommodate every *corollary* of Baudelaire's or Valéry's aesthetic doctrines, will yet at least allow us to see what is common both to them and to us in our attitude to poetry?

To suggest that the former alternative is the only one open to us, is to admit in so many words that there is a difference in kind between the artistic phenomena of the nineteenth-century tradition and those of our own or of earlier times: a difference so basic that either the activities the nineteenth century indulged in must cease to count with us as art or we ourselves must admit to having lost the tradition of poetry. Equally, if of any two protagonists of the possible definitions listed above we say that one was describing a thing we call art (or part of it) and the other was not, we must go on from there to show that the art of the one was *in principle* more artistic than that of the other. In short, either there must be a grain of truth in every one of the definitions ventured in the course of this chapter, or else the champion of the 'erroneous' view was not only a mischievous disseminator of wrong opinions but also working from data fundamentally irrelevant to art.

To advance a theory of literary symbolism that will do justice to the whole symbolist movement does not, we have already said, mean that we shall passively accept the theories which symbolists themselves have offered about their symbols: just as justice is not an affair of finding a principle to condone all deeds, good and bad, that men have committed. Rather we shall have to take note of the *data* on which theorizing has taken place, in all its diversity, and see if it offers any hope of our bringing it into a single perspective.

The data are set out in the list on pages 306–7 (above). Is there any single concept in the arts, literary, plastic, musical, and architectural, under which all these very diverse phenomena used by artists, and especially poets, can be equally subsumed? I have offered the answer, 'Language'.

Language, in the wide sense in which it was proposed in the last chapter to use this term, embraces everything and anything which an artist appropriates to himself from tradition and uses as a vehicle of expression. It embraces not only the application by the artist of a certain kind of chemical paint in a certain way to canvas to produce 'this patch of colour': it embraces, in addition, the poet's use of the word 'white' and the semantic reference of 'this white in this context'. It includes not only such utterances as 'I am happy', and the successive stages of elaboration and precision that the lyric poem can give it, but such more intellectually complicated utterances as 'the world is a sorry fiction', in which the poet aims not so much to convince us of the truth of a proposition as to say truthfully how he feels when he thinks a Schopenhauerian thought.

Speech has this added complexity, when compared with music, that precisely because of its derivative functions as a sign-language, which is a function at least as old as reason in the history of man, it always presents itself as a complex act of expression, with a referential aspect comprised within its expressive potentialities. A man playing tunes on the horn is an artist, a musician expressing, within the range of his instrument's capabilities, an attitude—already in a complex way as compared to wordless singing or yodelling, for instance. A man sounding a hunting-call on the same instrument has subordinated the expressiveness of musical utterance to the exigencies of sign discourse, arrived at by arbitrary convention. The expressive range of the stereotyped call is infinitely less than, say, that of the traditional tunes one may still hear in the evening in some European countrysides. Nevertheless, such a call can again be taken up into music, and it will take with it a whole aura of associated emotions to make up its intrinsic expressiveness—echoes of the excitement of hunting; a faintly archaic flavour; emotions fed by experience and by former artistic uses. And the new piece of language formed by the passage of a snatch of music through these phases will have its own place in the range of linguistic resources: though now no longer in the company of pure music, simple utterance, but in the sphere of music as part of the utterances of attitudes and emotions into which enters an intellectual element. The hunting-call music in *Tristan* or *Les Troyens* offers examples of music so constituted.

As in music, so in poetry. Every word in speech is the mark of an abstraction, language on the level of the hunting call; it marks the fact that language subserves the needs of reason, and that language which serves as the expressive form of an imaginative utterance is a language that has already served as signs, but which has been taken up together with its reference as a fresh (and no longer abstract) single element of language. The poet now stands in the same relation to it as a whole that he stands in to a modulated expressive cry or a snatch of song, despite the vastly greater complexity of its structure: when he says 'Good dog', for instance, he is expressing an attitude through language, part of which at any rate has been through the stage of being a sign; and his approval has to that extent a greater specialization, and is also more adequate, than would be an appreciate cry of 'ah', but it is not wholly different in kind. In either case, he stands in the relation of user and creator of attitude to a linguistic resource which tradition has handed him and which he, by using it, modifies, be it by ever so little; the relation which characterizes the creation of art, and is present in both 'ah', and in 'good', and in 'good dog', is also present when Eumaeus delivers his eulogy of Argos.

This, then, disposes of the trap in which Baudelaire and his successors tend to get caught when they speak of symbols; and which result in Baudelaire's inability to say how composition, the 'sorcellerie évocatoire' and the formal construction of parts, enters into the production of aesthetic value, otherwise than in Poe's crude dogma; and in the young Yeats' inability to relate the poetic role of symbol-images to the expressive power of words. For if, in fact, both elements—word and references—are equally constitutive of language as the poet's medium, to pick on one to the exclusion of the other will plainly lead to trouble—the sort of trouble that results when a partial account of an event is forced to provide explanations of results that can only have followed from the event taken as a whole.

In this light, the event which Baudelaire pointed to by the use of the word symbol is a fragment of highly organized and expressive speech, swimming, as often happens, in a sea of much less expressive language: a formal monad, relatively far more 'poetic' than the formal constructs of ordinary discourse. One case of this kind, which particularly struck Baudelaire in the literary tradition which he inherited and contributed to, was that of a special kind of metaphor, in which elements of language were combined in ways not ordinarily attempted. Now for the purposes of art it matters not a halfpenny if a writer—or his audience—does or does not have an unwilled idea of violet when listening to the notes of a horn, or to words in which the vowel 'o'—'O, l'Oméga, rayon violet de ses Yeux!'—predominates; and so far as the philosophy—and the practice—of art is concerned, laborious experimental researchers are wasting their time when they try to establish 'L'audition colorée' as a psychological fact in such and such a percentage of humankind. It may well be that 'audition colorée' did suggest the new combination of resources to the man—whoever he was—who first introduced certain metaphors; but it need not have done; all that was necessary was for someone to cash in on the fact (which he need never have consciously thought of) that attitudes of mind are expressed in language, that whatever senses the attendant images of words are drawn from, language is a homogeneous unity appealing not to these discrete senses but to the imagination, and that although smells, colours, sounds, tastes, and tactile sensations are all qualitatively different, the attitudes that go with (or rather, *through*) them are all attitudes without differentiation. Art being grounded in linguistic attitude, and not simply in the data of the senses, there is no reason at all why a blind man should not talk of violet clarion-calls, or a deaf man of shrill colours. However, from

Baudelaire, standing at the confluence of romantic innovation and mystical theocracy, such an approach would have seemed cowardly, and succeeding generations were too greatly impressed with his poetic eminence to part from the doctrine of 'correspondances'. Through it, symbolism slides into an irrationalist wing. All we can accept from this early theorizing on symbols is the fact that certain pieces of language stand out as particularly expressive, and that these include metaphors—invariably the object of great care on the part of writers—of a sort specially, if rather unjustifiably, associated with his poetry. The special 'incantatory' virtue of certain words, the smallest monad of utterance normally recognized as speech, falls equally within this formal perspective, as examples somewhat similar to metaphors—both relatively simple (though, in fact, already enormously complicated) instances of formal application by the poet. We should not have to mention them, since the symbolists produced no poems of one word, but for the fact that Mallarmé's doctrine of 'pure ideas' shows that he recognized an element of expressiveness even at this low level of formal construction.

This disposes of the first two definitions on our list. Both of them start from data important to aesthetic—constituent elements of language—but are led into the wilderness by one or another irrationalist philosophy—the mysticisms of Schopenhauer or Swedenborg—and give exclusive use of the word 'symbol' to a feature of composition not entitled to this monopoly, thus producing nonsense when they stretch out to encompass myth. In both cases, too, there is a semblance of adhering to the traditional meaning of the word Symbol. But it will be noted that in each case that which is referred to by the symbol is so vague as hardly to be definable in positive terms; and the decision to make the symbol's aesthetic efficacy flow from this reference is no more than an act of faith. Ordinarily, what we mean by a symbol is something of which we can say, 'Let *this* be the symbol of *that*'. It is open to doubt whether we are entitled to use the same word when we say, 'This is aesthetically efficient; its efficiency flows *ex hypothesi* from some relationship between it and something else; and we shall assume this something else to be an undefined and unknowable supernatural agent and the relationship one of symbol to reference'. It seems to be essential to the nature of a symbol proper that everyone who uses it should be quite clear exactly what it does refer to.

We come next to those uses of the term which seem to bear a closer relationship to the conventional non-literary usage. The Fish or the Lamb of Christian tradition is a symbol by virtue of an intellectual act of some kind or another; in the one case, the Fish is *chosen* for its punning reference, and spelling is the link; in the other, the Lamb is *chosen* because both it and its reference are taken as having a limited number of characteristics in common. Relationships of this sort between Symbol and reference are the justification for just *these* symbols and no others having been chosen. Suppose now that a devout artist wishes to give voice to his religious experience. Nothing more natural than that he should paint a Gospel scene, every line and stroke of which serves as a vehicle by which he can express his devotion. Equally he might choose to paint the lamb, as a recognized 'symbol', and work with this lamb as a piece of pictural language standing in the same relation to his creative activity as does the language of his colours or the formal disposition of rocks and trees and rivers which he puts in his background. Or he might, less usually, it is true, express his feelings about his religion by the use of formal elements which are neither human nor a lamb: prophetic writings are full of this departure from traditional representations. So far as the intellectual side of the symbol is concerned, the picture loses all interest when the reference has been grasped. So far as it is a work of art, however, it has not yet even begun to be judged. The demands of the intellect are felt in our judgement of its worth: for instance, it would be impossible for the artist to make use in his picture of three identical lambs without upsetting the spectator: but that is because the lamb, as language, is an essentially singular piece of language, and three lambs would be as jarring as a false rime or a clumsy grammar mistake in a poem. Language imposes conditions on the artist which he cannot recklessly ignore; and for that reason, he is forced into certain uses of language, certain 'subjects' impose themselves as immutably— no more, no less—as conventions of syntax. Just as the grammarian abstracts certain 'regularities', so the art-school abstracts certain 'subjects' from the flux of language. Sometimes these are called myths, allegories, legends, and the like. For the artist they are as important and as necessary as any other formal elements that enter into his work. But they can only subserve the purposes of art on the same condition as all other elements of language: i.e. the artist must—and, of course, always does, to a greater or lesser extent—digest and modify them, not simply for the sake of modifying, but as part of the act of bringing his language into an organized, an expressive form.

As a constituent part in a poem or a picture, they are valuable not for their reference pure and simple, but for their adhesion, symbol and reference and all to the imaginative act. Mauclair is right in part when he says that allegory—purely as reference—gives nothing new and valuable to art: he would be equally right if he were to say that the alexandrine, as a pure convention, or metaphor, or fugal form, as such, is aesthetically null; but that all can enter into a creation in which they play a part.

The symbol as myth—e.g. Laforgue's *Hamlet*—has, then, nothing in common with the Baudelairean symbol, save its character as a formal element in literary creation; it is a more complex element, to be sure, it presupposes a wide literary culture of a different sort from Baudelaire's, and yet it occupies the same position in the act of writing—as part of the range of language. In principle, Laforgue finds in Hamlet the same kind of resources for the expression of cynical disillusion as Baudelaire finds in the *cheveux bleus, pavillon de ténèbres tendues* for the expression of love and awe.

Again, in this perspective, as we have seen that no issue of principle is at stake between the old-established and the new, more fluid and individualist mythical construct; divergence between the two tendencies is merely a matter of empirical boundary-drawing.

The realization that 'a symbol' is something as elastic as this in literary parlance, leads us forward inevitably to admit the validity of Gide's contention, that the 'symbol' is the form—and, of course, the content—of a book or other piece of writing. And seeing that the formal construction of a work of art is simply the way in which its creator expresses an attitude—*is* that concrete attitude—by these same tokens the 'Villes tentaculaires' of Verhaeren are equally entitled to be called 'literary symbols'.

Thus in poetry, to be a symbolist is merely to have a strong feeling for aesthetic qualities in writing: that is to say, to be a poet.

This feeling may manifest itself in a specially acute sense of metaphor, in a specially concentrated and powerful use of imagery, of taut and closely fused language, in the use of pieces of myth and allegory and emblem, either longstanding and traditional or freshly created, arising out of the linguistic consciousness of the moment. . . . As we go through the list, it is borne home on us that what we are enumerating as fields of 'symbols' are nothing more nor less than all the grades and levels and sorts of formal constructs in language. Suppose we were to transfer the whole argument into a world in which musical language was extensively used for imparting information, with a well-developed syntax and attendant paraphernalia: the artistic 'symbolist' then would be the man whose outlook on music and composition came in general closest to our own of to-day: if he concentrated his creative energies on the extreme development of harmonic resources and musical 'language' on the fairly low stage of forms, he would correspond perhaps to Baudelaire (that side of Baudelaire which we have taken notice of, at any rate); he might even describe his chromatic and enharmonic progressions as the music of the spheres, giving access to a world beyond the purely practical. Were he to develop the organic resources of musical form on a wider canvas, he would fall into the position of the later symbolists: his knitting together of fugal and other forms in something other than mere conformity with academic laws would correspond to the revival of a sense of the infinite possibilities for lyrical and, indeed, all literary forms (Viélé-Griffin, Verhaeren, Mallarmé, Rimbaud—all the giants of poetry).

So far as the criticism of art is concerned, these different interests and aptitudes are naturally of the highest significance: they make the poet what he is—even determine to some extent the attitude he can express through them; they *are* his art, and form the object of study of the critic. But from the point of view of the philosophy of art the differences between them are empirical only; they are all specific instances of complexes of language: the fact that they *are* diverse is no doubt important, as helping us to avoid thinking of 'form' as one thing, essentially, 'metaphor' another, and myth yet another when we are discussing poetry; but they all stand in the same position in the analysis of the creation of a work of art. That position, and the general nature of language *qua* language, will, we hope, have been made plain in the foregoing pages.

The literary symbol, then, is not simply an intellectual sign, nor does it derive aesthetic value from the sheer presence of one or another sort of reference element in it. It is a unity of poetic language. The implications of such a definition are such that to continue to apply the term 'symbol' to features of modern poetry and art generally provides a source of perennial confusion and misunderstanding of the main trends of lyric poetry from Baudelaire to the twentieth century. It is a far cry from the mathematician's or the philosopher's definition of a symbol to the final resting point of our inquiry into literary Symbols; and it is too much to hope that whoever talks of modern poetry will make the journey in the back of his mind each time he sets out to discuss the importance of the 'Symbolist' movement. It seems almost as though one sector of our intellectual field is doomed for ever to be haunted by 'utraquistic fallacies' based on ambiguities in the word 'symbol'. It would be desirable, then, if only for this reason, to expel the word from our histories of literature and our literary discussions, and try to find another to take its place: 'literary monad' or something of the sort, harsh though the word would sound on our unpractised ears. And there is another and more cogent reason still for ridding ourselves of a troublesome and misleading label. If we think of the literary monad or symbol as a genus of which the different species have been discussed by various nineteenth-century writers and critics, it appears at once that these critics have concentrated almost exclusively on the differentiae of the several species, and largely—if not entirely—neglected the underlying community of nature. This is constantly happening in the world of literary criticism, and is the source of all the fruitless arguments that go on there from year to year. Such eternal disagreement and argument at cross purposes cannot in the long run be good for the name of literary criticism; and if it becomes impossible to reconcile the claims of Baudelaire and Laforgue (say) to be regarded as 'symbolists', there is a tendency to conclude either that neither was, or that 'symbolism' means nothing. In each case a great deal of time is lost, and valuable aids and observations by the writers in question thrown wastefully away; what is more, no helpful pointers for a later solution are provided by a sterile controversy. Evidently the word 'symbol', with its various specifications, is partly to blame: it tells us too much—and too little. The same objection arises in the case of the stock question: 'Who is the *typical* symbolist?' As usually posed, this could demand one of two possible answers: either we should have to point to a man who created literary and formal 'monads' of outstanding interest in his poetry of absolutely every kind, who embraced the genius of Baudelaire, Laforgue, Mallarmé, Kahn, Verhaeren, Gide, Valéry, and a dozen others—an unimaginable monster—or else we could point to one poet, and designating the emphasis of his formal creativeness (as, for example, Laforgue and the mythical caricature) say, '*This* is the symbolist, because *that* is the aspect of literary form, the grade of constructs, which for purposes of your question I propose to call *symbols*'. The former course is impossible; the latter would never be accepted as an answer: but the real fault lies rather in the question, which is really of the same kind as 'Are fugues better than sonatas?' or, 'Are crowd scenes better than portraits of individuals?' or 'Are plays better than novels?'

8. CONCLUSION

Throughout the foregoing pages we have discussed the symbolist movement in the context of two contrasting moments of aesthetic history, the contemporary and the positivist; the twentieth century and the mid-nineteenth; and our constant effort has been to determine how far along the road from the earlier to the later moment it should be said to stand. In assessing its significance in this light, there is one thing to note: namely, that occupation of some such intermediate position as is suggested does not in any way limit its tools of analysis to those of its predecessor or of its successor. Two examples of peculiarly symbolist concepts are the *Idea* and the *Symbol*. By invoking them a new approach was made to a number of problems which positivism had left in an evidently unsatisfactory state; and we have seen how far they went in surpassing earlier intellectualist difficulties—only to be brought down by not enough, rather than too much, independence of outlook. The theory of Ideas, in one guise or another, argues the autonomy of art in a way long overdue; but in Schopenhauer's version it does this too successfully and makes it hard, if not impossible, for art to keep its grip upon the more plainly intellectual human interests; while in symbolist hands it became hopelessly involved between the intellectualist and anti-intellectualist horns of the dilemma. So, too, with the theory of Symbols, which has long since ceased to worry artists: it was invented piecemeal to cope with a range of questions about language which a naturalist aesthetic could hardly even propound; but it has since been shown to be unable to do more than carry the problems within the range of our vision.

The terms 'literary symbol' and 'symbolist' are terms which, introduced and fortified by a series of mischances, should never have been allowed to remain in usage: after all, Verlaine's 'décadence' was permitted to lapse after the brief outburst which gave it point; and between the two terms there is little to choose for inappropriateness. As we have attempted to show in the foregoing pages, Symbolism is a term of many parts; each of which was begotten on one section of a genuine literary revival by a doctrine of some sort—Swedenborgian mysticism, Wagnerian rodomontade, and the like—which contained the strains of a distorted account of art. The common underlying awareness of what art *is* appears, like the rock stratum of a geological area, in faults and sometimes unexpected turnings on the flat ground of criticism; most of all, of course, on the mountain ranges of poetry that run in all directions through the last seventy or eighty years, and whose sides stand well above the tangled woods of controversy that litter the lower ground. Just as those thickets are most impenetrable in which the indigenous flora mingles with uncontrolled and artificially introduced growths, so the imported doctrines that feature so largely in French nineteenth-century amateur aesthetics destroy all chance of our ever passing through these lands without a very powerful chopping-knife. Where we are able to study a single tree in the forest of post-Baudelaire criticism—Mallarmé, for example—it is much easier to separate what is meaningful from what is not; but if we look at the period as a whole, as a phase through which the aesthetic consciousness passes on its course towards the present, the distinction between native and imported, natural and artificial, becomes greatly blurred; and we may end by seeing no more than a mass of opinion out of which the less responsible critic may produce very much what he chooses for a new fancy theory of art and 'impressionistic' histories of literature.

And yet we are under the obligation of looking at more than single authors, single thinkers; for our heritage of poetry in the present time is indebted to more than just one or a couple of poets in the past, and our thoughts on what poetry is depend to a similar—if not identical—extent on the digestion and absorption of past thoughts on the subject. For the poet at work, the business of assimilation and rejection takes place almost automatically: no writer's imagination will be stirred by ineptitudes and blunders in his predecessors, and if no other way existed, we could tell bad art from good by its long-term sterility. But in the tradition of thinking about art no such hidden hand, no such intuitive judgement, readily exists; it is up to each one to think whether such and such a statement in an earlier view still seems alive to him; whether it falls naturally into place in a continuous and developing stream of aesthetic speculation; whether and how it has been absorbed within his own way of thinking. It is something of this sort that I have attempted in the foregoing pages; aware that the subject is one which, like all others of its kind, is inexhaustible; but daring at the same time to hope that a critical examination of the symbolists' aesthetic may escape being completely useless as the world of to-day comes to terms with its own art and literature, with a system of outlook and language which is, after all, at least in part owed to symbolism—

'Tel qu'en lui-même enfin l'éternité le change'.

FINIS

INDEX OF PROPER NAMES

SUBJECT-INDEX

(Works of literature and criticism quoted below appear, with their dates, in italics.)

A

Aesthetic
Principal functions of, 3, 184, 302;
historical nature of, 4, 8 *seq.*, 13;
not independent of artistic movements, 5;
formal character of, 7 *seq.*;
positivist, 21 *seq.*;
defined by Taine, 27;
rational, 32;
multiplicity denied, 99.
Affective factors, 65, 66.
Alexandrines, 11, 182.
Allegory, 210, 223n., 240n., 252, 260n., 272, 276, 282, 285 *seq.*;
held incompatible with symbolism, 299.
Alliteration, 160n.
Ambiguity, 92n., 103n.
Âme romantique et le rêve (l') (1937), 86, 94, 96n., 109n.
'Analogies,' 208, 282, 289;
identified with symbolism, 210;
distinguished from symbolism, 272.
Anarchy, 181n.;
significance of literary, 6;
reflected by art, 117;
in Laforgue, 183.
Anormal (l'), 36.
Antidotes, 53n.
Anti-intellectualism, 86, 121;
promoted by a theory of Ideas, 67–72.
Anti-socialism, 238.
Antonia (1886), 195.
Après-midi d'un faune (l'), 66, 68, 219, 294, 299, 307;
as a symbol, 70, 288;
as 'musical', 151;
its form, 182;
dramatic in substance, 227.
Architecture, 11, 216.
A Rebours (1884), 16, 186.
Aria, 203.
Art
social function of. 9–10, 14;
an inferior science, 25, 75;
for art's sake, 33;
not descriptive, 36;
independent of social progress, 36;
the creation of a world, 50;
intuition of the Divine, 53, 63;
an esoteric rite, 64;
'art pur' defined, 85n.;
its religious function, 106n., 240;

in Hartmann's philosophy, 115 *seq.*;
a self-critical activity, 121–2;
as a form of thought, 133 *seq.*
Art and the Material (1925), 80, 133, 134n., 271, 286.
Art au point de vue sociologique (l') (s.d.), 208.
Art en silence (l') (1901), 48, 136n., 272, 274, 290.
Art idéaliste et mystique (l'), 34, 106n., 180, 259n.
'Art intégral'—*See* Fusion of the arts.
Art Romantique (l'), 31, 54, 59n., 159n., 191, 207, 260, 296.
Art Symboliste (l') (1889), 144.
Asceticism, 55, 60, 102.
Association, 46;
procedure attributed to symbolists, 123.
Attitude, 32, 65, 158.
'Audition colorée,' 208–9, 310.
Aurélia, 87.
Autonomy of art, 30 *seq.*, 63.
Axel (1890), 43, 195, 229.

B

Bateau Ivre (Le), 93, 97, 225.
Bayreuth, 171, 195 *seq.*, 204, 247.
Beauty and other forms of value (1933), 56.
Belphégor (1918), 30n.
Bonhomet (Tribulat), 42.
'Bourgeois values,' 54, 184, 193, 241.
Byzantinism, 185.

C

Calepin d'un poète (Le), 78, 121, 132, 158n.
'Caractère essentiel,' 23, 75, 118-9.
Cathédrale symboliste (La) (1933), 52, 88.
Chemin de velours (Le) (1902), 17, 37, 111n., 288n., 290.
Chevauchée d'Yeldis (la), 247, 293.
Classicism, 243.
Classification of the arts, 60, ch. V, *passim.*
Cliché, 115, 178, 184.
Communication
problem of, 57, 103, 211;
linked with value, 130n.;
in symbolist literature, 135, 210n.;
regarded pessimistically, 155–6;
of music, 223.
Composition, 296, 301.
Concepts, distinguished from Ideas, 72.
'Conscience collective,' 145.
Consistency, 112.

S

Saison en enfer (Une) (1872), 67n., 94, 97n., 98.
Salammbô, 75, 77.
Sanglot de la Terre (Le), 48n., 99n., 183.
Sartor Resartus, 53n., 257 *seq.*
Science, 25, 30;
  an inferior art, 33;
  in the novel, 35;
  subordinated to literature, 76;
  offering sublime themes, 105.
Sensation, 27, 30n., 81, 88, 98, 118, 138, 144, 146;
  stuff of plastic arts, 198.
Sensibilité musicale et romantisme (1905), 66.
Sentiment de l'existence (Le), 82.
Siegfried, 275, 294, 295.
Sociocracy, 16.
Sociology, 21, 27.
Soleil des morts (Le), 91, 210.
Solipsism, 40 *seq.*, 76, 89, 107n., 288;
  in Laforgue's poetry, 48, 100.
Sonnet, 175–6, 182.
Soulier de Satin (Le), 241.
Subject, undifferentiated from object, 59.
Subject-matter, in abstraction valueless, 67, 312.
Subjective senses, 58.
Suggestion, 304;
  opposed to imitation, 65, 299;
  realm of music, 201n.
Surrealism, 30n., 72, 84, 86, 94, 95, 117, 121.
Symbol, 53, 64, 67, 69, 70, 101, 143n., ch. VI, *passim*;
  denounced by Schopenhauer, 67;
  universal significance, 76;
  mystical value of, 105n., 106n., 142–3;
  its imaginative nature, 114;
  two uses of the term, 129;
  arbitrary and natural, 258, 281;
  consecrated by age, 284;
  modified in time, 288.
Symbole chez Verhaeren (Le) (1924), 299.
Symbole littéraire (Le) (1945), 124.
Symboliques (Les), 16.
Symbolism, its meaning and uses (1926), 143.
Symbolist movement in literature (The) (1899), 240.
Synaesthesia, 199n., 207 *seq.*
Synonyms, 214, 218.
Synthetic art, 174n.
System in aesthetic, 15.

T

Technique, 11, 26, 58, 149, 173, 176 *seq.*, 180, 256, 279;
  in Mallarmé's aesthetic, 63;
  how developed, 122;
  a secondary refinement, 142;
  derided by Rimbaud, 185.

Teste (Edmond), 41, 78.
Théorie de l'unité universelle, 265.
Thomism, 78.
Three Lectures on Aesthetic (1915), 152.
Total art, 193, 198, 201n., 222, 229 *seq.*
Tradition, 185, 186, 238, 243.
Traité des sensations, 78.
Traité du Narcisse (1892), 49, 69, 300n.
Traité du verbe (1886), 101, 209.
Trois Portraits (1887), 290.
Truth, 75;
  imaginative, 79, 111–4.
Typography, 164.

U

Unconscious (The), 48, 111, 114–25;
  symbolized, 288.
Understanding, 24.
Unity, 158, 178–9, 302, 314.
Univers de la Parole (1944), 238n.

V

Value-judgements, 12, 112, 303;
  impossible in mystical aesthetics, 110.
Vanity of aesthetic, 20.
Verse
  Mallarmé's theory of, 155, 187 *seq.*;
  repairs defects of language, 158;
  and prose, 192;
  and drama, 192.
Vers libre, 11, 42, 46, 117, 119, 158n., 187–192, 200, 304;
  mistrusted by Mallarmé, 158, 188;
  in *Un Coup de Dés*, 236.
Victorieusement fui le suicide beau, 103.
Vie des Lettres (La), 123.
Vierge, le vivace, et le bel aujourd'hui (Le), 299, 300.
Vies encloses (Les) (1896), 288.
Villages Illusoires (Les) (1895), 299.
Villes Tentaculaires (Les) (1895), 313.
Vivante continuité du symbolisme (La), 109n., 123.
Vogue (La), 35, 65n., 89n., 150, 169, 187, 288.
Vowels, erroneously coloured by Rimbaud, 209.
Voyage d'Urien (Le) (1894), 69, 298, 300, 301.
'Voyant (Le),' 94, 96, 97, 185n.

W

Waste Land (The), 135n.
Welt als Wille und Vorstellung (Die) (1818), 40, 55 *seq.*
Wissenschaftslehre, 44.
Words, discordant with their meanings, 157–8.